Flying the Line

Flying the Line
The First Half Century
of the
Air Line Pilots Association

By George E. Hopkins

The Air Line Pilots Association
Washington, D.C.

International Standard Book Number: 0-9609708-1-9
Library of Congress Catalog Card Number: 82-073051

First Printing 1982
Second Printing 1986
Third Printing 1991
Fourth Printing 1996

CONTENTS

Illustrations: "Beginnings" following page 56; "The Behncke Era" following page 120; "The Sayen and Ruby Eras" following page 184; "ALPA's Fifth Decade" following page 248. (Credits: page 310.)

FOREWORD

I have this recurring Walter Mitty dream.

I'm a passenger on a 747 and all three pilots get food poisoning. Just before the captain passes out, he gasps to a flight attendant, "Find someone who can land this plane." She runs frantically through the cabin and, in true Walter Mitty-Arthur Hailey fashion, she finds me—the world's most frustrated would-be airline pilot. A man who got most of his flight training from watching *The High and the Mighty* 27 times. An aviation writer who in the course of research managed to set a world's record for crashing flight simulators.

I land the 747 without anyone getting a scratch.

I've never been psychoanalyzed, but I strongly suspect that this Mittyish dream simply reflects my long-standing hero worship of airline pilots. The truth is, I not only envy them but respect and admire them. Many have been close friends for years. I have not always agreed with them or the policies of their union, but I yield to no one in my defense of their professionalism and dedication. Pilots have taught me much about aviation and in doing so have made me a fairer, more balanced observer of the airline industry over the past 35 years.

This is why I consider George Hopkins's history of the Air Line Pilots Association a long-overdue addition to the annals of commercial aviation. For ALPA, like so many of its members, is a vastly misunderstood organization. Traditionally, it has worn two hats—that of a militant union and that of an underrated professional group which has contributed more to the advancement of civil aviation than many people realize or care to admit. What the public, the news media, and government and industry see too often is the ALPA with the union hat—"the only union in the world whose members ride to the picket line in Cadillacs," as some cynic once wrote. Quite literally, the union's long struggle in behalf of safety, better working conditions, and pay consistent with a professional's training and skill has been obscured by judging the end results. We look at today's $100,000 annual salaries for senior captains and forget too easily what it was like in the airlines' infant years.

Hopkins doesn't let us forget. Here is the story of ALPA's humble beginnings, by necessity a union so secret that its existence on one airline was not revealed until an ALPA membership card was found on the body of a pilot killed in a crash. Here, in prose whose objectivity never dilutes the basic drama, are the gallant pilot pioneers who formed the world's first real brotherhood of airmen. Here are the fascinating stories of the family feuds, the intraunion battles and bickering, the crippling strikes, the dogged steps toward safer air travel. Here are the finely etched portraits of ALPA's leaders through the years—controversial Dave Behncke, erudite

Clancy Sayen, stolid Charley Ruby, and the inheritor of both history and headaches, J. J. O'Donnell.

It's all in these pages, from the dramatic deposing of Behncke to the defection of American Airlines pilots, a move that almost wrecked ALPA. As a fellow writer and aviation historian, I salute Professor Hopkins for his incredibly detailed research; there will be some who disagree with his conclusions and interpretations of certain events, but history has always been seen through the eyes of the beholder and time can distort memory, particularly memory of controversy.

I began covering civil aviation in 1947 when I was assigned to report on the crash of a Pennsylvania Central Airlines DC-4 in the Virginia mountains. That was when I was first exposed to the sensitivity of airmen toward that damning phrase "pilot error." That was when I first became associated with airline crews, and I sensed the comradeship and unity of a fraternity with wings. They became my teachers as well as my friends, the innocent instigators of my Walter Mitty fantasy. They made a near-sighted, 5-foot, 6-inch writer feel like part of every cockpit crew who ever flew the line.

So I welcome this book as a long-delayed tribute to the union of U.S. airline pilots—each and every one of them sworn to uphold ALPA's motto: Schedule with Safety.

Robert J. Serling
Tucson, Ariz.

ACKNOWLEDGMENTS

It is always difficult for an author to acknowledge his indebtedness to those who have helped him, largely because limitation of space means he must omit many names. In an oral history such as this, those who submitted to tape recorded interviews can see in the pages of the book the fruit of their patience, but many others who sat for equally lengthy interviews will see no trace of their participation. These omissions do not mean, however, that the many dozens of sources for this book whose specific recollections do not appear herein have wasted their time. I have been helped greatly by all of them and were it not for their kindness, my understanding of the history of ALPA would be poorer, as would the story which follows.

That said, I must begin by paying tribute to Colonel Carroll V. Glines (USAF, Ret.), ALPA's director of communications, who first suggested in 1979 that I might like to undertake a commemorative history to mark the fiftieth anniversary of ALPA's founding. I was initially skeptical about the project, largely because I didn't want to jeopardize my scholarly independence by writing a captive history subject to narrow censorship. C. V. Glines put those fears to rest, and I can honestly say that in the three years I worked on *Flying the Line* not once did an ALPA officer or staff member interfere in any way with my interpretation of ALPA's history.

More fundamental to my skepticism about undertaking a history of ALPA was my doubt about completing the project in a mere three years. My first book on ALPA, *The Airline Pilots: A Study in Elite Unionization* (Harvard University Press, 1971), took four years to write, and it covered only the formative years through 1938! How, I wondered, could anyone do justice to the long sweep of years since then and still have a manuscript ready by 1981, the half-centennial of ALPA's founding?

After much discussion with C. V. Glines and a review of ALPA's archival material at Walter P. Reuther Library at Wayne State University in Detroit, I agreed to undertake the project. Professor Phil Mason, director of the Archives of Labor and Urban Affairs at Wayne State, had the foresight to collect ALPA's historical material in one place. Warner W. Pflug, assistant director of the archives, also rendered valuable service to me during the early stages of research.

The heart and soul of this history, however, lay not in the archives, but in the more than 100 hours of tape-recorded oral histories I collected. A special thanks to the ALPA Washington office secretaries who labored many long hours to transcribe the tapes. I must also thank the staff of *Air Line Pilot* magazine, especially editors Anne Kelleher and Joseph Younger. *Flying the Line* was originally published as a series in *Air Line Pilot*. Editing, design, and production of the book were also the work of the magazine staff. Esperison "Marty" Martinez, ALPA's manager of public relations, also displayed keen interest in the project.

One other ALPA staff member deserves special mention, even though he is also part of the story. Wally Anderson, who retired last year after 40 years at the center of ALPA affairs, provided invaluable assistance in reviewing the manuscript and setting the record of events straight.

Closer to home, I must acknowledge the help of my wife, Elaine; the hard work of my daughter Ginger, who toiled at several tasks connected with the book; and my son Paul, who had to postpone many events crucial to a 10 year old so that Daddy could write. Tom and Ginny Helm, faculty colleagues here at Western Illinois University, offered unending support as I worked on the project, and Spencer Brown, my department chairman, good naturedly arranged my teaching schedule to further progress on *Flying the Line*.

I must also say something about a few of the many professional airline pilots who helped out. Almost from the moment my first book on ALPA was published, pilots have written to me, each with a story or a point of view, often suggesting that I carry the history forward from 1938 into the years they personally remembered. Capt. Bill Himmelreich of Republic was only one of many who wrote during the 1970s, offering his files on an area of particular interest to him, the Southern Airways strike of 1960. Jim Damron of United, Dick Russell of Braniff, and Dave Ekleberry of TWA are also among those on the long list of active airline pilots who assisted in this history in one way or another.

But finally I must say something about the old-timers, many long retired who contributed to the foot-thick stack of letters I collected during the 1970s. Many of these letters are quite moving, often running to several single-spaced typed pages filled with intricate accounts of events long past. There was such a rich and varied history in these stories that I was always mindful of the human face behind this story as I wrote it. I cannot possibly acknowledge all the old-timers who helped me so much, but perhaps one of them will serve as surrogate for all the others. He is former Capt. Joe E. Miller, a man I never met, but who in his mid-70s wrote to recount his own experience as a Century Airlines pilot in 1932. "I was a good friend of Behncke's," Miller wrote, "and it was fun to read and remember those times. I only wish I could write. I have so much I would like to say, but I have tried and do not seem able to get it down on paper."

So for Joe Miller, who also flew for United when it was still called Boeing Air Transport, and all the others, here is my thanks, and here is your story.

George E. Hopkins
Western Illinois University
Macomb, Ill.
Aug. 4, 1982

Flying the Line

CHAPTER 1

What's a Pilot Worth?

"Sometimes we have to earn a whole year's pay on a single flight. That's why they pay us high salaries." So says the captain, a sudden celebrity following his miraculous feat of airmanship.

Many a pilot, over the last half century, has said something like this, usually amid glaring lights, thrusting microphones, and scribbling reporters.

In a modern setting, the press conference would follow an utterly routine flight that had abruptly turned sour. There would have been no prior hint of trouble. The cabin attendants would have been serving drinks, the second officer gazing contentedly at his gauges, the first officer monitoring the assigned frequency, and the captain keeping an experienced weather-eye on everything else. Not a worry in the world for these skilled people at the peak of their professions.

Then, suddenly, the moment of truth. It always comes without warning. It could be anything from an engine failure to a systems malfunction. The only common denominator in this little scenario, whether it happened aboard a Ford Trimotor in 1929 or on a widebody jumbo the day before yesterday, is that life and death hang precariously in the balance.

Airline pilots have created their own traditions. They see themselves as calm, mature individuals who leave nothing to chance, but who never panic if things go wrong. An important part of this self-image is, admittedly, an almost arrogant self-confidence, a feeling that if push ever comes to shove, "I can handle it!" This cocky self-image has sometimes led to trouble, but more often it has constituted that hidden reserve which has enabled quite ordinary pilots to accomplish amazing feats in a crisis, avert disaster, and return their shaken passengers, *somehow*, to mother earth. This attitude was born in the days of wooden wings and is still bred into airline pilots today.

The success of commercial air passenger service has always depended, to an extraordinary degree, on the public's acceptance of this special mystique. Even today, a passenger boarding an airliner believes, tucked away in the back of his mind, that his *particular* pilot on his *particular* flight will be able to handle the danger he half expects to occur. In short, a passenger bets his life that his pilot is a worthy heir to an ancient tradition of excellence and professionalism.

1

The public also believes that airline pilots earn high salaries *because* their employers appreciate their ability to overcome an occasional emergency. Pilots themselves often encourage this notion.

It ought to be true. Airline pilots should be well paid solely for the skills they possess and the responsibilities they bear, and in an ideal world they would be. But in the real world people get paid what they are worth only if they have the muscle to command it.

Skill, courage, and devotion to duty have less to do with why modern professional airline pilots have the best-salaried jobs in the world than do history and the Air Line Pilots Association. ALPA is first and foremost a labor union, an AFL-CIO affiliate. It is also a unique professional association that has made enormous contributions to the air transportation industry, particularly in the safety realm, but that is something of a by-product. ALPA's primary function has always been to make sure pilots got a decent wage. The corollary to this pursuit has been to see that they lived long enough to spend it.

In 1981, ALPA celebrated the 50th anniversary of its birth. The first half century had not been easy. ALPA's existence had often hung by a slender thread. It has never lacked enemies, either. Pilots themselves, against all logic, have sometimes been among the potential destroyers.

Dave Behncke's worst nightmare was that a disgruntled pilot group on a major airline would form a company union. Behncke ("BEN-key"), ALPA's founder and first president, knew from bitter experience how easily a clever airline boss could lure pilots away with sweetheart deals and personal plums. Behncke feared that if a major pilot group should ever defect from ALPA, others would inevitably follow. Then, when ALPA had ceased to represent the bulk of pilots on all airlines, the operators would crack back, reducing pilots to the kind of peonage they were flirting with when it all began.

Behncke fully expected disunity to come someday, and he dreaded it mightily. But he would never have expected it to come from the American Airlines group. In 1963, they bolted, nearly destroying ALPA in the process. Fortunately, Behncke wasn't alive to see it; he probably wouldn't have believed it anyway. The American pilots were Behncke's solid rock from the old days—the tough guys, ALPA's historic backbone, the first to organize 100 percent, and the first to negotiate a contract.

Despite the tragic defection of American's pilots, ALPA survived and grew. Someone picked up the pieces. For half a century now, someone always has. Behncke, who died in 1953, was gone, but Charley Ruby carried on, doing the best he could, as Clancy Sayen had before him, and J. J. O'Donnell has since.

What kind of people created ALPA and nurtured it through half a century? How do we explain the courage it took to hold the center when the flanks were giving way? Whence came the integrity of the Century Airlines pilots, who defied the industrial power of E. L. Cord in 1932? There was a depression on, with millions unemployed. Cord knew there were plenty of pilots out of work, so why shouldn't they be willing to work for a "competitive" wage? Cord figured a fair market wage, given the degree of unemployment, would be about $150 per month. When his ALPA pilots resisted the wage reduction, he replaced them. In the economic climate of 1932, it was no trick at all to get replacement pilots. It never has been. No concerted effort by an employer to replace his pilots has ever failed for want of eager applicants, or on economic grounds alone. But despite this, Cord's pilots fought him. Other pilots would fight other airlines in the future, on grounds almost as hopeless.

What made Howard E. "Sonnyboy" Hall challenge Jack Frye's company union on Transcontinental & Western Air (TWA) in 1933? Hall had been a loyal employee since the days when TWA was known as Transcontinental Air Transport and stopped flying at dusk to transfer passengers from Ford Trimotors to trains. He had helped organize ALPA on TWA during a frenetic burst of activity in 1932. Then he made the mistake of going on a two-week vacation. When he came back to work, everyone who declined to join the new "TWA Pilots Association" was in trouble. Some got fired. Others simply ducked, paid their ALPA dues quietly, and gave lip service to the company-approved "association." Hall did none of these things, and because he was so senior and respected by his fellow pilots, Jack Frye dared not fire him openly. There was a simpler solution. TWA transferred Hall to an unfamiliar route half a continent away, flying open cockpit planes (he had been flying Fords), over terrain unfamiliar to him *at night!*

"They hoped I'd either quit, or worse yet, get killed," Hall remembers. "My wife cried when I was transferred from Kansas City to Newark. She thought she was going to be a widow for sure."

They played hardball in those days, but Hall wouldn't quit *or* get killed. He had some help by 1933. ALPA was flexing its muscles and beginning to have some influence in Washington. Hall survived; he retired from TWA, after a full career.

While some pilots hung tough, others folded, and it is a mistake to view ALPA's early history as an uninterrupted success story. There was a lot of human wreckage in the beginning. Pilots who were out front serving as ALPA officers were really asking for trouble. Of the first three national officers, Behncke, Homer Cole of Northwest Airlines, and John Huber of Thompson Aeronautical Corporation (later American), *not one* kept his airline job. And it wasn't because they were incompetent.

Homer Cole was a Canadian who enlisted during the patriotic fervor of 1914 and went off to serve king and country in the trenches of France. Cole quickly discovered the gap between reality and recruiting posters. Mud, misery, and boredom were the lot of combat infantrymen.

"I got sick and tired of the rats and rotten food," Cole said in a taped interview in 1967. "For six months I went without taking off my outer coat, let alone my underwear. We were lousy, had crabs, and in the trenches around Vimy Ridge I would look up and see aeroplanes buzzing around. They, on the other hand, never flew unless the sun was shining, and I said, 'Well, if I have to die it might as well be on a nice clear day.'"

After the war he came to the United States and began barnstorming in the company of his brother-in-law, Walter Bullock (another ALPA founder). Cole and Bullock went to work for Northwest Airlines in the late 1920s; both had a hand in organizing ALPA and both lost their jobs. In Bullock's case it was temporary. Now retired, he recalls that Cole wasn't the keenest weather pilot, but they did so little weather flying in those days that it didn't matter. "They were pretty much out to get him, I think," said Bullock. "It was a kind of *pressure* thing." Cole died in 1978 after a long career with the Federal Aviation Administration (FAA).

John Huber's case was more direct. In 1929 he was Thompson Aeronautical's top pilot, the one other pilots referred to as "the weatherman." Jerry Wood, who later went to work for Eastern, was a hustling young aviation entrepreneur at the time, and he remembers the near-legendary status of pilots like Huber, who could always get the mail through. "Johnny was a pilot of exceptional ability," Wood said.

But skill didn't save Johnny Huber's job. At first the airmail contractors desperately needed pilots like Huber, but later, when flying became a little more routine, they no longer had the need for such expertise. That's when the harassment began. After American gobbled up Thompson, Huber was just another pilot—and a union member, at that.

American had a straightforward policy of frightening pilots away from ALPA. It never worked very well, serving only to make the American pilots more militant in their support of ALPA. Other airlines at that time were engaging in selective firing of ALPA officers. United's W. A. "Pat" Patterson had recently been slapped down hard by the National Labor Board (a predecessor of the National Labor Relations Board) for trying to sack Dave Behncke. C. R. Smith, American's president, was too clever for that. Instead of firing Huber outright, Smith simply saw to it that the pilot's life was miserable. The company transferred Huber around on the spur of the moment, once sending him from Chicago to Albany on notice so short he didn't even have time to go home for a change of clothes.

"I had to call my wife to tell her we were moving," Huber said. "I told her to send some clothes and that I'd see her as soon as she could pack the household goods and get to Albany. She couldn't believe it."

Of course, American offered Huber an option—he could quit. It was rough, and Huber's health began to fail. In 1935 he resigned, unable to take it anymore. He went on to a distinguished career in air traffic control with FAA. Now retired and living in Florida, Huber feels that modern airline pilots do not appreciate the price he paid in helping to establish ALPA.

What made these people tick? What made a man like Byron S. "Pop" Warner defy the conventional wisdom of the era? In 1929 Warner had what he wanted above all else, a pilot's job with National Air Transport (NAT, later part of United). He was a university graduate, a trained engineer, and although he loved flying, the relatively low pay, poor working conditions, and the company's lack of appreciation for the pilots' contributions bothered him. When he met Dave Behncke, the hulking six-footer who was "talking up" a new pilots' association, Warner knew immediately it had to be a _union,_ not another toothless, semisocial pilots' club.

"I could see that unless we got a pilots' association with real power," Warner remembers, "there wouldn't be enough money in airline flying to make it worth my effort. I would have to go back to slipsticking at a desk, and I didn't want that—I wanted to keep flying."

So Warner was a rapid convert to Behncke's cause. He could readily see that all this talk about airline pilots being "high-class professionals who didn't need a union" was just so much blather. Operating under the code name "Mr. A," Warner successfully organized the pilots of NAT in 1931. Then he got fired. Management's spies were good at figuring out the cover names of ALPA's "Key Men," as Behncke called them.

It was an angry, frustrating time. Warner was among the lucky ones. He got another airline job and went on to fly a full career. Now retired and living in California, he can still remember the devastating effect of being fired without just cause. "I pretty well kept my head down after that," Warner admits.

Then there are the unlucky ones like George L. Hays. He stood up for ALPA during the Long & Harmon fight in 1934, and, like Warner, he too was fired. By 1934, the New Deal's labor protective machinery was operating effectively, so Hays appealed his dismissal. In one of its first uses of professional staff, ALPA sent a representative down from Chicago to Fort Worth where NLB held hearings on the dismissal of Hays and two other pilots.

On paper it was a great success. ALPA won the legal battle when NLB ordered Hays reinstated. Another pilot, Maurice M. Kay, also won reinstatement. (A third, L. S. Turner, a previous winner of the Air Mail Pilot Medal of Honor, declined reinstatement in order to pursue other business opportunities.) But while ALPA was busily contesting the illegal firing of pilots for union activities, Long & Harmon sold out to Braniff. The Braniff brothers took over the Post Office airmail routes, but not the pilots. There was nothing ALPA could do.

Kay found another airline job after a long period of unemployment, but George Hays had no luck. ALPA was supporting him with a meager monthly payment raised from members by a special assessment. That was embarrassing enough, but even worse was the humiliating fact that Hays had to fall back on his parents for support at the age of 28.

We must remember that this was happening in the midst of the Great

Depression, when the despair of unemployment was epidemic, and that there were other things eating at George Hays. He feared that standing up for his legal rights had caused other airlines to blacklist him and that he would never be able to find another flying job. One day, George Hays went out to his car, sat down in the front seat, and shot himself through the head. It was 1936.

These hard times required some sassy politicking on Behncke's part, and it always bothered some pilots, who liked to think of themselves as nonpartisan. Behncke spent much of his life trying to educate pilots. The airline business was highly political, unable to survive in those days without direct government subsidy, and Behncke (who was from Chicago, after all) knew about the role clout played. As Behncke began to take his first, halting steps toward representing pilots in Washington, D.C., he found himself facing people with formidable political connections—hard characters like the legendary Eddie Rickenbacker of Eastern and American's steely eyed C. R. Smith.

Many pilots didn't like the way Behncke criticized their employers when testifying before congressional committees. Nor did they like the way he glorified politicians who aided him. Behncke found this kind of political soft-headedness contemptible. He openly pursued a shifting series of alliances based on the Machiavellian principle that "my enemy's enemy is my friend." His approach to politics was always frankly opportunistic. "It doesn't matter where the coal comes from," Behncke once said, "as long as it gets on the fire."

Politically, the bane of Behncke's existence (and of other ALPA leaders to come) was the kind of pilot who could not understand that there was no political safe ground and that ALPA must choose on some issues. "Most pilots don't know any more about politics than they do pink tights," Behncke once grumbled.

The Old Man had a way with words.

Behncke was a quick study at the game of politics, learning to play it masterfully over the years. Airline bosses hated him for that, especially Eddie Rickenbacker, who bore an ancient grudge against him and had once tried to punch him out. "They hated each other because they were so much alike," says Eastern's Jerry Wood of the perennial feud between Rickenbacker and Behncke. Eventually Behncke and Rickenbacker mellowed, each coming to have a grudging respect for the other's abilities.

But that never happened with National Airlines' George T. "Ted" Baker. Behncke's last, and in some ways his toughest, political fight was with Baker. There was no quarter given, and none asked.

It began in 1948, when Ted Baker goaded his pilots into a strike. A nasty situation had developed on National in 1945, following the dismissal of a pilot for questionable reasons. Behncke, who prided himself on working things out, proceeded deliberately, without panic, to settle it through the

National Mediation Board. National's pilots were certainly in no hurry to strike, owing to the large surplus of trained military pilots hungering for their jobs. But then the mechanics got into it. Baker had been abusing them for some time, so they went on strike; the National pilots naturally felt sympathy for them. In addition, there was a safety question involved.

"Baker had a bunch of typewriter ribbon clerks out there working on the planes," Charles Ruby recalls. "The real reason for the strike was that our planes were a bunch of accidents just waiting to happen."

When it became apparent to Behncke that Ted Baker was engaging in a calculated effort to break ALPA, there was no alternative to a fight. One thing is clear; ALPA never wanted the National Airlines strike of 1948. Ted Baker provoked it and there is strong evidence that he had the tacit approval of other airlines. Their theory was that if ALPA could be broken on a major trunk airline (albeit one of the smallest), it could be broken elsewhere.

The National Airlines strike lasted nine months. To the pilots it seemed like forever—picketing, towing banners behind an old T-6 Texan, writing in smoke across the skies of a dozen cities: "Don't Fly National."

It was great theater, for a while. Then the public, ever fickle, lost interest. The spectacle of uniformed airline pilots carrying placards, handing out leaflets, and talking on any local radio show that would have them was unusual, but how could it compete with Milton Berle on the hot new medium of television? The new pilots working for National wore uniforms just like the old pilots, though of a different color. It was all very confusing to the man in the street.

In short order, Baker had fleshed out his crews with a full complement of strikebreakers and it was pretty much business as usual. ALPA was all but beaten, "scabbed out." Baker had won every aspect of the strike except the purely political one, and that decision awaited only the outcome of the 1948 presidential election between Truman and Dewey. Mr. Gallup had already stopped taking polls by October, calling Dewey's two-to-one lead over Truman "insurmountable." Dewey was so certain of victory that he announced his cabinet appointments in advance and allowed bands to play *Hail to the Chief* wherever he went. Ted Baker and Tom Dewey were great friends.

Behncke, already slowing down from the heart condition that would eventually kill him, backed Truman and the Democrats in 1948 against all odds. Many pilots thought he was crazy. When it was over, and Truman had pulled the greatest upset in American political history, Behncke looked wiser than a tree full of owls. He held Truman's political IOU, and Harry Truman was a man who paid his debts.

Now it was shell-shocked Ted Baker's turn to sweat it out. He had to admit defeat and settle with ALPA. Truman had left no doubt that if the National strikers didn't get their jobs back, Ted Baker wouldn't have an airline. Baker may have been mean and shifty, but nobody ever called him stupid.

In 1960, politics was once again the determining factor in the defeat of Southern Airways' Frank W. Hulse, a spiritual descendant of Ted Baker. Beginning in the summer of 1960 Southern's pilots walked the picket lines for more than two years. Like the National pilots in 1948, they were completely "scabbed out." To be out of work is bad enough, but to see others take your job, fly your trips, and draw your salary is even worse. A complacent FAA bent the rules to help Hulse, actually allowing one strikebreaker who held only a private license with no instrument rating to slip into the cockpit. He flew for several months as a captain! There were plenty of bureaucratic red faces over that one, especially since it was ALPA, not the government, that uncovered this incredible dereliction.

The Southern strike of 1960 was no mere local dispute, despite the fact that Southern was a local service carrier. It employed more pilots in 1960 than National had in 1948, and there were other local service carriers that were even bigger.

"If Mr. Hulse had won," says John Boyd (whose fellow Southern pilots dubbed him "Senator" because he spent so much time lobbying in Washington), "the regional carriers' association would have broken ALPA on every feeder line, Trans-Texas, all of them."

Everything hinged on a presidential election, just as it did in 1948, this time John F. Kennedy's. The Southern strikers formally endorsed him after Richard Nixon crossed their picket lines.

The gamble paid off. After his election, Kennedy paid his debts to organized labor, of which ALPA was one cog, by appointing a prolabor Democrat to the Civil Aeronautics Board (CAB). One must remember that CAB held the power of life and death over airlines like Southern, owing to the fact that they could not sustain themselves without government subsidy. In 1962, after the long drawn-out series of lawyerly confrontations called "due process" had run its course, CAB ruled that Frank Hulse had "bargained unfairly" and must either reinstate his pilots or lose his operating certificate. The crucial vote was along straight party lines, three Democrats to two Republicans.

"If Richard Nixon had won the election of 1960," says Harry F. Susemihl, former Southern master executive council chairman, "neither I nor any other Southern pilot would ever have worked again."

Close calls like that dot ALPA's history. They were interesting times, but it is well to remember that interesting times are usually gut-wrenchingly grim to live through.

Every airline pilot working today owes a substantial debt to those who came before, men whose names they do not know, who sweated and fought to make ALPA what it is today, sometimes at great personal cost.

A long series of beacons winks out of the past at modern airline pilots.

They mark a rough and perilous course. Flying it again would be tough. Modern airline pilots owe it to themselves to know their own history—warts and all. ✈

CHAPTER 2

Stepping on Toes

They were called "troublemakers." Who did they think they were, butting in where they had no business, presuming to form an "association"? Airline owners weren't fooled by the fancy name and the talk about ALPA being "like the American Medical Association." They knew the shape and smell of a union, and they were having none of it in 1931.

"I won't have any union man working for me," said W. A. "Pat" Patterson when he first heard of ALPA. "Nobody can belong to a union and fly for United!"

It was no idle threat, as the example of Byron S. "Pop" Warner made clear. Warner ("Mr. A") got the ax for ALPA activities on the National Air Transport (NAT) division of United, just after the convention of "Key Men." That meeting, held at the Morrison Hotel in Chicago on July 27, 1931, was ALPA's official moment of birth. Reuben Wagner ("Mr. P"), in charge of organizing the Omaha-based pilots of Boeing Air Transport, was one of several very nervous young men who had made that meeting possible. Why did they risk their careers by listening to Dave Behncke?

"We were just worn out," Wagner explains of the way airline flying was developing as the depression deepened. "We all wanted to fly, we *liked* to fly. Everyone in those days was flying because they liked to fly, not for the money. But we thought we weren't getting what we should."

Of the 24 pilots who acted as Key Men during the birth of ALPA, only 6 remain. They are old men now, mostly in their 80s, and the state of their health varies, as does the clarity of their memories.

Johnny Huber is the only one who gave up his airline job prior to reaching mandatory retirement, and he was forced out because of C. R. Smith's vendetta against ALPA. At 74, Huber is the junior surviving Key Man, a year younger than Byron Warner, who managed to land and keep a flying job with American after he was fired from United. Warner is still alert and articulate, still working regularly as an aeronautical engineer, still passing his Federal Aviation Administration (FAA) medicals with ease, and still flying his own lightplane regularly. He is the only one of the six surviving Key Men who does; the others have had enough flying. Nearly all of their 18 deceased colleagues died in crashes.

Walter Bullock ("Mr. C"), born in 1899, flew his last DC-7 trip for North-

10

west Airlines in 1961. He collected "pledges," as the first ALPA recruits were called, on what would ultimately be Northwest's Council 1. He is, in effect, the dean of all master executive council chairmen, although they weren't called that then. After being forced into retirement by FAA Administrator Quesada's age-60 edict, Bullock remained actively a part of aviation well into his 70s, founding a company in Lakeville, Minn., to build classic aircraft replicas. He also flew exhibitions at county fairs in a 1911 Bleriot Model 11 monoplane, a throwback to his early days as a barnstormer. Bullock learned to fly at the Curtiss School in Virginia in 1916. In 1918 he flew a 1910 Curtiss Model D pusher from the outfield grass at a Boston Braves Fourth of July doubleheader before thousands of gaping baseball fans.

He quit flying about 10 years ago. "It was time to hang 'em up," he says, rather wistfully. His logbook shows 34,000 hours in 102 different aircraft. Now in his eighty-second year, Walt Bullock is thinner than old photos show him. As the shadows lengthen over the patio of his Florida retirement home, he gradually forgets about the tape recorder, which inhibited him at first. With the help of his wife Lillian, and a massive collection of well-thumbed photographs to trigger remembrance, the stories tumble out.

Reuben Wagner is the picture of radiant health in his eighty-fourth year. He was one of the old Post Office Air Mail pilots who formed their own association as far back as 1919 and who later provided a granite base of support for Behncke's idea of unionization. To watch "Rube" Wagner enter the crowded grand ballroom at Reno's ornate El Dorado Hotel during a Retired United Pilots Association cocktail hour is to understand the term legendary. Mere striplings of 75 approach him as they would royalty, touching his elbow cautiously, eager to share some treasured memory of the days when they served as his copilots on trimotor Boeing 80s. Rube Wagner, of course, was never anybody's copilot.

For Ralph Johnson ("Mr. Q") the years haven't been so kind. Called "Little Ralph" to distinguish him from the other Ralph Johnson flying for United, he lives quietly in California, coping as best he can with the debilitating effects of a stroke as he approaches his eighty-fifth year. He remembers little now, which is a pity since no man contributed more to the creation of ALPA. Back in 1930, he advocated linking ALPA to the Railroad Brotherhoods until Dave Behncke won him over to the idea of affiliating with the American Federation of Labor. After that, Ralph Johnson became one of Behncke's rocks, a close friend and confidante.

George Douglass ("Mr. V") is also living in California retirement. He goes back to the days before W. A. Patterson and P. G. Johnson's developing monolith swallowed up little Varney Air Transport, his airline, and made it part of United. "The wife and I are pretty much on the sick list these days," Douglass says good-naturedly. But fortunately, his physical ailments have not affected his memory. George Douglass talks lucidly about men long dead and events long past. The only hindrance to communication is his deafness, a problem he shares with other early birds who spent long hours exposed to unmuffled engine blast in open cockpits.

Their wives help them answer questions they cannot quite hear through the assortment of hearing aids they carry. Some, like Virginia Huber, remember almost as much about the early days of ALPA as do their husbands. Virginia was working as a stenographer in 1929 when she married Johnny Huber (then a dashing young airmail pilot) and, like Gladys Behncke, she did a lot of notetaking and typing for ALPA—all for free.

Just these six were left in 1981 as the fiftieth year approached.* (R. Lee Smith of Northwest Airlines, one of the original movers of ALPA, is still alive, but he did not act as a Key Man.)

In the memories of these men the truly important things remain bright. A man's personality and his values, the shape of his face, the way he talked and thought and acted half a century ago, these things they still remember. Principles last forever, but specific details no longer matter much—who was at a meeting, when it took place. The shape and course of debates, once passionately contested, seem with the passage of time unimportant, perhaps even faintly ridiculous.

Every man is his own historian, extracting from the past that which he finds useful and worthy of preservation for posterity. What fundamental truths do these survivors still treasure? What aspect of their experience during the creation of ALPA do they deem most worthy of passing along to the current generation of airline pilots?

Above all else, ALPA's founders want modern airline pilots to know the sense of satisfaction they feel for having secured their future with their own hands at a time when nearly everybody, including their fellow pilots, thought it could not be done. A tone of calm satisfaction pervades the stories these old men tell. To overcome great obstacles, to participate in an enduring act of creation, to build something lasting with one's own sweat, these things are sufficient to maintain the fires of satisfaction during the winter of any man's life. And if the price is to remember being called a troublemaker by those you outwitted, well, that makes it all the sweeter.

The men who helped Dave Behncke create ALPA never thought of themselves as troublemakers. They were, in fact, good "company men," loyal and conscientious, with more of a stake in the survival of the airlines for which they worked than the owners themselves had. As Rube Wagner put it: "We pilots *were* the company. Some pilots who didn't want to join ALPA tried to make believe that if the pilots were for a union, they weren't for the company. But ALPA pilots were for the company way ahead of the company!"

*Originally published as a series in *Air Line Pilot* magazine beginning in January 1981, *Flying the Line* is based on interviews with ALPA's founders and principal figures conducted during 1980. In midsummer 1982, as this version was going to press, we learned that George Douglass had died on June 19 at age 86.

The people who owned airlines in those days usually had something else going for them. Most of them had already made it big, thanks to previous success, or birth, or both. The same couldn't be said for the first generation of airline pilots. Very few early pilots took up regular airline flying because they were bored by hanging around country clubs. Aristocratic celebrity aviators back then, the Howard Hugheses and Harry Richmans, usually flew somewhere once, perhaps even around the world, collected their headlines and tickertape parades down Broadway, and then left the day-in, day-out humdrum battles with fog and thunderstorms to people like Eastern's Dick Merrill. Showing his good sense, Harry Richman (actually a professional musician) took Merrill with him when he tackled the Atlantic. Guess who did the flying.

The first generation of airline pilots, the ones who managed to live through the 1920s against all odds, saw the future only dimly. Indeed, the nature of their work precluded long-term planning. Some of them, however, had the idea that air transportation would one day become something more than a curiosity, perhaps even the dominant mode of passenger travel, and they had an inkling that those who flew the airliners of the future would occupy a critical position in the industry.

This foresight was remarkable considering management's arrogance in those days, the cocksure belief of most early airline operators that *they* were the industry and that pilots were dime-a-dozen technicians doing a job *anybody* could do.

The airline operators were just a bit premature in this judgment. In a few years, airline flying would become a rather ordinary exercise, still requiring considerable technical skill but sufficiently routine that almost any young pilot coming out of military flight school could, with proper training, undertake it. The operators failed to recognize that the piloting skills necessary for successful scheduled airline operations in the late 1920s were anything but ordinary. An airline's success was heavily dependent upon the skill of pilots who knew intimately the contact landmarks of their routes, who knew every fence, every mountain pass, every bend and kink in every river and lake between lighted beacons. They flew contact over these "lighted airways" in weather modern pilots wouldn't touch, conditions sometimes measured in terms of how many telephone poles were visible from a railroad telegrapher's office. There are cases on record in which pilots only narrowly averted head-on collisions with onrushing locomotives.

The first generation of airline pilots had learned these extraordinary contact flying skills in open cockpit biplanes flown in every conceivable weather condition, often as government airmail pilots. When the first multiengine transports became available, the skills early pilots had honed under circumstances that absolutely precluded carrying passengers were easily translatable into regular passenger operations. The ability of these old barnstormers to get a Fokker or Ford Trimotor through on schedule bred a false confidence among their employers—a feeling that there really was nothing much to flying an airliner in 1929.

The pilots themselves knew better, especially the first generation who had not flown the mail but who were expected to fly single-engine aircraft. Jim Belding, who learned his trade at the Boeing School of Aeronautics in 1929, managed to win a job on Boeing Air Transport against the stiff competition of Army Air Corps flying school graduates. The parting advice Belding's instructor gave him and Bert Ball prior to their departure for their first regular airline job was, "Boys, don't try to follow Rube Wagner!"

New pilots who tried to match the record of veterans such as Ham Lee and Rube Wagner usually came to grief.

The go-getter businessmen who began taking over aviation in the late 1920s were largely ignorant of flying skill. Many of them were opportunists who had come into the business following Lindbergh's celebrated flight to Paris in 1927, their primary goal being to harness the torrent of money unleashed by that epochal event. Wall Streeters called it "The Lindbergh Boom." There was big money available in the free-wheeling atmosphere of 1927—a choking glut of it, in fact—for anybody who could put together a stock prospectus with the magic word "aero" somewhere in it. The movers and shakers in this scene were usually young men who hoped to make their mark exploiting the commercial possibilities of aviation as the previous generation of entrepreneurs had exploited steamships and rails. They had no real love for aviation otherwise.

Harris M. "Pop" Hanshue, the operator of Western Air Express, for example, hated airplanes and never flew, *even as a passenger,* unless he had no other choice. W. A. "Pat" Patterson of United was a banker who never so much as touched the controls of an airplane. Delta's C. E. Woolman briefly played around with airplanes as a young man, but he was essentially a promoter who stumbled into airline operations via his accidental control of a crop-dusting outfit. Even some legendary aviation personalities, like Eastern's Eddie Rickenbacker, had only "public relations" flying experience. Although he carried a great reputation from his combat days in World War I, Rickenbacker's total pilot time did not exceed 200 hours, and he never held a civil license. Juan Trippe of Pan American flew the same way the notorious E. L. Cord of Century Airlines flew—only when the weather was perfect and only with an experienced professional pilot along.

Cord had a pivotal role in the pilots' growing support for ALPA, because nobody better exemplified the contempt for pilots that most operators hardly bothered to conceal. Cord had risen rapidly into the rarefied heights of 1920s-style finance capitalism, dealing mostly with automotive stocks. In 1929 he acquired his first aircraft operation, the struggling Stinson Aircraft Corporation, and shortly thereafter added Lycoming to his stable. Already equipped with engines and airframes, all Cord needed for an airline was pilots, which he proceeded to hire as the depression deepened at wages of $150 per month. Cord had no trouble staffing Century Airlines at that price.

"Any normal person can handle an airplane," Cord said in 1930.

Virtually the only genuine airman among airline executives was Jack Frye of Transcontinental & Western Air (TWA). Capitalizing on this unique fact, TWA used to advertize itself as "The Airline Run by Airmen." All the other airline owner-operators were pilots in the sense that George T. Baker of National and Paul Braniff were pilots—fair-weather amateurs.

The hard fact is that by the late 1920s a clear clash of values had set in between pilots and management—one that almost amounted to a class conflict. When all the romantic myths are punctured, the typical airline owner-operator of that era can be seen as possessing some very unlovely characteristics. He was less interested in pioneering than he was in his bank account, less interested in the welfare of his employees than he was in his stockholders' dividends, and less concerned with the safety of flight than he was with its profitability.

To the pioneer airline pilots of the 1920s, men who had flown the airmail for the Post Office, who knew the ins-and-outs of making a buck with an airplane through barnstorming, it was profoundly disillusioning to discover the true nature of their new employers. After the disillusionment wore off, the pilots were just plain mad. It was pilots, real airmen, who had brought aviation into prominence by the late 1920s — not bankers and Wall Street wheeler-dealers with their fancy connections and silk suits. To pioneer pilots, flying airplanes was a way of life, something they did because they loved it. To be in an open cockpit, to smell the seductive odor of doped wings and oiled machinery, to cast free from earthly restraint with a water-cooled Liberty's 12 drumming cylinders up front and a challenging DH-4 beneath them, *that* was what aviation was about. It didn't matter that they could have earned far more money on the ground selling insurance. Airplanes mattered—more than life. Certainly more than mere money.

That didn't mean, though, that early airline pilots were going to work for peanuts. It was obvious that the men who signed their paychecks had plenty of money. Aviation was a gusher that returned unimaginable profits, at least percentagewise, on the amount invested.

From the moment the Post Office proved that an airmail service was feasible, certain well-heeled gentlemen were using their influence with powerful congressmen to have it transferred to private contractors. To get some idea of just how lucrative a government mail contract could be, consider the following example. In 1926, the year Congress authorized private bidding for mail contracts, one Charles Deeds, son of a powerfully connected East Coast financier, invested a mere $253 in the stock of Frederick B. Rentschler's United Aircraft. The initial stock issue was closely held, available only to insiders with the right connections. Only three years later, through repeated splits on the great bull market of the late 1920s, Deeds' original $253 investment was worth nearly $36 million—most of it thanks to government mail payments.

The Post Office pilots themselves were aware of the financial possibilities. Acting through their association, they hired former Superintendent of the Air Mail Carl F. Egge to head a pilot-owned corporation created for the specific purpose of bidding on a contract.

"Well, we really got in high gear on that," Rube Wagner declares. "We went to bankers, mortgaged our homes. They said, 'Oh no, that won't work.' We couldn't do a thing about it."

The message was clear—only the big boys need apply for a mail contract.

Early airline pilots, aware that they weren't getting much money for doing the flying that was earning desk-bound manipulators fat profits, were highly irritated. They naturally resented being exploited by people who never flew, who never risked their own necks. And there were shennanigans going on after 1926 that the pilots found very distasteful.

"We were carrying little bolts through for several hundred dollars," Reuben Wagner recalls. "With a postage tag on it and everything, and it was fraud, yeah, it was." The operators got paid for more than the price of postage stamps, so they made sure there was plenty of mail.

Walt Bullock had made a good living for 11 years as a barnstormer. "Sometimes we had hungry winters," Bullock recalls, "but we usually did so good we didn't need to work but half a year." But after going to work for Northwest in 1927, Bullock found himself earning much less. In 1928 Bullock was one of several pilots who approached the owner of Northwest, a Minneapolis banker named Lilly, for a raise. Their reception was humiliating.

"He said he'd quit, disband the airline, if he had any labor trouble," Bullock remembers. Northwest's pilots got a flat salary of $350 per month for five trips a week between Chicago and the Twin Cities, with neither hourly limitations nor regular vacations. "The speed of the J-4 Stinsons we flew was only 83½ miles per hour, so that made for some long days," says Bullock.

Following their first meeting with Lilly, Bullock and the other NWA pilots knew something had to be done:

> That was the main reason the NWA pilots were interested in forming a union. Lilly would say he was rich, didn't need the airline, that it was just a plaything to him. This was foolish. Even then it was a pretty big airline as airlines went. And this was our whole future, you know, and it didn't sit so good to have him sit here and tell us it was just a plaything to him.

Were Bullock and his fellow pilots intimidated by Lilly's threats to disband the airline and fire them if he had any labor trouble?

We knew he wasn't about to close it up. No, it actually made us more determined, I think, because we weren't afraid, we really didn't believe that. By that time [1928], it was a pretty big business and it was making 25 percent per year on the original investment, right through when the only revenue was mostly mail. Mail used to pay very well, you know. He saw to it that there was plenty of mail. It wasn't like a man like Lilly to pass up a profit, believe me. He didn't get to be president of that bank by passing up profits.

Rube Wagner confirms Walt Bullock's description of airmail profits. "P. G. Johnson bought the best equipment he could buy," Wagner says. "He bought the best automobiles and trucks and everything. In six months, the first six months, they paid everything off. They paid for the whole thing and they still were making money."

Still, only by dint of repeated pressure could the pilot groups get any pay raises. On NWA, following the introduction of Ford Trimotors in 1928, Lilly agreed to a small raise. "We got a whole $25 more a month," Bullock says. "We all just kept coming in as a group and we'd haggle. Lilly wasn't about to give away anything.

"When ALPA was fully organized Lilly threatened dire results to anybody who joined. But that never materialized. We got $775 a month for flying Fords." Leaning back in his chair, Walt Bullock's eyes twinkle, and there is a trace of wonder in his voice.

Behncke, old Dave, he was a great one for that. I can't say I liked the guy that much, personally. He was a hot air kind of guy but he had a lot of guts and he knew every politician in the country. Behncke always painted a picture of how rough it was in those days, and it was rough. But he exaggerated, for a reason I guess, so people wouldn't think it was easy to buck bankers like Lilly. Hell, we'd have been dead without Behncke.

Rube Wagner agrees about the combination of political and public relations pressures that Behncke brought to bear. "After the convention of Key Men at the Morrison," Wagner says, "I figured my job was gone. Then Roosevelt took over and Patterson changed, he was all for the unions, said that if he were a pilot, the first thing he'd do would be join ALPA." Wagner slaps his knee and laughs. "We got along fine after that."

Earning a decent salary was one thing; living to spend it was another. While the pilots were fighting for ALPA's right to exist, a new battle loomed. It was about safety, and the pilots had a word for it—they called it "pushing." ✦

CHAPTER 3

Pilot Pushing

For the first generation of professional airline pilots, the most persistent problem was not low pay, but safety—and the related question of job security. A pilot who played it *too* safe, who canceled flights too often because of weather or some other consideration, could get fired.

Airline operators had a hard-nosed attitude about schedule completion in those days and tended to regard overly conservative pilots as "slackers." This kind of thinking was an outgrowth of the contemporary notion regarding competition, the belief that people had to be "pushed" to achieve a satisfactory competitive edge. From the operators' point of view, the fledgling airline industry had to meet the competition, meaning railroads. Unless airlines, like railroads, ran on schedule, no one would take them seriously.

The pilots were skeptical about entering a competition with the railroads for the sensible reason that it could get them killed. Any serious effort to compete with the railroads in the area of schedule reliability, the pilots knew, would fall most heavily upon them and would put pressure on them to take risks. More bluntly, the pilots worried less about being taken seriously by business moguls of the 1920s, than about being taken advantage of by them.

In truth, there were two sides to this question. Some pilots *were* overly timid, reluctant to adopt the new instrument flying techniques as they began to appear during the late 1920s and early 1930s. They were slow to abandon the old-fashioned contact-flying techniques that had seen them through so many flights before. On the other hand, some operators were too ready to adopt new flying techniques and equipment that later turned out to have serious flaws. They may also have been too hasty in their dismissal of the pilots' weather-related complaints.

Although conflict between pilots and their superiors over when and how to fly is an old story, going back almost to the beginning of regular airmail flying, the pace of technological change in the late 1920s and early 1930s aggravated the situation. Pilots and operations managers could not agree on the issue of pilots' authority to cancel a flight because of unsafe conditions. In a sense, it was a question of *image*.

By the early 1930s, the operators preferred to promote commercial aviation as an industry that had arrived, that was fully developed, mature, and no longer experimental. The pilots knew better and preferred a more conservative image, one that portrayed the industry as it really was, essentially a tax-supported public service. Because it was still heavily dependent upon the government airmail subsidy, the pilots insisted that airline service should be seen as a regulated public utility, with safety dominant over every other consideration.

This conflict of assumptions and image set the stage for a battle over safety that continues to this day. Its roots are deep in the history of commercial aviation, and one of the keys to ALPA's growth and success lies in the way Dave Behncke utilized the safety issue in the 1930s.

In theory, airline owners agreed with their pilots that safety was the paramount goal; in practice, it was a different story. Early airline pilots were made to feel that arriving on time counted for more than arriving safely, but late. Of course everyone wanted both safety and regularity of schedules, but to the pilots it was evident that the two were not always compatible. The operators agreed in principle, although in specific cases the reasons given by pilots for canceling flights were not always acceptable to them, particularly if it cost the company money. It all boiled down to the question of "command authority"—who had it and when.

The issue of "pilot pushing," or forcing a pilot to fly against his better judgment, was acute, particularly in the last days of single-engine airmail operations when passengers were still scarce. In the easy money climate of the 1920s, a time of cheap nonunion labor and readily available materials, the operators could well afford an occasional smashed airplane and dead pilot. On the Boeing Air Transport Division of what later became United Airlines, the Cheyenne repair and maintenance base would frequently salvage only the registration number of a crashed aircraft and then proceed to build an entirely new airplane around it. "They could go rebuild a Boeing 40B4 far better, stronger than before," Rube Wagner says. "I don't think anybody ever bothered to tell the Bureau of Air Commerce either."

With the arrival of very expensive multiengine equipment, airline owners became less casual about the loss of aircraft and hence of pilots. But even then, a pilot had no recourse but to fly if a determined operations manager disputed his decision to cancel.

"The operators fired at the drop of a hat," says Pan Am's Roy Keeler, one of the first group of largely ceremonial vice-presidents elected at ALPA's 1932 convention. Keeler, who retired in 1960, had gone to work for Pan Am in 1929. "The operators always talked safety. Juan Trippe and Musick, sure they wanted it. But they had short memories, and when things would go along well—no accidents—they'd forget. Just a little line of thunderstorms,' sure. They're not flying it. But you'd better go if they said to," Keeler remembers of the days when ALPA was still too weak to contest every dismissal from an airline. "We were all subject to dismissal for most anything anybody could think of," says former President Charles Ruby of his experience on National during the 1930s.

Closely allied to the issue of pilot pushing was the related one of competitive flying, a managerial technique that took advantage of the natural desire of pilots to compete with each other—to see who could get through fastest or perform under the most trying circumstances, most often. Operations managers, themselves pilots, used this device to urge their pilots into flying contests. Some pilots liked it; most didn't.

Dave Behncke's earliest known utterances on the subject of pilot unionization stemmed directly from the sour feeling competitive flying instilled in most pilots. In 1928, Behncke was elected "governor" of the Central District of the National Air Pilots Association (NAPA), one of several semisocial pilots' organizations that flourished in the 1920s. Some airlines were using cash incentives to encourage pilots to fly in marginal weather, and Behncke was speaking for the sober majority when he urged NAPA to adopt the slogan: "Don't overfly a brother pilot!" By that, Behncke meant that if one working pilot refused to fly the mail, then his brother pilots should support him. Unfortunately, working pilots made up only a tiny percentage of those who claimed membership in NAPA, so Behncke got nowhere with his campaign. In a sense, Behncke's failure to accomplish anything useful through NAPA, particularly in the area of curbing competitive flying was one of the reasons he began the agitation that later led to the creation of ALPA.

Jim Belding (UAL) remembers Behncke's denunciation of the evils of competitive flying as one of the main reasons junior pilots were attracted to ALPA in the beginning:

> Behncke and the senior guys didn't include really junior pilots in ALPA when they started it up in 1931, because they had no protection to offer us. The company could find copilots off the street if they had to. Then in January 1933, when I got my first command, flying single-engine night mail, I was transferred to Omaha. Dave Behncke met me one night when I came in off the line at Chicago and we talked in his car. I hadn't really been approached before. Behncke said they couldn't guarantee too much for a newly promoted pilot. But I went ALPA because there was one management pilot who was not instrument trained, who was notorious for pushing pilots. He was a good example of a weather pusher, pushing pilots to make his record look good. We had a case of competitive flying start up that was the cause of a serious accident. One senior pilot would go out and he would get through because he knew everything, and the next man up, who wasn't as familiar with the route, was intimidated into taking the mail out, and we picked a bunch of them up off the top of hills. I blame it on the intimidation of [the management pilot], but you had to kill somebody be-

fore you really got the problem solved. They finally caught up with [the management pilot] and he got fired.

Thus, to get through the 1920s in one piece and stay on the payroll, was no mean feat. But the first generation of professional pilots accepted the risks of the flying game the way it was, often flying under circumstances modern pilots would never accept.

They flew when some unknown railway telegrapher said he could see five, maybe six telephone poles down the track. How good was his eyesight? And would you have company somewhere along the route? Early pilots learned to fly slightly to the right of the tracks just in case a brother pilot might be fumbling along in the opposite direction.

The mortality rates that resulted from this kind of flying were staggering. An airmail pilot working for the Post Office Department in 1918 stood only one chance in four of surviving until 1926, when the private contractors took over. The situation improved only slightly thereafter, and as late as the mid-1930s, Behncke was scoring well in debates with the operators by citing the risk factor. A favorite rhetorical device of his was to intone solemnly, at appropriate intervals, that one airline pilot perished in the line of duty every so many days.

One of Behncke's greatest political achievements was to convince President Roosevelt that the high level of risk working pilots encountered on an everyday basis justified their getting federal protection. In 1934, FDR's cancellation of the airmail contracts opened the door for Behncke. Most pilots weren't surprised that FDR took this drastic action. For months, the Senate investigation into the awarding of the 1930 airmail contracts had filled headlines with charges of fraud and collusion between postal officials and airline executives. And, we have seen, most pilots were aware of something peculiar in the way the airmail operation was being run. Perhaps, in a moral sense, a case could be made that the major operators deserved to have their airmail contracts canceled. But most pilots opposed the cancellation because since mail was the airlines' principal source of income, "justice" meant that they were going to get laid off—as indeed many were.

In what can only be called an inspired act of political legerdemain, Behncke turned this dark hour in the history of commercial aviation to ALPA's advantage. Behncke was the only industry spokesman to support FDR's decision to cancel the airmail contracts. While Lindbergh, Rickenbacker, and other aviators by the score were howling for FDR's scalp, Behncke won the President's gratitude by standing behind him. FDR rewarded Behncke by inserting the following language into the message he sent Congress requesting new airmail legislation to restore the contracts to private bidders: "Public safety calls for pilots of high character and great skill. . . . The occupation is a hazardous one. Therefore the law should provide for a method to fix maximum hours and minimum pay."

21

Airline executives were appalled when they saw Behncke's rhetoric enshrined in the President's special message. A hazardous occupation! To say that pilots deserved special treatment because they weren't going to be around very long was hardly calculated to get people on airliners.

In a tactical sense, though, Behncke's harping on the dangers of flying, on the peril a pilot faced each time he went aloft, was the correct thing for him to do at that time. The airlines' principal business then was mail, not passengers. Scaring people about flying wasn't going to materially damage any airline's business. In the future, however, when passengers would inevitably surpass mail as the airlines' mainstay, ALPA would be able to damage an airline merely by publicizing the safety angle. In effect, Behncke was saying to the operators: "Look! Either you take us in as a full partner in this business, now, or we're going to be damned disruptive. This is just a sample."

He made his point. By 1934, Behncke had considerable political support. Most airline executives knew full well that he was becoming the kind of talented polemicist it didn't pay to fool around with. After 1934 the operators started praising their pilots to congressmen of all political stripes, agreeing that they needed federal protection. Since Congress was obviously going to insert protective provisions for pilots into the Air Mail Act of 1934 anyway, it made sense for the operators to be good sports about it. Besides, they hoped to pass along the increase in pilot salaries to the taxpayers. This turned out to be only partly true, as we shall see, and hence a source of much future friction. But no one could see this in the spring of 1934, when there was a lot of congressional talk about "socializing" the airmail, recreating the Post Office's old Air Mail Service. The operators wanted their airmail contracts back on any terms, even if it meant having Behncke and ALPA as de facto partners.

What Behncke proved was that he knew how to play hardball with the big boys, and he did it brilliantly.

Of course there was grumbling among some ALPA members that Behncke was getting awfully big for his britches, attacking their employers like that in Washington. The airlines were, after all, the pilots' bread and butter, and many pilots disliked undermining them, even for temporary tactical advantage. But this was a minority point of view, coming mostly from pilots so devoted to their employers, perhaps out of fear, that they could not properly distinguish their own interests. And in any case, Behncke had exceptionally good insight into the mental processes of the typical pilot of that era, knowing that when he stressed the dangers of flying, he was on perfectly safe ground.

The truth was that early airline pilots enjoyed wearing the mantle of danger. The devil-may-care attitudes usually associated with flying were a part of the mystique of aviation. Of course, by the late 1920s, much of this kind of thinking among pilots was mostly sham; they were already in the process of becoming quite ordinary technocrats—sober family men, regular in their habits. But airline flying was still an exotic occupation.

It could hardly have hurt Behncke's cause to emphasize the "danger theme" because it was a major factor in the public's fascination with flying, and one that pilots encouraged. In the 1920s, particularly following Lindbergh's flight, professional airmen were socially "in" because the public was absolutely air crazy. Any schoolboy of the time could tell you about the aviation feats of Acosta, the Hunter brothers, and countless others.

Although early pilots faced long odds on living to fill a nursing home bed, there were other, nonmonetary compensations. The way kids looked up to you, the thrill of handling the most advanced airplanes in the world, the knowledge that you had a job most men envied. We must remember that the typical airline pilot of that era was a very young man, far younger than the typical airline pilot of today. For young men, mortality is only an abstraction, and the bottom line isn't always what's on a paycheck. The pay wasn't really that bad either, even during the depression. It was the threat of pay cuts, rather than the fact of them, that worried most pilots. The hours were reasonably short, compared with the usual lot of the working class, from which most pilots came, and working pilots were beginning to move well up into the middle class—a far cry from their gypsy status as barnstormers a few years before. Many a pilot was the first in his family line to have the leisure to take up the previously aristocratic game of golf. Or, if improving a golf swing wasn't a concern, there was time enough to run a business.

Airline flying was, in short, just the same then as it is today, in some respects. It was a good job a lot of people wanted badly—wanted to get paid for what they'd gladly do for free; wanted the romance of skull-hugging cap and goggles; wanted the looks they got from attractive young women. And that brings us to another fringe benefit—it could get a fellow married.

On the other hand, flying could get a girl widowed.

The issue of pilot pushing came to a head when just such a widow filed a lawsuit, charging that her airline pilot husband had been pushed to his death by an overzealous superior. The pilot's name was Joe Livermore, the airline was Northwest, and the year was 1936. The roots of the Livermore case go back to 1919, when the pilots of the Post Office's Air Mail Service went on strike rather than submit to "weather pushing."

The airline pilot of today, who wishes to know his own professional roots, must return now to 1919—the first full year of peace following World War I.

CHAPTER 4

The Airmail Pilots' Strike of 1919

Leon D. Smith was known as "Bonehead," but not because he was stupid. He got that nickname after walking into a whirling prop, and living to tell about it—stunned, bloody, and partially scalped.

On the morning of July 22, 1919, Leon Smith was about to prove that there was nothing wrong with his mental processes. He reported for work before dawn at the Belmont flying field in suburban New York City, ready to assume his duties as a Post Office Air Mail Service pilot. After loading seven sacks of first-class mail in the forward locker of his de Havilland DH-4, Smith paused, lit a cigarette, and waited. His scheduled takeoff time came and went, and still Smith sat there on the muddy tire of the DH-4, pondering.

In the previous two weeks, 15 Air Mail Service planes had crashed, killing two pilots and seriously injuring others. In every instance, fog was the culprit, and as Smith sat there a thick, murky blanket of it obscured his vision. Horizontal visibility was so bad that he could see only about 100 yards—not even to the field boundary. So Smith waited, hoping the fog would lift.

Of all the hazards early pilots feared, fog was the worst, even more so than thunderstorms. A man could see a thunderstorm and avoid it in those days by flying underneath right down on the deck. The DH-4 was built like a brick, double strutted, but if the turbulence got too heavy, you could set it down on those big balloon tires almost anywhere. Farmers seldom complained about the few feet of crops the landing gear might flatten. Having one of the celebrated airmail pilots land in your field was an event well worth a few ears of corn.

Fog was different. It could sneak up on you almost instantaneously, and then there was big trouble, as you tried to get a few feet lower where you *might* be able to pick up that familiar windmill that was your next checkpoint. The panic set in when you realized that you ought to be just about to the windmill *now*, and you still couldn't see anything except a blur of row crops straight down. That's when you yanked back the throttle and set her down.

But what if the blur below you turned out to be trees instead of a nice flat farmer's field? Then you would be faced with an Air Mail Service pilot's worst choice—either a crash landing or a blind climb into the soup, without instruments, relying on the seat of your pants, or the sound of the engine, or a change in the pitch of the wind through the wing guy wires. Anything to tell you that you were still right side up.

Air Mail Service pilots were, by their nature, brave men. But bitter experience had taught them to avoid fog at any cost.

That's why Leon Smith was still sitting there when his boss, a Post Office supervisor who was not a pilot, shouted at him to get moving.

"I'll be damned if I'll kill myself for a sack of two-bit letters," Smith said, trying to explain to his nonflying superior that the weather was unflyable. Smith allegedly used "abusive language" in challenging the supervisor to find a pilot, *any pilot,* who would fly that day.

The supervisor fired Smith on the spot, turned to the back-up pilot, E. Hamilton "Ham" Lee, and ordered him to take to the air. He too refused to fly and was also fired.

Actually, the pilots had been unhappy over wages and working conditions for a long time before the flap at Belmont erupted, but it seemed impossible that they would ever cause any real labor problem for the Post Office, let alone go on strike, because they just didn't seem to be that type.

Certainly there had been no hint of future trouble when the airmail was inaugurated amid gala ceremonies in Washington the year before. On that day, May 15, 1918, President and Mrs. Woodrow Wilson were present, chatting with Major Reuben Fleet, the commander of Army pilots temporarily detailed to the Post Office, and Lieutenant George Boyle, who was scheduled to fly the first sacks of mail out of Washington to Philadelphia. Political bigwigs milled around the old Polo Grounds, which were being pressed temporarily into service as a flying field, while nervous functionaries self-consciously loaded sacks of mail aboard the JN4D-2 Jenny and the two pilots posed stiffly in front of the plane for newspaper photographers.

Meanwhile, in Philadelphia, a similar scene was in progress, with Lieutenant James C. Edgerton accepting a lavish bouquet from his kid sister prior to departing for Washington and bearing, among other things, a letter from John S. Wanamaker, the famous department store owner and former postmaster general, to his successor Albert Sydney Burleson.

In the first years of operation the Air Mail Service proved remarkably efficient as it expanded westward to Chicago via Cleveland. The crucial ingredient in its success was the skill of the pilots who flew the antiquated war-surplus Jennys and DH-4s.

Most of the pilots were ex-military men who had resigned their commissions to take civil service appointments, and many of them had become pilots prior to World War I. Smith had been the senior instructor in charge of pilot training for the Army during the war and had learned his trade at the Curtiss Flying School in 1913. Lee was a veteran who held the world record for consecutive loops, set on June 18, 1918. He landed his Jenny when it ran out of gas on the 105th loop.

Because Americans have always been fascinated by speed and the technology of transportation, Air Mail Service pilots were the objects of genuine adulation. Their exploits were regular fare in newspapers and magazines by the early 1920s.

Their superiors in the Post Office Department in Washington also praised the pilots in the early phases of the service, when their skill at "contour" or "terrain" flying, as it was called then, enabled them to complete over 90 percent of their scheduled flights. But Post Office bureaucrats became openly critical of the pilots when the service expanded westward across the "hell stretch" of the Alleghenies, and the efficiency norms established on the original Washington–New York corridor proved impossible to maintain. All-weather capability was only a distant dream in 1919, despite what the bureaucrats thought.

In the second year of airmail operations government officials came to expect and demand a high percentage of completed flights. Most of the pressure came from two men: Postmaster General Burleson and Otto Praeger, the assistant postmaster general in charge of the airmail.

Burleson was a politician from Texas whose loyalty to Woodrow Wilson had won him the Post Office appointment in 1913. Early in Wilson's first administration, Burleson had been an important man, but as time passed and weightier matters (such as the World War) occupied the President, Burleson found himself increasingly pushed into the background.

Burleson was looking for a scheme by which he could regain his lost clout. He decided upon the Air Mail Service. Together Burleson and his crony Praeger, a paunchy, bespectacled newspaperman from Texas whose only qualification for office was his friendship with Burleson, pushed hard to make the airmail a success.

Burleson never tired of bragging that under his administration the Post Office had produced annual surpluses of as high as $20 million, and he claimed he had accomplished this by "eliminating wasteful and extravagant methods of operation and making no expenditure for which adequate service has not been rendered." In his annual message to Congress in June 1919, Burleson declared: "The high standard of daily perfect flight is being maintained regardless of weather conditions."

Praeger was a carbon copy of his boss when it came to pinching pennies, and he was equally ignorant of aviation. He once told a convention of aeronautical engineers that "a commercial flying machine should be able to land in a city lot near the heart of town, instead of on a 40-acre field out where the commuters live." This combination of ignorance and tight-fistedness set Burleson and Praeger on a collision course with the pilots.

In midsummer 1919, the East Coast experienced a period of extremely bad weather, but Post Office supervisors, most of whom were not pilots, insisted that the pilots fly as usual. As a result, there were 15 crashes, two of them fatal, in the two-week period just before Smith refused to fly. The deaths forced the pilots of the Eastern Division to hold a series of meetings during which they decided to assert what they regarded as the pilot's prerogative to determine whether or not the weather was flyable. They had precedent on their side, for even the Army allowed its pilots some discretion in this area. The pilots agreed that if one pilot refused to fly, all of them would refuse to fly. When Leon Smith said "no," they were as good as their word, and the strike was on.

Post Office officials knew there was some discontent among the pilots, chiefly because of problems with the aircraft, but they routinely brushed aside complaints. The pilots wanted to continue using both DH-4s and Jennys because the lighter and smaller Jenny was better for low-altitude flight in bad weather. The Jenny carried the lightweight, dependable Hispano-Suiza 150-horsepower engine, and it could fly much more slowly, thereby giving the pilot greater reaction time when hedgehopping under a low-cloud ceiling.

The Post Office wanted to phase out the Jenny in order to standardize its operations with the larger and faster DH-4, which the government had available in considerable surplus from the war. A further complication arose because the Curtiss Company had modified the DH-4 to carry the liquid-cooled Liberty engine, which had also been mass produced too late in the war to see service. The trouble was that the Curtiss modification didn't work very well, and the Liberty-equipped DH-4s had a nasty habit of overheating, especially at low altitude. Pilots with gallows humor sometimes referred to the DH-4s as "flaming coffins."

Eventually, and partly because of the fuss they were making, the pilots got the DH-4 modified to suit them, and toward the end of its service career they were very pleased with it. Rube Wagner, who joined the Air Mail Service in 1923 recalls:

> The DH had big wheels on it, so you could land it anyplace where you'd land a Jenny. But it was heavy, the engine was over 400 pounds sitting big and long out in the nose. Eventually it worked all right, when they got the timing gear fixed. They built a stub-tooth gear for it and made that engine all but foolproof. That Liberty 12 engine was running just like a clock toward the end. We hated to give it up.

What the pilots really wanted, of course, was a completely new mail plane designed and built specifically for their use. J. L. (Larry) Driggs, president of The American Flying Club, an association of aeronautical engineers, supported the pilots' criticism of the DH-4 by declaring: "If the pilots themselves have found the DH-4 unfit and unsafe, then their word should be taken in preference to that of the engineers at Curtiss who supervised the alterations." But Driggs's sensible advice made no impact on the economy-minded Burleson and Praeger, who were determined to use up the available supply of surplus Liberty-equipped DH-4s.

But if the Post Office wouldn't buy new aircraft, the pilots at least wanted the DH-4s properly equipped with instruments. Here too they ran into opposition. Because they were expected to fly in bad weather, the pilots requested that the Post Office purchase "stabilators," primitive needle-and-ball-type turn-and-bank indicators for their aircraft. The devices cost only about $75 each, but Praeger turned down the request, advising the pilots: "Steer by compass. Turn indicators are too expensive." This was almost the last straw.

Praeger had heard that the pilots were in a fighting mood, and he was more than ready to tangle with them. When he learned that Smith and Lee had refused to fly, he issued a press release approving their firing, citing postal regulations for letter carriers as justification.

Upon receiving a telegram of protest signed only "Air Pilots," Praeger warned the pilots that by sending an anonymous telegram they were "conspiring against the government." The pilots replied in an open letter released to the press that it was not conspiracy "to avoid killing oneself for the sake of a two-cent stamp," whereupon Praeger huffily informed the press that the Post Office would be master in its own house. "These pilots came into the service as every other pilot," he said, "with knowledge that they must comply with orders, and where flying conditions are such that they cannot operate, they have the option to resign. If they refuse, removal must be made!"

Sympathizing with the underdog pilots, the reporters asked a series of hostile, probing questions that succeeded in nettling Praeger. Finally, flustered and angered, Praeger admitted that there had been a series of bad crashes in the weeks preceding the strike, but he shrugged it off as "something which happens all the time." When asked a question about stabilators, Praeger insisted that they were not commercially available. He added pompously that he would never recognize a pilots' union, nor would he ever have to, because there were "other pilots aplenty." All in all, Praeger's performance was a public relations disaster.

Praeger had a long history of hostility to labor organizations as might be expected of a former editor of the conservative _Dallas Morning News_. He was apparently resolute in his intention to break the strike by replacing every pilot, if it came to that. Indeed, the Post Office had a backlog of hundreds of applications from pilots who wanted work.

Praeger even tried to arouse patriotic resentment against the pilots by saying that criticism of the DH-4 constituted a "calumny on our aeroplane industry." In so doing, he revealed his own ignorance. Most of the pilots had distinguished war records, and the DH-4 was not an American plane at all. It was a British design manufactured under license in the United States.

The upshot of Praeger's pomposity and bungling, which the press faithfully reported in headline stories, was that public opinion shifted strongly in favor of the pilots. The pilots were popular and glamorous figures. There was strong support for them in Congress and growing criticism of Praeger.

Two standing committees in the House announced that they would investigate, and Halvor Steenerson, chairman of the powerful Post Office Committee, announced that he would personally investigate the firings, which under Civil Service rules required a hearing that Praeger had refused to grant. In general, the pilots struck a sympathetic chord when they issued a public manifesto declaring: "We will insist that the man who risks his own life be the judge—not somebody who stays on the ground and risks other people's lives."

Burleson and Praeger were considerably taken aback by the adverse reaction to their hard line against the pilots. Although they had wanted to attract the President's attention, this wasn't exactly what they had had in mind. In response to a request from the White House for information, Praeger tried to smooth the whole thing over by saying: "This represents one of those cases where the newspapers misled the public by printing only one side of a case" (a lament that has a curiously modern ring). But he quickly backed down under the mounting pressure and showed signs of adopting a more moderate tone in his dealings with the pilots.

Largely because of the efforts of Charles I. Stanton, the superintendent of the airmail (himself a pilot, although not a regular airmail pilot), the pilots went back to work on July 26, four days after Smith had refused to fly. Working feverishly behind the scenes while Praeger made a fool of himself in public, Stanton had arranged a deal whereby if the pilots went back to work, either Praeger or the postmaster general would meet with a committee of their representatives to discuss grievances.

By the time the conference between Praeger and the pilot committee was held in Washington on July 27, the pilots' position had been greatly strengthened by events reported the previous day in the *New York Times*. A reporter had investigated Praeger's earlier assertion that he had not bought stabilators because they were not available and found that, as the pilots insisted all along, they were commercially available. He reported: "Today they [the Post Office] agreed to buy some." The story made Praeger appear to be either a fool or a liar. Many pilots insisted that he was both.

Despite the pilots' strong position, however, they emerged from the conference with only half a victory. Praeger had agreed in advance to discuss a pay raise, although pay had not been directly at issue in the dispute, perhaps because he wanted to use the carrot-and-stick technique on the pilots. The pay raise was to be his carrot. On the crucial question of weather, there was a compromise. Praeger agreed to hire as field managers, pilots who would, in case of dispute, go aloft to demonstrate that the weather was flyable.

Praeger then agreed to a small pay raise, but there was a quid pro quo: there had to be a sacrificial lamb to satisfy his pride. That lamb was to be Leon Smith, who had earlier described Praeger as a "damned donkey." Lee was rehired, and the pilot committee wanted to hang tough on Smith, but it finally agreed to make his rehiring the "subject of further discussion." Pending that discussion, Smith took to barnstorming, making news when he took a 106-year-old Indian woman for a ride at a county fair in Batavia, N.Y., a few months later.

The pilots learned two crucial lessons from the strike: first, they needed some kind of organization, or structure, through which they could communicate with each other and protect themselves; second, they needed a leader, someone from among their own number who was willing to step forward and stick his neck out by acting as spokesman.

They tried to satisfy the first requirement by forming the Air Mail Pilots of America, but it was a weak, unaffiliated organization that soon folded. They tried to get around the leadership problem by hiring a lawyer, but that proved too expensive. The pilots did little else, and as a result, within a few months they were faced again with the same old problem of officials making decisions that showed no understanding of the risks of flying. In one case, an "efficiency rating system" was instituted based on ground speed, which forced the pilots to compete with each other and obviously encouraged them to take chances.

Despite their failure to put together any lasting organization, the pilots knew what needed to be done. Years later, after the Air Mail Service had been phased out and most airmail pilots had gone to work for the new private airlines, most of them strongly supported some kind of pilots' association.

At the time of the strike, Dave Behncke was an unknown pilot trying to make a living selling rides and barnstorming in his surplus Jenny. When he emerged to assume the crucial leadership role in forming the organization that became the Air Line Pilots Association, the old airmail pilots were the rock upon which he built. They remembered the strike of 1919, and Behncke could always depend on them to sell the concept. Stories about "Fat Otto" Praeger usually got the point across to younger pilots that unionization was the key to survival.

As for Leon Smith, he was never rehired despite Praeger's promise that there would be further discussions. Eventually he disappeared into obscurity—the first martyr in the struggle of the piloting profession to protect itself. He would not be the last. ✦

CHAPTER 5

The Livermore Affair

What sent Joe Livermore and his copilot Art Haid into the midst of an 80-mile-per-hour winter gale on the night of Dec. 18, 1936? Enroute from St. Paul, Minn., to Spokane, Wash., in a Northwest Airlines (NWA) Lockheed 10 and carrying a cargo consisting solely of Christmas mail, they made their last radio contact at 3:00 a.m., reporting over what they thought might be Elk River, Idaho. They were off course, overdue, and nowhere near their destination.

From Seattle, the western terminus of NWA's "northern transcontinental" route, Operations Manager A. R. "Bob" Mensing told newsmen the next morning that he felt confident the plane had been forced down northwest of Elk River, and that the pilots had been unable to reach a telephone.

Newsmen in Seattle were particularly interested in the overdue NWA plane because it was the second such mysterious airliner disappearance in a week. A Western Air Express (WAE) plane with seven people aboard, four of them passengers, was missing somewhere along the Nevada-Utah border. It was presumed that there were survivors because two radio stations had heard weak distress calls claiming to be from the downed plane. It was front-page drama—the possibility that somewhere there were injured people desperately trying to summon help. In a race against time, over 8,000 searchers scoured the wild terrain, trying to find the WAE plane before a predicted killer blizzard hit the area. After 24 hours, the faint radio signals, which had stirred hope, were heard no more. Later, WAE officials surmised that the distress messages were probably a hoax —some amateur radio operator's idea of a joke.

The reporters besieging NWA's Bob Mensing for news of his overdue plane didn't know that yet. Consequently, they spent the day of December 19 camped outside his Seattle office, hoping to get a story that would scoop the reporters covering the WAE plane search several hundred miles away in Salt Lake City.

Then, on the following day something happened on the East Coast that upstaged everybody: Henry T. "Dick" Merrill, celebrated transatlantic flier, bon vivant, and Eastern Air Lines (EAL) pilot, disappeared somewhere in the mountains of southern New York. He was flying a DC-3 with a full load of passengers.

Of the three airline disappearances in the nation's news that week, only Merrill's had a happy ending. Owing to static that rendered his radios useless, Merrill had become lost in heavy fog. Just before running out of gas he managed to set his DC-3 down on the side of a 1,500-foot mountain near Port Jervis, N.Y. The plane was demolished, but the only person injured was Merrill, who had several teeth knocked out and a broken ankle.

Spokesmen for WAE dampened the high spirits raised by Merrill's good fortune when they announced that they "had given up hope days ago" of finding any of their people alive. A crushing blizzard had descended on the probable crash site in northern Nevada, convincing them that there was no longer any use in holding out the possibility of rescuing survivors. "We doubt that the plane will be found before the snow melts next spring —if ever," a WAE executive said.

But there was still hope for the NWA plane and its two pilots. Rescuers had narrowed their search to a series of unnamed ridges along the Wyoming-Idaho border. A ranger in the Gallatin National Forest reported seeing the plane at 4:00 a.m. on December 19, an hour after its last radio transmission. On December 21, a pilot spotted wreckage near Kellogg, Idaho. He thought there might have been survivors, but before ground parties could work their way up to the nearly inaccessible site, another blizzard hit.

There was nothing to do but wait.

On December 26, a fur trapper who had volunteered to snowshoe his way up to the wreckage mushed out to report that there were no survivors—both Livermore and Haid were dead.

When reporters asked Bob Mensing how copilot Haid's young widow was taking it, he said: "She's true blue. She simply asked that Art's body be sent home to Seattle."

Mensing said nothing about Lorna Livermore, Joe's widow. He had good reason, for an angry Lorna Livermore had already sent a notarized statement to the Department of Commerce (DOC), the principal federal agency regulating aviation in those days, all but accusing Bob Mensing of murdering her husband.

Any roster listing airlines with the worst pilot-management relations records would show Northwest Airlines somewhere near the top. On other airlines, bad blood between pilots and supervisory personnel would ebb and flow, but on NWA it seemed to stay pretty much at flood stage. Before catching on with United Airlines (UAL), Dave Behncke himself had worked for NWA. In fact, he would have been first on the seniority list if he hadn't gotten fired and if NWA paid any attention to seniority.

So it came as no surprise that something like the Livermore case happened on NWA.

Joe Livermore was an "old" pilot.

"I would say that he was maybe in his late 30s," says R. Lee Smith of NWA, one of six pilots who met secretly with Dave Behncke in 1930 to begin planning what would later become ALPA.

Livermore lived in Spokane with his wife Lorna, flying a regular section between there and St. Paul, with stops at places like Missoula and Billings, in the twin-engine Lockheed 10, a low-wing all-metal airplane called the "Electra." It carried 10 passengers.

The Lockheed 10 could operate IFR (instrument flight rules), but the state of the electronic airways was still so rudimentary over NWA's routes that in a crunch many pilots still preferred to fly visually, relying on the Post Office's old lighted airways with their reassuring beacons winking every few miles. Joe Livermore was one of them, and he is a classic case of an older pilot caught in the transitionary bind between what pilots still called "contact" flying and instrument or "blind" flying.

In the late 1920s, when the first practical passenger aircraft, such as the Ford and Fokker Trimotors, began to appear in regular airline service, the instrument panels already had a modern look. They usually sported a complete array of instruments, including even the revolutionary gyro-driven artificial horizon, so a pilot could easily keep his plane right side up when he inadvertently ventured into clouds. The problem was navigation. Effective IFR operations were still impossible because the electronic airways were not yet complete.

Even as late as the 1930s, after low-frequency ranges began dotting the nation's airways and suitable inflight radios were available, the all-weather concept could still be hindered by elements such as static.

In those days, a pilot navigated under instrument conditions largely by his ears—like a bat. Each low-frequency range transmitted steady "As" and "Ns" in Morse code, in alternating 90-degree quadrants. That is, if you were flying in an "A" quadrant, you would only be able to hear "A," "dit-dah." In the next quadrant, the "N" quadrant, you would hear a "dah-dit"—"N."

At the point of juncture between these "A" and "N" quadrants, the Morse code signals blended to form a steady aural "tone," which designated the airway. So each low-frequency radio range was capable of producing only four airways (or "legs"), and static could play havoc with the radio reception necessary to delineate them. And that wasn't the only problem.

The feature of early IFR flying that drove the first generation of airline pilots crazy was "ambiguity." Each 90-degree "A" and "N" quadrant had a mirror image exactly opposite. Which "leg" were they on? Were they going *toward* the station, or away from it? (There were no convenient "to" and "from" flags.) Did they have the range correctly identified by its Morse code call sign, or was a similar station in Calcutta skipping around the world to deceive them? (There were cases on record in which a phantom station created by skip waves lured pilots to their deaths.)

The most troubling aspect of early IFR flight was the approach—what pilots called the "let down through" procedure. It was one thing to sit up high, clear of surrounding terrain, and take a chance that the "beam" was on course. But when it came to dipping down into the soup, trying to fly the beam into the field, that was something else. A pilot had to be absolutely certain he had gotten station passage during the approach, and the *only* way he could determine that was, again, with his ears—something called "the cone of silence." Directly over the station there was an electronic null that could be either very small or very large, depending on your altitude and atmospheric conditions. Static could have a number of effects on a low-frequency radio range, but from the point of view of early airline pilots, the worst thing it did was to interfere with reception to the point where they could not determine the cone of silence.

In theory, the low-frequency radio ranges worked well enough that airline executives and government officials declared that the age of all-weather flying had arrived. Working pilots knew it wasn't true. They knew from firsthand experience how vulnerable to such factors as atmospherics and poor maintenance the early IFR system was. They knew the terrors of wandering ranges and all the other problems they encountered on an everyday basis. Most pilots developed their own tricks to avoid betting their lives on their ears. Some only grudgingly endured the new instrument training and rarely flew "blind." They would take off and submit fraudulent position reports, saying they were at "9,000 instruments," when actually they were dodging sagebrush, flying visually underneath, just like they used to in the old days. How was anyone to know before radar?

Joe Livermore was such a pilot. On the night of Dec. 13, 1936, he did something that got him in serious trouble with Bob Mensing, his immediate superior. Livermore abandoned the electronic airway early that night because of static and thunderstorms. Maybe he was right in doing so, and the chances are good that Bob Mensing wouldn't have made a fuss had Livermore not had a long history of going off the beam.

Livermore worked his flight safely into Missoula. But it was a turbulent trip at low altitude, and Livermore's passengers were airsick and scared. The night was turning ugly with lots of lightning visible on the horizon. Livermore did what he thought was the responsible thing under the circumstances—he "trained" his passengers. Then he checked into a Missoula hotel to get some sleep and to wait out the weather.

Bob Mensing was furious with Livermore for two reasons: first, because he had trained his passengers, thus depriving NWA of much-needed revenue and second, because he had gotten off the electronic beam to fly contact, *again!* Mensing had previously warned Livermore about flying into low turbulence because of the upsetting effect it had on passengers. NWA was trying to get all of its pilots to fly on instruments up high where passengers could have a smooth ride. It was company policy not to go contact unless there was no other choice. Mensing was convinced that Livermore had canceled instruments prematurely. Or maybe Mensing was just angry because Livermore had gone into town, casually leaving word at the field to call when the weather got better, instead of staying by the plane to assess the weather for himself.

So Bob Mensing exercised his managerial prerogative by chewing out Joe Livermore over the telephone. "What in the hell is the matter with you? Is your job too tough for you?" Mensing demanded of Livermore (according to his widow's deposition). "You bring that section through or I will accept your resignation!"

"You mean I must either take this ship out *now* or resign?" Livermore asked. But Mensing refused to answer the question directly, according to Lorna Livermore's reconstruction, thus indicating that the ancient concept of a pilot's command authority was still basically intact. Nevertheless, Joe Livermore checked out of his hotel room, returned to the field, and took off into what ground personnel later described as "bad weather." He successfully made it home to Spokane—for the last time.

Lorna Livermore's notarized deposition stated that Joe was highly upset by the dressing-down Mensing had given him over the phone in Missoula. "Joe came home very late, tired and worried," she said. "He didn't want to talk about it. Finally he told me that he had been 'given hell' by Bob Mensing. Joe said that it came down to the fact that he had to fly in any weather or lose his job."

Five days later Livermore was airborne once more on his regular run. The weather was bad again, a solid IFR night, with a winter storm slamming across the northern Great Plains at winds clocked at up to 80 miles per hour. Copilot Art Haid might well have been better qualified to fly the gauges than Livermore, owing to his recent Army stint where he had learned the most up-to-date IFR techniques.

It is apparent that Joe Livermore, on the night of Dec. 18, 1936, should probably have canceled his flight. But he was so depressed, under pressure, and fearful of losing his job that he didn't. He and Art Haid would pay with their lives for that error in judgment.

If it were not for the use Dave Behncke made of the Livermore "pilot pushing" case, nobody would care about it today—except perhaps the heirs of Joe Livermore and Art Haid. But the Livermore affair came at a crucial point in American aviation history. Congress was in the process of writing a sweeping new law that would ultimately be called the Civil Aeronautics Act of 1938. The Livermore affair became the dramatic centerpiece of Behncke's campaign to protect pilots from the arbitrary dictates of officialdom, both government and corporate, at least when *safety* was at stake.

Between 1934 and 1938, from the airmail cancellations crisis to the passage of the cornerstone legislation of 1938, the air transport industry was in constant turmoil. In Washington, the heavyweights were sparring over the shape of future federal law. ALPA began as a lightweight in 1934, and moved rapidly up to about middleweight status by 1938. It wasn't an easy climb. Nothing about the future was certain except that one bad error, one poorly chosen fight, one major political mistake would finish ALPA. It was a perilous time for the pilots who were struggling so hard to create a "voice" in Washington—footing their own bills, giving up their free time, and appearing as a chorus of moral support for Behncke on the innumerable occasions when he testified before congressional committees.

The National Recovery Administration (NRA) "code" hearings of 1933 provide a good example of Behncke's use of a phalanx of uniformed airline pilots to establish an ALPA "presence" in Washington. The NRA was the New Deal's big gun during the early war on the depression. It was premised on the notion that cooperation, rather than competition, could get the country back on its feet economically. In June 1933, President Roosevelt signed legislation permitting the government to oversee the creation of industrywide "Codes of Fair Competition." The crucial part of an industry's code was the hearing during which a mutual voluntary agreement on prices, profits, wages, and working conditions would be reached between representatives of management, labor, and consumers. At the August 1933 Air Transport Code hearings, Behncke pulled out all the stops to keep airline pilots exempt from any control by the code.

John H. Neale, who stood No. 1 on the seniority list of Capital Airlines prior to its merger with UAL in 1961, remembers what it was like to help Behncke during these trying times:

> Almost my first contact with Dave after joining the union was when he asked me to sit with him before a hearing on the National Recovery Administration Code Authority. Our good friend Mayor LaGuardia of New York came down and sat with us at the hearing. He was always willing to help us at any time. Dave Behncke did nearly all the talking; in fact I can't remember ever opening my mouth. I just sat there in my uniform providing moral support. I can't remember the gist of his thinking now, but Dave was adamantly opposed to our being included in the code. He knew a great deal about it, so I was willing to trust his judgment, as were the other pilots from several airlines who were there.

Many pilots were puzzled by Behncke's opposition to the inclusion of pilots in the code. On the surface, having their wages and working conditions spelled out in the code appeared advantageous, as did the contractual provision requiring employers to bargain collectively with their employees and to recognize the right of labor unions to exist. (Later, after the NRA was declared unconstitutional, Senator Wagner of New York would extract these labor provisions from the NRA legislation and salvage them in the Wagner Labor Relations Act of 1935.) But Behncke became alarmed when he discovered that the operators were proposing ridiculously high maximums of 140 hours per month as in the Air Transport Code, higher than the 110 hours per month the Commerce Department established as the monthly maximum in 1931. Behncke had been battling to lower the maximum to 85 hours, so he fought hard to stay out of the code, preferring instead to seek specific congressional action on pilots' wages and hours.

The NRA code hearings were held in the ballroom of the Mayflower Hotel, under the supervision of Malcolm Muir, deputy director of the NRA. There was an all-star cast of airline executives present, so Behncke made sure that well-known airline pilots, such as E. Hamilton Lee of UAL (probably the senior professional pilot in the country) and Mal Freeburg of NWA (recent recipient of the Air Mail Pilot Medal of Honor), were present. La-Guardia flew down from New York on August 30, and Behncke met him at the Washington Hoover airport with a contingent of airline pilots in full uniform. Among them were Sam Carson of Kohler Airlines (later UAL), Walter Hunter of American Airways (AAL), Homer Cole (NWA), and E. Hamilton Lee, Charles Drayton, and John Tilton of Pan American (PAA). Behncke rotated these pilots at various hearing sessions and added Howard "Sonnyboy" Hall of TWA, Gene Brown of EAL, Clyde Holbrook of AAL, and John Neale of Capital Airlines.

The primary fear haunting these men was that if they did not succeed in establishing ALPA as an effective vehicle for pilot representation, pilots would almost certainly never get another chance. The 1920s were littered with failed experiments like ALPA, short-lived organizations bearing prestigious names like the Air Mail Pilots of America, the National Air Pilots Association, and the Professional Pilots of America. As we have seen, the first airline pilots were under no illusions about their economic vulnerability or the ease with which their employers could replace them. They knew a prestigious name wasn't enough, nor was a glamorous image. Leadership, the ability to function as a group, and timing were everything.

Leadership was something Dave Behncke supplied, sometimes brilliantly. Functioning as a group was something the pilots were doing on two levels: first, with their peers, their fellow pilots, and second, as part of the American Federation of Labor, identifying themselves with the political and economic aspirations of the labor movement. Timing, although hard to categorize, essentially meant knowing when the iron was hot, and how to strike it cold-bloodedly in your own interest.

Of the three, timing was probably the most important factor, because even brilliant leadership and aggressive group action cannot succeed in the absence of opportunities. Dave Behncke's genius lay in knowing when to press the issue of safety. Thanks to Lorna Livermore and his own gift for theatrics, Behncke made the safety issue almost irresistible by 1938.

In the anti-big business climate of the depression years, Behncke was adept at hitting the right rhetorical notes with his charges that the operators cared less about safety than about their profits. He did this in speeches that, despite their occasionally shrill, ungrammatical, and overly sentimental content, never struck people as being particularly "radical." Partly, it was because of the way Behncke looked. Although he seldom wore a tie, he had a well-manicured appearance, reminding some people of a Philadelphia Main Liner. He was, as more than one airline executive discovered, an exasperating foe to tangle with before a congressional committee.

In another sense, Behncke was something of a pioneer, thanks to a devastating new wrinkle he injected into the debate over airline safety—an attack on government bureaucrats. The feeling of ordinary people in the 1930s was that government power was good, but Behncke argued that it was rather like Frankenstein's monster—it needed watching. Specifically, Behncke was highly critical of the stewardship DOC exerted over aviation, particularly in the area of accident investigation. On that point, Behncke caught the public's fancy, for he had survived a crash and walked with a limp and a heavy cane, which served as constant reminders.

In a 1937 article published in *Liberty* magazine, Behncke wrote:

> On Dec. 21, 1934, I took off from Chicago on my regular run, and after proceeding 10 minutes westward found my hands filled with dead throttles. Both motors had quit with every instrument in the cockpit registering normal. The result was a forced landing into treetops at night with injury to no one but myself. It was even possible to rebuild the airplane. That was my first serious accident in nearly 20 years of flying, but I have no doubt that if my copilot and I had not lived to defend ourselves, "pilot error" would have been given as the cause of the crash.

The thrust of Behncke's argument was that only pilots could speak for safety, because only pilots had the same interests as the traveling public. Government officials, Behncke insisted, were too closely tied to the industry they supposedly regulated, and when it came to investigating accidents, they often conspired with the airline operators to fix the blame on dead pilots. His argument was plausible because of a long history of interchangeable personnel moving through a revolving door between DOC and the airlines.

The worst conflict of interest, Behncke maintained, was that DOC, which maintained the airways and wrote the regulations governing commercial aviation, was allowed to investigate itself. Behncke wanted an independent federal agency to investigate accidents. He was the first to advocate the concept that would ultimately become, in 1966, the National Transportation Safety Board (NTSB).

The Livermore crash provided Behncke with a forum from which to attack both the operators and government bureaucrats on the safety issue. DOC's Bureau of Air Commerce, under severe pressure since mid-1936 owing to a Senate investigation into the death of Sen. Bronson Cutting of New Mexico on a TWA plane the previous year, held a public hearing on airline safety in February 1937. The combination conference and investigation permitted interested parties to appear, but it discouraged those whose direct interest was not in air safety. Too often in the past, DOC hearings such as this had degenerated into wide-ranging, unfocused "bull sessions," featuring all sorts of aviation cranks and self-appointed experts. For this reason DOC narrowly restricted those who could participate. That Behncke was included on the list was a measure of ALPA's growing influence. Not too long before, DOC had excluded ALPA from participating in its accident investigations, contending that it was not an interested party.

Behncke appeared on February 6, the final day of the conference. Pointing out that DOC had attributed 16 of the last 27 airline crashes to pilot error, Behncke raised publicly, for the first time, the issue of "pilot pushing." Gung ho supervisors were regularly intimidating their pilots into dangerous flights under threat of dismissal, Behncke testified, and DOC was doing nothing to stop the practice. Furthermore, Behncke said he had affidavits to prove his charges.

Behncke's testimony provoked anger from airline executives in attendance, among whom were C. R. Smith, W. A. Patterson, and Eddie Rickenbacker.

Patterson, Behncke's old boss, who had recently reversed himself on the subject of pilot unionization, nevertheless disputed charges of pilot pushing on United. The *New York Times* called the interchange between the two men "a lively battle of words."

Eddie Rickenbacker all but snarled at Behncke: "If you've got proof of pilot pushing, then produce it." Rickenbacker said he was confident Behncke had no such proof.

With a small secret smile, Behncke listened to the various airline executives heatedly deny any pilot pushing on their lines. When they were finished, Behncke asked chief of the Airline Inspection Division, Major R. W. Schroeder, to confirm the existence of Lorna Livermore's deposition, which had not yet been made public because the investigation was still incomplete. The reluctant Schroeder had no choice but to make the information public. He read selected portions, including the closing sentence of Lorna Livermore's deposition: "I am writing this letter so that the Department of Commerce will have an understanding of the attitude of the operators. This attitude can be verified very easily."

Behncke then called attention to an affidavit from Roy P. Warner, a recently fired NWA pilot, that supported Mrs. Livermore's charges.

Behncke had succeeded in putting the operators on the defensive about the safety issue, and in so doing he had seized the initiative. He now had his choice of two mutually exclusive courses of action. The first choice would be to grab all the headlines he could, levy a barrage of additional charges, and try to make more waves in commercial aviation's already troubled pond. The second choice would be to play ball with the industry, making a reasonable deal in exchange for defusing the pilot pushing controversy. He chose the latter.

"The companies have seen the error of their ways," Behncke testified. "Northwest has seen their mistakes, and they have eradicated them."

What did Behncke mean by this enigmatic statement?

In effect, Behncke was using the Livermore crash, and poor Lorna Livermore as well, to further ALPA's interests. He was saying to the airline executives assembled, "Look! This is another example where we could have been as radical as the devil and blown this thing sky high. But we are going to back off and play ball with you. Now give us what we want in return." (Behncke actually used just these words in a private conversation.) What he wanted was some kind of judicial device that would take account of the pilots' point of view. In short, Behncke was cutting a deal with the operators, and the Livermore affair was just the last in a series of complex maneuvers. The ultimate goal was an independent accident investigation board.

The upshot was that Lorna Livermore would have to shift for herself on the pilot pushing lawsuit against NWA. "Old" Joe Livermore might well have been totally wrong. Rather than Bob Mensing killing Joe Livermore, it might well have been Joe Livermore who killed copilot Art Haid by willfully getting off the electronic airways to fly contact too soon.

It was admittedly a murky case, but the facts are that NWA's young copilots were up in arms about Joe Livermore and two other "old" captains, both of whom later got fired. The copilots did not have bidding rights in those days, so they flew with whichever captain they were assigned. Several of them had already flatly refused to fly with Livermore again because of his reputation for premature termination of IFR flights. In fact, it was said that he sometimes simply took off his headset under IFR conditions and continued flying blind by the seat of his pants.

Speaking for the majority of NWA pilots, R. Lee Smith sums up the Livermore case this way:

> I suppose Joe was pushed. We were just beginning to fly instruments, and he was reluctant. The copilots had complained about him and [two unnamed pilots]. They were really unhappy. They complained through ALPA, in fact. Livermore and [the unnamed pilots] only got away with it because Fred Whittemore, who was general manager, was the same way. He wouldn't fly instruments either. Of course, he didn't fly every day, but when he did it was all contact. Mensing wanted to fire Livermore, but Whittemore wouldn't back him up. Not too much later, Whittemore did the same thing. He picked up a new Lockheed 14H at the factory in California, it was his baby anyway, the 14H, an abortion of an airplane, unstable as all get out. Planeload of company employees, wives and kids mostly, and the guy wouldn't fly IFR. Hell, he wouldn't even practice! So he wound up getting lost in one of those box canyons; he could have punched through that overcast and been in the clear. Killed the whole damn planeload because

he wouldn't fly instruments. Joe Livermore was the same. The night he got killed he reported Elk River because he was lost trying to fly visual and he spent time circling there at Elk River because he had earlier mistaken the glow of a forest fire, of all damned things, for the lights of Spokane, and he let down too soon and got lost.

Behncke knew what he was doing when he refused to render any further assistance to Lorna Livermore after having exploited the issue raised by her husband's death. She wanted ALPA to appear on her behalf in the legal action she brought against NWA, alleging wrongful death under Washington State law. Both the Central Executive Council and the NWA pilots agreed that ALPA should ignore her and do nothing further in the pilot pushing case.

Despite all this, Lorna Livermore won her lawsuit. Her victory came early in 1939, at the end of another very bad year for NWA. The cause of NWA's trouble was the Lockheed 14H, successor to the 10A, called the Super Electra and a real loser according to many old-timers.

"What nobody could figure out," says R. Lee Smith, "was why Whittemore didn't insist on the kind of structural changes on the 14H other airlines did—the Dutch on KLM, for instance. That was the mystery. We were strongly suspicious of that plane long before Nick Mamer had one come apart on him at Bozeman. ALPA was going to have to get into aircraft certification someday, that was for sure."

The trouble with the 14H was control surface flutter, which increased in harmonic series, quickly becoming uncontrollable (in perhaps a second or so), until it wrenched the double vertical stabilizers completely off the aircraft. When it happened to Nick Mamer on Jan. 11, 1938, he had a planeload of passengers. Everyone died. The weather was clear and there were eyewitnesses on the ground, so there wouldn't be any pilot error findings on this one. They saw the tail come off during straight and level flight. Subsequent investigation of the wreckage confirmed it.

Somebody had to be at fault, and since it couldn't be a dead pilot this time, NWA itself was the prime candidate. DOC came down hard, sending in a special team to conduct what Secretary of Commerce Daniel C. Roper promised would be a "thorough investigation." As a first step Roper, no longer trusting his beleaguered Aviation Branch to calm public apprehension, personally announced the grounding of all NWA's Lockheed 14Hs. Then, on Feb. 4, 1938, citing "failure to comply with regulations for aircraft maintenance," Roper suspended NWA's operating certificate, grounding the whole airline. It was an unprecedented action. On February 6, Roper permitted NWA to begin carrying mail and express freight again, but not passengers. Finally, on February 10, NWA passed muster and Roper allowed passenger service to resume, but there were few takers.

NWA's unsavory reputation almost surely had an effect on the Spokane jury, which awarded Lorna Livermore $37,500 in damages on Jan. 17, 1939.

Although the jury gave her only half the $75,000 she had asked for, NWA stood legally convicted of pilot pushing in the death of Joe Livermore. NWA's legal counsel promised to appeal all the way to the Supreme Court, if necessary, but NWA didn't. Enough was enough. An appeal could only cause more bad publicity. You can't win beating upon the widow of a martyred pilot. And it didn't matter that much anyway. Pilot pushing was a dead issue—that was the Livermore affair's ironic legacy.

By 1938, ALPA had positioned itself so favorably in Washington, thanks to Behncke's adroit exploitation of episodes like the Livermore affair, that it really couldn't lose. Everything was guaranteed—collective bargaining contracts over and above federal minimum guarantees, a full partnership in the new aviation establishment called the Civil Aeronautics Administration—everything. Particularly in the area of safety, ALPA had it made. The Livermore affair was crucial in Behncke's successful drive to make an independent safety board part of the Civil Aeronautics Act of 1938. Tom Hardin, an American Airlines pilot who was ALPA's first vice-president (second in command to Behncke), was FDR's first appointee to the new Air Safety Board. Nothing demonstrated ALPA's new muscle better than Tom Hardin's appointment.

But it hadn't come about overnight. No single issue, not even one as flashy as the Livermore sideshow, or the safety angle, can account for ALPA's extraordinary political success in Washington up to 1938.

In order to understand that, we must go back to the beginning of the decade. ✦

CHAPTER 6

The Trouble with E. L. Cord

E rrett Lobban Cord was to ALPA what Satan was to the early Christian church—both encouraged membership. Ask any pilot who flew for the airlines prior to 1932 about the origin of ALPA, and more than likely he'll say something about E. L. Cord, usually punctuated by the kind of stately profanity that went out of vogue with Harry Truman. These pioneer pilots have neither forgiven nor forgotten what Cord tried to do to them so long ago, and it behooves every member of the profession today to know about it. Forewarned is forearmed—a modern-day Cord is still possible.

Actually, Cord had nothing to do with the origin of ALPA. The first "formal" discussion among six pilots representing three airlines was held at the old Troy Lane Hotel in Chicago in 1930 a year before Cord founded Century Airlines.

"Dave [Behncke] selected the five of us because he thought he could trust us, and he started from there," remembers R. Lee Smith of Northwest Airlines, probably the only surviving participant in that meeting. "E. L. Cord came into the picture a little bit later. We had been talking about a new pilots' association since at least 1929, but we really got rolling on it in 1930 because that was when the airlines got together on reducing pay. They felt we were overpaid and underworked, and they were going to chop us down to size."

The others who met with Behncke and Smith were Lawrence W. Harris and Walter A. Hallgren of American Airways (AAL), J. L. "Monty" Brandon of United Airlines (UAL), and one other UAL pilot whose name Behncke erased from ALPA's records because he went over to management a few days following the founding meeting. Although his memory is extraordinarily good, Smith cannot recall the identity of ALPA's "lost" founder. He attended the Chicago meeting just after completing a rough flight, he was tired, and he wasn't acquainted with anyone in the room except Behncke.

E. L. Cord's real value was to make working pilots of that era realize just how ruthless their employers could be, thereby encouraging the growth of unionism. Not that flying for one of the major airlines was any piece of cake to start with.

"I can show you in my logbook," says James H. Roe of Trans World Airlines (TWA), who retired in 1965, "where I flew part of *every* day in June

1932. I reached the Department of Commerce limit, 110 hours, on the last day."

But at least Jimmy Roe was getting paid well for flying—Cord's design was to put a stop to that.

Because he was a quiet man who shunned publicity, Cord never achieved anything like the notoriety his wealth and success would otherwise have commanded. He preferred to remain in the background, functioning as the gray eminence behind such corporate subordinates as C. R. Smith, the hard-driving young Texan who rose through Cord's empire to head AAL after Cord gained control of it.

Cord appeared out of nowhere during the Great Depression to head a series of automotive enterprises, the major ones being the Auburn Automobile Company and Checker, the taxicab manufacturer. Generally, he was best known for a short-lived car design called the Cord, which featured the revolutionary concept of front-wheel drive. Airline pilots knew about him principally because of his ownership of two regional airlines, each bearing the name Century. Cord won their attention because he offered employment to pilots at wages as low as $150 per month and got all the applicants he wanted at that price. That was drastically below the prevailing wage rate for airline pilots, but because Cord had no airmail contract, he saw no reason to follow the Post Office Department pilot pay scales. The Post Office paid its pilots as much as $1,000 per month under certain "bonus" circumstances. The private contractors who took over the mail routes in the late 1920s generally continued to pay similar wages, at least for awhile.

Anyone familiar with Cord's history as an employer knew there was bound to be trouble. His industrial enterprises were notorious for low wages, union-busting, and poor working conditions. But personally Cord was a charmer, a characteristic he shared with a great many other early airline owners.

A. M. "Breezy" Wynne, who went to work for AAL in 1934 after a stint in the Army Air Corps, remembers this contradictory aspect of Cord's personality well:

> If you got him by himself, E. L. Cord was just as down-to-earth as anybody you ever saw, a nice guy to talk to. But he was a bastard when it came to business. At the time I went to work for American, there was still a lot of disgruntlement over what Cord had pulled on Century. We knew there had been a bad situation there in Chicago, but we were on the West Coast and didn't know all the details. When Behncke came out to the West Coast to explain it, a lot of us hadn't joined ALPA yet. We didn't know enough about it. Dave got a hotel room, and all of us who were in town, United pilots, and TWA pilots, and Western Air, all the ones who operated out of Burbank or Grand Central Air Terminal at Glendale, went over to talk to

him. So he explained the situation on Century, and what E. L. Cord was up to.

Well, our mothers didn't raise stupid children! We could see that what Cord had done on Century he'd sure as hell wind up doing to us on American. After Dave explained the thing to us, we *all* signed up, captains and copilots—*all* of us.

The trouble with E. L. Cord began abruptly in 1932, just when Dave Behncke needed it least. At the time he was trying to organize pilots on airlines scattered all over the country, juggle several apples simultaneously in Washington, and maintain some kind of order in his personal life. The last thing Behncke wanted was a war with somebody like E. L. Cord over a hip-pocket operation like Century Airlines. Century employed about 20 pilots to fly Stinson Model T trimotors over what was little more than a commuter route serving Chicago, Springfield, and St. Louis, with an occasional flight into Cleveland. Yet this relatively insignificant strike (or "lockout," as Behncke always called it) was the first genuine labor dispute in modern aviation history, and it would become the single most important event in the development of airline flying as a profession and the establishment of ALPA as a force to be reckoned with in the future.

It began on a gray February evening in 1932 as Behncke sat in his office on the second floor of Chicago's Troy Lane Hotel. The Troy Lane had seen better days, but it seemed like heaven to Behncke, who had run ALPA's affairs out of the front bedroom of his south-side Chicago bungalow for the previous two years, amid clattering typewriters, racing mimeograph machines, ringing telephones, and people coming and going at all hours. Understandably, the clutter annoyed his wife Gladys, so it was a relief when Dave scraped up enough dues money to rent the two-room hotel suite and remove ALPA's operation from their home.

ALPA was Behncke's full-time preoccupation. He spent almost every hour when he wasn't sleeping or flying at the Troy Lane, where he and his fellow pilots could make plans far into the night without bothering Gladys.

Dave was feeling pretty good about the world that evening. He had good reason to be pleased, for in the space of a year he had organized nearly half the working airline pilots in the country into a real honest-to-goodness union, complete with an American Federation of Labor (AF of L) affiliation.

Of course, there was some grousing about the tie to organized labor, because some pilots already thought of themselves as "professionals," the equivalent of doctors and lawyers, who had no need for the protection of the AF of L. Behncke had done it anyway, despite what people said about pilots being too individualistic, too cantankerous ever to submit to union discipline. They even said Behncke would surely lose his own job flying for United if he persisted in his obsessive quest to create a union.

The crushing depression that followed the stock market crash of 1929 eased Behncke's task. As bread lines lengthened, pilots became a little less cocky, a little more willing to listen to his arguments, as Behncke button-holed them in airports and hotels.

Behncke's reverie that evening was interrupted when a snow-bedraggled band of 23 Century Airlines pilots trooped in, led by a Michigan Dutchman named J. H. S. "Duke" Skonning. "Well, here we are," he declared. "We have been locked out. Now what is the Association going to do about it?" Behncke suddenly found himself in the middle of a dispute that would command national attention.

Trouble had been brewing on Century Airlines for some time, but Behncke had paid it little attention, for there were weightier matters on his mind. The situations on Eastern Air Transport and TWA, for instance, were far more critical, for both were big, important airlines employing many pilots, few of whom were ALPA members. Eddie Rickenbacker's tough anti-union stance at Eastern frightened away many potential ALPA converts, and TWA's management had a nasty habit of changing a pilot's domicile if they suspected him of belonging to ALPA. Needless to say, the mere thought of having to uproot wife and kids, sell a house, and move was enough to discourage TWA pilots from joining. At a time when he was fighting some real toughies, Behncke didn't need a two-bit sideshow like Century to contend with. Still, the Century boys were ALPA members. They needed help and there was no way Behncke could dodge the issue.

Both Behncke and Cord had come from hardscrabble backgrounds. Neither had much formal education, and they were about the same age. But, while Behncke had been rising slowly from Army private to commissioned aviator during World War I, Cord had avoided service, emerging instead as the most successful automobile salesman in a large Chicago firm dealing in Auburn autos.

During the 1920s, while Behncke was trying to make a living by turns as barnstormer, airport operator, and airmail pilot, Cord was steadily expanding his business influence, seemingly leading a charmed life as he climbed into the rarefied world of 1920s-style finance. He got control of Auburn Auto in 1924, reversing its fortunes by ruthlessly reducing labor costs while introducing several new automobiles.

Although the depression blighted most careers, it seemed to act as a tonic for Cord's. It wasn't until after the crash that he began to achieve notoriety as a tycoon, dealing mostly in aviation, automotive, and related corporate operations. By the time of the Century strike, his stable of industries included Auburn Auto, Duesenberg, Yellow Cab, Checker Cab, dozens of lesser manufacturing enterprises, and, of course, Century Airlines.

Cord's decision to go into the airline business stemmed from his control of Stinson Aircraft Corporation and later acquisition of Lycoming Aircraft Engine Company. Cord had learned to fly in 1929, taught by his personal pilot J. C. Kelley, and he owned a Stinson Detroiter. He flew only when the weather was perfect, and he always had Kelley along with him. Nevertheless, Cord professed to believe that anybody could fly an airplane.

In 1930 Cord declared, "I feel that 'aviators' have fostered an erroneous conception of flying. There was a time when I was no different from any other person who looks upon flying as something for especially gifted 'birdmen.'"

Cord was trying to sell Stinsons by convincing people that it was no more difficult to fly an airplane than to crank up the family Chevy. "It is my conviction," Cord told the press, "that any normal person can easily and safely handle an airplane." Frankly, Cord was contemptuous of pilots, with their scarves, goggles, and pretensions. Such attitudes stood in the way of selling "personal" Stinsons, and Cord would have none of it.

The depression put a stop to Cord's plan to put an airplane in every garage; people could barely afford garages, let alone airplanes. But, being a versatile and clever man, he saw an opening. The government's decision to release military aviators from active duty in an economy move swelled the ranks of unemployed pilots. Cord had airplanes and engines. All he needed to start an airline was pilots, now available in abundance.

Cord's Stinson trimotored airliner was originally known as the Corman 3000, but when equipped with three Lycoming engines it became the Stinson SM6000B, commonly referred to as either the Model "T" or "U," depending upon modifications. It was a high-wing aircraft (in contrast to the later low-wing versions), carried 10 passengers, and required only one pilot (so Cord claimed). The Stinson Trimotor sold for less than $25,000. Its competition, the Bach Trimotor, also carried 10 passengers but sold for $30,000. (Ford Trimotors cost $40,000 and carried only four more passengers.) It was a good airplane and became a profit-maker for Luddington Airlines, the first to adopt it. Luddington, a commuter airline serving Washington, D.C., Philadelphia, and New York, began operating early in 1930. Cord was impressed with Luddington and decided to copy it.

The result was Century Airlines, which began flying in March 1931, offering three round trips daily between Chicago and St. Louis via Springfield, Ill., and four round trips daily between Chicago and Cleveland by way of Toledo, Ohio. The basic fare was $15.95 to St. Louis and $13.95 to Cleveland. On opening day, Cord sold 163 out of 180 seats available, later settling down to an average load factor of 80 percent, respectable by the standards of any era.

Although Century Airlines was only a small part of his empire, Cord was intrigued by its profit potential, especially if he could get his hands on an airmail contract. Most of his profit resulted from substandard wages, especially for his pilots, whose pay was well below the average annual salary of $7,000 then prevailing on the major airlines. Cord paid his pilots a flat $350 per month, plus $3 per hour for daytime and $5 per hour for nighttime flying.

Cord, however, believed his pilots' salaries were too high. When he started Century Pacific Airlines between Los Angeles and San Francisco a few months later, he reduced the basic salary to a flat $150 per month and was still able to find plenty of willing pilots. It was Cord's threat to reduce the Century pilots' salaries in the Midwest to match the lower salaries he paid in California that brought Duke Skonning and his band of pilots to Behncke that night in February 1932 where they told an amazing story.

It seems that Cord had in mind a nationwide network of airlines, all named Century, but with regional designations such as "Century Southwest," operating at the bare bones cost of 38 cents per mile, which was roughly one-half the amount the Post Office airmail contractors were paid. Cord reasoned that if he could prove to Congress that he could fly the mail at half the going rate, then the chances were good that Congress would cancel the old contracts and reopen them for competitive bidding. When this happened, Cord was sure he could underbid everyone else, win a contract, and make a killing.

To get his costs down Cord planned to lower the Century pilots' salaries to the standard $150 per month he paid on Century Pacific (and planned to pay on Century Southwest, which was due to begin operating soon). The Century pilots balked, pointing out that they already worked for below-average wages, and that to lower them further would result in a considerable hardship. "Starvation wages," Duke Skonning called them.

They wanted to bargain with Cord, and although Cord agreed to a 10-day delay in instituting the new salaries, he had no intention of backing down. Too much was at stake here, he believed, to let the pilots foul it up. When the 10-day "truce" was over, Cord hired armed guards to meet each pilot as he reported for work at Chicago's Municipal Airport. The guards escorted the bewildered pilots into the presence of a company official, who brusquely handed them a sheet of paper that was both a resignation and an application for reemployment at the lower rate of pay. Century's president, a Cord man named Lucius B. Manning, explained that because "the old man" was angry with the pilots for not cooperating, they would have to compete with other pilots for the jobs they now held. If they signed the paper immediately and stopped making trouble, then *perhaps* Mr. Cord would retain them. The whole scene was humiliating, and every one of the pilots refused to sign. Manning fired them all on the spot.

Actually, Behncke relished the Century explosion because it gave him a chance to try his hand as a negotiator. He prided himself on being reasonable and persuasive and he thought he could talk Cord out of it. But he hit a stone wall; he tried to make an appointment to see Cord and got nowhere. Nor would Cord's secretary put through Behncke's phone calls. There was nothing to do but fight.

When the unusual spectacle of a strike by airline pilots hit the newspapers, the connection with the AF of L began to pay off. AF of L President

William Green publicly blasted Cord, citing substandard wages in his various manufacturing enterprises, and ordered the Illinois State Federation of Labor into action on ALPA's behalf.

Victor Olander, secretary of the state federation, promptly went to work with Behncke to devise a publicity campaign, set up a strike fund, and map strategy. He secured free time on WCFL, a Chicago radio station controlled by organized labor, where Behncke and several Century strikers told their story, and even verbally took listeners on imaginary flights. The broadcasts were very good, surprising even the station's staff with their descriptions of flights through thunderstorms, landings against crosswinds, and other technically accurate accounts of flying.

The popular nightly broadcasts generated a surge of public support for the Century strikers, but they didn't pay the grocery bills. Behncke assessed every ALPA member $25 a month, raising nearly $5,000 the first month, to distribute among the strikers. They used part of the money to rent an airplane that strikers took turns flying alongside every Century plane arriving in Chicago—a unique attempt to persuade passengers to boycott the airline through the use of aerial picketing.

Within a week, however, Cord had managed to resume daylight flights, as out-of-work pilots quickly responded to his advertisements. Before Century could resume its night schedules, however, the new pilots would have to "night qualify," which involved making five landings at each airport along the route. The Department of Commerce obligingly agreed to send a special team of flight examiners to check out Cord's new hires, and, even worse, the Army and Navy released a number of qualified military pilots from active duty, specifically so they could go to work for Cord.

Behncke then tried a new tactic. He sent squads of Century strikers to politely persuade the strikebreakers to come to the Troy Lane Hotel where Behncke would explain the issues. Behncke promised to use ALPA's influence to find jobs for any of the strikebreakers who joined ALPA, but most of these appeals fell on deaf ears. Only a few of Cord's new hires joined the boycott.

Nevertheless, Behncke's attempt to contact his pilots directly worried Cord, forcing him into his first mistake. In an attempt to insulate his new hires from contact with the strikers, Cord forced them to live in a guarded dormitory, take their meals together, and ride to and from the field on a bus with an armed guard. He also stationed armed guards to keep the strikers off the airfield.

Behncke checked the Chicago city ordinances and found that there was no justification for this action because the airfield was public property. The newspapers began to question Cord's high-handed actions and shortly thereafter the city council, which was favorably disposed toward organized labor, got into the act.

The city council invited Cord to appear before one of its sessions to explain himself. Cord ignored them. After this, ALPA's fortunes began to improve, for elected officials dislike being snubbed.

News of the Century squabble did Cord no good in Washington, where his proposal to carry the airmail at half the prevailing rate was then under serious consideration. The AF of L marshaled support among prolabor congressmen and senators, urging them to resist Cord's proposal unless he settled with the striking pilots.

Rep. Fiorello LaGuardia, known as "The Little Flower" among New York City's Italian-American population, emerged as the chief anti-Cord spokesman, largely because he and Behncke were personal friends. After LaGuardia became mayor of New York, he paid Behncke the signal honor of inviting him to join in leading the New York State Labor Day parade.

It would be a mistake to think that the Century strike was a burning issue in Washington, however, for it was a small strike on a small airline, affecting only a few people. LaGuardia made several speeches on the House floor without attracting much attention, arguing that "piloting requires the highest degree of skill," and asking his fellow lawmakers how the traveling public would ever "get trustworthy pilots for less than a union truck driver gets in the City of New York."

LaGuardia's speechmaking worried Cord and forced his second great mistake: he persuaded a congressman from Indiana, where the largest Cord manufacturing enterprises were located, to attack ALPA. Cord feared LaGuardia and Behncke might drum up enough support to deny him a mail contract. It was one thing to ignore Chicago aldermen (who had no mail contracts to bestow), and quite another to ignore congressmen. So he sent Rep. William Wood onto the floor to answer LaGuardia and to declare that ALPA was not only "associated with the racketeers and plug-uglies of Chicago," but was also "communistic!"

This action enraged LaGuardia. Whatever Dave Behncke was he certainly was not a racketeer. And since most airline pilots were military-trained, many still holding reserve commissions, it stood to reason that they were not communists either. This assault on war veterans, especially in view of Cord's own conspicuous lack of service, brought several congressmen down on him, including Rep. William Larson of Georgia, who accused Cord of being "a notorious exploiter of labor" whose airline did not "have satisfactory men to man the ships." Rep. Melvin Maas of Minnesota, who called himself the "flying congressman" and took off at every available opportunity for Randolph Field in Texas to "inspect" (i.e., go flying in) the latest pursuit aircraft, urged the secretaries of the Army and the Navy to deny leaves of absence to military pilots who planned to work for Cord.

Things were snowballing against Cord, and he was seriously worried. On Feb. 29, 1932, he sent every member of Congress a printed statement of his position in the dispute, entitled "A Patriotic Interview with E. L. Cord."

He declared flatly that most pilots were opposed to unionization and that ALPA was "infiltrated by Reds engaging in anarchistic activities," and asked for federal protection of his planes and pilots.

LaGuardia was furious. Taking the House floor on the day after Cord's "patriotic interview" was circulated, LaGuardia described him as "low, dishonest, a liar and a gangster." In the course of his speech, LaGuardia introduced a committee of Century strikers who were present in the House gallery, led by "Duke" Skonning and "Red" Williams.

"Gentlemen," LaGuardia said as he introduced the men, "over 50 percent of the pilots referred to as 'Reds' by this miserable person are ex-servicemen who served as fliers in our Army during the World War." He insisted that Cord's airplanes were unsafe, his mechanics poorly paid, and his pilots unqualified. "There is not a meaner employer of scab labor than this man who disregards the truth and calls it a 'patriotic interview,'" LaGuardia concluded, "and I hope to express the sense of this House when I say that we shall expect and insist that all operators of airplane companies having contracts with the government shall operate their planes safely and skillfully and shall treat their pilots and labor decently." LaGuardia sat down to an ovation from his fellow congressmen. Cord's hopes for an airmail contract were dead.

Shortly afterward one of Cord's airplanes crashed in St. Louis while practicing night landings, killing several pilot trainees. The crash seemed to confirm that Cord's equipment was unsafe. It also accomplished what aerial picketing had been unable to do: discourage business. Boardings dropped so drastically that Cord began hauling his own clerical employes around in an effort to persuade people that there were still plenty of passengers. No one was fooled, however, and in April Cord closed Century Airlines for good.

Cord was enough of a gambler to see that his luck was running out, so he cashed in all of his airline operations, selling Century Pacific to American Airways. Cord gave up his aircraft, equipment, and personnel in exchange for 140,000 shares of stock in Aviation Corporation (AVCO—the parent company of American). Within a year Cord had parlayed this block of stock into effective control of AVCO and hence American. He dared not take personal control of the airline, however, for he had too many enemies in Congress. In order not to endanger American's airmail contract, Cord placed another of his lieutenants, C. R. Smith, in charge of operations. But Cord remained the force behind the scenes.

ALPA proved that it could effectively arouse public and congressional support during the Century strike, but in some respects the outcome was not altogether satisfactory. Neither the Chicago strikers nor the strikebreakers were included in the merger with American, for Cord had closed down Century and released the pilots prior to the merger. Only Century Pacific's pilots automatically gained new jobs.

Behncke worked hard to find jobs for ALPA's Century stalwarts, placing all of them by 1936, despite the tight job market. The luckless strikebreakers were in deep trouble, however, because Behncke saw to it that their names were published in boldface type in every issue of ALPA's monthly publication, *The Air Line Pilot.* "The vilest enemy of the morale of aeronautics is a scab," Behncke once editorialized in *The Air Line Pilot.* "Those scabs recently let out by Mr. Cord will start floating around the country, making every effort to find employment. It will be our duty to see they don't get it. Their plea may be that of need! Match that with the fact that it took guts, faith, and sacrifice for the Century pilots to fight something they knew was wrong."

Although ALPA could not prevent an airline from hiring a Century strikebreaker, everybody knew their names, and no ALPA member, which by the late 1930s included nearly every pilot, would work with them. Behncke eventually relented and allowed a few of them to join ALPA, but not until all the Century pilots had been placed, and only then, as he put it, "to prove definitely ALPA has a heart."

Through a combination of clever public relations and support in Congress, Behncke managed to turn the Century strike into a victory for ALPA, emerging from it as a labor leader of national reputation. Postmaster General Brown, in reality the czar of the airlines because of his control of airmail contracts, flew with Behncke from Chicago to Washington shortly after the strike, and declared that Behncke was "a very good fellow, a splendid pilot. These pilots are the cream of the profession," he added, "the fine type of men I am personally willing to trust my neck with." Brown readily agreed when Rep. James M. Mead, the powerful chairman of the House Post Office Committee, urged him to withhold mail contracts from any airline that did not "accord the privilege of collective representation to its pilots."

This kind of support offered enormous opportunity for Behncke to pursue his goals in Washington, where he lobbied effectively throughout the 1930s to gain protective federal legislation for his pilots. The Century strike turned out to be the catalyst because when the Century pilots struck, they thought Cord would have to come to terms, that he could not replace them. After E. L. Cord showed what he could do to them, they came to realize that they would need friends.

That friend was the AF of L. Without its support, it is unlikely that Behncke and ALPA would have been able to sustain themselves during the strike. As Behncke once put it: "If we had gone down there to Washington as a weak, unaffiliated organization, about all we would have gotten was 'It's a nice day. How does it seem to fly?'"

Most pilots realized that Behncke was right, and that they could not depend upon their skills alone to protect their livelihoods. After their encounter with the likes of E. L. Cord, most pilots came to accept unionization as a necessity of life.

Cord likewise came away from his encounter with ALPA considerably chastened and, one might speculate, angry enough to try to settle scores. Certainly the first generation of airline pilots believed Cord would try to get them later, if the opportunity presented itself. The fact that ALPA had miraculously managed to thwart Cord by establishing a presence in Washington during the Century flap was no guarantee that that presence would be permanent, nor did it mean that Cord's money and power would not someday turn events around.

For the moment, ALPA held the upper hand over Cord and others like him who would try to increase their profits at the pilots' expense. But one thing was certain: the fight was not yet won, and ALPA's only sure path to survival led through Washington, D.C.

And what of the principals in this long-forgotten affair? E. L. Cord lived for many years in seclusion in Reno, Nev., before dying at the age of 80 in 1974. Dave Behncke died of a heart attack at age 53 in 1953. "Dave was a workaholic by any standard you'd care to use," remembers Charley Ruby, another of ALPA's former presidents. "I know personally that he went year-in and year-out without ever taking a vacation."

That pattern of overwork began during the intense battle with E. L. Cord, and it would continue. Behncke was driven to see to it that ALPA would survive, and it is no exaggeration to say that he was the only pilot in America with the skills and contacts to complete the job successfully.

There would be no rest for Dave Behncke. Events were moving rapidly in Washington, and ALPA would have to move with them—or die.

CHAPTER 7

The Perils of Washington

The idea of establishing a political presence in Washington was an obsession with Dave Behncke. His scrape with E. L. Cord had convinced him that ALPA's primary purpose should be to lobby Congress to pass protective legislation for airline pilots. Employment contracts could wait, Behncke believed, while he marshaled his forces to build a case for federal legislation guaranteeing certain minimum standards for pilot pay and working conditions. He knew that his fledgling outfit would never be able to make even the best employment contract stand up against the legal assaults his powerful corporate opponents would surely launch.

Behncke had, in short, chosen to live by the sword of political influence. It was a risky step because ALPA's enemies were big corporations with deep pockets, batteries of lawyers, and lines of connections. There was a possibility that, having chosen to live by the sword of politics, Behncke and ALPA might wind up dying by it.

Although Behncke was the star in those early days, he had an effective supporting cast. What kind of pilot gave up his free time for the headaches of ALPA work—all unpaid in those days?

James H. Roe of Trans World Airlines (TWA) was typical. Now in his 70s and living in Arizona, Roe learned to fly in the Army Air Corps after graduating with an engineering degree from the University of North Dakota. He was exactly the kind of articulate, attractive young pilot Behncke needed as a part-time lobbyist for ALPA. Roe remembers:

> Within a month of the time I went to work in 1932, a couple of pilots approached me about ALPA. They didn't ask me to join, they just mentioned it during a layover at Salt Lake City in a hotel room. They were sounding me out about it, I guess, because there was no recourse if you were to be fired, and they couldn't be sure about us new pilots. Everything was undercover, you know, and you never knew who was a member and who wasn't in those days. About three months passed, and I let people know I would be interested in joining.
>
> I didn't actually meet Dave Behncke until I volunteered to go to Washington on my vacation to help him lobby the National Labor Board [NLB] on Decision 83. We met in Chicago to map strategy

54

about the kind of pay scale we wanted and the number of hours and so forth. That was in 1933. Later I was in a group that William Randolph Hearst, the newspaper baron, called "The Lobby to Save Lives!" We were mostly doing free-lance lobbying on the safety issue, trying to get the independent safety board established to investigate accidents.

One man can't cover Congress, so 10 or 15 of us would map out the group of people we wanted to see and we would just go in. We got to know a lot of politicians, and some of them became our good friends. We always wore our uniforms; Behncke asked us to. I think it was effective, although most of us would rather not have. You could get into an office a little easier and get an appointment. As you know, senators and congressmen are busy people, and that was especially true during the 1930s when so much was happening.

For congressional committee hearings, Behncke always liked to bring along a chorus of uniformed pilots for moral support. Usually Behncke did the talking, with occasional help from Eddie Hamilton, an ex-airline pilot who worked as ALPA's full-time Washington representative, or John Dickerman, a Washington lawyer who took his place. Behncke discouraged pilots from speaking up because an ordinary line pilot who was too outspoken in Washington could get himself into serious trouble. Alexis Klotz, who started flying with Western Air Express (WAE) in 1927, and later went to work for TWA, has vivid memories of crossing TWA chief Jack Frye during the 1933 NLB hearings:

Jack Frye got up and told them we shouldn't be paid more for flying faster equipment, that it was not dangerous to cover more miles and fly through more weather. We had just started flying new Lockheeds, so I said, "Will you please tell us why four pilots have been killed in them recently?"

Well, that did it! Frye was waiting for me out in the hall. I had come to the hearings on a pass. Frye said, "I'm yanking your pass!" Then Pat Patterson, who was president on United, came up to me and said "Lex, you come back to Chicago with me on my private plane. Then we will send you back on United to Los Angeles." I went with Patterson to Chicago where a guy from TWA was waiting. He said "Mr. Frye would appreciate it if you would continue on TWA instead of United."

In the history of ALPA's struggle to create a presence in Washington, no episode is more crucial than the airmail cancellations of 1934. Dave Behncke and the pilots who helped him capitalized on this event to secure the future of the profession.

It began as a seemingly classic case of the good guys vs. the bad guys, with FDR and the New Deal playing hero while Herbert Hoover and the airline operators played villain. After a series of spectacular hearings chaired by Sen. (later Supreme Court Justice) Hugo A. Black, FDR canceled the airmail contracts Hoover had awarded in 1930 on the grounds that they had been fraudulently let.

Postmaster General Jim Farley had urged FDR to cancel the airmail contracts, but he miscalculated. Farley had intended to reopen the contracts after a short interval, and this time to make sure the airmail money was spread around. On the other hand, FDR, who loved to experiment, started toying with the idea of reestablishing the old Post Office Air Mail Service, complete with its own pilots, planes, and airfields. In the interim, FDR ordered the Army to fly the mail.

After a rocky start, the Army did a pretty good job. In the beginning Army pilots were poorly prepared to fly the mail regularly, and there were some fatal crashes. Because of the depression, peacetime Army pilots were limited to about four hours of flying a month. Even that had to be in good weather because the Army feared that bad weather flying might result in the loss of scarce aircraft. Although most Army pilots had received some rudimentary instrument instruction during flight training, most of the operational aircraft they flew in those days had no modern instrumentation. A few Army pilots managed to stay current by volunteering for Department of Commerce weather research flying, but such billets were extremely scarce. As a result, only a few Army pilots had flown any instruments at all after winning their wings. To complicate matters, the winter of 1934 was exceptionally severe.

"There we were," wrote Robert L. Scott, a West Pointer who had been assigned to a Curtiss Falcon squadron after training, "about to start flying the mail in tactical planes with open cockpits in the blizzards of the Great Lakes. It must have looked peculiar to airline pilots to see us taxiing out to take off in P-12s and P-26s holding some 50 pounds."

Although the Army pilots learned to cope with the airmail on a reduced schedule after they got better equipment, there was an immediate outcry over the fatal crashes. Historian Arthur Schlesinger, Jr., calls this outcry the New Deal's first public relations setback. It seemed that every prominent aviator in America was mad at FDR. Capt. Eddie Rickenbacker, the World War I ace, denounced him for committing "legalized murder." Charles Lindbergh flatly refused to serve on a special committee investigating the airmail crisis and accused the New Deal of being "socialistic." Lindbergh declared that he would not "directly or indirectly" lend his support to "the operation by military forces of American business and commerce." Republican Sen. Simeon D. Fess of Ohio, a stalwart enemy of FDR, called the airmail cancellations "the most important single issue since the Civil War."

It was front-page stuff—a lot of heavy debate, wild charges, and good old-fashioned political hot air. In this volatile environment, when it seemed that everyone else was losing his head, Dave Behncke kept his. Cooly and calmly, he almost single-handedly turned the airmail crisis of

As the first to fly the line, the airmail pilots established a legacy of courage and commitment to safety inherited by the airline pilots of today. William C. "Big Bill" Hopson *(left, in winter flying gear)* was one of those pioneers, helping establish the transcontinental airmail route for the Post Office in 1921. He died when his plane crashed at Polk, Pa., Oct. 18, 1927.

Taking aloft a single-engine biplane like the Laird Swallow *(above)* alone over the new airmail routes offered the opportunity for adventure and fame to the Air Mail Service's early pilots. Jack Knight *(opposite, bottom)*—pioneer airmail pilot and later, as a United Airlines captain, one of ALPA's first members—proved the dependability of airmail service and became a national hero in the process. Knight fought darkness and freezing temperatures to be the first to complete the night leg of a transcontinental airmail route. His 435-mile flight from North Platte, Neb., to Chicago earned him the epithet "ace of the Air Mail Service." Even with the few amenities offered passengers on early flights *(opposite, top)*, the airlines found that passenger fees alone could not sustain operations; government airmail subsidies would be essential to the airlines' survival for the next 50 years. The spareness of the Omaha office *(right)* was typical of the Air Mail Service's offices.

A NEW SCHEDULE
AIR MAIL
NEW YORK SAN FRANCISCO
STARTS JULY 1
ASK YOUR POSTMASTER

The glamorous reputations of early airmail pilots were earned not only by their courage and sacrifices but also by those of their fellow pilots who did not live to share the glory. Pilots working for the Post Office Department in 1918 stood only a one-in-four chance of surviving until the private contractors took over in 1926. Fog, which obscured this Jenny's takeoff *(opposite, top)*, presented the direst threat. Safety concerns over flying in fog led to the first pilot strike in 1919. The fortunate pilot found himself grounded in a cornfield *(opposite, inset)*; the less fortunate didn't survive. The lucky one who lived through this serious crash *(opposite, bottom)* went on to even wider fame: Charles Lindbergh.

Buck Private David L. Behncke's dream of becoming an Army aviator was earthbound when he served support duty for General Pershing's Mexican campaign in 1916 *(left)*, but took off when he entered flight training in San Diego in 1918 *(below)*. His other dream—that of making the military his career—continued to be frustrated, though Behncke held on to it even after he became president of ALPA.

In the early 1920s, Behncke won recognition as a part-time aerial daredevil *(right)* and as full-time manager of Checkerboard Field in Chicago *(below)*.

Behncke had a knack for attracting press coverage of his exploits, not only during his tenure as ALPA's first president but also during his earlier stints as a member of a "flying circus" troupe and as an airmail pilot *(opposite, clockwise from left):* setting an airmail speed record, buzzing the homestead in Wisconsin, or performing with wing walker Lela Davidson.

BANG **LETS ALL GO**
Sunday, Aug. 13
Checkerboard's
— FIRST —
AERIAL REVUE
Exciting — Thrilling — Educational

Spend an afternoon at Chicago's foremost airdrome. See the largest congress of record-holding and nationally known aviators and aerial dare-devil performers ever brought together at one time. See America's best airplane pilots compete for liberal cash prizes on the famous Checkerboard low altitude racing course.

E. HAMILTON LEE, star air mail pilot, holder of the Chicago to Washington flight record 6 hours.

J. NELSON KELLY, famous Kelly field stunt flyer.

MAJOR SCHROEDER, one time holder of the world's altitude record.

SHIRLEY SHORT, known as America's most daring stunt flier. The man who flew for Locklear.

SEE SOMETHING NEW! INTREPID DAREDEVIL PERFORMERS WILL DEFY DEATH MANY TIMES IN THE FOLLOWING EVENTS

BEN GREW will perform the most daring feat known to the flying world. Grew will hurl himself through space in a thousand foot leap saving himself by a small, pack parachute. This act alone is worth many times the price of admission.

CHIC WHEELER, Chicago's own daredevil, will demonstrate how the pilot of the modern battle plane escapes certain death, after his plane has been disabled in combat.

BERT BLAIR, known as one of Chicago's best, who hopes to add to his laurels by winning this race.

JOHN SCHROEDER, winner of the American Legion derby.

TONY YACKEY, the famous Italian ace, holder of Chicago to Detroit record, will fly his Breguet bombing plane.

DAVID L. BEHNCKE, manager of Checkerboard Flying Field, known as one of the oldest and most capable pilots in the business

JACK COPE, late of the RUTH LAW flying circus, will show you how a farmer boy would break into the flying game. Thrilling as well as amusing.

GORDEN (DAREDEVIL) HOLDER who will escape from an exploding balloon after being bombed by an airplane piloted by David Behncke. Weather permitting. Holder will also walk on the wings of a speeding airplane many feet above the earth.

This meet is being held for the purpose of furthering the science of aviation and the public is cordially invited to co-operate in making it a success

Behncke's Checkerboard Aeroplane Service, Inc.
Admission Adults 50c Children 25c

METROPOLITAN "L" GARFIELD PARK TO FOREST PARK STATION. MOTOR BUS TO FIELD
Auto Route: West to Jackson Blvd. to Kenton Ave., south to Harrison Road, west 3 blocks to Checkerboard Aerodrome.
DON'T FORGET THE GREAT AIR MEET, COME EARLY. September 4th.

Airmail Pilot Thrills His Family, Flying Over Farm Home Each Trip

DAVE BEHNCKE.

170 Miles An Hour

Across the broad state of Wisconsin in seventy-five min utes! That record was made yesterday by David L. Behncke, air mail pilot, who is shown standing by the plane which brought him from La Crosse at the rate of two and a third miles a minute.

175 MILES — 75 MINUTES

The route taken by Behncke in his record

YOUTH, BEAUTY AND AGE FLY

CHICAGO

Accompanied by Miss Lela Davidson, the veteran pilot David L. Behncke won the air race yesterday against a swift field of fliers.

Behncke's seemingly happy employment with NWA was unfortunately short-lived. Exhibiting the overriding concern for safety that was characteristic of his career, Behncke refused to pilot a passenger flight in a plane that Charles R. "Speed" Holman *(left)* had "warmed up" aerobatically earlier in the day. Behncke argued that Holman may have overstressed the plane, but Holman won; Behncke got fired. Subsequently, Behncke's third try at the Army was not entirely charmed *(below, Behncke fourth from left)*. Despite his best efforts, the Army refused him a regular commission and the military career he longed for.

1934 to the benefit of ALPA and the fledgling profession of airline piloting.

From Behncke's point of view it was all a matter of power: FDR had it and Behncke wanted a share of it. He knew that FDR would come out on top of this little battle, and he wanted ALPA to be in the winner's corner.

For this reason Behncke publicly applauded FDR. The President's actions, Behncke told a press conference, "are regarded by the pilots, who are perhaps closer to the industry than any other group, as being the soundest and most constructive move yet taken in the entire history of air commerce."

With every prominent aviator in the country screaming for FDR's blood, Behncke figured it wouldn't make much sense to join the pack. FDR was notorious for punishing his enemies and rewarding his friends. When the dust finally cleared, ALPA stood out as the only group inside the industry supporting FDR. Behncke got his reward—a federally guaranteed minimum wage for airline pilots in the new Air Mail Act of 1935. Behind these simple facts, however, lies a plan carefully calculated and skillfully played out by ALPA's founder.

The cancellations had come as a great shock to Behncke. He was in Omaha when he learned about them and promptly telephoned the *New York Times* to say that the pilots were "entirely innocent of any fraud." He insisted that most airline operators were honest and that "the graft of a few government officials and air operators ought not to discredit the entire industry."

Behncke had no alternative but to return to Washington. He had spent so much time there since the beginning of the New Deal that W. A. "Pat" Patterson, his boss at United, had fired him for absenteeism. Only by taking his own case before the NLB had Behncke won back his job. The last thing he wanted was to jeopardize it again, but the future of the profession, ALPA, and the industry itself was at stake. This time, Patterson approved Behncke's request for a leave of absence.

Behncke had become a familiar figure in Washington, appearing at countless hearings, stating the pilots' position to anyone who would listen; but he never had much influence. ALPA, after all, was a small union with no real power. What muscle Behncke had came mostly from the fact that William Green, the president of the American Federation of Labor (AF of L), liked Behncke and lent his support. Behncke hated being away from Chicago, waiting around endlessly for a chance to testify before congressional committees, but he kept "boring in" and whenever an opportunity presented itself would "start talking and waving my arms," as he put it.

The cancellations had thrown many pilots out of work. The Army took back on active duty some who still held reserve commissions, but most found themselves either on reduced work schedules or not flying at all. WAE furloughed its entire pilot force and ceased all operations. By early March 1934 nearly one-third of ALPA's members were out of work.

Despite considerable grumbling in the ranks, Behncke stood firm in his support of FDR. He tried to alleviate the unemployment problem by encouraging the Army to hire all airline pilots as a temporary reserve force for flying the mail. But most airline pilots didn't want to become government pilots again. They much preferred working for their civilian employers.

Behncke repeatedly told his pilots to lay low, to trust his judgment, to put up with being temporarily out of work. He was on thin ice, but he insisted that FDR would take care of them if they remained loyal and did not join the attacks on the New Deal. "I'm a strong Roosevelt man," Behncke declared. Few pilots understood what Behncke had in mind, but because he had been right so often in the past, they went along with him.

Behncke figured that FDR would eventually be forced to restore the airmail contracts to the private operators. The crucial thing, from ALPA's point of view, was to make sure that when the airmail contracts were written, the pilots would receive a slice of the pie; only FDR could guarantee that result.

While Behncke publicly sided with the President, privately he was urging that the established airlines be given another chance. Underneath the public show of support for FDR, Behncke was alarmed at the prospect of Postmaster General Farley allowing the small operators back into the airmail business. The small airlines paid notoriously low wages, and they were difficult to organize. So with masterful equivocation, Behncke urged that when new contracts were awarded, the government set "minimum specifications" to keep out "shoestring" operators.

Behncke's position was almost identical to that of Walter F. Brown, Herbert Hoover's much-abused postmaster general. The only difference was that Behncke stressed safety, while Brown stressed efficiency. In essence, ALPA's welfare and the welfare of the old, established operators were mutual. Once again, as in the Century strike of 1932, Behncke and the established airline operators who had lost their contracts joined forces in a temporary alliance.

Behncke guessed right: In March 1934 FDR announced that he would restore the airmail service to private operators. He really had no choice. The Army's business, after all, was national defense, not flying the mail. And with the country in the midst of its worst depression, it didn't make much sense to spend a lot of money recreating the old Post Office Air Mail Service.

When FDR reopened the airmail contract bidding, he exacted his political revenge in two ways. First, he insisted on the reorganization of the airlines involved in the so-called "spoils conferences" that preceded Hoover's airmail contract awards in 1930, and he banned airline executives who had participated in those conferences from taking part in the new bidding.

Second, he insisted that the new airmail contracts specify wages and working conditions for pilots. Of all the operators, only Patterson of United, Behncke's boss, supported the inclusion of a minimum wage law.

Behncke stayed in Washington from February to June 1934, assisted by a committee of pilots whose routes included stops in there. "We began to see," Behncke said, "that we could not get anything definite unless we had something definite for these people to put in the new airmail law." That "something definite" was Decision 83 of the old NLB—the cornerstone of the modern system of airline pilot compensation.

Anybody who has ever delved even superficially into ALPA's history or into the subject of pilot compensation has heard about Decision 83. What was it, and why was it so important?

ALPA owes its existence to the desire of the early operators to abolish, once and for all, the old Post Office system of pilot compensation. Some of the new private contractors continued paying their pilots (many of whom had been flying the routes for the Air Mail Service) in the same way as the Post Office. That is, they paid their pilots a monthly base (or minimum guarantee), plus so much per mile, with added increments for night and hazardous terrain flying. A Post Office pilot could earn as much as $1,000 per month, and salary levels stayed pretty much the same on some airlines until the bottom dropped out of the economy in 1929. Suddenly, operators had to cut costs, and pilots salaries were first on their hit list.

When rumors of the impending "pay adjustment" began circulating in 1929, talk of forming a union gained momentum. By the time talk had given way to action and Dave Behncke and his cohorts were secretly collecting signed, undated letters of resignation (or "pledges"), most pilots would probably have accepted some reduction in pay if the old Post Office system had remained basically intact. But the operators were having none of that. They wanted either a straight hourly or monthly wage, stripped of all the little extras that in their opinion made pilot salaries so excessive. From the pilots' point of view, a straight monthly salary was unacceptable because it made no allowance for different types of flying, routes, or equipment. A few airlines, such as Northwest Airlines (NWA) and Pan American Airways (PAA), had used the monthly basis of pay from the beginning, and the pilots there definitely did not like it.

For pilots with foresight, an hourly system was no good because in the future it would almost surely deprive them of productivity gains associated with flying new, faster aircraft. They resolved to fight.

The focal point of this resistance was on TWA and UAL (United Aircraft Corporation; later United Airlines). On TWA, a pilot named Hal George led the resistance. He had nearly as much to do with creating ALPA as Dave Behncke did. Had he lived the TWA pilots might well have been spared a lot of misery. Howard Hall remembers Hal George well:

He was a very purposeful man, very good at the word-of-mouth stuff it took to get things rolling. He got killed because of a fluke. He was flying the Northrop Alpha from Columbus to Newark. One night a woman came out to the field and demanded that she be permitted to ride on the night mail flight, which normally didn't carry any passengers. It was dangerous flying, winter as I recall, open cockpit; the pilot wore a parachute, and more than one had to get out when the ice got real bad in that kind of flying. This woman insisted that she be allowed to board, said her daughter was seriously ill. George permitted her on the airplane on the condition that she wear a parachute.

Well, the weather was bad and he got into a bunch of ice. He got down in the Allegheny River over just east of Pittsburgh and he never got out. The woman wouldn't, or couldn't bail out, and I guess he wouldn't leave her. He crashed, killing both the woman and himself.

After Hal's death, I became the primary go-between for ALPA on TWA. Based at Kansas City, I wasn't nearly as well situated as he [Hal George] had been at Columbus to act as a go-between. TWA was divided, and the company wanted to keep it that way, and there's no doubt that the company had made promises of executive positions to a lot of pilots, if they would stay out of ALPA. Anyway, that's the way it was on TWA—tough.

On UAL, Dave Behncke had much better luck collecting the letters of resignation he intended to use as bargaining chips. In fact, Behncke's activities on UAL provided something of a laboratory for the techniques he would use later to create ALPA on a broader stage. He rented a room in the Morrison Hotel on June 19, 1931, and surreptitiously spread the word that every UAL pilot interested in stopping the pay cut should meet there at a designated hour. The pilots who showed up to hear what Behncke planned to do with their pledges were so afraid of being discovered they blocked the keyholes with toilet paper.

Behncke had a lot going for him—a wide acquaintance among pilots, a reputation for trustworthiness, and demonstrated leadership qualities from his days in the late 1920s as governor of the Central District of the old National Air Pilots Association. Also working in his favor was the general decline in pilots' working conditions, pay, and status during the first full year of the depression.

At the Morrison Hotel meeting, Behncke got the assent of his fellow UAL pilots to confront management directly. The plan was for Behncke to present their signed, undated "escrow" resignations to management, with the warning that if their salaries were cut, they would shut down the airline. They knew it was a long shot, that they could not win a protracted struggle and would eventually have no choice but to come back to work at a lower salary and on the company's terms, if it would have them, but they signed up anyway. The mimeographed pledge Behncke persuaded his fellow UAL pilots to sign read as follows:

> Enclosed you will find my letter of resignation. The time of the resignation is left blank. I hereby empower you to deliver my resignation to said employer anytime you see fit. Particularly in the event that any United Aircraft Corporation pilot should be discharged because of the movement now under way to protect the interests, working conditions, wages, and hours of pilots. I hereby authorize you to negotiate for and on my behalf with my employer in all matters concerning my working conditions, wages, and hours, and to enter into an agreement with my employer binding myself to service when agreed to by majority vote.
>
> In the event that you should see fit to deliver the enclosed resignation, I hereby agree to cease working at the time designated by you and not to return to work until your committee has so desired. The above authority is granted to you for a period of one year from date.

The mock legalese of this pledge bears the unmistakable stamp of Behncke's rambling rhetorical style. Behncke, as the ringleader and spokesman, was in grave danger. He fully expected his brother UAL pilots to stand behind him, but obviously could not be sure that they would.

Behncke was gambling his whole career at this point, and he knew it. It was a nervy, courageous, possibly foolhardy move, but something in Behncke's psychological makeup drove him to accept this kind of challenge, perhaps even to relish it. In a May 31, 1931, letter to George Douglass ("Mr. V"—from Varney Airlines), Behncke wrote grimly:

> The slight standards we have maintained in the past have been maintained only at the expense of a few leaders fighting fearlessly and alone for the good of all. About half have the guts to stand in line, and the other half must be kept there through the medium of a heavy boot. I feel that the right kind of organization will serve as the boot.
>
> Personally, I am either going to nail this fight up for good and all through the medium of an effective line pilot's organization, or fold up for all time and start selling peanuts—and I don't like peanuts!!

Behncke's vision of this new airline pilots' organization was that it would be *solely* for working airline pilots—barnstormers, crop dusters, and miscellaneous commercial pilots need not apply. Furthermore, he insisted that it cut across company lines to include all airline pilots, regardless of their employer. He was also determined that all airline pilots receive the same pay for flying similar routes and equipment, regardless of which airline he worked for, whether it was a major "trunk" carrier or a fly-by-night "shoestring" outfit such as Long & Harmon down in Texas.

In early July 1931, just before rumor had it that UAL was going to unilaterally impose the new "reformed" pay scale, Behncke asked for and received an audience with the Chicago operations manager. Behncke was accompanied by a committee of pilots, who stood resolutely behind him as he solemnly presented his collection of escrow resignations and asked that they be forwarded up the line.

UAL's management was flabbergasted. They had no idea that the long-rumored unionization of their pilots had gotten so far, and they were hesitant to stick their necks out by reacting to it too quickly. For reasons that have never been fully explained, UAL's management proved conciliatory. They didn't promise *not* to reduce pay, but they did promise to consult with the pilots before instituting any changes. Compared with the negative reception Hal George and the TWA pilots received at Kansas City, Behncke and the UAL pilots scored a great success. These meetings took place in either late June or early July, barely a month before ALPA's official birth at the Morrison Hotel on July 27, 1931.

Clearly, the pay issue underlay the creation of ALPA, but the mere existence of a union, particularly a small unaffiliated one, would never be enough to thwart a major corporation. If ALPA were to survive and be effective, it had to have the backing of the larger labor movement, either an affiliation with the AF of L or the Railroad Brotherhoods. Behncke ultimately decided on the AF of L and proceeded to get a "charter" from it at the annual meeting in Atlantic City, N.J., which luckily was to convene in early July. Behncke went personally to Atlantic City, got the international charter to organize the craft of cockpit workers, and then kept it secret while he awaited the upcoming convention of Key Men, where he hoped to have it ratified.

The Key Men ultimately ratified the affiliation with the AF of L (although at first they kept it a secret from the rest of the membership), and this act was the key to ALPA's entry into the NLB's jurisdiction and, finally, Decision 83. If ALPA had not joined the AF of L, it would have lacked the necessary connections to have its case heard.

In December 1932, during the dying days of Herbert Hoover's administration, Postmaster General Walter F. Brown announced sharply reduced airmail subsidies to the contractors. This move was undeniably political, made in direct response to President-elect Roosevelt's criticism of Hoover's budget deficit and his announced intention to balance the budget with his New Deal.

The immediate impact of this subsidy reduction was to pinch the airmail operators so hard that they had no choice but to cut pilot salaries to the bone. It was either that or reduce stockholders' dividends, which was unthinkable.

The average pilot of that era was intimately concerned with his airline's economic survival and at times would be willing to make substantial sacrifices to help his employer. The focal point of this managerial mentality among airline pilots was on the small airlines, whose owners often poor-mouthed their pilots into believing that any raise or failure to accept a reduction in pay would lead to the company's speedy collapse.

Combating this kind of thinking was one of Behncke's early challenges. Behncke probably distrusted airline managers more than any pilot in America. To him, it was evident that companies with similar sources of income should pay similar salaries. When managers poor-mouthed, Behncke automatically assumed they were lying, and he couldn't understand why pilots were so easily taken in. A uniform national pay scale for all pilots, regardless of the airline they worked for, was the rock upon which Behncke built all other ALPA policies. The only problem was, how could he get it?

The August 1933 National Recovery Administration (NRA) "Code" hearings did indeed propose a uniform national pay scale for airline pilots. But that scale was so low and the monthly hourly requirements so high that Behncke fought successfully to have the pilots excluded from it.

Title III of the operators' draft proposal code called for 140 hours per month as the maximum a pilot could fly, and $250 per month as the minimum salary. President Lester D. Seymour of AAL (American Airways; later American Airlines) testified that these figures were "fixed with consideration for the smaller operators," and he insisted that the major operators would never pay their pilots such low salaries or work them so hard.

Fiorello LaGuardia, who was then running for mayor of New York City, attacked Seymour's proposals. He also pointed out that in the codes so far adopted by the NRA, the wages and working conditions specified usually corresponded closely to those being paid.

With ALPA out of the Air Transport Code, the operators, who had been talking about reducing pilot salaries for so long, saw no reason to delay it any further. Now Behncke was faced with a genuine dilemma.

The NLB, which was the logical place for Behncke to appeal, was set up as an agency of the NRA *solely* to adjudicate differences arising under different interpretations of the code—*which ALPA wasn't in!* How, then, could Behncke possibly expect the NLB to hear ALPA's case?

Behncke was determined to have his cake and eat it too. Early in September 1933, just after the signing of the Air Transport Code, the operators formally announced that they were instituting the new pay system, and ALPA be damned. Behncke played his last card—he threatened a national strike!

It was a desperate gamble, one which would have wrecked ALPA completely had it come to pass. Fortunately, the operators took it seriously. As UAL's James Belding recalls:

I think it was about September 1933 when the threatened national strike came along. I was flying the Monomail down in Kansas City, and I remember to this day, vividly, I landed at the terminal there, taxied up, unloaded my mail, and taxied the airplane in the hangar and shut it down. As I came around the corner of the hangar, there were two Pinkerton guards with shotguns. They walked the wing all the way around into the hangar and waited for me to get out and put my parachute and gear away, and followed me until I got into a cab. They were afraid I was going to blow the goddamn place up! This was the evening of the strike. Out of our whole group of people, all the pilots and copilots combined on all of United, the company only found 11 people that were willing to break the strike, and they were all in Chicago waiting for the deadline of midnight.

I came back out to the field that night to take my return trip to Omaha; it was due out a few minutes after midnight. I reported because I didn't know if the strike was on or not.

Well, no sooner did I hit the field than they said, "Well, the National Labor Board has taken over and the strike is off."

William M. Leiserson, secretary of NLB, had agreed to take on the airline pay dispute because Secretary of Labor Frances Perkins had been persuaded by William Green, president of the AF of L, to ask him to do so. The reasoning under which the NLB adopted the case lay in an obscure clause of NRA's enabling legislation that "no industry operating under a code shall reduce pay levels below the precode level." It was of no consequence that the intent of the act was clearly to cover workers _in_ a code, which pilots weren't. What mattered were the connections and the muscle of the AF of L, which Behncke made use of—and not for the last time either.

After the crisis had passed Behncke admitted that if it had actually come to a strike, ALPA would have been finished:

I believe that American Airways was the best balanced. They were pretty much together, and I believe they would have walked out to the last man. TWA would have collapsed completely, and I know that on United everything south and east of Chicago would have gone out, and west of Chicago it would have been just about half.

The only way you can keep a striking element in line is to keep them informed. I figured it would cost $1,000 a day to conduct the strike, and our treasury had $5,000, so we would have lasted about five days. After that, our communications would have been cut. We would have been completely broken.

Once again, under nearly impossible odds, Behncke had staved off defeat. There was big trouble in ALPA, nevertheless, for the mere threat of a nationwide strike had been sufficient to unravel some shaky locals, particularly on TWA. It was at this time that one of ALPA's early stalwarts, Waldon "Swede" Golien, charter member and then current master executive council chairman, led the defection to a company union, "The TWA Pilots Association."

Things went poorly for the operators from the very beginning of the NLB hearings, mostly because of the situation on TWA. There was a predisposition in the early New Deal years for government agencies to favor labor over management, and the underdog aviators caught the fancy of several NLB members, particularly Sen. Robert Wagner of New York, who wanted to know more about this "TWA Pilots' Association." A TWA lawyer named Henry Hogan all but ruined the operators during one exchange over the legitimacy of the company union. Hogan's curiously detailed knowledge of the TWA pilots' letters of resignation from ALPA provoked this exchange:

WAGNER: How did you happen to see these letters of resignation?
HOGAN: Because I represent the company and the letters were sent to us.
WAGNER: You are not an officer of the Association. Why should they send letters to you? How did they know the company was interested in them?
HOGAN: If you were a pilot you could answer that.
WAGNER: What? No. It might indicate that the company was evidencing a little interest in their resigning, and that is something you ought not to be interested in because it is none of your business. When a man working for a concern is a member of a union and he resigns and then hurries to tell his employer—well now, I am not a child! That sort of thing must stop. Certain rights are given to them under the law, to organize, and you must not discriminate against them. This is a new era. We are not living in an old century. You must not intimidate them.

The various airline presidents in attendance squirmed in their seats as their high-priced legal talent, hired to keep them out of trouble, proceeded to get them in it. J. Bruce Kremer, a managerial spokesman for UAL told Wagner: "Candidly, Senator, knowing their fearless spirit, I think a man shows a great deal of temerity who tries to intimidate any of them."

To which Wagner replied: "It doesn't take much courage to fire a man, and this sort of thing must stop or we will see to it that there are no more liberal subsidies."

Now that was a threat, to cut off mail subsidies—enough to make any airline operator pro-union. The assembled airline managers promptly assured Wagner that on their lines, nobody was intimidating pilots. "We consider our pilots to be in a class *at least semiprofessional*," one executive explained (italics added).

The NLB hearing before Judge Bernard Shientag of the New York State Supreme Court subsequently arrived at Decision 83. His compromise decision set the monthly maximum flight time at 85 hours, which was what Behncke had been pushing for all along. On the troublesome pay question he gave in to the operators by establishing a basic hourly pay, which would increase with the speed of the aircraft, *plus* a small mileage increment.

The operators were shocked. Decision 83 gave the pilots an automatic share of any productivity gains associated with new aircraft, something they believed should accrue exclusively to stockholders. Although Behncke had originally opposed a straight hourly wage, he was willing to accept one because it was geared to the speed of the aircraft.

The NLB staff subsequently converted Judge Shientag's formula into a scale matched to each aircraft type, and on Dec. 15, 1933, they presented it to the full NLB. Although Behncke was pleased with it, the operators were not, but there was really nothing they could do about it.

By the time Behncke decided that Decision 83 was the "something definite" about pilot pay he wanted included in the new Air Mail Act of 1935, the very existence of NRA, and all its subsidiaries like NLB, was under legal challenge in the courts. Eventually the entire NRA would be declared unconstitutional by the Supreme Court. Behncke had to hurry if he was going to salvage the pilots' pay provisions from the sinking ship.

By 1934 NLB was practically defunct, and Decision 83 had no legal standing. It was for this reason that Behncke stayed in Washington and worked so hard to have it included in the new Air Mail Act. Subsequently, the substance of Decision 83 was placed into the Civil Aeronautics Act of 1938. Behncke told his fellow airline pilots: "They are never going to try to replace you again."

In May 1934 the private operators were once again flying the mail and ALPA's members were back at work. Behncke's strategy had paid off. Largely because Behncke and ALPA were his only supporters inside the industry during the airmail crisis, FDR paid his debt to Behncke by calling for the inclusion of the Decision 83 formula in any new airmail legislation passed by Congress.

By early 1934 a consensus was forming in favor of a full-time professional staff for ALPA. Everyone knew that satisfactory progress would be much more difficult in the future if ALPA continued doing things as cheaply as it had in the past. As a growing membership increased dues revenue, most pilots seemed ready to fulfill a prophecy made by the legendary AAL pilot M.D. "Doc" Ator, who told the 1931 convention of Key Men: "I do not think we should be lenient on dues. This organization has got to be high-class. I might be wrong, but I think we are going to need high-powered men, and they are going to cost us money. This is going to be a damned expensive organization, but we can afford to put this money out for future protection."

In March 1934 the Central Executive Council authorized a mail ballot on the question of making Behncke the full-time president of ALPA. The response was overwhelmingly in the affirmative. Even the most uninvolved airline pilot of 1934 could hardly help but appreciate the things Behncke had achieved since 1931. Likewise, the nation's airline pilots realized it wasn't fair to expect "old Dave" to spend his days getting a Boeing 247D to Omaha only to come home to Chicago for another long night of unpaid ALPA work down at the Troy Lane Hotel.

No one could be certain what the future held, but it was obvious that more battles lay ahead and that the gains of the past year were far from secure. ALPA's workload would surely increase, and a part-time operation wouldn't be able to handle it. Already looming were potential enforcement problems. What could ALPA do if some hard-nosed bush-league airline simply refused to pay its pilots the scale mandated by Decision 83? The question was about to become more than rhetorical. ✈

CHAPTER 8

Flying for a Rogue Airline

Dave Behncke was determined that there should be no second-class citizens in the ranks of airline pilots. He understood that there was bound to be some expression of chauvinist pride, that natural rivalries would exist among different airlines and their pilots. Nevertheless, Behncke could get feisty when it came to "competitive flying"—pilots of one airline recklessly boasting that they could fly in weather too tough for pilots of other airlines. From the very first issue of *The Air Line Pilot*, which appeared in newspaper format in April 1932, Behncke warned his fellow pilots:

> Faced with the fear of losing his job, even the pilot who knows bet-
> ter will engage in cutthroat flying, and fly on in the spirit of foolish
> rivalry. This present reckless competition is setting a dangerous
> standard. The tougher you fly, the tougher your employer is going
> to expect you to fly.
>
> Modern business may demand a 100 percent schedule, but this
> is commerce, not war. The smart pilot knows when to quit, and he
> doesn't take pride in flying over or through tougher weather than
> his brother pilots.
>
> As pilots, we are no longer individuals. We are a group, and as
> such we must think collectively and work collectively.

Behncke's remarks struck a responsive chord, particularly among the pilots of the smaller airlines. As W. J. Fry of Pacific Seaboard Airlines (which later became Chicago & Southern and then Delta) put it in the December 1934 issue of *The Air Line Pilot*:

> In airline piloting, there has been a great deal of undue criticism
> and friction between pilots working for different companies. Re-
> cently a pilot made the remark to me that the pilots of one com-
> pany could not work for another company because they were not
> capable. This pilot had no reason to run down these pilots. Some
> of us seem to have the idea that we are a little bit better than any
> other pilot because we happen to be working for a certain com-
> pany or flying a certain plane.
>
> This is entirely wrong. We will accomplish a great deal more and
> have a finer and stronger organization in ALPA if each pilot will

work with and help other pilots, rather than create a lot of petty jealousy among ourselves.

Fine words, but in a country dominated by marketplace considerations the bottom line would always be salaries. The pilot who worked for substandard wages on a small airline was, in fact, a second-class citizen economically, and everyone knew it. That's why Behncke resolved that the small airlines should pay the same salaries as the large ones.

That was easier said than done.

ALPA's battle to equalize pilot salaries began in an obscure confrontation on an obscure airline. Forget, for a moment, today's fast-paced world of jet equipment and crowded terminal control areas, and put yourself in another time and place. Imagine yourself in 1934 working for an airline called Long & Harmon, flying mail and an occasional passenger through the virtually empty skies between Brownsville and Amarillo, Tex., in a single-engine Stinson "Reliant." Put yourself in the place of Long & Harmon's pilots, whose names nobody remembers today and whose forgotten ordeal appears in no history book. After you've read their story, perhaps you will understand why every pilot working today owes them something—particularly those who work for the smaller airlines.

When FDR announced his intention to return the airmail to private contractors, Dave Behncke knew there was bound to be trouble with the undercapitalized little airlines, fixed-based operators, and crop-dusting outfits, which were submitting bids in competition with the majors.

The nation's small operators, led by the Braniff brothers in Texas, had been screaming since 1930 that they had been frozen out by Hoover, the Republicans, and the big corporations. They charged fraud and collusion, arguing that the "little man" had been victimized by rigged bidding.

The alleged villains, Hoover and his postmaster general, Walter F. Brown, had been trying to create an airline system with passenger-carrying capability. They knew that the small operators would be content merely to fly the mail in small aircraft and would never risk their limited capital to purchase the new trimotor aircraft that were becoming available in the late 1920s. The small-fry had no stomach for competing with the railroads for passengers. Hoover and Brown reasoned that without the modern equipment that passenger service required, the small operators would never get off the government dole.

In an effort to force the shoestring operators into upgrading their equipment, Brown required all bidders for mail contracts in 1930 to either meet certain minimum specifications or be forced out of business. Because of these requirements, the small operators denounced the bidding session of 1930 as a "spoils conference." Actually, it was no such thing: the small-fry had the same opportunity as the big fellows—they just didn't have the money to buy the new multiengine aircraft Brown demanded. Admittedly, there was an element of ruthlessness in the way he proceeded, but it was not illegal. Brown succeeded in creating the genesis of a regulated, integrated airline system—a system that FDR would eventually copy.

Dave Behncke and his union of airline pilots were in complete agreement with the policies of Hoover and Brown. Behncke disliked most small operators because they were almost impossible to organize and quick to fire any pilot who so much as flirted with the idea of unionization. In addition, it angered Behncke that most of the small airlines were owned by men who didn't work every day as pilots, but who nevertheless came to Washington to speak for pilots during congressional hearings. When the Democrats took office in March 1933, the small operators expected to have their day. The Braniff brothers, it was said, had ensured a favorable hearing from the new administration by liberally contributing to certain powerful Democrats. Delta's C. E. Woolman was playing the same game.

Behncke won FDR's gratitude by publicly supporting him. Privately, however, Behncke supported the old operators, doing everything he could to get their contracts restored. The last thing he wanted was for the shoestring operators to get a new foothold in the industry.

It proved impossible to keep all the small operators out of the business when the new contracts were let in April 1934. At high noon on an unseasonably warm day, more than 150 people crowded into the office of Superintendent of the Airmail Stephen A. Cisler to see the bids opened. Among those present were heavyweights like Paul Braniff, W. A. "Pat" Patterson of United (UAL) and Lester D. Seymour of American Airways (AAL, later reorganized as American Airlines). They were bidding for a one-year contract under an interim law that would apply while Congress was in the process of writing permanent legislation (eventually the Air Mail Act of 1935). The new bids were stated in terms of a flat amount of money per mile over each route. The tension in the room, heightened by full press coverage and a battery of photographers, was largely due to the knowledge that of the 45 bidders only half would be successful. Behncke's worst fears seemed about to materialize when the final bids were posted. The major airlines suffered severe losses to the small operators, whose bids were unrealistically low. The major operators had to face the tough decision either to compete with the small-fry by also submitting unrealistically low bids, or to stand by while the small operators again filled the nation's airways with open-cockpit biplanes. The majors had no choice—they had to retain control of some of their old routes, even if it meant accepting substantial losses in the short run. But they dared not underbid the small operators on *every* route—that could lead to bankruptcy.

As a result of this dilemma, the small operators were able to pick off a number of choice routes. When private contractors once again began flying the nation's airmail on May 20, 1934, some of them had new, unfamiliar names like Braniff, Hanford Tri-State, Kohler, and Long & Harmon, Inc. At an absurdly low 19.75 cents per mile, Long & Harmon was the lowest bidder for the 1,125-mile route serving Brownsville and Amarillo at each terminus. American, which had to reserve its low bids for more crucial routes, was the high bidder at a realistic 39.5 cents per mile, while Braniff lost out with a bid of 20 cents per mile. Long & Harmon's winning bid came as a nasty surprise to the Braniff brothers, who regarded Texas as their private turf. A strong suspicion persists among old-timers that William F. "Bill" Long somehow got inside information on Braniff's bid, and then cagily slid under it with the idea of eventually selling out to either Braniff or American.

Long first had to prove to the Post Office that he could actually serve the route during a probationary period ending Aug. 31, 1934. He was in a good position to do it. Having learned to fly in World War I, Long had seen some combat and then come home to Dallas where he dabbled in the aviation business. His largest enterprise was a Dallas flying school that employed over 100 people, including 40 pilots. It was from his flying school that he intended to staff his "airline"—which at the time of his successful bid existed only on paper. He had already teamed up with C. E. Harmon, a restaurateur who had run a small airline in Nebraska.

Harmon would serve as general manager of the new airline, which would consist of three divisions: Amarillo-Dallas with stops at Wichita Falls and Fort Worth; Dallas-Brownsville via Fort Worth, Waco, Austin, San Antonio, and Corpus Christi; and Dallas Galveston via Fort Worth, Waco, and Houston. The Post Office agreed to pay Long & Harmon $443.88 per day for serving these routes, requiring a round trip on each division daily in one of Long & Harmon's five Stinson Reliants or in the six-passenger, single-engine Travel Air 6000 that the airline planned to hold in reserve. To fulfill their contract, Long & Harmon's planes had to fly 2,250 miles every day.

Experienced airline men shook their heads at Long & Harmon's folly. They knew that no one could make a profit flying so far for so little money without supplementing the airmail subsidy with passenger revenues. They also knew that successful passenger operations required modern, multi-engine equipment—of which Long & Harmon had none.

Within a month of beginning operations, Long & Harmon realized what they were up against. The story goes that one day Long started tallying up his receipts, which he carried around in his hip pocket, and determined he would soon go broke unless he got some kind of passenger service going in a hurry. Harmon disagreed and a violent argument ensued, which Long won with his fists. After Harmon agreed to the purchase of a used Ford Trimotor, the little airline began aggressively advertising its new passenger service in Texas newspapers.

For a brief period things improved. Long & Harmon lured 391 paying customers into the air in June and July and began to think they just might succeed in the airline business after all. Had it not been for Behncke and his feisty union, Long & Harmon might be as familiar a name today as Delta or TWA. But it was not to be, because when Long & Harmon got into multi-engine equipment they set in motion a series of events that finally brought them down.

The problem was that none of their pilots were Ford-qualified. Even though there was a major depression in the country, the pool of available trimotor-qualified pilots was fairly small. But Long & Harmon found three pilots—Maurice M. Kay, George L. Hays, and Lewis S. Turner—who were Ford-qualified. They were the crucial ingredient in the airline's successful passenger operation. The pilots took their jobs in good faith, assuming that Long and his chief pilot were honorable men—a handshake was contract enough for them in that simpler, more trusting day. At the end of June, when they received their first paychecks, they realized that the figures were far too low. Long & Harmon ignored their complaints, so the three pilots appealed to Behncke and ALPA in faraway Chicago.

Because of ALPA's steadfast support of FDR during the airmail crisis, the President subsequently showed his gratitude by insisting that the temporary mail contractors pay their pilots by the formula specified in Decision 83 of the National Labor Board (NLB). Decision 83 required airlines to compensate their pilots on the basis of both the mileage and the time they flew. This formula guaranteed pilots a share in the increased productivity of the equipment they flew. In short, a pilot flying Long & Harmon's Ford Trimotor might not work any more hours than one flying a Stinson Reliant, but the law required that he be paid more because the Ford flew faster.

Long & Harmon refused to comply. Admittedly, the verbal agreement under which the three pilots went to work was vague, but the law was the law, and they expected their employer to honor it. When Long heard that his three Ford pilots had asked ALPA for help, he exploded with anger, denouncing unions in general and government bureaucrats in particular. He also boasted that he could, as he put it, "move Washington by contacting the right man." Long informed Kay, who was acting as the pilots' spokesman, that he already had a "fix" worked out. ALPA couldn't help them, Long told his pilots, so they might as well forget about it.

Of the three Long & Harmon strikers, Maurice M. Kay is the only one left. Now 75 years old and living in Texas, he has been retired from American Airlines since 1966. He well remembers the troubles with Long & Harmon.

> I learned to fly at Major Long's flying school in the early 1920s and then bought an airplane and went barnstorming. After that I flew for the Major as a flight instructor in the Dallas school, and I also did cross-country flying, charter work, and so forth. I flew for him up until June 1930, when I resigned to go to work for Bowen Airlines in Fort Worth.
>
> Bowen was a feeder line and I flew from Dallas to Houston, San

Antonio, Oklahoma City, and Tulsa in the Ford Trimotor. That's where I got the qualifications at that time and that's why the Major needed me. There were five of us on the airline roster, including George Hays, Lew Turner, Burns Ramsey, and Dick Lowrey. There were several more on the flight instructor roster in the school. They opened up without a Ford, and later added one when they hired me. They were only operating the Ford between Dallas and San Antonio, and they just couldn't make it pay, but they reneged on the agreement with us, so we had this labor dispute.

Now, I liked the Major, he was a nice man. My personal impression was that he was influenced by Mr. Harmon, who was very tight with a dollar. He wanted you to do this and that. He might pay you for it or he might not, but it wasn't very much he wanted to pay you, let's put it that way.

Now, I wasn't a member of ALPA at the time, I didn't become a member until I went to work for American. But I said my part. We all three met together and decided—Turner, Hayes, and myself. Lowrey and Ramsey didn't want to get in bad, so they continued to work without saying anything about it.

Things were pretty tough, employment-wise in 1934, but we agreed that we would not work—gave our word. George Hays had been a copilot with American Airways before it became American Airlines, you know, and Turner had been with American too, the Southern Air Transport division, and they knew Behncke, and that's how he got involved.

If there was one thing Behncke seemed to love, it was a good fight. With Long & Harmon he was about to get a dandy, and for a change he held all the chips. The company, by its insistence on paying all pilots the same regardless of the equipment they flew, was clearly in violation of the law. The only problem was, how could ALPA get the government to enforce it? In a case like this, you could not simply go to the local sheriff.

NLB could only enforce its edicts through the courts—a lengthy, uncertain, and expensive process. The Post Office, on the other hand, had no way of enforcing the law other than outright cancellation of Long & Harmon's mail contract. This alternative was obviously unsatisfactory, because it would result in putting the pilots out of work. Then Long & Harmon solved Behncke's dilemma.

On the kind of August day when the sun will fry an egg on a Texas runway, Harmon summoned all his pilots to a meeting in a stuffy room in the airline's Dallas headquarters. He told them that, as of August 31, they were all fired, but he offered each reemployment if they would agree to work for a flat monthly rate. Of the pilots working for Long & Harmon at the time, only the Ford-qualified pilots were relatively secure; the single-engine pilots would be willing to scab. Antiunion sentiment was so strong in Dallas and organized labor so weak at that time that employers habitually flaunted their union-busting activities.

Despite everything, the Long & Harmon pilots decided to fight. The burning sense of righteous indignation over promises broken and a good job unappreciated made them ripe for ALPA.

Behncke had other problems. He was trying to run ALPA almost single-handedly. While spending time in Washington seeing to it that the pilot pay provisions of Decision 83 would be included in the new, permanent airmail legislation that Congress was then considering, Behncke was also trying to hold down a cockpit job with United, flying a regular route between Chicago and Omaha.

As a result, Behncke told Turner to begin negotiations himself, without waiting for help from headquarters. This came as a shock to the Long & Harmon pilots. They knew that if they became publicly identified as union troublemakers they would probably be fired; they could expect no sympathy or support in conservative Dallas. But still, right was right, and they decided they couldn't let Long & Harmon get away with it. Turner called a meeting of all the pilots, and after lengthy discussions, they all agreed that the least vulnerable pilots—the trimotor pilots—should be up front.

Although Kay sympathized with his fellow pilots, he disliked unions and steadfastly refused to join ALPA. If Kay acquiesced to Long & Harmon, the airline could continue to operate the Ford, since it required only a single qualified pilot. But if they all stood together, they could ground the airline and perhaps force Long & Harmon to obey the law. After many agonizing meetings, Kay finally agreed to go along and even to act as the spokesman, although he still refused to join the union. It was a courageous act, undertaken in the hope that Long & Harmon might at least listen to their only non-ALPA Ford pilot. They hoped in vain, however, because not only did Harmon refuse to meet with Kay, he also insisted that all the pilots sign their contracts _before_ reading them.

It is clear from subsequent investigations by federal agencies (most notably the Post Office) that Long & Harmon knew its course of action was illegal. Long's behavior has never been satisfactorily explained. He obviously needed to cut costs, but to do so by reducing pilot salaries, which was clearly illegal, seems inexplicable. In any case, Harmon began searching for another Ford pilot. When he found one, a man named George E. Halsey (whom ALPA subsequently designated a "professional strikebreaker" because he had previously scabbed for E. L. Cord's Century Airlines), Long & Harmon fired Kay, Hays, and Turner outright. The single-engine pilots then caved in and signed contracts.

At this point, Behncke had no choice but to drop everything else and devote his full attention to the Long & Harmon affair. Because he now had little interest in what happened to the scabs working for the airline, Behncke asked the Post Office to cancel its mail contract. At the same time,

Behncke brought the cases of Kay, Hays, and Turner before NLB. Shortly thereafter, both the Post Office and the Commerce Department announced formal investigations of Long & Harmon.

By early October, Long and Harmon were seriously worried, despite all their tough talk. ALPA's Washington representative, Edward G. Hamilton, had interested Sen. Hugo Black, who was responsible for the original cancellations, in the Long & Harmon case. Eddie Hamilton worked like a demon on this case because, as one of the former Century strikers who had not yet managed to get a flying job, he felt a keen sense of identification with the strikers. There was also a general fear that if Long & Harmon got away with defying Decision 83, other airlines would follow its example. Rumor had it that the Long & Harmon affair was a deliberate setup for just this purpose.

Thanks to Eddie Hamilton's activities in Washington, Long & Harmon did not get away with it. Hamilton managed to get Senator Black to personally take up the matter with Postmaster General Farley who, knowing the President's wishes that the wages of airline pilots be guaranteed, had no choice but to crack down. From then on, the blows against Long & Harmon fell heavy and fast. A regional labor board meeting in Fort Worth ordered reinstatement for Hays and Kay and three months' back pay to Turner, who by then had found another job. A lawyer representing Long & Harmon denied that the three pilots had been fired for union activity, citing a number of other reasons. But the NLB report declared: "We are not impressed by Long & Harmon's arguments. These men were able pilots. During his employment, Turner flew more hours than any other pilot. The record shows that Long & Harmon was hostile to these pilots because of their union affiliation."

Next, the Post Office opened formal hearings in Washington, during which Long & Harmon was asked to "show cause" why its airmail contract should not be canceled for violations of Section 13 of the Air Mail Act of 1934 (the provisions relating to pilot pay). ALPA sent its lawyer, Lionel G. Thorsness, to the November hearings, and in one of his first uses of a full-time staff member outside of Chicago, Behncke sent Jack Oates to Dallas, where he took depositions from all Long & Harmon pilots. Thorsness was able to make good use of those depositions, which clearly showed the airline's attempt to reduce pilot salaries.

Long & Harmon's lawyer argued that its reduction of pilot wages was undertaken "as a service to taxpayers," and threatened to challenge the constitutionality of the pilot-pay provisions in the courts. This threat to Decision 83 injected a new note of urgency. Following a day-long recess, ALPA's representative persuaded Rep. James M. Mead, chairman of the powerful House Post Office Committee, to testify. As chairman of the committee that approved the Post Office budget, he was somebody to whom postal officials would listen.

Mead explained to the postal investigators that the purpose of the pilot-pay provision, as embodied in Decision 83, was "to attract the highest type of citizen to this calling [of airline piloting]. By specifying pilot wages and hours, it was our intent that the operating companies would take this fixed cost into consideration.

"If this were not done, it is obvious that unfair operators like Long & Harmon would take advantage of their more conscientious competitors, resulting in the employment of cheap help, which would have ultimate evil effects, and which certainly was not desired by Congress."

Faced with this kind of overwhelming pressure, the Post Office investigators formally ordered Long & Harmon to comply by Jan. 15, 1935, or face cancellation of its contract. The final Post Office report, issued in December 1934, condemned the company for "willful disregard of the law." Furthermore, in answer to Long & Harmon's threat to appeal to the courts the constitutionality of Decision 83 on the grounds that it was an "unwarranted expense to the taxpayers," the Post Office declared: "It was never the intention of the President or the Congress to achieve such savings through contracts based upon bids having in contemplation profits to the bidders based on speculation with respect to the cost of labor." So it would appear that Behncke and ALPA had won a complete victory, as indeed they had in the long run. But for the Long & Harmon pilots it was cold comfort that the price they paid would eventually benefit other airline pilots whose employers realized that they could not get away with defying the government's wage edicts. Long ignored NLB, the Post Office, and the Commerce Department, and continued to operate while conducting feverish negotiations with Braniff and American to sell the route he would surely lose on January 15.

Long & Harmon was officially an outlaw airline, but that didn't help its courageous "three musketeers," as Behncke called Kay, Hays, and Turner. Lewis Turner seemed not to care particularly about returning to flying. At the age of 39, he was considered somewhat "over the hill" by the standards of that day. Flying was a young man's game, people believed, and the fact that Turner had received the highest civilian award for heroism, the Air Mail Pilot Medal of Honor, did not make him any more employable. He eventually went home to Louisiana, where he engaged in farming until his death in 1939.

For George L. Hays, the outcome was far more tragic. In the words of Maurice Kay:

> In the aftermath of that dispute, we used to wonder if we did the right thing, you know. ALPA did a good job for us, under the circumstances. We would either carpool or ride over to the hearing sessions in Fort Worth every day. I remember the hearings were held in the Post Office building, and the Labor Board officer there was a Mr. Elliott. We would have a meeting and they would go off

and study exhibits, and then Elliot would say they'd have to consult with somebody. We might have a couple of meetings a week, and then go a week before we would have another meeting. It dragged on for about three months. We didn't know where our next nickel was coming from, that was for sure. We did attend all of the meetings, because Carl Miller, the attorney ALPA hired for us, had an office over in Fort Worth, and he wanted us there.

It was a terrific blow to George Hays. He had been with American for two or three years, flying the Fokker F-10, and I don't know why he left for sure, but I don't think it was just the airmail cancellations. They let off a lot of pilots, and they only took back the ones with pull, you know, because there was no seniority or guarantee—like in Lew's case, and he had flown with them for a long time, about six years.

Now, I got on with American because I knew somebody who knew somebody, but neither Lew nor George could get back on, and it was a blow to them, particularly George, who was a quiet, introverted type.

You see, the problem was that we went through all this, and we won, and we didn't win. We stood up and fought for our principles, but it didn't get us our jobs back. We thought we were doing what was right. I never felt badly about it, and I'm glad we did it. But George, well, he was troubled.

George Hays was living with his parents in St. Louis. With a young wife to support, falling back on his parents must have been humiliating. Sure, everybody knew it was hard times, the depression, that a lot of people were out of work through no fault of their own. But still they felt guilty.

Probably other things were eating at George Hays too. He was having no luck finding a job, and despite the special fund Behncke set up to support the Long & Harmon strikers, he probably felt abandoned, felt that standing up for his rights had left him an outcast, perhaps forever blacklisted by the airlines as a troublemaker. Behncke's letters assuring Hays that ALPA was using its influence to find him a job were cold comfort in those troubled times.

So George Hays broke. He went out to his car, parked in the front yard of his parents' St. Louis home, sat down behind the steering wheel, put a pistol to his temple, and pulled the trigger.

And what of Long and Harmon? They succeeded in unloading their route to Braniff. As of Jan. 1, 1935, Braniff assumed all of Long & Harmon's obligations to the Post Office under the contract let in April 1934. Why would the Post Office permit these outlaws to escape? No satisfactory explanation has ever been advanced, and some old-timers were known to mutter that perhaps there had been something to Long's boast that he had the "fix" in with some high official in Washington.

Despite the paper gains ALPA achieved in the wake of the airmail crisis of

1934, most working pilots came to realize as a result of the Long & Harmon affair that a determined, unscrupulous employer could turn victory into ashes unless there was a more effective way to enforce compliance with the law.

The professional livelihood earned by today's airline pilot was paid for, in part, by sacrifices like those of pilots Kay, Hays, and Turner—ALPA's first martyrs. They had no intention of becoming heroes; they were ordinary men who just wanted to work. But they met the challenge and paid the price. They should not be forgotten. ✦

CHAPTER 9

The Rise and Fall
of the TWA Pilots Association

Harvey Bolton refused to join Jack Frye's company union. He was one of only 17 Transcontinental & Western Air (TWA) pilots who remained loyal to ALPA in 1933 when Waldon "Swede" Golien led out the rest. Of course Bolton kept quiet about it—on TWA, silence was the price you paid to keep your job if you were an ALPA member.

But we can't ask Harvey Bolton for his reminiscences during this year of ALPA's half-centennial. Bolton's been dead since May 6, 1935, when his DC-2 crashed near Kirksville, Mo.

As fatal accidents go, the crash that claimed Harvey Bolton and his co-pilot Ken Greeson wasn't too disastrous. Of 13 on board that night, only five died. Under ordinary circumstances the accident would have made only a headline or two and quickly faded.

It didn't fade, however. Owing to the identity of one of the deceased passengers, the crash that killed Bolton, Greeson, and three passengers was still in the news nearly three years later. Sen. Bronson Cutting of New Mexico had boarded the plane earlier that evening at Albuquerque and gone to sleep. Because Bolton missed his approach at Kansas City and subsequently failed to find his alternate at Kirksville, the senator never woke up.

Senator Cutting was the first prominent politician to die in an airline crash. His death triggered a full-scale congressional investigation into airline safety that would ultimately revolutionize the industry and indirectly bring about the passage of the Civil Aeronautics Act of 1938.

For ALPA, the "Cutting crash" would have two important side effects. As a consequence of a muddled investigation by five separate governmental bodies, the accident would provide Behncke with a perfect forum from which to argue for something he had long dreamed of—an independent Air Safety Board, which would investigate accidents in order to fix their probable cause. It also set in motion a chain of events that brought down the TWA Pilots Association, Jack Frye's company union.

The TWA Pilots Association was born in December 1933 at a time when Dave Behncke was threatening a national strike. Behncke's strike threat was a desperate last gamble to keep the operators from "reforming" the wage structure, and it almost certainly would not have succeeded. Even knowing they could not win, a surprising number of pilots would have walked out anyway largely because they felt the operators had left them no choice. At the last minute, Behncke's adroit manipulation of his political connections got the issue before the National Labor Board (NLB), thus averting the strike. But the pressure of the moment was too much for TWA's pilots, who were badly intimidated and all but leaderless owing to the death of Hal George. In a case that foreshadowed the actions of the American Airlines (AAL) master executive council (MEC) three decades later, TWA's MEC Chairman "Swede" Golien led the defection. The average TWA pilot went along with it because he was bewildered, fearful of losing his job, and prone to following his local leaders.

Swede Golien wasn't really a bad guy, and to this day ALPA loyalists refuse to speak ill of him. An affable, easy-going sort, Golien was well-liked by his fellow TWA pilots. The idea of directly confronting men like company chief Jack Frye and head of operations Paul Richter in a strike situation was abhorrent to him. Although Golien knew that Frye and Richter were his superiors, he thought of them as his colleagues. Behncke's maneuvering in Washington, coupled with his threat to call a nationwide strike, was too much for Golien and many pilots shared his views. As Howard Hall remembers:

> You see, most pilots then, and I suppose today for that matter, didn't really understand what was at stake during the time when ALPA was being formed. We had to do it, and people today better believe we had to do it. I didn't like belonging to a union, but on the other hand I could certainly see the handwriting on the wall, that if we didn't have a union the profession wasn't going to be worth a damn.
>
> I think Golien was a man who just couldn't see that. He sincerely believed that the company union was the best thing. Other men joined him, and naturally Jack Frye and the company helped them out.
>
> I went on a two-week vacation during the time when the company union was being formed. When I came back, I was taken to the office TWA had opened for them. On the door in gold leaf was "TWA Pilots Association." I was taken there and told that I would be furnished a secretary and everything necessary.
>
> Swede led the walkout, but he wouldn't be president of the new company union. The company wanted me to do it, because they knew I had been a good ALPA man. When I said no, I would have no part in it, the next word was from Mr. Frye. He said, "Hall, if you lead a strike against this company, you'll never work for another airline as long as you live."
>
> Now, Frye was an excellent pilot, and later I got to be good friends with him. I don't think that Jack Frye was doing anything that any executive would not have done. But if he'd succeeded with that company union, pilots as a _profession_ would have gone down

the drain. We would have been the same as taxicab drivers. That company union would have provided no protection whatsoever.

Because Howard Hall refused to have anything to do with the company union, Harlan Hull, a TWA executive pilot, became the titular president. The TWA Pilots Association was so obviously a creation of management that few pains were taken to conceal it.

Still, the TWA separatist movement was a serious threat to ALPA. In the absence of contractual guarantees, even committed and loyal ALPA members would have no choice but to join a company union should their employers follow the TWA example. In late 1933 ALPA was still far too weak in numbers to seek collective bargaining agreements, and in any case the machinery for selecting a bargaining agent through a representative election was not yet in place. That would come later, as the New Deal matured.

For the moment, Behncke knew that he must devote all his energies to stamping out the virus of company unionism that had broken out on TWA before it spread to other airlines. His chosen method, as we have seen, was to establish a political presence in Washington. If he could convince airline executives that ALPA could make trouble for their airmail appropriations by influencing key legislators, Behncke believed they would hesitate before undercutting ALPA with company unions.

But politics by itself would not be enough. Behncke knew that ALPA would have to survive on its own merits, that it would have to perform, produce salary increases, win grievances, help pilots in trouble with the government—the whole gamut of job-related assistance that modern pilots take for granted. And that's where the Long & Harmon affair proved helpful.

Behncke fought like a bulldog against Long & Harmon, the rogue airline where unreasonable working conditions for pilots posed a clear-cut threat to safety. His victory there, which actually led to shutting down the airline, impressed pilots everywhere.

The episode rippled through the industry and first manifested itself on Braniff and Delta, neither of which was complying with Decision 83 before the Long & Harmon crackdown. Both airlines began paying their pilots the prescribed scale shortly thereafter, and by threatening to bring another action through the Post Office, Behncke got Braniff to distribute $30,000 in back pay to its pilots.

Vernon I. "Whitey" Powers, one of the early Braniff pilots, who later served repeatedly as Braniff's local ALPA chairman in Kansas City and also became one of the first regional vice-presidents, is now 84 and living in retirement in Mississippi. Powers remembers Braniff's financial maneuvers in those early days all too well:

> Braniff never met its payrolls. When I first started to work it was called the Braniff *division* of Universal Airlines, but that ceased op-

erations in December 1929. I flew for Braniff *Airways* from March to May 1931, but the pay was so slow in coming I quit to go to work for Century Airlines in Chicago. That strike on Century, we called it that, but it was really a *lockout.* Cord locked us out. That's where I met Dave Behncke and became an ALPA member. Then I caught on with Braniff again in July 1932, and flew for them until I retired.

Until Behncke forced Braniff to start paying the labor board scale, we never saw any cash money, and they were always trying to get us to do something contrary to the labor board's decrees. They tried to get each of us to sign a contract whereby we *voluntarily* agreed not to get the labor board scale.

But Behncke kept Tom Braniff so busy in Washington he forgot all about us boys down here, and he had to get about the best law firm in Washington to save that airmail contract.

Behncke's case for ALPA was helped even further when a group of small operators created "The Independent Operators Association," an entity whose ostensible goal was to lobby the Post Office for increased airmail compensation and more favorable routes. By the fall of 1934, Behncke was regularly castigating this group, contending that its real purpose was to seek "ways and means of violating the new law [Decision 83]." Thanks to an anonymous airline executive who leaked memos to him, Behncke was able to document his claims.

ALPA's proven effectiveness as an agent for pilots was in direct contrast to the public record of the TWA Pilots Association. The differing testimonies of Behncke and Harlan Hull before the Howell commission bring those differences into clear focus.

The commission, chaired by Clark Howell, editor of the *Atlanta Constitution,* had as its primary purpose the study of airmail subsidies. In the aftermath of the airmail cancellations in February 1934, FDR had asked Congress for specific legislation authorizing him to appoint a study commission to update the work done by the Morrow board, a similar study commission appointed by President Coolidge in 1925 and named for its chairman, Dwight Morrow. Since Morrow was a powerhouse Wall Streeter, it was no surprise that his board's findings favored heavy investment in commercial aviation, with strong subsidy support from the government (via airmail contracts), guaranteeing private risk capital. The Morrow board's work laid the groundwork for the whole edifice of early commercial aviation, including de facto control by the Postmaster General—the system, in short, which FDR dismantled when he canceled the airmail contracts. The Howell commission's job was to erect another structure, one which eventually turned out to be the Civil Aeronautics Act of 1938, the cornerstone of the industry until the arrival of airline deregulation in 1978.

Although Charles Lindbergh refused to serve on the Howell commission, thus earning FDR's enmity, several other prestigious persons were associated with it, including Edward P. Warner, an M.I.T. professor and aviation expert with a worldwide reputation. The Howell commission began its work in July 1934 and submitted its report in January 1935.

In his testimony before the Howell commission in November 1934, Behncke was, in effect, addressing his fellow pilots on the dangers of company unionism:

> Among the so-called pilots who will testify before this commission, you will seldom find one who will raise his hand in protection of or in the interest of his brother pilot. They are practically all employed by the airline interest. Some of them are so-called famous pilots who seem to forget that they were ever pilots. The commission will find that these pilots who usually do the talking are not even licensed, and for that reason, due to the rapidly changing style of flying, are not qualified to render an opinion.
>
> Airline flying is no different than any other profession. In order to know about it you must do it actively, continuously. The least you can do is be actively flying the line.

Behncke was making this point by way of rebuttal to the testimony of celebrity aviators, like Amelia Earhart, who had unanimously opposed minimum wage and working conditions guarantees in testimony before the Howell commission. He succeeded well in linking this "managerial mentality" to the TWA Pilots Association. When Harlan Hull appeared before the Howell commission in his capacity as president of the TWA company union, his testimony was indistinguishable from any airline executive's. He opposed minimum guarantees of wages and working conditions and he also protested against a provision proposed by Behncke whereby a federal agency like NLB would be established to hear grievances in the case of a pilot being fired. Hull had, in short, totally discredited the TWA Pilots Association by his testimony, because if there was one thing every airline pilot wanted, it was some safeguard against capricious dismissal.

Behncke and Hull differed on one other issue as well. Behncke was foursquare in favor of an independent safety board to investigate accidents; Hull was lukewarm, leaning toward opposition. Another issue agreed upon by every pilot was that the existing system of accident investigation was much in need of reform. "Pilot error" appeared far too often as the probable cause of accidents, and early airline pilots wanted that stopped.

By early 1935, Behncke's files were beginning to bulge with letters from TWA pilots filled with a variety of grievances. The TWA Pilots Association had proved utterly worthless as a watchdog. Many of these writers rather shamefacedly admitted the error of having supported the company union.

"You were right," wrote one furloughed TWA pilot. "A lot of us out here have been wrong. We fell for it and resigned from ALPA feeling that the new organization would recognize seniority. Yesterday 20 of us were laid off, although at least seven copilots junior to us were retained."

TWA pilot Jimmy Roe, as perceptive in 1934 as he is today, never had any illusions about the company union:

> I would say that accident over at Kirksville was a definite turning point. In the aftermath of that crash, a circular went out from Richter and Frye ordering all TWA pilots and employees not to talk to the press.
>
> Of course, pilot error is one thing, and company error, like maintenance or lack of facilities or breaking some federal rules, is another. They could live with pilot error, because that didn't cost the airline companies money. From the start, ALPA was putting 50 percent of its dues money into safety. The TWA Pilots Association really didn't amount to much in the safety area. How could they? They were completely under the company's thumb.
>
> So we weren't supposed to talk to anybody, and I didn't, I followed orders. There was a big hullabaloo in the company over that one. They'd fire anybody, and the so-called officials of the company union went along. They were riding high up till that crash, so we stayed pretty much in the shadow.
>
> Now, as I told you, we never knew exactly who was a member of ALPA and who wasn't, and neither did the company. I never said I was and I never said I wasn't. But they thought I was, and Behncke was making big trouble for them over this crash.
>
> So Paul Richter, vice-president in charge of operations, called me up and gave me hell about ALPA. I just sat there and listened and never said a word, and when he got through he asked me if I had anything to say. I said no. I left that office and shortly afterward called a meeting of ALPA pilots. I knew a few who were members, word of mouth, friends like Dan Medler and Fred Richardson, but I didn't know all. And I told the guys who came to the meeting what had happened, that Richter had called me on the carpet and threatened to dismiss me. They said they were behind me. Several who had gone over to the company union more or less to save their jobs came over secretly. Right then we started getting ALPA active again on TWA. Just about all of them eventually came back and paid dues and fines, even "Swede" Golien.
>
> Anyway, after that crash that killed Senator Cutting, the company union started to fold. After 1936 you never heard any more about it, although they still had an office. No members, just an office.

What about "that crash that killed Senator Cutting"?

At first glance, Harvey Bolton would seem an unlikely pilot to have blundered into the fog-shrouded hills of northeast Missouri. He had accumulated over 2,000 hours of pilot time (a respectable total for that day), of which 714 were in the DC-2 that he was flying the night his career ended.

The company regarded Bolton as one of its best pilots. TWA prided itself on the IFR (instrument flight rules) competency of its pilots, and Bolton was a crackerjack. He had scored 100 percent on a series of written instrument tests in late 1934, and navigation instructor Pete Redpath had noted on his TWA "qualifications certificate": "His general navigation ability in the air was observed to be very thorough."

As a reward for his proficiency and skill, TWA had assigned Bolton to special charters, flying VIPs. The flight that claimed his life began as a charter on April 30, 1935, carrying a party of Hearst newspaper executives from New York to California, where they met with press lord William Randolph Hearst at his San Simeon estate. When the Hearst party canceled the return portion, Bolton was assigned to an extra section of the regular run from Los Angeles to Kansas City.

The passengers who boarded Bolton's aircraft at 4:00 p.m. on May 5, 1935, at the old Glendale Central Air Terminal were not what you'd call ordinary. Common folk took the train in that era. People who flew by commercial air were usually smart, worldly, and accustomed to the best that money could buy.

Two of the passengers were on TWA nonrevenue passes. June Mesker, the wife of TWA pilot "Doc" Mesker, was an experienced air traveler, as was Virginia Hillias, sister of TWA dispatcher Duke Hillias. They occupied seats 1 and 2, directly across the aisle from each other. June Mesker, who would survive another 32 years, owed her life to the fact that she was sleepy and that the forward two seats didn't fully recline because of a wall separating the passenger cabin from the DC-2's cockpit. After takeoff, Ken Greeson, the copilot, helped her move aft to Seat 10 on the right side. TWA didn't use cabin attendants, so passenger comfort was the copilot's responsibility. Virginia Hillias was wide awake, so she stayed put on the left side. It was a fatal choice.

The next two pairs of seats, numbers 3 through 6, were occupied by Paramount movie executives. The next two were occupied by Mr. and Mrs. William Kaplan of Los Angeles, enroute to New York on business. Midway through the flight they exchanged seats so that each could enjoy a different view. This casual exchange would prove fatal to Mrs. Kaplan, while enabling her husband to survive.

Seat 9, also on the ill-fated left side of the cabin, was reserved for Senator Cutting, who would board Flight 6 at Albuquerque. Seats 11 and 12 were empty. The last two seats, 14 and 15 (TWA never numbered any seat 13!) were occupied by Mrs. Dora Metzger and her 15-month-old daughter. During the first part of the flight the baby girl slept peacefully, while Mrs. Metzger enjoyed the panoramic view out the left window. When the baby became fretful, Mrs. Metzger moved to the right seat to hold the child in her arms. Had she stayed on the left side, they would both have died.

"It was perfect flying," June Mesker said later. "Very smooth, not a bump

85

over the mountains. The passengers, a congenial group, were apparently enjoying themselves. One man took pictures. Kenny Greeson served supper around 6 o'clock." Senator Cutting boarded the plane at Albuquerque just after 9:00 p.m. Some of the passengers went to sleep.

The flight from Albuquerque to Kansas City was routine. Bolton and Greeson were trailing a few minutes behind another TWA aircraft piloted by J. D. Graves. Graves could hear Bolton communicating with TWA's ground stations enroute, but neither flight contacted the other. The weather was clear until just after they passed Wichita. Then both planes entered instrument conditions.

From that point on, nothing is clear except that Bolton failed to get into Kansas City, diverted to Kirksville, and had trouble locating the low-power NDB (nondirectional radio beacon) there. (Its normal operating range was only 25 miles, and evidence developed during the Senate investigation indicates the possibility that its effective range was only two miles.) We can never know for sure the sequence of events that followed, but there is enough circumstantial evidence to reconstruct the final moments of Flight 6, at least partially.

Because the crash occurred within the normal range of the Kirksville NDB, it is possible that Bolton deduced that the beacon was malfunctioning once he reached his dead-reckoning estimated time of arrival. He might well have reversed course in an effort to descend to contact conditions. The last weather reports from Kirksville called for a ceiling of 1,200 feet and visibility of five miles, so it should have been at least a possible approach. Because the country was flat and docile, there was a satisfactory margin for error.

But something went wrong. At less than 200 feet AGL (above ground level) by the altimeter, TWA Flight 6 was still in and out, unable to establish firm contact flight, and in the few clear pockets there was no sign of the beacon.

Bolton and Greeson were probably straining every nerve, employing the lateral vision technique used by early pilots to locate a beacon's "mushover effect"—the faint aura that a rotating light spreads through fog. They were probably too far south of Kirksville to locate the beacon, but the Department of Commerce (DOC) had made their chances even slimmer through what an investigator subsequently called "a niggling economy." Director Vidal had earlier ordered airport keepers at secondary fields to reduce their beacon wattage. By so doing, DOC saved nearly $2,000 per year in electric bills. That bit of penny-wise and pound-foolishness may well have caused Flight 6 to lose its race with destiny.

"I had a bad feeling that we were losing altitude," June Mesker said later. Mr. Kaplan, the Los Angeles lawyer, agreed. So did Pat Drew, one of the Paramount movie executives. "We were looking out the window into the fog," Kaplan testified later. "Suddenly Pat said 'Say! Did you see that?' We had just passed over a very white house!" Alarmed, the two men woke up the rest of the passengers.

Finally, one of two things happened—no one will ever know precisely which. Either Bolton saw what he thought was a suitable precautionary landing field and tried to land before he ran his tanks completely dry, or he inadvertently flew the DC-2 into the ground. The evidence for the former is that Bolton turned on the "Fasten Seat Belts" light shortly before the impact. The evidence for the latter is that there was no noticeable power reduction. There was no cabin address system by which the pilots could communicate with the passengers; nor was there a cabin attendant who could pass the word.

Kaplan said he noticed some kind of aircraft light come on once, probably landing lights, but thought they were off just prior to the crash.

The DC-2 slammed to earth, flipped, and broke apart. The cockpit was smashed, but miraculously, Bolton survived the impact, although he was badly hurt.

"It was all over in an instant," said June Mesker, who found herself lying in mud, thrown clear of the aircraft. "I could hear people crying and moaning," she said.

"My God, these poor people," Bolton said over and over as he moved painfully among the injured. Bolton explained that he had "run out of gas." Technically this wasn't true. Later tests would show that he still had 30 gallons remaining. But Bolton was in pain, and apparently unwilling to be more specific about the nature of the landing.

The survivors focused their attention on trying to get help. It would be a while in coming, and for some, already too late. Kenny Greeson died instantly, his neck broken and one leg severed. Mrs. Kaplan's back was broken—she would die the next day following emergency surgery at Samaritan Hospital in nearby Macon, Mo. Virginia Hillias and Senator Cutting died of massive injuries where they sat. Everybody else had major injuries, except the fortunate June Mesker, who, having only slight fractures, could still walk.

Bolton, who refused medical attention until all the other injured were removed, died enroute to the hospital of massive internal injuries.

It is almost a certainty that Bolton was an ALPA member, because Behncke promptly included his name in the "In Memoriam" list of the deceased in the next issue of _The Air Line Pilot_. (Ordinarily, Behncke excluded non-ALPA members from the column, at least temporarily.) Furthermore, in the September 1934 issue, Bolton's name appeared in a routine social activities column. "TWA pilot Harvey Bolton had an opportunity to express his ideas when he paid a visit to the submarine S49 moored in the Chicago River."

There is no way to be absolutely sure because, as we have seen, even pilots like Jimmy Roe didn't know who all the ALPA men were. Behncke kept the list under tight security, and it has never come to light since. The truth is that Behncke would have made a huge fuss over the Cutting crash even if Harvey Bolton hadn't been one of ALPA's secret supporters on TWA, especially once the DOC findings of "pilot error" appeared three weeks after the crash.

For airline pilots of the 1930s, the frequency of "pilot error" findings was a source of constant irritation. They believed the investigatory process was rigged against them and in favor of the companies and the government. Early airline pilots wanted to subject the bureaucrats of DOC to the same rigorous investigation they had to undergo following an accident. At the time of the Cutting crash, DOC still investigated itself. Could the truth emerge from such an investigation? Many people, including Dave Behncke, wanted the answer to that question. It seemed unlikely. Out of a total of 101 fatal accidents between 1927 and 1935, DOC attributed the majority to "pilot error," with a few other causes making up the remainder. Not once did DOC attribute the "probable cause" of an accident to its own areas of responsibility.

Because Behncke suspected that Bolton had not been completely at fault in the accident—that a combination of poor weather forecasting and worse radio maintenance at Kirksville was responsible, he gambled that an early publicity campaign hinting at a cover-up would put DOC on the defensive. "A tired pilot is an unsafe pilot," Behncke informed the press in the first few hours after the accident. "The pilots believe that fatigue is an important factor in accidents."

Behncke went on to inform the press that Harvey Bolton had been flying more than eight hours and that there was a DOC regulation prohibiting this. "TWA regularly flies its pilots more than eight hours," Behncke said, "under a special waiver" granted to it by Director Eugene Vidal of DOC's Bureau of Air Commerce. "ALPA had made a detailed survey of waivers of flying hours following the recent crash on TWA," Behncke continued. "We believe the 8-hour maximum-flight rule out of any 24 should be hard and fast, with no waivers."

Behncke also flooded the newspapers of the country with letters attacking the investigatory process in general, DOC in particular, and especially Eugene Vidal, whom he regarded as being in cahoots with the operators. Behncke's incessant drum beating did not fall on deaf ears because the powerful Hearst newspapers soon took up the cry. "President Behncke of the ALPA makes it plain questions of serious moment are involved in crash which killed Senator Cutting," said a standard editorial which ran nationwide. "They must be searchingly investigated by competent and disinterested experts."

On May 28, 1935, faced with mounting criticism from congressmen who were unaware that he had the power to waive the eight-hour rule, Vidal canceled all such waivers. Round one to Behncke. The second round would be a fight over an "independent" investigation of the accident.

After initially dismissing Behncke's call for an independent investigation as "mere window dressing" and expressing "complete confidence" in DOC's accident investigation procedures, Frye and Richter began to have second thoughts. It dawned on them that the Cutting crash had heavy political overtones and that as a consequence the bureaucrats weren't to be trusted entirely. So the canny airline executives became quiet, while allowing the TWA Pilots Association to continue prattling in news releases about how wonderful the "system" was and occasionally taking a slap at Behncke. The TWA leaders suspected that the bureaucrats were unlikely to admit error themselves and might be searching for a candidate to throw to the wolves. With a pilot scapegoat ruled out (thanks to the fuss Behncke was making), that left very few candidates, and Frye and Richter had the uneasy feeling it was going to be them.

If Behncke and the Senate hadn't been breathing down DOC's neck, chances are that the old "gentleman's agreement" between management and DOC would have held, and the whole scandal would have been smothered. Bolton and Greeson would have been blamed and that would have been the end of it. TWA knew that Bolton had done nothing wrong, but it was for management to keep silent in cases like this. Frye and Richter couldn't be sure that this comfortable arrangement wouldn't hold once more, and so they had to play the string out.

As May blossomed into June of 1935, everybody waited for DOC's formal report. The accident board heard testimony from 35 witnesses in six days. Nobody had an inkling what its verdict would be. Then on June 15, 1935, it hit like a bombshell. DOC placed the entire blame on TWA *and* its pilots, citing a long string of "rules violations." Oddly enough, in announcing the verdict, Secretary of Commerce Daniel Roper, Vidal's boss, told reporters: "In my opinion the crash was due chiefly to bad weather." In the next breath, however, Roper levied several thousand dollars in fines against TWA. The airline would almost certainly be sued for negligence as well.

DOC's report focused on trivial infractions unrelated to the crash. For example, the principal cause cited by DOC was that TWA had cleared the flight from Albuquerque to Kansas City "with the radio transmitter not functioning on night frequency." TWA argued fruitlessly that the applicable rules simply required a functioning transmitter, and the DC-2's "day" frequency was working fine.

There was conflicting testimony as to whether anyone had actually talked to Bolton, and TWA officials began to suspect perjured testimony on the part of DOC underlings. DOC even disputed that Bolton had actually received radioed instructions to proceed to Kirksville.

DOC admitted that many of the infractions had nothing to do with the crash, but they were added to the report anyway, thus making the case against TWA look stronger. For example, Harvey Bolton had been a few days overdue on his quarterly physical. Also, the DOC waiver that permitted flights in excess of eight hours required the copilot to have a Scheduled Air Transport Rating (the equivalent, in 1935, of an ATP). Greeson didn't have one.

It was obvious to Frye and Richter that they were going to need the public investigation Behncke had been insisting upon. Luckily for them, the Senate had already authorized it. But before the Senate inquiry could get under way, something curious happened. Because a malfunctioning radio had allegedly caused the crash, an unimportant federal agency known as the Communications Commission on Radio Broadcasting (a predecessor of the Federal Communications Commission) issued a report. The agency, staffed largely by political hacks, accused TWA of another 45 "rules violations" and flatly declared that "the root cause of the crash was due to the company's radio system."

Not only was aviation outside this agency's area of responsibility, but it also appeared that the report was timed to appear just after DOC's and had been instigated by DOC. It certainly reinforced their report. Frye and Richter were furious over what they saw as a concerted bureaucratic effort to frame TWA.

Sen. Royal S. Copeland of New York headed the Senate's inquiry into the death of Bronson Cutting. At the first public session, Senator Copeland declared the purpose of the committee to be "a sweeping investigation of the present standards of safety in commercial aviation." To achieve that end, Copeland vowed to take testimony from "cabinet officers from all government departments, and experts in every field of aviation."

Copeland's handling of the probe won plaudits from the *New York Times*, which had been openly critical at first. After a week of public hearings, the newspaper complimented Senator Copeland for his "careful groundwork." For the next seven months, every witness who had something relevant to say about aviation safety or the Cutting crash got a respectful hearing from the Copeland committee.

The final report of the Copeland committee was an almost complete vindication of TWA and its pilots. The committee cited DOC inefficiency as the principal cause of the accident, and TWA's errors as merely "contributing." The report had nothing but praise for Harvey Bolton and Ken Greeson, however. "No one could possibly allege carelessness, lack of loyalty to duty, selfishness, or a character that would shirk," the report said of the two dead airmen. "They were 'let down', the victims of fallible ground aids to navigation in which they trusted implicitly."

Following the report of the Copeland committee, President Roosevelt ordered a shakeup in DOC. Vidal was the first to go, resigning in disgrace. This was not altogether to Behncke's liking because although he had differed with Vidal, the two men respected each other and Vidal had at least been willing to learn from his mistakes. Furthermore, Behncke began to suspect that the Copeland committee had fallen into the hands of FDR's enemies, and indeed the final report focused heavily on the administration's shortcomings. Ed Hamilton, ALPA's Washington representative, criticized the Copeland committee for "making personal attacks on individuals which may not have been warranted and did not reach the seat of the trouble. The fault lies more with the system than it does with individuals."

The Copeland committee generated a reform movement in Congress that eventually brought about the Civil Aeronautics Act of 1938. So in the final analysis, Senator Cutting's death served a purpose, for it indirectly brought about a new regulatory agency to control commercial aviation completely outside DOC.

It also brought about an indirect meeting of the minds between airline operators and their pilots. Following their harrowing encounter with professional bureaucrats out to save their own necks by blaming somebody else, TWA management dropped their opposition to Behncke's pet project, the Air Safety Board (ASB). It was clearly not in the industry's interest to have any regulatory agency investigating its own failures. ASB was thus an integral part of the Civil Aeronautics Act package, and with the appointment of ALPA First Vice-President Tom Hardin of American Airlines as one of its three members, Behncke had achieved a cherished goal. The ASB is a direct ancestor of today's National Transportation Safety Board.

The Cutting crash also spurred TWA to begin using cabin attendants once more. It had been the first airline (during its earlier incarnation as Transcontinental Air Transport [TAT]) to do so, but in keeping with the macho image of 1920s aviation, they had been men. They were also considered a "frill." Following TAT's near bankruptcy, such "frills" were dropped. United later began using young women as cabin attendants, but TWA resisted doing so, preferring instead to have copilots double as stewards.

During TWA's intensive internal investigation, their thinking about cabin attendants began to change. TWA's investigation reconstructed the flight in minute detail, and its technical analysis was far in advance of anything DOC's "official" investigation attempted. Consequently Frye and Richter knew much more about the crash than DOC. They were also airmen first, and businessmen second. Their handwritten notes on the flight, still available in TWA's archives, reveal an almost palpable anguish. They *knew* what Bolton and Greeson went through during the final moments, almost as if they had been with them, looking over their shoulders. Frye recognized that if a cabin attendant had been aboard, maybe he or she could have helped. Before the year was out, TWA had graduated its first class of "stews"—copying United this time, by using young women who also knew a good deal about airplanes.

Finally, one curious result of the Cutting crash deserves mention. In 1935 there was still very little difference on TWA between the men who managed an airline and those who did its day-to-day work in the cockpit.

Some airline bosses flew regularly, and they thought like pilots; many pilots exercised management functions and thought like managers. The welfare of the company was never far from the mind of a pioneer airline pilot. Circumstances were beginning to drive these two similar kinds of men apart. It came down to the ancient questions of autonomy and control. Managers wanted to control things; so did pilots. Differences were bound to emerge. This didn't mean that they weren't all still a "band of brothers," imbued with the mystique of what was one of the most romantic episodes in the history of American business.

The Cutting crash shocked Frye and Richter back to a stark realization of their almost total dependence on the men who actually made the machines go, who controlled the largest part of their corporate assets in the form of a fleet of very expensive aircraft. They needed to communicate with these men, freely and openly, without the hindrance of a "superior-inferior" relationship. In short, the Cutting crash helped TWA's higher management accept the necessity of a strong, independent pilot voice in the industry. They might not like that voice. It would sometimes cause frustration and delay. But it was a safeguard the industry needed, and captive outfits like the TWA Pilots Association simply could not provide it.

Perhaps as a consequence of this realization, TWA softened its attitude. A de facto truce with ALPA ensued, and the TWA Pilots Association faded away without a trace. Within a year, TWA's pilots were nearly 100 percent in the ALPA fold.

CHAPTER 10

Dave Behncke—An American Success Story

Who was Dave Behncke? To the public at large he was practically an unknown, bearing a name so peculiar that many people who saw it in the news thought is was a misprint.

Everybody in air transportation knew who Behncke was, though, and what he had done. They knew Behncke as the obscure United Airlines (UAL) pilot who came out of nowhere to forge a labor organization rivaling in power the industry's corporate giants.

But who was he? What were the wellsprings of his beliefs, the roots that made him such a striver?

Few people know the answers to these questions. Even his closest professional associates admit they hardly knew Behncke beyond the most superficial of levels. A few old-timers speculate that this may have been the result of Behncke's having lost so many close friends, men like H. A. "Collision" Collison of UAL, Hal George of Trans World Airways (TWA), or Clyde Holbrook of American Airlines (AAL), who were killed in crashes in the early 1930s. Behncke himself used to encourage people to believe that his early friendships with these men were so deep that they were past replacing.

Although there is probably an element of truth to this idea, it is also true that Behncke's friendships always tended to be more professional than personal. He was reserved and distant from beginning to end. Those who associated most closely with him in the formation of ALPA unanimously agree that they never really understood what made Dave Bchncke "tick," that he was driven by intense, compulsive forces that he himself understood only poorly. Many could predict Behncke's behavior, his probable reaction to an event, or his way of dealing with a crisis. But those who worked with him admit that they never knew the whys of this strange man—why he had risked his chosen career to embark upon the risky seas of labor organization, why he was at once the most generous of souls and the most vindictive, why his judgment could be so sure in some areas and so faulty in others, why he was a leader.

Behncke did leave some clues. To follow them we must return to 1938, Behncke's shining hour of triumph, the last full year of peace before Hitler's panzers shattered Poland and launched World War II.

By 1938 Behncke could look back with satisfaction on nearly a decade of achievement. The capstone of his success was the passage of the Civil Aeronautics Act of 1938, with its full federal guarantee of wages and working conditions for airline pilots. Starting in 1931, with nothing but a pilot's job on Boeing Air Transport and an idea, Behncke had wrought dramatic changes.

Despite opposition from the Air Transport Association (ATA hastily formed in 1935 to lobby Congress and oppose ALPA), Behncke won battle after battle in Washington. He secured passage of the "pilots' amendment" to the Railway Labor Act in 1936, thus removing the necessity for any more panicky strike confrontations. The inclusion of airline pilots under this law, with its machinery of conciliation and adjustment boards to hear grievances (originally written in 1926 to prevent strikes on the railroads), was probably Behncke's most longstanding achievement. Airline pilots today still benefit directly from the provisions of this act. Without Behncke's careful political legwork, it would never have come about.

Thanks to ALPA's activities, Congress had come to regard the professional airline pilot as the indispensable cog without which the system could not function. Behncke had succeeded in portraying the professional airline pilot as an individual whose personal welfare was in the nation's general interest.

As Rep. John Martin of Colorado said when Congress passed the pilot pay and working conditions section of the new law:

> In my opinion, the piloting of these great airplanes is the most responsible, the most skillful occupation mankind has ever engaged in. They are the picked men of the country. It is a profession to which many are called but few chosen. These men ought to be as free from worry about their economic condition or future as it is humanly or legislatively possible to accomplish. If there is anything we can put in the legislation that will keep worry from the airline pilots, it ought to be done.

Behncke was at the pinnacle of his success in late 1938, looking to a future of limitless possibilities. He had already begun the final countdown on collective bargaining agreements with each airline, and by now it was simply a matter of circumstance and timing as to which pilot group would be first to have a contract. The slow pace of contract negotiations bothered some ALPA members, but Behncke was in no hurry.

The 1936 ALPA convention had taken up the subject of collective bargaining in earnest, agreeing on a standard set of negotiating points, principal of which was, in Behncke's words, "a bulletproof seniority plan." That Behncke proceeded so slowly indicates his caution, especially since passage of the Railway Labor Act amendment made his bargaining base essentially secure. In May 1936 Behncke told the Central Executive Council that he feared Col. Edgar S. Gorell, head of ATA, had outsmarted him on the

Railway Labor Act. What if ALPA signed a contract and the operators followed the procedures specified in the Railway Labor Act for breaking a contract, and a court subsequently upheld it? Would a contract supersede the pilot protective provisions in the Airmail Acts of 1934 and 1935, he wondered? If so, would he not be jeopardizing those laws by negotiating a contract—any contract? It was farfetched, but this kind of thinking reveals Behncke's inveterate suspiciousness and caution. Behncke deliberately waited another three years before finally approving a collective bargaining agreement—well after passage of the 1938 legislation was complete and legal counsel had advised him that his fears of an end-run by the operators to kill Decision 83 were groundless.

By March 1939, a close race had developed between Panagra, Braniff, and American for the honor of signing the first contract, with TWA also in the running. In May 1939, American won the race. C. R. Smith signed for the company, while Behncke, W. P. McFail, Walter Hughen, and copilot representative Harry L. Clark signed for the pilots. This first working agreement between American and its 279 pilots covered not only pay, but also expenses, hours on duty, seniority rights on "bulletined runs" (a primitive "bid" system for preferred routes), leaves of absence, promotions, and provisions for investigations and grievance settling.

A milestone had been reached. Behncke, a farmboy from Wisconsin with a grade school education, now headed a union representing the majority of the nation's airline pilots. He had been in the Oval Office of the President of the United States for the ceremonial signings of important pieces of legislation on several occasions. His testimony was usually the high point of the dozens of congressional hearings he attended. Newspapers sought him out for comment, prestigious groups such as the Aeromedical Association invited him to speak at their annual conventions, and learned publications, such as the _Journal of Air Law and Commerce,_ named him to their boards of editorial advisers. Behncke was a success in the classic American way—by his own hands. His standing was so high that the 1938 ALPA convention reelected him without a single dissenting vote.

Born on May 1, 1897, in a farmhouse near Cambria, Wis., David Lewis Behncke's early years were similar to those of any son of a hardscrabble farmer of German immigrant ancestry. Money was tight, the family atmosphere was austere, and education was a rare privilege, clearly secondary to long hours of farm drudgery. Recreation consisted of weekly attendance at church services.

Sometime in his early adolescence Behncke attended a county fair that featured one of the era's typical commercial exhibitions of flying. Behncke was thrilled by what he saw. It was a common dream among rural youth of that era to go flying, to soar across mountains and rivers, to be free. No more tedious farm chores, no more rules laid down by strict parents, no more ordinary worries, only those that really mattered—like life and death. Not one youngster in a thousand who entertained these fantasies ever acted upon them, but Behncke would. Already, he was breaking out of the pack.

Young men yearning to fly but lacking the financial resources had only one path open to them—the U.S. Army. Because he needed help on the farm, young Behncke's father angrily denied him permission to enlist in the Army. Although he was just 16 years old and had only a smattering of formal education, Behncke ran away from home, displaying early the steely will that was to characterize him in adulthood.

He headed for Milwaukee to enlist, but his undocumented claim to 18 years didn't jibe with his juvenile face, so the Army turned him down. Having nowhere to go and fearful of facing his father's wrath, Behncke turned to the only thing he knew—dairying. He got a low-paying job doing the most menial work in a big dairy on the outskirts of town, toiled unremittingly for six months, contracted tuberculosis, and was sent home to die. The atmosphere was strained at first, but Behncke and his father made their peace.

In 1914, Behncke's father began reaping the benefits of the economic bonanza that to this day marks "parity" for American agriculture. The outbreak of war in Europe spurred demands for American products of all kinds, and farmers got more than their share. The Behncke family rapidly advanced from near poverty into the comfortable middle class. Simultaneously, young Dave Behncke surprised his doctors by making a dramatic recovery from TB.

By 1915, Behncke was on good enough terms with his now-prosperous father to secure his blessings for an Army enlistment. His goal was to become an enlisted pilot in the Signal Corps, but the closest Behncke got to an airplane was peeling potatoes in an aviation unit, and the most thrilling thing that happened to him was rear-area-support duty during General Pershing's pursuit of Pancho Villa into Mexico in 1916. But because he had established a good reputation as a buck private, Behncke was sent to San Diego for flight instruction after the Pershing expedition came to an end. While there, he became a corporal and a designated pilot.

Thanks to World War I, the gates of aviation opportunity swung wider for young Behncke. He was able to parlay his new piloting skill and native ability into a commission and an instructor's billet.

Had Behncke had his wishes, he would have stayed in the Army. But his lack of formal education made him a poor choice to the selection boards that determined such things. In 1919, the Army released Behncke to make his way in the world of civilian aviation. There can be no doubt that Behncke was disappointed. Over the next few years he would request active duty several times.

After the armistice, Behncke, like thousands of other young men, began the familiar pattern of barnstorming and gypsy aviating. He bought a surplus Jenny and did the country fair circuit for a while, joining temporarily with a company of daredevils in a "flying circus" that wowed the locals with wing-walking, parachute jumping, and other aeronautical exotica. His goal was to earn a decent living while at the same time continuing in aviation. No mean feat that, for the woods were full of young men with similar ideas. After the number of people willing to pay five dollars for a ride dwindled, he tried to make it as a freight operator. That didn't work, so he tried teaching, aerial mapping, and aerial advertising, painting the sides of his aircraft with the names of various Chicago businesses. The only kind of aviation activity he avoided was the one that paid best—rum running. Not that he wouldn't occasionally haul a few gallons over to Rockford when he was really hard up, but Behncke wanted nothing to do with bootlegging on a regular basis. In the unanimous opinion of the surviving old-timers who knew him, Behncke was a moral man, particularly when it came to booze and women.

By 1921, Behncke had fared better than most. He owned a couple of nickel-plate Jennies and had a reputation as one of Chicago's best airmen. In September 1921, he won the Chicago Air Derby, covering a 55-mile course in just 49 minutes. That gave him name recognition, so through the next four years, until 1925, he was able to make ends meet running Checkerboard Field. By this time, Behncke's parents had joined him in Chicago and were operating a boarding house in which Behncke also lived.

For Dave Behncke, being an independent businessman wasn't all it was cracked up to be. He longed to return to the military, to participate in the great things Billy Mitchell had begun. In any case, the Cook County Forest Preservation Society, which owned the land Checkerboard Field was on, was threatening to cancel his lease. So Behncke was eager to bail out when Tony Yackey made him an offer.

Something else was on Behncke's mind by 1925. Her name was Gladys Mae Hensen and she became his wife early that year. Soon after the Army accepted Behncke's application to return to active duty. Behncke set off for Langley Field in Virginia with his new bride for what he hoped would be a lifetime career in uniform. After six months, however, Behncke found himself back in civvies looking for any job that would support him and his young wife, provided it was in flying. Behncke wanted desperately to stay in the flying game, primarily because it would enhance his chances of returning to military duty. Upon his release from active duty in early 1926, Behncke got a job with Charles Dickenson, a Minneapolis-based entrepreneur who held the first private contract for airmail service to Chicago. Behncke was first on the pilot list of what would eventually become Northwest Airlines (NWA). Throughout the remainder of 1926, Dave Behncke flew a single-engine Stinson "Detroiter," an enclosed-cabin monoplane, back and forth between Chicago and the Twin Cities. He was one of three pilots working for Dickenson who picked up three spanking new Detroiters in the city for which they were named. Behncke then led a formation flight to Chicago, where they picked up a full load (12 passengers on three airplanes), and proceeded on to St. Paul. The other pilots were Eddie Stinson himself and Raymond B. Collins, an executive who specialized in aviation finances. Among the passengers was Charles R. "Speed" Holman, a newly hired pilot. Behncke's path would cross Holman's again, with unfortunate results.

"The Northwest Airways," as it was called in late 1926 after a name change from "Dickenson Air Lines," made stops at La Crosse and Milwaukee, Wis., in each direction. In the beginning, it was strictly a mail service, but on Feb. 1, 1927, it carried its first paying passengers. The pilot was Dave Behncke.

Behncke might have ended his career as an NWA pilot, might well have been an executive of the airline. He got along exceedingly well with Col. L. H. Brittin, the developer of the St. Paul airport who subsequently became NWA's operations manager. It was a tough life, one which required pilots to fly two days out of three, but Behncke loved flying and also the technical aspects of the airline's operations. In May 1927 he wrote an article that was published in *Aviation* magazine (predecessor of today's *Aviation Week*), titled "The Cabin Monoplane." The gist of this piece was that pilots need not fear flying "out of the slipstream." Many early pilots insisted that a pilot must always be in an open cockpit, even if the passengers had to be out of the weather. There was no other way to get the "feel" of an airplane, they contended. Behncke dismissed this kind of thinking, pointing out that the comfort and convenience to the pilot was a safety factor.

In stressing safety, Behncke was ahead of his time, and in direct conflict with pilots like Speed Holman, a daredevil who insisted that the natural employment for an aircraft was aerobatics, that all pilots should prefer to fly inverted, and that every plane should be periodically tested out with a few loops—just to warm it up for a passenger flight later in the day.

Holman on one occasion took a Stinson Detroiter up for such a flight just before Behncke was scheduled to take it out on a regular run. A confrontation followed, with Behncke getting the worst of it—Holman got Behncke fired. It was a shattering blow to Behncke, who expected Operations Manager Brittin to back him up on what was obviously a safety violation. Holman might well have overstressed the airplane by flying maneuvers for which it was not designed, Behncke argued, but to no avail.

Consequently, in early 1927 Behncke was once more unemployed. Holman would shortly kill himself doing acrobatic maneuvers in Omaha, while Behncke would get one more crack at a military career. The Army accepted him for a full year of active duty. Once again he was off to Langley Field, this time posted as executive officer of the newly formed Second Bombardment Group. Gladys was pregnant with their first child, and Dave

Behncke was determined to succeed this time, his third chance, in the Army.

"Me and Dave Behncke was happy fellows," remembers Werner O. Bunge of his days with Behncke at Langley Field in 1927. Bunge, who flew as a commercial pilot for United and later KLM, died in 1981 at the age of 82. "Our wives both had babies in the post hospital at the same time and we lived in the same house. I was a second lieutenant and so was he, and we had a pretty close association. We both learned to fly Martin bombers. But then the money ran out, the Army had no more money for active duty, so he had to go back to Chicago and I went into the regular Army as a staff sergeant, enlisted flight instructor."

That, in a nutshell, sums up Behncke's last chance at a regular commission and the military career he coveted. Not that he hadn't done well. He had won a promotion to first lieutenant, functioned exceptionally well as an administrator of the group's affairs, and was officially credited with taking out the Pee Dee River concrete bridge after MacArthur's artillery failed to do it during war games in late 1927.

The problem for aspiring career officers like Behncke and Bunge (both of whom were from Wisconsin and of German heritage) was twofold: first, the military was short of money; second, neither had the requisite educational background for a regular commission. It was common knowledge that moss-backed antiaviation careerists were trying to keep the Army's aviation branch small, and they frowned on commissioning mere pilots in the first place.

One key to understanding Dave Behncke is his Army experience. He had worked hard, had overcome severe educational handicaps, had painfully clawed his way up from being a nobody to rather substantial achievements, both in civil and military aviation. Yet he was getting nowhere. On Northwest Airlines he had been fired unjustly, and the Army, despite his best efforts and excellent performance, had once more rebuffed him. That Behncke was disillusioned there can be no doubt. That these painful experiences caused him to reject the stereotypical notion that success comes in due course if you work hard enough, there can also be no doubt. Behncke had had enough of the Horatio Alger success myth, the idea that any young man can go from rags to riches, from a log cabin to the White House. The decks were stacked against him, it seemed, with educated, patrician elitists getting all the plums in life, regardless of how they actually performed.

When you add this set of experiences to Behncke's natural doggedness and determination, you get a man who was willing to found a labor union. When the Army released him from active duty in late 1928, he got a job flying for Boeing Air Transport on the Chicago-Omaha run. This subsidiary of United Aircraft had no way of knowing it was hiring a man who had all the prerequisites for a successful labor leader—suspiciousness, lack of sentimentality, and a good deal of personal drive.

This still leaves unresolved the question why Dave Behncke would expose himself to yet another firing by leading the drive to unionization. Perhaps it was precisely because he had been fired before, and had survived, that he was willing to risk being fired again. Like many airmen, Behncke believed the propaganda of that time, which depicted pilots as extraordinary individuals. He also understood that his fellow pilots were, at that particular moment in history, ripe for the undertaking he had in mind. They seemed to understand that the privileged few, the ones from good homes with good educations who got the regular commissions and the executive jobs with airlines, were going to milk this commercial aviation bonanza for all it was worth, and ordinary pilots were not included in their plans.

Perhaps George Douglass, the Mr. "V" of the organizational period, sums it up best:

> I don't really know why Behncke was the leader, and I don't know why he picked me out as the Key Man on Varney. He must have had a crystal ball. I had met him just once or twice, but he was sharp enough to size me up as a working stiff who understood we needed a union. He didn't have to explain it to me. When he asked, I said, 'Fine and dandy, I believe in it.'
>
> As to why Behncke was successful, boy, that's a tough one. He was able to see that there's something in human nature that wants to join something, to be _associated_. It's the same old story, in unity there is strength. I sure as hell believe that.
>
> I hate to think where we'd be if Dave Behncke hadn't been there to put it all together. ✦

CHAPTER 11

Wartime

The key to understanding what happened to the airline piloting profession during World War II lies in recognizing the amount and rapidity of aviation's wartime growth. From a time when a pilot could expect to know every pilot working for his own airline and a great many working for others as well, aviation became, almost overnight, a globe-girdling business with an expansion in personnel to match. Pilots could no longer expect to know their contemporaries, even at the same domicile, unless they happened to attend school together. The number of pilots working for the airline-military contract operation doubled and quadrupled. The far-flung overwater operations of airline pilots who had never before been out of sight of land was a harbinger of things to come in the postwar world.

War and technological development have always had a curious relationship, almost as if humans' destructive urges somehow feed their creative ones. World War I spurred aviation's development, but World War II skyrocketed it. Fueled by unlimited government spending, aircraft designers and manufacturers burst brilliantly into the struggle against Hitler and Tojo. The advances in aircraft, engines, electronic communication, and weather forecasting were phenomenal. Even turbine-powered aircraft, considered a technical stunt with only remote possibilities in the 1930s, had by the end of the war become an operational fact of life.

For ALPA, the biggest problem posed by wartime was one of adapting. As part of the labor movement, ALPA was in an awkward position. Labor, although a crucial commodity, clearly took a backseat to the managerial and industrial skills necessary for America's becoming, in the words of FDR, the "arsenal of democracy." The titans of industry and commerce, who had been pretty much out of power during the early New Deal years, returned triumphantly to Washington after war clouds began forming on the Asian and European horizons, and the New Deal made its peace with them. For the labor movement as a whole, the question was one of maintaining its position, rather than of making new gains. The union leader who ordered his workers to strike for a pay raise at a time when young men were dying in foxholes and on a hundred battlefields around the world risked not only a crackdown by the combined power of government and industry, but repudiation by the public and his rank and file as well.

ALPA entered the post-1938 period in excellent shape. As the possibility of war increased, the military services began denying pilot requests for release from active duty, thus cutting off the supply of labor on which the airlines had always depended. This worked to ALPA's advantage as the contract process went forward.

The military further tightened the supply of pilots by allowing junior airline pilots with a hankering for a military career to return to active duty. *The Air Line Pilot* began carrying an ever-lengthening list of active airline pilots killed in crashes while serving with the reserves. The shortage of pilots was becoming so acute by late 1938 that FDR created the Civilian Pilot Training Program (CPT) to train 20,000 pilots. ALPA worried about this kind of competition. "Who is going to provide jobs, retirement, and benefits for these pilots?" the lead article in the December 1938 issue of *The Air Line Pilot* asked. Behncke couldn't really try to stop CPT, for it was clearly in the national interest, should war come, to have adequate manpower in the nation's cockpits.

In terms of membership, ALPA was growing all the time. An overwhelming majority of working airline pilots paid dues, with the percentage of nonmembers dropping every year. Back in 1932, the 19 delegates who assembled at Chicago for the convention represented just 344 dues-paying members. By 1940, 70 delegates represented 1,400 airline pilots, roughly 90 percent of the total then working. At the end of World War II, ALPA's dues-paying membership had increased to 5,730, or over 90 percent of all airline pilots.

As early as 1939, the few pilots who were not ALPA members were primarily either junior copilots, not yet eligible, or a handful of senior holdouts, many of whom were also ineligible for membership because they had fought some ALPA policy over the years, or more commonly, because they had gotten badly in arrears on dues.

For most new hires, it was considered a sign of acceptance when the veterans asked them to fill out an ALPA application form. Junior pilots who refused to join were rare. "If a fellow is not going to join," one delegate to the 1936 convention said, "he is not going to get a lot of instruction from the first pilots. If he joins, we will help him along and do everything we can for him." The old-timers who had put their necks on the line for ALPA weren't about to let fuzz-cheeked newcomers have a free ride.

Most junior pilots understood this and could see other advantages to belonging to ALPA as well. W. T. "Slim" Babbitt of Eastern Air Lines (EAL) remembers his decision to join:

> I went to work for Eastern in 1935, and I learned about ALPA from the senior people. But by no means were all of them in ALPA; none of the supervisors was. Of course, I was very interested in how you got to be a captain. Every now and then I'd see a copilot disappear. I'd say, "What happened to him?" Somebody'd say, "Well, he's not

here anymore. A couple of supervisors said he couldn't do it." And I figured, hell, this is on a personality basis. That's what got me interested in ALPA. I mean the union was what gave us an orderly procedure for checking out as a captain based solely on your ability as a pilot. It was very evident to me that if I was going to take this as my profession, I'd better stay close to ALPA.

The senior holdouts were a tiny minority, and Behncke didn't worry about them. Of course, if they got in trouble he wouldn't do anything for them either. By 1938, when ALPA first began appearing on behalf of pilots with grievances, that counted for a lot, as a group of senior holdouts on United Airlines (UAL) was about to discover. The affair was known as "The Purge of '39." After it was over, most pilots knew that ALPA was worth the dues—even back dues, if it came to that.

The genesis of the purge on United was an accident at Point Reyes, Calif., in February of that year. The pilot in command of a flight from Medford, Ore., to Oakland misinterpreted signals from the Point Reyes low-frequency range, went in the wrong direction, ran out of gas over the ocean, and crashed at sea. Everyone aboard died except for a passenger and the captain, Charles B. Stead, a veteran who had been with UAL.

Stead was not much of an instrument pilot. He had a lot of company in this respect, particularly among veterans. Unlike so many others, Stead had the questionable good fortune of surviving his error. He had no alternative but to face a federal investigation, which, partly owing to the new pressure generated by the Air Safety Board (ASB), found that he was incompetent and had used "bad judgment."

For UAL's higher brass, the Point Reyes crash was the last straw. W. A. "Pat" Patterson had always treated his pilots rather gingerly, whether they were ALPA or non-ALPA. As the new-fangled instrument flying developed in the 1930s, many old-timers either chose to ignore it, or did the bare minimum to comply with the new rules without getting fired. On UAL, there were about a dozen such pilots who were targeted for dismissal in the wake of the Point Reyes crash as an object lesson to other reluctant instrument fliers. Many old-timers suspected that UAL wanted to get rid of them because of their high salaries rather than because of their alleged inability to fly instruments. The company had already proved that it was no respecter of legendary names when Jack Knight, the hero of the first transcontinental night airmail flight in 1921, got kicked upstairs to a meaningless (and temporary) executive position in 1937. That was a clear indication to older line pilots that they had better stay close to ALPA for self-preservation. Still there were a few who perversely refused to join. They were about to learn the full measure of their antiunion folly, for the only qualification an older pilot needed for inclusion on the purge list was that he *not* be an ALPA member.

The company appointed Ragnar T. Freng to head the purge. Among its victims were some exceptional pilots, such as the legendary Al De Garmo, whose skill at contact flying dated back to the days of open cockpits. Behncke's buddy from Langley Field, Werner O. Bunge, got caught in the purge and hauled before what he called a "monkey trial," or pilot disposition board. Bunge's case is unusual, for he was a charter member of ALPA who had resigned after things settled down.

Werner Bunge told his story of the purge:

> Freng had been ordered by Mr. Patterson to get rid of us old guys who didn't care to learn instrument flying. A lot of them said, "If I can't see where I'm going, I don't fly." I wasn't like them, I'd fly instruments.
>
> I had learned instrument flying while we were at Langley Field on active duty. I did, and so did Behncke. While I was based at Cheyenne in the early days, I had a conversation with Pat Patterson. He asked me, "You're a leader, aren't you?" So I guess people there had told him that I was a president of the ALPA local council. It was very touchy. This was in 1933, and we were pretty much on the spot, because they called us in one by one and said, "We understand you are liable to strike. If a strike is called, will you fly?"
>
> Well, all I could say was that I'd strike. We beat them on that, and Mr. Patterson humbly recognized ALPA. After that, I said "Well, I am not going to fight anymore, I'm going to stay out of this in the future." The fight was over, see, and I have a document signed by Ralph Johnson, George Douglass, and Rube Wagner saying they appreciated the fact that I stood up when so few would. Then I resigned because I didn't really believe in unions.
>
> Then when Stead crashed, the company said, "These old fellows don't know how to fly instruments." They called seven of us to the Oakland base and asked us to resign, said if we would we'd get six months' base pay— that was $250 a month. Now if I had been in ALPA, they wouldn't have bothered me, because they never called George Douglas or Rube Wagner or any of the older guys who were in ALPA. They were let alone. Along about 1937 I began to think I'd like to get back in ALPA, but with the back dues I had to pay since I got out in 1934, well, I guess I should have.
>
> Harry Huking was my superior and since I wouldn't resign like they asked, he gave me a flight check. He admitted that I had been singled out because I was an old-timer and not in ALPA. So I knew at that point it didn't matter what I did, but I went up in a 247 and we did all these fancy maneuvers while Harry kept writing down these things in his little book. So I was fired like that.

Although ALPA was quiet during World War II, it was not altogether inactive. Dave Behncke had reached an achievement plateau in 1938, and in the months of peace remaining he devoted himself to completing employment agreements, one by one, with each airline. Almost simultaneously with the completion of the last contract, the Japanese bombed Pearl Harbor, and Dave Behncke faced pressure to relax standards for pilot working conditions because of the wartime emergency. The airlines were going to war, and they expected the nation's airline pilots to salute smartly and toe the mark.

In the beginning, this was not an altogether unsatisfactory idea to Behncke. As we have seen, he had a lifelong love affair with the military that left him predisposed toward some kind of militarization of airline pilots in time of war. As far back as 1932, Behncke had persuaded his fellow ALPA members to support something he called "The Legion of the Air," designed primarily to give airline pilots a quasi-military status. The "Executive Board" (a group of Chicago-area pilots he assembled, temporarily, for advice) formally petitioned the Democratic party's national convention in 1932 to adopt a platform plank that would give *all* active airline pilots reserve commissions or, failing that, to support a new organization of airline pilots that would be available for call-up in time of national emergency. In 1934 the second ALPA convention voted unanimously that "recognition be given to ALPA by the government as a reserve air unit, due to the fact that our members are in continuous training in the most advanced phases of flying, especially night and instrument and bad weather flying."

Over the years, a number of bills were introduced in Congress to give airline pilots reserve military status, but without exception they failed to pass. As late as June 1939, Behncke was still pushing this idea, calling airline pilots "the minutemen of air defense."

There is no doubt, however, that a great many airline pilots were leery of the military. Most of them had been soldiers at one time or another and, like most veterans, much preferred civilian life. Behncke was clearly more gung-ho than the average airline pilot, but he persuaded them to back his military idea as politically expedient. In that highly patriotic era it was crucial for ALPA to present a public service image.

In any case, Behncke had more pressing problems to contend with than the rather improbable one that masses of airline pilots would be drafted as buck privates, handed rifles, and sent off to the trenches. Even with World War II looming, Behncke's strongest efforts weren't in military preparedness, but in contract negotiations. ALPA had its own business to attend to in Kansas City, Dallas, and New York. TWA signed ALPA's second contract on July 18, 1939, having been narrowly nosed out for first by American.

While British and French armies crumbled on the continent of Europe, Dave Behncke continued knocking down contracts. Penn Central Airlines (later merged with UAL in 1961) became the fourth company to sign an ALPA contract.

In the midst of the contract successes, a purely political battle erupted in Washington—one that ALPA would eventually lose. A prelude to Behncke's decline, it heralded the erosion of his political base in Washington. It began in a curious way, with the failure of what had been, in its time, one of ALPA's greatest successes—ASB.

The creation of the independent ASB was the political high-water mark for ALPA in the Behncke era. He had beaten the Air Transport Association (ATA) solidly on this one; they fought against ASB all the way. But, despite the initial enthusiasm for it and the fact that Behncke's idea of an independent safety board to investigate accidents was so obviously in the public interest, ASB fell victim to the war years and was not revived until 1966 with the creation of the National Transportation Safety Board (NTSB).

The two factors primarily responsible for ASB's demise were the new whip hand held by the operators over the Roosevelt administration because of the wartime buildup and the personality of Thomas O. Hardin, former ALPA first vice-president and the dominant member of ASB.

Jimmy Roe, who was on both the first and second "Lobby to Save Lives," striving first to secure passage of ASB in 1938 and second to prevent its being abolished in 1940, remembers:

> The first thing you have to understand is that real safety costs money, and that's why they were out to get ASB in 1940. In the old days, before that crash that killed Senator Cutting, the first thing the government would come up with was pilot error, it was just about automatic. Of course pilot error does happen, but what if it was _company_ error, or more likely an error in the government-run facilities? Did they ever come up with _government error?_
>
> When we got the independent safety board in 1938, we thought our troubles were over because we had one of our own men in there, Tom Hardin. Now, Tom Hardin didn't make too many friends in Washington, and maybe if we'd had somebody else it would have been different, but that's just my opinion in hindsight. I thought Tom would be all right, and I thought at the time he was doing OK. I knew him particularly well. We'd been in the Air Corps together at Kelly Field, and after he went with American Airlines I worked with him a lot. In fact, we roomed together for weeks in Washington during hearings and meetings. Maybe we lost the independent safety board because of his personality or because of the way he was carrying out his duties as chairman.
>
> I do know that Hardin cost the airline companies some money, and he certainly wasn't popular with them because of that. Roosevelt had the power to abolish the safety board. Congress could stop it, but it did not do so. So after two years of the independent safety board, from 1938 to 1940, it was abolished by presidential order.

Behncke couldn't believe that FDR, the man who had so often supported policies favorable to ALPA in the past, would let its cherished ASB slip away. Behncke had made safety the cornerstone of ALPA's public relations policy, emblazoning the motto "Schedule with Safety" on ALPA's letterhead. He had manipulated the ASB law so that one of its three members would have to be an active airline pilot, and had personally selected Tom Hardin to be the airline pilot member. He probably made a mistake for, as Jimmy Roe noted, Hardin had more than a few rough edges.

Hardin was a Texan who had been, variously, a soldier, a barnstormer, a local aviation entrepreneur, and a 10,000-hour American Airways, later American Airlines (AAL), pilot. Like Behncke, he had been involved in General Pershing's expedition into Mexico after Pancho Villa in 1916, but there is no indication the two met at that time. He served for seven years on active duty as a commissioned aviator before resigning to form his own airline, which he headquartered in Fort Worth and christened Texas Air Transport. He won the first Texas airmail contract in 1927, and in 1929 sold out to Aviation Corporation of America in a deal that left him financially secure. In 1930, apparently bored with the life of idle wealth or broke because of the stock market crash, he went to work for AAL, first as an executive, and subsequently as a line pilot. Hardin took an active interest in ALPA's affairs almost from the beginning, and Behncke considered him an asset to ALPA because of his previous success in management. During the 1930s, Hardin held practically every ALPA office, finally winding up as first vice-president, second only to Behncke.

In June 1938, during the closing days of the congressional session, Hardin had led the first Lobby to Save Lives in its efforts to save the independent ASB in the Civil Aeronautics Act of 1938 from a last-minute revision proposed by ATA. ATA had tried to dilute the airline pilot member's authority by weakening ASB's mandate and, when that failed, to substitute a one-man safety director in lieu of a multimember ASB. The newspapers had learned of this proposed revision in the law and had given the Lobby to Save Lives a fair amount of publicity. ALPA had won the battle, and the future of ASB seemed secure.

Had it not been for the war in Europe, ATA would probably never have been able to destroy ASB. The problem was that FDR needed the support of the executives his New Deal had previously opposed. In order to win them to his service in wartime, there had to be a quid pro quo, a token of good faith. Throughout every area of governmental authority, the weakening of New Deal reforms was apparent as the "dollar-a-year" men (who were, in reality, merely executives on fully paid leave) flooded Washington and began taking the measure of their old opponents, particularly the labor union leaders. Thus a softening of the New Deal's prolabor policies was an early and obvious casualty of the wartime situation. For air transport management, nullification of the costly ASB idea was a primary target. FDR, canny politician that he was, understood the give-and-take nature of the political game. What he had given, he would now take, and so ASB was dead.

Behncke was stunned at the elimination of ASB in FDR's Reorganization

Plan No. 4 when it was announced in April 1940. During the months ASB had been in existence, it had done an excellent job. The number of pure pilot error findings had dropped sharply, and the airlines had had to spend a large amount of money complying with ASB safety recommendations. Airline safety began to improve dramatically. By June 1939, after the completion of the first full season of cold-weather operations (traditionally the most dangerous time), the accident rate was down sharply, with only a single fatal accident, on Northwest Airlines (NWA) at Miles City, Mont., which resulted in four deaths. Figures for the previous three years showed an annual average of 22 fatalities.

FDR's proposed reorganization would transfer ASB's investigatory function, together with all its personnel, to a newly restructured Civil Aeronautics Board (CAB). Behncke learned about the abolition of ASB like everybody else—by reading the newspapers. Fiercely angry at what he considered a betrayal by FDR, Behncke resolved to fight.

He put up a good one, earning wide popular support in the press. Personally leading a second Lobby to Save Lives to Washington in late April 1940, he tried to persuade Congress to block Reorganization Plan No. 4.

Carl Luethi, a charter ALPA member who went to work for NWA in 1931 and retired in 1963, remembers being tapped by Behncke to replace Cash Chamberlain as NWA's member of the second Lobby to Save Lives:

> I think Behncke asked me to come on down to Washington to walk the halls of Congress because I was local council chairman at Minneapolis. When Cash Chamberlain got killed at Miles City, I was the logical one to do it.
>
> What happened to Cash was they had a fire. The Lockheed 14 had this little step between the pilot and cockpit, which covered a fuel transfer valve, and it never should have been routed through the cockpit like that. Well, the speculation is that they got a fuel leak in there and it caught a spark somehow. It was a poor design, and they changed it afterward, and I think ASB's investigation made them do it. In the old days, they'd have just written it off as 'pilot error' and let it go.
>
> We all thought ASB was doing a good job, and the trip down to Washington to try to save it was well worth our effort. But we just couldn't get anywhere, we came away feeling very frustrated, like the administration wanted ASB out, they had the power to do it, and that was that.

ALPA's only hope of stopping FDR's reorganization of ASB lay in persuading key legislators to block it. As Behncke and his fellow airline pilots were discovering, being right wasn't enough.

U.S. aviation had gone an entire year (1940) without a single fatal accident, but when the President issued a formal statement commending the air transport industry he omitted any mention of ASB, which most airline pilots believed was directly responsible for the good record. "This safety record," FDR declared, "has been achieved through cooperation and team-work between the personnel of the airlines and the workers in the federal government."

Behncke wondered editorially why FDR would abolish "the principal contributor to the world's best air safety record," and so the controversy continued to swirl, eventually spurring FDR's enemies to the attack. Among them was Rep. Clarence Lea of Minnesota, whose support of ALPA extended back to the early 1930s. "I raise no question about good intentions," Lea said on the floor of the House. "But when the history of aviation in this country shall finally be written, it must contain chapters showing the dark side of the picture, particularly the President's decision to cancel the independent safety board."

Stung, FDR replied with uncharacteristic rancor, accusing his critics during a press conference on April 30, 1940, of being "ignorant, gullible, and politically misled." He reserved some particularly harsh words for Dave Behncke and ALPA: "I am standing behind the plan to reorganize ASB. A flood of misinformation has engulfed this issue, much of it absurd. This morning, we saw a group of well-intentioned people staking out an exclusive claim as the so-called Lobby to Save Lives. Their implication is that *we* are not interested in saving lives." The President assured the assembled reporters that such was not the case, and there is little doubt that these tough words had a chastening effect on Behncke. He had been in FDR's corner for so long, on so many issues, that the thought of having him as an enemy was unnerving. Congress refused to block FDR's plan for ASB, and in May 1940 it went out of business.

Behncke seemed to realize that he was outmatched, politically in over his head, and in danger of alienating a man who could do ALPA irreparable harm. So he made his peace with FDR, at least for the time being. He still hoped that reason would prevail and that the special relationship he had previously enjoyed with the Roosevelt administration would be rekindled. It was in this mood that he wrote: "Now war clouds loom. Local problems should be made secondary. There is a bigger job to be done. We must prepare quickly. There is no other way to stay safe from the dictator-controlled machines of Europe."

Once again, as in the crisis over the airmail in 1934, Behncke pledged his support to FDR. Behncke hoped that history would repeat itself and that ALPA would emerge victorious by tying itself to FDR's apron strings. Behncke also had personal goals in mind, goals he could hardly hope to achieve if he alienated FDR.

Sometime in early 1940, at the age of 43, Dave Behncke took one last shot at the military career that had eluded him in the 1920s. Although he had not flown at all since his near-fatal accident in December 1934, he got back in the cockpit. He was considered a bit old by the standards of that time, but through judicious string-pulling with friends in the Army Air Corps reserves, Behncke managed to get checked out in Boeing P-26 fighters. He still held a first lieutenant reserve commission but he was obviously angling for bigger things.

Rumors were rife in mid-1940 that in the event of war the airlines and all their pilots would be called to the colors. Behncke expected to be offered a significant jump in rank when that happened, and he wanted to be an active aviator.

While everybody waited on events, Behncke tried hard to mold ALPA into a more modern, technocratic entity. He began forming special committees of airline pilots to serve as his technical advisers, partly because he felt that lack of this kind of expertise had hampered the effort to save ASB. Behncke was beginning to put together the committee infrastructure that would one day be the domain of the "nuts-and-bolts" types, airline pilots whose personal and technical bents inclined them toward the nonpolitical side of ALPA activity. In May 1940, just after the ASB battle was lost, Behncke announced the formation of ALPA's first Engineering and Airworthiness Advisory Committee.

Behncke knew, however, that airline pilots alone, for all their practical experience with airplanes, would not give him sufficient weight when combating the airlines' technical personnel, who usually sported an impressive array of fancy engineering degrees from prestigious universities. In 1940 Behncke began to search for a suitably degreed aeronautical engineer. The search finally bore fruit after the start of the war when he hired Ted Linnert to be ALPA's first full-time staff engineer.

"Mr. Behncke said he wasn't looking for an airline pilot type," Linnert remembers. "He said he had plenty of flying talent, and he could get all the lawyers he wanted for the legal department, and in any case Mr. Behncke was pretty much of a one-man gang over there when negotiations were in progress. 'What we need is aeronautical engineering talent to go along with certification,' he said, 'because all these aircraft being developed during the war have to be licensed, certificated by doing flight test work, and so forth.'"

By early 1941, ALPA's Air Traffic Control and Airway Aids Advisory Committee was also functional, but its contributions were muted because, like the Engineering and Airworthiness Committee, it suffered from lack of technical engineering help.

All the while, the employment contracts continued to mount. Each one represented something of a scalp for ALPA's trophy belt, particularly Delta Air Lines. This southern airline, with its strong regional tradition of antiunionism, proved surprisingly easy to conquer. When the Delta pilots under Charles Dolson got moving, they did a thorough job of it. Delta had a reputation for being a paternalistic "one big happy family." Consequently, it must have come as a shock to C. E. Woolman when his pilots unionized.

"I don't think he ever forgave me for getting ALPA started on Delta," Dolson said later. Nevertheless, after a hard, four-day bargaining session in Atlanta, Woolman himself signed for the company. "All arguments were cut to a minimum," Behncke admitted happily. He was used to far more strenuous, long drawn-out sessions. In fact, some pilots were beginning to think Behncke rather enjoyed them and felt cheated when the negotiations went too easily.

UAL fell into the hopper on Sept. 25, 1940, after nearly a year of negotiations. The agreement covered the airline's 359 pilots, which made it second in size only to AAL. It was the eleventh ALPA contract.

Northwest and Western Air Express (soon to be renamed with its modern title, Western Air Lines) had already completed contract negotiations, but final signing was being delayed owing to a few minor points that were under National Mediation Board (NMB) jurisdiction. Of the nation's major carriers, only EAL and PAA (Pan American World Airways) were still without contracts, and the prospects on EAL looked bleak.

One of the EAL pilots involved with that first contract, Vern Peterson, remembers what it was like to challenge Eddie Rickenbacker:

> The thing that really got us interested in ALPA to begin with on Eastern was when the company bought some multiengine airplanes and brought in new pilots to fly them. Well, Gene Brown was No. 1 on our seniority list, but the concept of upgrading people according to seniority had not yet been established. So Gene Brown took the bull by the horns, got out early one morning, had some of the mechanics crank up one of the new multiengine airplanes, and then he went out and checked himself. Before ALPA was founded, that was an offense which would have been followed by firing.
>
> I was attracted to ALPA from the beginning because of what happened to a friend of mine who was working for a little fly-by-night outfit right after the mail cancellations in 1934 for $120 per month. My friend cracked up and broke a leg and was in horrible shape.
>
> Then Behncke got into my friend's case and was able to get his hospital bills paid and his salary paid while he was in the hospital. I thought that was quite an achievement. When I finally managed to get a job here on Eastern and the boys asked me to join ALPA, I said it was a darn good thing and I would be glad to join. The trouble with talking like that is that you get elected to something. The next thing I knew I was elected copilot representative.
>
> But anyhow, by 1940 we were long overdue to have a contract. Now, some coordination was necessary, and when I brought this to the attention of other local council chairmen on our line, they elected me to be the guy to carry the ball on this first contract. It wasn't easy, some of the pilots would get me off in a corner and tell me I shouldn't rock the boat. We had opposition.
>
> Time went on and Behncke requested a date to start negotiations, but this was stalled month after month. Finally, I got

exasperated and decided to go directly to Capt. Eddie Ricken-backer. My opportunity came at the dedication of the Eastern Air Lines building in Rockefeller Plaza in New York. This was attended by several of the Rockefellers, Eddie Rickenbacker, and all kinds of celebrities.

When it was over, I approached Captain Eddie, asking when we could meet with him to discuss the contract. His response started off with, "Why you little whipper-snapper," and ended up with a statement that hell would freeze over before he would do any negotiating.

I reported this lack of progress to Behncke, and he went to Washington. Eventually, through some political pressure, we got a contract.

In July 1941, EAL became the last major domestic airline to sign an employment agreement. Only National, among domestic airlines, lacked a contract. Panagra and Pan Am presented special negotiating problems because of their unique status under federal law, but in October 1941 Panagra signed.

Because of the far-flung nature of Pan Am's operations, plus an innate streak of conservatism among its mostly ex-Navy pilots, Pan Am would not sign a contract until June 1945. Its 1,000 pilots lagged nearly five years behind their domestic contemporaries.

It was a hard contract, requiring repeated intervention by NMB. The first actual negotiating did not take place until August 1943, and the need to involve pilots at dispersed domiciles made subsequent sessions the most expensive in ALPA's history, costing in excess of $50,000.

And then it was Dec. 7, 1941—the day of the attack on Pearl Harbor. For Dave Behncke, the first few months of the U.S. involvement in World War II held bitter personal disappointment. He was so ready for the call to active duty that he had prepared himself for it by requalifying as an Army pilot in the reserves. The new Air Transport Command (ATC) was going to war, with deskbound executives like C. R. Smith of AAL, who had no previous military experience, claiming high rank and important positions. During the first few weeks of war Behncke anxiously awaited his call to serve. All around him airline pilots were returning to active duty, and Behncke's hunger to be part of it was intense. When his orders to active duty finally came, however, they were shattering.

Behncke had expected that he would be assigned to a job commensurate with his civilian experience. He had, in fact, told his friends that he expected no less than a colonelcy and hoped he would be billeted to personnel duties in the ATC. What he got was a measly promotion to _captain_ with orders to a flight instructor's billet in Texas.

Once more Behncke enlisted the aid of Fiorello LaGuardia, who managed to get the offensive orders canceled. In fighting them, Behncke learned that his old enemies in management had contrived the orders to get him out of the way and had on at least one occasion bragged about it publicly.

So Behncke embarked upon his great crusade—to protect airline pilots from the use of what he called "war hysteria to tear down our hard-won gains." The first battle would be over extending the limitation on pilots' hours from 85 to 100 "for the duration." Publicly Behncke went along, while privately he did everything he could to sabotage it. He told the 1940 convention: "They're using 'patriotism' as an excuse to tear down the 85-hour law, and on most of the smaller airlines it's just about dead. It will be hard to get back."

Behncke never blamed FDR personally for these reverses. "He is a great President who has done many good things," Behncke said. "But he has also made a few bad mistakes and he has certainly received plenty of bad advice."

Behncke seemed to understand that both he and FDR were now prisoners of forces neither could control. Behncke had to float with the prevailing antilabor tides that were then at flood stage in Washington. FDR, in order to win the war, had to allow a free hand to Behncke's old enemies. Believing that it was the airline executives who were the villains, Behncke resolved to fight a subtle, behind-the-scenes guerrilla war. Its object was to protect the pilots working for the ATC in the various companies' military contract operations from being excessively exploited. As Behncke said: "President Roosevelt himself had made it clear that his national defense program is not to be done with the sacrifice of wages and working limitations which labor has made."

The airline managers who flocked to Washington after Pearl Harbor expected to eliminate the federal 85-hour law entirely. Behncke was willing to extend the 85-hour limit to 100, but would go no farther. Behncke's hard-nosed attitude infuriated Eddie Rickenbacker, whom Behncke accused of using the war to "continually peck away" at the EAL contract Rickenbacker had signed so reluctantly in 1941. The crunch came in 1942 when a committee of airline executives invited Behncke to Washington to confer on an "intercontinental supplement" to cover pilots working overseas for various airlines under contract to it. Behncke smelled a rat—industrywide bargaining.

Actually, Behncke didn't want to go to the August 1942 meeting at Washington's Carlton Hotel but he felt obligated to because of the war. ATA had named the committee of company executives. In his first attempts to negotiate "supplementals" for the pilots of AAL and UAL, Behncke had hit a stone wall, so he knew something like this ATA attempt at a uniform contract was coming. For moral support, Behncke took along ALPA's lawyer, Daniel D. Carmel, plus EAL pilot leader W. B. Inman.

Behncke began the meeting by warning the assembled executives that they would get nowhere with him talking of sacrifices and weeping "crocodile tears" because he knew they were making a ton of money on their contract operations. Furthermore, he said that if they tried, he would go public with a campaign to have _everyone_ drafted for the duration of the war—executives, pilots, and _whole corporations_. They could all draw military pay, Behncke said, with all profits going back to the government or to the families of the killed and wounded. The meeting was off to a rocky start and got worse. As Behncke described it to the 1942 convention:

> This was just a friendly little get-together they said, but when we got there, they suddenly decided that they were going to do their negotiating collectively. Monro acted as their chairman, but Rickenbacker did most of the loud talking. It was the most peculiar and strained meeting I ever attended.
>
> After I said my piece, Rickenbacker walked over and pointed a finger in my face, saying he was going to fight me and if I wanted to start now to go ahead but he would still be standing when it was over!
>
> He was very much worked up, and that little meeting didn't end very well. That afternoon we met again and everybody was a lot less inclined toward fisticuffs. Monro was elected chairman, and he started out by saying he was sorry, but some of the things they were going to propose were not their own ideas but those of the Army. Then he walked over and apologetically laid a piece of paper down which contained the Army's pay scale for ocean flying. I told them we'd go back to Chicago and think about it.

Behncke was under extreme pressure. One high-ranking ATC colonel and a former airline executive told him to "play ball or else!" Behncke told the 1942 convention: "They have been after us with everything they could lay their hands on to try and tear us down and destroy our salaries and working conditions. We must defend the rights of our members in military service so they will have something to come home to."

This was not entirely idle rhetoric, as the death of W. B. Inman proved. Inman had less than a year to live when Rickenbacker threatened to thrash him along with Behncke for his "unpatriotic attitude" in 1942. On May 7, 1943, Inman's last radio message reported an engine on fire and a planned ditching midway across the South Atlantic enroute to Africa on the military contract run from Natal. There were no survivors. To prove his point that people like Rickenbacker, for all their efforts to force pilots to fly for "Army pay scales," were unwilling to do so themselves, Behncke ran an article in _The Air Line Pilot_ calling attention to CAB figures for 1942. These figures showed that the airlines were cleaning up, with Ted Baker's National topping the list by earning 53.76 percent on its total investment _in just one year._ The lesson Behncke made clear was that in war some get killed while others get rich.

Although it was not an easy thing to do, given Behncke's natural tendency to be a flag-waver, he hung tough during World War II, grudgingly giving ground on standards, but always warily angling for advantage. He won a few, lost more. ALPA beat back a wartime attempt by ATA and the government to raise the certificated maximum gross weight for the DC-3, correctly pointing out that the new standards would mean that a DC-3 that lost an engine on takeoff at many ordinary airports would have a single engine ceiling _below_ the runway it had just left. But there was very little ALPA could do about routine violations of federal standards and contract provisions when they occurred under crisis conditions just behind the battlefronts.

Behncke knew the real crunch would come when the guns fell silent. ALPA would then have to contend not only with the great technological changes wrought by the war, but also with the airlines' demand for industrywide bargaining. Behncke wasn't about to surrender the privilege of negotiating with one airline at a time, a technique which permitted "jacking up the house," as one airline executive complained. Management surfaced the notion of industrywide bargaining in earnest for the first time at the Carlton Hotel, using the Army's pay scale as cover.

Behncke would see it again in 1946 on TWA. It would cause ALPA's first real nationwide strike. ✦

CHAPTER 12

The TWA Strike of 1946

"Golden Boys," sneered *Time* magazine, as ALPA neared the deadline for its first true strike in the fall of 1946. For John Q. Citizen, the notion of well-paid airline pilots going out on strike was incomprehensible. The average American, although irritated with organized labor because of the great wave of postwar strikes, could understand why an ordinary working stiff would hit the bricks. Inflation was raging, wages hadn't kept up, and it was hard to make ends meet. But to be inconvenienced by "the world's most gilded and exclusive labor union," as *Time* unflatteringly described ALPA, was another matter entirely.

To say that ALPA lacked broad support for its strike against Transcontinental & Western Air (TWA) would be a considerable understatement. The average newspaper reporter did not understand the issues, and for that reason news stories were often more confusing than informative. Nor were many labor leaders sympathetic. When *Time* referred to Dave Behncke as "a suave, self-assured retired pilot who looks about as radical as a Philadelphia Main Liner," it played on the prejudices of ordinary working people, who couldn't understand why pilots earning as much as $10,000 a year should be out on a picket line. Speaking to this blue collar attitude, Phillip Murray of the Congress of Industrialized Organizations snapped: "Labor dispute hell! That's a row between capitalists."

In order to understand the roots of the TWA strike, we must first delve into three complicated issues: the four-engine pay dispute; the airlines' attempt to negotiate on an industrywide basis; and the nature of Behncke's leadership in the post-World War II period.

Beginning with the latter, let us turn to the recollections of Henry Weiss, the New York labor lawyer Behncke selected (on the advice of Fiorello LaGuardia) to assist him when the legal tangles got too intense for ALPA's staff. Weiss's perceptions of Behncke are important because as an outsider he could view Behncke without the hero worship many airline pilots felt for him.

> The Dave Behncke I met in the late 1940s was an intractable negotiator whose tendency to see conspiracies everywhere convinced me that he was suffering from paranoia or some deteriorating mental condition. The Airlines Negotiating Committee had an al-

most traumatizing effect on him. All this began during the strike on TWA in 1946. Although Dave was an interesting man, he was difficult to deal with. After our initial confrontation he never gave me any more trouble.

The confrontation occurred down at Miami during an arbitration. I had traveled all night by plane to arrive there at 7:00 a.m. Dave Behncke handed me a long statement to be read to the arbitrator—it may have run 40 pages—full of rambling, empty phrases. He pushed it into my hands, but I edited it as I went along, rather severely in fact. He was very unhappy with me, but by that time he was so deeply committed to me in front of the arbitrator that he couldn't pull away, not without a great loss of position.

In any event, that was when we had our break and I stood my ground. Afterward he just kind of grinned at me. Eventually he and I got quite close, as close as anybody could get to Dave. He never abused me, never challenged me again, although I must say he could be quite abusive to the people around him, to his lawyers from the Chicago headquarters particularly. He would fire them on the spot, literally. So with Behncke it was a rough go. By nature he was a hard-driving, suspicious, withdrawn person.

I think in the immediate post-World War II period, when aviation was really ready to go, more complicated, more sophisticated, he couldn't cope. I think he was suffering the fate of many union leaders who had the drive and regularity of purpose to launch an organization, but who didn't really have the ability to run it successfully once it got under way.

Behncke's good fortune during the 1946 TWA strike was to be surrounded by pilots who carried him at a time when his shortcomings were becoming obvious. Jim Roe was one of these pilots:

> I was mustered out of the Army on Dec. 25, 1945, and I returned to the home base at Kansas City. I don't think I was home much over a day or two when Bill Judd [who had taken Roe's place as master executive council chairman when he got called to active duty] said, "I'm sure glad to see you. You have it, take over."
>
> Well, Bill Judd went off to fly on ICD [TWA's "Intercontinental Division" operating transatlantic out of New York], and I walked into a hornet's nest. It was all new to me. I had been gone nearly 43 months, and I hadn't heard anything at all about the four-engine pay problem.
>
> Everything was boiling, so I got started with some old friends, people like Red Foster and Dan Medler, trying to see if we couldn't get this thing straightened out. I went up to Chicago to see Dave Behncke. The TWA problem was the only thing on Dave's mind. It was serious and he was trying his best to cope with it before something drastic happened. We talked for hours, trying to see how we could figure this thing out and try to solve it. Behncke was *not* for a

strike. That was absolutely his last desire, because he was aware of the tremendous impact a strike would have on an airline as big as TWA, with 30,000 employees. There were some pilots smart enough to invest their money and they had no problem. But there were others who couldn't make the next payment on the house. Behncke also worried about the hostesses, the copilots, and the mechanics. Before the strike, he set up a kitty of several thousand dollars for anybody who needed money. People would come in and sign and pay us back when they could.

Behncke had aged since I last saw him; he had more responsibilities on his mind. He should have delegated power to his trusted people, but he didn't. It took its toll on him, but in late 1945 I can't say that he looked particularly sick, or worse than he had before. That came later, the next year.

The four-engine pay controversy on TWA had a long gestation period. It began when Boeing introduced the prototype 307 Stratoliner in 1939. This revolutionary pressurized aircraft had enormous possibilities. It could fly well over most weather, above the airsickness-inducing turbulence that had always bedeviled passenger operations. For Jack Frye and for TWA, the airline that prided itself on always being one technological step ahead of the competition, an aircraft like the Boeing 307 was irresistible. With the help of Howard Hughes's millions, Frye had committed TWA to the purchase of five Stratoliners in 1939, but the aircraft were not delivered until just before World War II. The Army drafted all five shortly thereafter, but in the brief period the Stratoliners operated for TWA, they set new standards for comfort and luxury. United Airlines (UAL) announced in August 1939 that it too was entering the four-engine era with the purchase of six Douglas DC-4s. The Stratoliner would lose out to Douglas's DC-4 after the war, but it was the Stratoliner that first got Dave Behncke's attention.

Behncke moved immediately to negotiate amendments to TWA's contract when the Stratoliner appeared. Technically, only an amendment to the existing contract was necessary. TWA resisted, and so no contract amendment was signed by the time the military commandeered the aircraft.

Despite repeated efforts to negotiate pay scales for these new aircraft, ALPA got nowhere. There were two arbitration awards, in 1941 and again in 1945 (which increased pay slightly *only* for the Stratoliner), but pay scales for the DC-4 and the Lockheed Constellation were still unsettled when these aircraft were ready to enter service. ALPA's first attempt to deal with the four-engine issue came at the Central Executive Council (CEC) meeting of April 29, 1939. After a good deal of wrangling, several CEC members expressed the opinion that Behncke should approach the pay issue on the basis of the weight of the aircraft, not the number of engines.

Behncke disapproved of this notion, preferring instead to stress the *dangers* of operating four-engine aircraft. Despite the dissension among CEC members, Behncke persisted in his argument that since the new aircraft would fly faster, encountering more weather and covering more miles, the pilots would necessarily encounter increased hazards, and so they deserved higher pay. Behncke also believed that having two additional engines to monitor would add to the distractions present, increasing the work load and offsetting any absolute gain in safety. His thinking was already outdated in 1939, and it would get worse.

Historical accident was on Behncke's side, however, for although most pilots were already uncomfortable with some of his archaic notions about "hazard pay," the shakedown days of every four-engine aircraft introduced on the airlines after World War II were marred by fatal accidents, often caused by design errors. Both the Lockheed Constellation and the pressurized version of the DC-4, the DC-6, were temporarily grounded following fatal accidents.

Philosophical considerations aside, every pilot agreed that the new aircraft should pay more than the old ones. The problem was how to negotiate pay scales that would take into account the new complexities of the aircraft—their heavier weight, higher passenger loads, and increased takeoff and landing speeds—without doing harm to certain positive aspects of Decision 83, ALPA's historic security blanket.

And here, ALPA was hoisted with its own petard, for the companies suddenly became zealous defenders of Decision 83, arguing that it provided a "more than fair [and] practical system [for determing pay on] large or small, fast or slow aircraft." As the Airlines Negotiating Committee put it during the presidential emergency board hearing of July 1946: "The committee believes that the flexibility of Decision 83 automatically compensating for all types of aircraft is in the continued interest of the air transport industry."

Why this great turnaround? The answer lay in the fact that Decision 83, which the operators had so hotly opposed in the past, had an hourly pay scale that paid more incrementally for faster equipment, but the scale topped out at only 200 miles per hour. In 1934 no one thought airplanes could fly much faster than that, but four-engine aircraft easily exceeded the scale. So Decision 83's speed-pegged component automatically guaranteeing pilots an increased share of an aircraft's productivity was something of a time bomb.

Had Behncke been willing to compromise on the issue of industrywide bargaining, the companies might in turn have been willing to renegotiate the Decision 83 pay scales. They might even have been willing to change Decision 83's copilot pay scales, which were set at straight monthly amounts according to seniority, topping out at only $225 per month. These were admittedly only minimum guarantees, which could be raised by contract negotiations. Copilots on TWA were earning $380 per month in 1946, with those on the ICD's over-ocean routes eligible to earn another $30 per month if they qualified as navigators. In fact, pilot pay had risen generally since Decision 83 went into effect, largely because the average speed of aircraft kept increasing during the 1930s. But Behncke was technically correct when he insisted that airline pilots had not had a basic pay raise since 1934.

During this period the airline industry was attempting to negotiate one contract covering all airlines, while Behncke wanted to continue negotiating one airline at a time—the familiar "jacking up the house" routine, which allowed the pilots of one airline to get a little something, thus providing their fellows on another airline a target to shoot for in their own negotiations. Although, historically, labor unions have favored industrywide bargaining while employers have opposed it, in the air transport industry it was just the opposite.

One of Dave Behncke's most brilliant maneuvers had been to include the pilots under the 1926 law designed to prevent the halting of interstate commerce. The 1936 "pilot's amendment" to the Railway Labor Act of 1926 gave Behncke a technical argument in favor of airline-by-airline negotiations, and he clung to it tenaciously. The airline companies did not realize the disadvantage of the one-by-one negotiating arrangement until the first contracts started coming in. They resolved to fight it when they saw how adroitly Behncke used the technique of exploiting a special circumstance on one line to win what another line would never have given up. That second airline would subsequently feel pressure to concede, however, because a competitor would have given the game away earlier. As recounted in Chapter 10, Behncke's first encounter with the airlines' demand for industrywide bargaining came at the 1942 conference in Washington. It had produced plenty of angry, fist-shaking rhetoric on Eddie Rickenbacker's part, but Behncke stood his ground. It did throw a scare into him, though, and the fact that the airlines stonewalled him so consistently during World War II when he tried to open negotiations on the new four-engine aircraft definitely had a "traumatizing effect" on Behncke, as Henry Weiss put it.

The period leading up to the TWA strike was replete with fruitless negotiations, endless mediation, and unsuccessful maneuvers. Neither side was willing to give on the fundamentals. Even the presidential emergency board, appointed in May 1946 by Harry Truman, couldn't solve the problem. The Airlines Negotiating Committee, chaired by Ralph S. Damon, hung tough; so did Behncke. Any mediation that involved more than one airline resulted in an ALPA walkout and vice-versa on the part of the companies. Behncke once startled a group of airline executives who had assembled to attend a mediation covering more than one airline by saying: "I'm here to deal with one outfit. If the rest of you fellows want to look on, that's all right with me. If that one outfit wants all of you to represent it, that's all right with me. But remember, I'm dealing with one, only one." Un-

ALPA's founders, the Key Men *(clockwise from upper left):* Byron S. Warner (Mr. A, United), Walter Hallgreen (Mr. G, American), John Huber (Mr. T, Trans-American), Dave Behncke (Mr. K, United), Walter Bullock (Mr. C, Northwest), Homer Cole (Mr. S, Northwest), and M. D. "Doc" Ator (Mr. H, American).

ALPA's founders and key figures during its formative years *(left to right, top row):* Jim Roe (TWA), A. M. "Breezy" Wynne (American), Clyde Holbrook (American), Key Man J. H. Burns (Mr. I, American), Key Man Glenn Fields (Mr. W, American), and Willis Proctor (American); *(left to right, bottom row):* Tom Hardin (American), R. Lee Smith (Northwest), Key Man John S. Pricer (Mr. J, American), Key Man Usher Rousch (Mr. M, American), L. W. Harris (American), and Key Man Verne E. Treat (Mr. U, Eastern).

Much of ALPA's early political clout came from the certificate of affiliation with the AF of L *(right).*

Behncke's spirited defense of pilots involved in mishaps grew from bitter personal experience. On Dec. 21, 1934, finding both engines dead with every instrument in the cockpit registering normal, Behncke managed a treetop landing *(opposite, center)* that injured only himself. He would later write, "I have no doubt that if my copilot and I had not lived to defend ourselves, 'pilot error' would have been given as the cause of the crash."

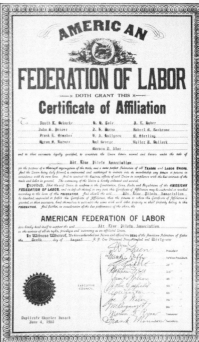

At the 1939 Labor Day Parade in New York City *(right)*, Mayor Fiorello LaGuardia *(in white suit)* chose ALPA President Behncke to march at his side, leading a contingent of uniformed ALPA pilots at the head of the parade. LaGuardia's friendship with Behncke proved invaluable during the Association's early years.

Behncke was elected to his second term at the second biennial meeting of the ALPA Board of Directors in 1934 *(opposite, top right)*, which also adopted the first budget plan and the complete bylaws. The ornate display at the 1947 Board of Directors meeting *(opposite, center)* indicates the intricacies of the issues discussed.

The Air Line Pilot began as a confidential, mimeographed bulletin to members and grew to a tabloid *(opposite, bottom)* and finally to a magazine.

T.W.A. Skymaster C-54 and Lockheed Constellation Emergency Board and Arbitration Proceedings

THE AIR LINE PILOT

Vol. 1—No. 2   Published by The Air Line Pilots Association, International, 3145 W. 63rd St., Chicago, Ill.   April 20, 1932

PILOT SAVES 8 PASSENGERS BY HEROIC ACT

A. F. of L. Gives Promotion For Arizona Victory

D. OF C. MEETS WITH ALPA

Skoning Relates Conditions on Century-Pacific

Motor Tears Loose; Stays on Landing Strut Till Dumped Off

"MAL" FREEBURG DUE CITATION

Radios Cause to Clear Mystery in Event Crash Kills All

KILLEN GOES TO CAPITOL AFTER BEATING C-P

L. A. Cottrell, Asst. Chief Air Line Inspector and Division Inspector George West of the Department of Commerce confer with David L. Behncke, A. L. P. A. President on pilots' requirements under proposed Scheduled Air Transport Rating at ALPA Headquarters.

RESOLUTION BY MEAD PASSED

Statement Made by Congressman Seen as Reaction to Card Methods

"AIRLINE PILOT" FOR LITERAL USE

RETURNS FROM COAST TO MAKE REPORT

By C. H. S. SKONING

MEMBER'S MILITARY STATUS WANTED

DUES SOON DELINQUENT

The crash of the TWA DC-2 *(above)* piloted by Harvey Bolton near Kirksville, Mo., on May 6, 1935, killed Sen. Bronson Cutting *(inset)* and four others but provoked reforms of accident investigation that survive today. As the first aviation accident to claim a prominent politician, the Cutting crash induced investigations by five government agencies, provided ALPA with evidence for the need to establish an independent safety board, and led to the Civil Aeronautics Act of 1938.

In the TWA strike of 1946, pilots and management first confronted the complex issues of pay scales and productivity that followed advances in aviation technology, specifically the introduction of four-engine equipment. TWA President Jack Frye *(below, left)* and Behncke *(right)* finally reached a settlement, with the help of Judge Frank P. Douglass *(center)*, but the protracted conflict revealed the first signs of Behncke's deteriorating ability to lead. Jim Roe *(below right, in cockpit)* was one of the pilots who served as catalysts to keep negotiations going.

National pilots, including future ALPA President Charley Ruby *(left, at typewriter)*, found time to spoof their own exhaustion during the 1948 strike, but their sacrifices were all too real; ALPA waged what was then its longest and costliest strike to reaffirm the union's integrity despite Ted Baker's attempt to break it.

The rapaciousness of E. L. Cord *(above, left)* moved Fiorello LaGuardia to denounce him as "low, dishonest, a liar, and a gangster" on the floor of the House.

Even today, E. P. McDonald *(above, right)* remains grateful to the ALPA national office for saving his job: "Without them I'd have been a goner, without old Dave Behncke, God bless him."

In 1932, ALPA's headquarters moved from a rented room in Chicago's Troy Lane Hotel to a walkup office at 3145 West 63rd Street *(top)*; President Behncke's personal office, the "cage" behind the filing cabinets, can be seen in the background. From that tiny enclosure, Behncke planned what he hoped would be a monument to himself: ALPA's first headquarters building on Cicero Avenue in Chicago. "He wanted the coping on the roof to be the exact slant of the pyramids and the color of the . . . partitions to be 'Cadillac' gray," remembers retired ALPA staffer Scruggs Colvin. Behncke broke ground for the new building *(above)* on April 28, 1949.

til Behncke agreed to recognize the Airlines Negotiating Committee, a new four-engine contract would not exist for anybody. There was such a deadlock that even a strike vote couldn't shake them loose. TWA's pilots took a strike authorization vote on March 26, 1946, approving it by a margin of 812 to 9. Truman's presidential emergency board delayed it, but couldn't stop it.

Robert N. "Bob" Buck, who went to work for TWA in 1937 and later played a major role in ALPA affairs, remembers that management didn't take the strike vote seriously: "Frye was in Washington trying to get international routes, and John Collings [TWA's vice-president for operations] was running the airline. Collings never believed the pilots were so adamant about getting better wages. When he heard strike talk he didn't realize 'his boys' weren't his boys.'"

With his tendency to "live in the past," as Henry Weiss saw it, Behncke had a hard time assimilating the myriad details associated with the incessant maneuvering, mediating, and negotiating. He began reverting to old tactics, sending out long, rambling denunciations of TWA's management and of the Airlines Negotiating Committee and flooding the newspapers with vitriolic press releases, much as he had done back in 1933. He was fixed on TWA, unable to concentrate on major issues because he was so intimately wrapped up in minor ones. In the meantime, the day of reckoning kept getting closer, the new four-engine aircraft kept arriving, the pilots kept checking out. Perhaps it was too much for any man. Certainly it was too much for Behncke.

On May 21, 1946, during the height of the controversy, Behncke collapsed and had to be taken to the hospital. Many pilots suspected that Behncke had had a heart attack. Actually, it was a severe insulin deficiency brought on by a chronic diabetic condition he had concealed for years. It was probably aggravated by the strain of the accumulating troubles on TWA. Behncke kept it secret.

Dave Richwine, who went to work for TWA in 1940 only to have his career interrupted by military service in World War II, became involved in ALPA work for the first time by serving as an observer during several mediation sessions in 1946. His perspective on them is worth hearing:

> We could have settled things early if everything hadn't been conditioned on industrywide negotiating. All these negotiations, mediations—the company just wouldn't make any decisions. They often sent in lawyers who had no other purpose than to talk and prolong without any resolution, and we couldn't do it by ourselves. We'd agree to something and then they'd renege.
>
> The first few months after the war, I was concerned most about getting myself qualified and back into operation. I was making $190 a month and I had a family so I was naturally very interested. I guess that's why I was selected as one of the 12 or so pilots to help

prepare exhibits, coordinate testimony, just generally witness things.

In the beginning I thought Dave Behncke was everything a labor leader should be. He was verbose and muddled sometimes, but generally I thought he was doing pretty well. One thing that struck me, though, was that when we went into these presidential emergency board hearings, a couple of the pilots gave Behncke a talking to. They told him, "Look, two things you're going to do everyday. One is you're going to wear a tie, and the other is you're not going to say anything. We've got the best lawyer we can get, we've got a good list of witnesses. You're not to get in there and louse it up."

To his credit, Behncke never once interfered, and maybe that was the first time in his life.

But nothing worked. Every avenue led to another dead end. Finally, ALPA had no alternative but to strike. Behncke tried one last desperate ploy, sending Jimmy Roe to talk to Jack Frye personally. Jim Roe remembers:

The main conversation I had was with Mr. Frye. We were in Washington; Behncke and I and the other negotiators were there trying to avert the strike. We had set a deadline of midnight. The night before we went out on strike, I talked to Jack Frye. I told him, "We just can't go on this way. It's going to go unless we change."

He said, "I can't change it. I can't do anything about it." I went back and talked to Behncke and told him the situation and he said, "Well, that looks like the end of it."

So I called the chairmen at the various councils and told them that midnight was the deadline. And we went out on strike.

On Oct. 21, 1946, ALPA struck TWA, breaking relations between labor and management. From then on it was economic warfare, a raw contest to see who ultimately had the power. Could ALPA withstand the forces of the marketplace? Would ALPA members hold the line and refuse to fly? Would TWA's management try to break the union in 1946, as it had done once before in 1933? These were not idle questions, for in the long history of pilot-management relations, the economic position of management has nearly always been stronger. In 1946 the labor market was bloated, with many thousands of ex-military pilots who had recent experience in four-engine aircraft looking for jobs. If the work stoppage on TWA went on long enough, there was a good possibility that an outfit calling itself the Military Pilots Association (MPA) might try to break the strike.

MPA turned out to be more formidable in appearance than in fact, but it gave ALPA loyalists a few uneasy moments in 1946 (in 1948 on National Airlines [NAL] it would cause serious trouble). It claimed 13,000 members, all of whom had allegedly flown for the Air Transport Command. "While we are not now seeking jobs at the expense of airline pilots employed before

Pearl Harbor," an MPA spokesman in New York said on October 7, just as the strike became inevitable, "we believe that military pilots who served patriotically in the war deserve equal seniority with those who were hired as civilians during the war." The implication was clear—anyone who didn't wear a uniform during World War II was a draft dodger and didn't deserve to be in an airline cockpit.

Fortunately, the strike didn't last long enough to allow MPA an opening. On Nov. 16, 1946, the strike ended with an agreement to arbitrate. Paul Richter signed for TWA, and Behncke signed for ALPA. The strike lasted just three weeks, but it had dominated the national newswires, prompting a good deal of heated argument in Congress. Judge Frank P. Douglass of the National Mediation Board (NMB) selected F. M. Swacker as the neutral arbitrator on a three-man panel. George Spater represented TWA. Bob Buck, ALPA's representative, remembers the arbitration process as a very trying one:

> Dealing with TWA was always difficult because there was constant turmoil in the executive suite. New people would come in and get hard-nosed and negotiations would drag out. If you look at the executives of Delta, for example, there isn't a guy in any spot who hasn't been there for 20 years, and that brings consistency, stability. On TWA we'd hear "bankruptcy" one day, then "things are getting better" the next. The Hughes takeover thing was boiling in 1946.
>
> I knew being the principal arbitrator after that 1946 strike wasn't going to be easy. Most of my earlier work with ALPA had been on the technical side. Dave called me at home and said Jim Roe and the boys wanted me to be the arbitrator. I argued, then said OK. For three solid months I sat out in Chicago, preparing the case. We hired Willard McEwen, an attorney who specialized in arbitrations, and he gave me an education in what it was all about. The actual arbitration took just about a week. We settled the biggest portion of it ourselves without ever using the neutral.
>
> Copilot pay was a big issue. This was a transition period for the whole industry. Prior to that time the copilot had been considered an apprentice, much as I had been when the captain kept saying, "Don't touch anything or I will break your arm." We were claiming that the copilot was an important part of the crew, not just a trainee. The guy had to know how to fly the airplane. Back when I started, if the captain had died, I would have had a hell of a time getting back on the ground.
>
> Well, the neutral in this case, Judge Swacker, was an old-fashioned guy well into his 70s, and he was convinced that the copilot was just an apprentice. We got down tight in the area of copilots' pay, deciding how much money it was, and thinking of Swacker's attitude, I took a big gulp and said, "OK, I'll sign for that amount." That night I went back to the ALPA group and they just tore me up and down. Next day we took it up to Judge Swacker. He

was sitting in his room up in the Blackstone Hotel when we handed him the copilots' settlement. The judge looked it over and said, "Bob, you sure screwed them."

The strike settlement was at best a mixed bag, but it did provide for across-the-board pay increases. Essentially, Judge Swacker extended the old Decision 83 formula up to 300 miles per hour, made minor pay adjustments in each category, and set a minimum monthly figure for ICD. Many TWA pilots were unhappy with the settlement, while others accepted it as reasonable. Everyone found something to grumble about. "It isn't all we wanted," Bob Buck admitted to his fellow pilots, "but it's upward, and for an international pilot it's the highest salary paid anywhere on earth." Buck estimated that the settlement would enable an eight-year captain flying 1,000 hours per year to earn $14,550.

By 1947, it began to dawn on some copilots that they might never make captain, that their number might never come up. On Pan American in particular, copilots with gray whiskers were becoming commonplace. If the industry continued to modernize, continually introducing ever faster and larger aircraft, promotion in the cockpit might cease on every airline. The specter of a lengthy career in the right seat loomed, and many copilots wanted to make that unpleasant prospect as financially secure as possible.

Consequently, the factor in the 1947 TWA arbitration that raised the most hackles was probably the settlement on copilot pay. Although it increased salaries, the settlement did nothing to change the old flat monthly salary system. Copilots in that era wanted increment pay based on a percentage of the captain's pay, but that idea was still ahead of its time. Although no one could know it, the vexing problem of proper compensation was still years away from a solution, too. A great deal of internal turmoil lay in ALPA's immediate future, some of it owing to the intractable nature of the opposition, some of it to the nature of Behncke's leadership.

As 1947 dawned, many pilots were increasingly uneasy about Behncke, but the idea of bringing down this mighty old oak of a man was something everybody shrank from. Bob Buck tells why:

> Dave was the greatest, but he was a man of his time, and his time ran out. He was a loner who had to know every single thing that was going on in ALPA. That was fine when it was small enough, but as the industry grew he couldn't do this anymore. Dave didn't know how to delegate authority, and this gave him a tremendous workload. He worked day and night, wore himself to a nub.
>
> His handling of the TWA strike was OK as far as it went, but he just couldn't drop everything for it. But he did, and consequently things weren't getting done, particularly over on American where they had a lot of trouble.
>
> It was during this period that the American guys started after Dave. Willis Proctor was after his job, and that bothered the hell

out of Dave. He mustered his horses and Proctor lost, but Proctor trying to get in was a recognition that Dave was not handling things well.

A little story about the arbitration held that wintertime will illustrate it for you. I was domiciled in New York, so I was living in a hotel during the arbitration. I walked into Dave's office late one night, and he was sitting there looking like a big lion, poring over papers. Everyone had gone home. I said, "Dave, I'm going home for a couple of days."

He looked up and said, "My God, what are you going home for? We're right in the middle of this thing."

I said, "Dave, tomorrow's Christmas."

CHAPTER 13

The National Airlines Strike of 1948

November 1979. The penthouse suite atop the Americana Hotel on Miami Beach is full. The bar is open, but business isn't particularly brisk. After downing the first one for old time's sake, there's a lot of nursing on seconds among the predominantly gray-haired crowd.

Jack Pitts, an energetic, fast-talking man whose coal-black hair belies his 64 years, moves rapidly around the room, slapping backs, laughing. This is his show. Having put it all together, he's anxious for the "NAL Buccaneers" to have a good time and worried that they won't.

"There will still be some bitterness tonight," Pitts had explained earlier in the day. "I came to work in 1951 after the strike, so I feel no personal animosity toward any of the scabs. I figured they had as much right as anybody else who retired from NAL [National Airlines] to join our group when I drew up the charter. But boy, you'd better believe there are some guys who disagree. I can understand why they do, and I'm not trying to justify what the scabs did either. Anytime you take a bunch of guys doing a good job and put them out for nine months—and all the hassle they went through with the physicals and check rides—there's sure to be bitterness. These guys will never kiss and make up."

Jack Pitts's anxiety is heightened by one of those classic blunders that just couldn't happen, but did. As the prime organizer of both the NAL retired group and the Retired Airline Pilots Association (RAPA), the umbrella organization comprising retired pilot groups, Pitts is an activist accustomed to keeping tabs on several projects at once. This time, however, one little detail has gotten away from him.

While walking through the lobby of the Americana, Pitts noticed hotel employees putting up banners that read "Welcome National Pilots Association."

Thunderstruck, he hurried to find the hotel manager to insist the banners be changed to "Welcome NAL Buccaneers." But because it was late in the day and the banners had been prepared weeks in advance, the hotel's harried manager could do nothing about the mistake.

Jack Pitts had no alternative but to brazen it out, hoping no one would get too upset with the banners welcoming the "National Pilots Association," a name full of painful memories for ALPA loyalists. He was certain they'd notice, and he was right.

"Look at that!" snorts Sid Wilson, trim and elegantly dressed, as he pauses outside the main ballroom to stare at the banner. "National Pilots Association! Can you believe it? That's what the scabs called themselves in 1948!"

"You ought to hear what we called them!" exclaims Earl Marx, at 83 one of NAL's oldest retirees.

Bruce Wilson (no relation to Sid) and Ed Brown laugh with Earl Marx, whom they call the "Owl Man" because he always bid night flights. Bruce Wilson, whose horn-rimmed glasses give him a professorial air, gestures to the sign, saying, "We really don't attach much importance to the fact that scabs are eligible for the Buccaneers. But let them get into ALPA, get the ALPA benefits, just by paying a fine and back dues? No way!"

"ALPA wouldn't permit it," says Ed Brown. "Some of them tried several times—one even offered to pay $5,000 to get into ALPA."

"You forgive, but you never forget," adds Bruce Wilson. "Certainly time is a great healer of everything, but our gut feelings about scabs will always be there. They tried to ruin this profession."

"Some guys won't join because the scabs are allowed," says Ed McDonald.

"Right," agrees Sid Wilson. "Bobby Rohan says he won't, and he's been the heart and soul of ALPA on National ever since Charley Ruby left."

"You notice who's not here?" asks Ed McDonald.

"Charley Ruby," several voices answer at once. The knot of talking men is conspicuous because of its ALPA lapel emblems.

Throughout the remainder of the evening, at the banquet and at the cocktail party that follows, the stories flow. But always there is a certain tension, slight but palpable. No one in the room who walked a picket line in 1948 will ever be more than merely polite to the tiny contingent of scabs braving the obvious displeasure of those whose jobs they took in 1948. Such are the wages of strikebreaking.

The NAL strike of 1948 was like World War II—a good fight, a just cause, an evil foe. George T. "Ted" Baker, founder of NAL and its president during the strike, played Hitler to Behncke's Winston Churchill.

"If Ted Baker were here tonight," Sid Wilson says, "he'd walk in this room, charm the socks off everybody here, *if he wanted to,* buy drinks, waltz the ladies, you'd think he was the greatest guy in the world. He'd have everybody eating out of his hand. Tomorrow, he wouldn't know you, cut your throat in a second."

"Once I bought 150 gallons of gas on my own Texaco credit card," says Ed McDonald. "I was flying copilot for Herschel Clark. We were on the ground at Atlanta, and Herschel said, 'Put 75 gallons in each main.' And the gas man said, 'Who pays for it?' Herschel said, 'What do you mean who pays for it? National Airlines pays for it.' The gas man said, 'No, National's cut off:

we can't charge any more to National.' So Herschel climbed out of the cockpit and called Jacksonville, and sure enough, it's no mistake, our plane is full of passengers, we're out of gas, and our credit's cut off. So I bought the gasoline. And you know what? It took Baker _four_ months to pay my money back!" McDonald concludes to laughter from his friends.

"Ted Baker got religion once, right after the strike," Bruce Wilson remarks. "I was on a layover in Detroit, got hit by a car, and was out for 15 months. Mr. Baker came to my house and said, 'Bruce, I am going to pay your salary for as long as you are off.' So I said 'Gee Mr. Baker, thanks a million.' And he told all sorts of people he was going to pay my full salary, and everybody was so happy we gave him a big party out at the Coral Gables Country club and . . ."

"Boy, was _that_ ever a waste of money," interjects Earl Marx.

"Anyway, there must have been a dozen company executives who came around and said, 'Well, Bruce, you're going to get your full salary,' and during that party Baker even autographed my cast."

"Well, maybe a month had gone by after I got back to flying the line when one day my phone rang and it was Mr. Baker. 'Bruce, I was wondering how you wanted to pay back your loan?' And I said, 'What loan, Mr. Baker?' He said, 'Why, that money I loaned you while you were off.' I said, 'For crying out loud, Mr. Baker, I never asked you for a loan while I was off!' He said, 'Oh yes, that money was just a loan. I thought you understood that.'

"So I argued with him, trying not to get him irritated, because he was easy to irritate. I said, 'Mr. Baker, would you do me a favor and just think about this—think about the fact that it wasn't a loan, that you agreed to pay me?' I was hoping he might be in a good mood and change his mind. And Baker said, 'Bruce, I am not going to change my mind. I thought this all over before I ever paid you the money in the first place. Besides, Bruce, with the money you're making, you will never miss it.' He took every penny of it out of my salary."

Everyone has a story to tell about incidents on the picket line, about harassment from local southern police departments unfriendly to "communistic" labor unions. It took guts to walk a picket line in the South in the late 1940s, and NAL's routes were predominantly southern.

"Palmer Holmes rented two apartments in New Orleans," Bruce Wilson recalls, "and there must have been a dozen of us living there while we picketed. Well, we'd had some trouble with the scabs—the airport manager at New Orleans had complained to the police that we were harassing the scabs, and he wanted us arrested. Bill Bruen had a convertible, a Hudson, and we used to drive it to the airport from the apartment, which was on Royal, to picket. One morning the police came blazing up the stairs, started asking questions. 'Are you so-and-so? Come on, you're under arrest!' Everybody got put in jail: Bruen, Dean Cooper. Jerry Kepner was the only guy left to tell where we were.

"To make a long story short, somebody had murdered a prostitute and dumped her body in the back of Bruen's car parked out there on the street. Everyone was innocent, but of course the police didn't know that, and anyway they were looking for an excuse to get us off the picket lines. But that kind of thing will throw a scare into you."

As Charley Ruby can testify, the longer the strike went on, the greater was the possibility of real violence. "We had only 126 pilots available for picketing," Ruby remembers during an interview at his home in Jacksonville. "We were stretched thin; sometimes we could have only a couple of guys at a station for a week, then nobody. Mr. Behncke had good contacts with other labor unions, particularly the Seafarers International. They offered to help us, and at Norfolk they joined us on the picket line for a while. One tough old seaman asked me once, 'Can a guy fly with a broken leg?' Well, I knew what he was getting at, but I told him, 'No thanks,' we didn't need that kind of help just yet."

The first thing any student of the 1948 NAL strike has to understand is that the reason for the strike wasn't *really* what it seemed. Ostensibly, the strike was over the arbitrary dismissal of a pilot named Maston G. O'Neal, who damaged one of Baker's Lodestars during a landing at Tampa in September 1945. Tampa's Peter O. Knight Airport was only 3,500 feet long, with a dangerous seawall at one end, and there was a thunderstorm in progress. NAL old-timers think O'Neal did an excellent job that night and that he was almost certainly a victim of the then poorly understood phenomenon of hydroplaning. He touched down easily in the first third of the runway, but couldn't get braking action, so he initiated a ground loop to stop the aircraft short of the seawall. No one was injured. The Civil Aeronautics Board (CAB) found nothing amiss with O'Neal's landing, and at first it appeared that neither would NAL. Baker had a standing rule that "anybody who skins one of my airplanes is grounded for two weeks," so when Operations Chief E. J. Kershaw told O'Neal to take two weeks off, no one thought much about it.

The accident happened at 3:13 a.m. on Friday the 13th, and what was about to happen to 28-year-old Maston O'Neal would be enough to make anybody superstitious. Within a month, two more NAL Lodestars crashed, and although both pilots were guiltier of error than O'Neal had been, the fact that he was first roused Baker's ire.

Old-timers on NAL offered a more gossipy explanation for O'Neal's firing. "Maston was movie-star handsome, a former football player at the University of Miami, and he had a reputation with the ladies," remembers Edythe McDonald, wife of NAL retired pilot Ed McDonald. "George Baker also liked the ladies, and he was something of a rover." Mrs. McDonald pauses, a distant look in her eyes. Outside the McDonalds' Vero Beach apartment the surf pounds ceaselessly. "The stories were that he and Baker were in some kind of conflict over a woman. It might have been true, and that might have been what got him fired."

Those who knew Ted Baker even slightly admit that he was a free-wheeler in an era when that kind of behavior was uncommon. Indeed, the name of the NAL retired group, the "Buccaneers," stems directly from Baker's philosophy and reputation—wine, women, and song, except that NAL always came first.

"He was a skirt chaser, a notorious womanizer," Charley Ruby agrees, with more than a hint of contempt.

Did Maston O'Neal get fired because he beat Baker's time with a woman? "Hell no!" says Maston O'Neal heatedly. "There's absolutely nothing to that." A self-made millionaire, O'Neal lives in Miami and is anxious to tell the *real* story of what occurred in 1948:

> I was dating a girl, a secretary to one of Baker's buddies. There was nothing wrong with it—I was single and so was she. Now, it later turned out that this friend of Baker's was sweet on her, but I didn't know it at the time. The stories that I was romancing his wife, who was a wonderful, lovely lady, are just crazy gossip.
>
> The day after the crash at Tampa, I was back over at Miami, where there was an illegal gambling club. I had a date with this girl that night, and I was playing the craps table, and there across the table was Ted Baker, slapping down a 5 while I was slapping down a 20. He gave me a funny look. I guess maybe he thought I should have been back in my room doing penance for breaking one of his airplanes. Here I was out having a good time with one of his buddies' secretaries, and he obviously didn't like it. *That* is where those woman stories came from, and that's the absolute truth. Maybe Baker's buddy whispered in his ear, but I never stole a woman from Ted Baker.
>
> And I'm gonna tell you something else: that strike wasn't over Maston O'Neal. Boy, it really burns me up when some guy comes up and says, "So you're the one they went out on strike for in 1948." ALPA didn't go out on strike because of me. They went out because Ted Baker treated the pilots *like dogs!* But you can't strike because somebody abuses the hell out of you, you've got to have a legal reason. My firing was the only *legal* reason ALPA had for a strike. Little pebbles, if you pile them up long enough, make big fences, and there was one hell of a big fence between Baker and the pilots. It's like Dan Carmel, the ALPA lawyer, said to me during the presidential emergency board hearings up in Washington, "You're the Dreyfuss of the airlines." He meant I was just the symbol, not the real reason. [The Dreyfuss Case, in pre-World War I France, was a symbol of corruption because after a proven case of espionage, high-ranking politicians and military officers conspired to frame an innocent Jewish officer in order to divert attention from their own shortcomings.]

Dan Carmel was a brilliant guy. I lived up in Washington for six weeks during these hearings, and I got to know him quite well. He worked for Behncke, who was totally dedicated to getting me my job back. But that still doesn't alter the fact that my firing was just a symbol, like the Dreyfuss case.

Maston O'Neal is right. Behncke's first public statement on the strike cited "increasing apprehension on the part of pilots about flying planes whose safety aspects from the standpoint of maintenance are open to serious doubts." Baker promptly slapped Behncke with a $5 million slander suit, claiming that ALPA's use of safety as an issue was a "smokescreen."

A mechanics' strike had triggered the safety issue. NAL pilots hated crossing their picket lines. The pilots also feared that the airplanes were unsafe, and they were more than a little anxious about some hotheaded striking mechanic sabotaging a plane. In addition, ALPA was under pressure, having a terribly difficult time with the four-engine issue, and there was evidence that the Air Transport Association (ATA) was encouraging Ted Baker to be as obstinate as possible to provoke a strike. If ALPA could be broken by a lost strike on NAL, it could be broken elsewhere by similar means. If high management was ever going to rid itself of ALPA, now was the time.

NAL was the seventeenth airline to sign an employment agreement with ALPA. On Dec. 9, 1941, two days after Pearl Harbor and after a last-ditch resistance that had lasted nearly two years, Ted Baker allowed E. J. Kershaw to sign. Mac Gilmour, chairman of NAL's Council 8 at the time, signed for ALPA, as did Ernest A. Springer, Stroube Lander, and Charley Ruby. During the protracted contract negotiations, which began on June 16, 1941, Baker fired two pilots who had acted as negotiators. Almost immediately after the signing, Baker began violating the contract, so Behncke appealed to the National Mediation Board (NMB). One of the violations involved pilots who held reserve military commissions and who wanted to return voluntarily to active duty. Baker, who was notoriously unpatriotic, threatened to fire anybody who voluntarily went into uniform. Ed McDonald first roused Baker's ire by appealing to Behncke in Chicago when Baker refused McDonald's request for a military leave.

By June 1942, under the cover of wartime emergency, Baker began paying his pilots a lump sum monthly in an unorthodox arrangement that clearly violated the contract. He at first appeared indifferent to Behncke's threat of legal action, but later modified his attitude when Behncke made it clear that he was not bluffing. In addition, on April 26, 1942, CAB announced an investigation of NAL's pay policies and implied that Baker stood in jeopardy of losing his certificate. Baker announced publicly that he had had "a change of heart." It would not be the last time that he feigned a conversion.

Behncke told the meeting of ALPA's Central Executive Council (CEC), on

Jan. 22, 1942, that Ted Baker was "a tough one" who was unscrupulous enough to "take advantage of the President's proclamation against wartime strikes." In a typical maneuver, Baker had laid off a copilot named R. D. Fordyce, who had only one day remaining in his probationary copilot period, and then offered to rehire him as a new copilot. Baker once declared that copilots should pay *him* for flying. "He did this simply to materially reduce the copilot's pay scale," Behncke said. The CEC voted Fordyce a salary of $105 a month while ALPA appealed his case to the NMB. "Baker is an SOB, everybody hates him, including the neutral assigned by the NMB," Behncke said. As a warning to Baker that ALPA would no longer put up with his petty "contract chiseling," the CEC authorized a strike vote by NAL's pilots—a very unusual step in wartime. Baker pulled in his horns at this point, and things quieted down for a while.

In 1944, trouble again erupted on NAL when Baker hired a group of ex-Pan American Air Ferries pilots and slotted them as captains. Some NAL copilots were eligible for promotion to captain, but Baker ignored the seniority rule spelled out in the contract, contemptuously daring Behncke to take him before the NMB again. Behncke traveled to Jacksonville twice during January 1944, trying to straighten out the seniority problem on NAL. Baker and Behncke were taking an increasing dislike to each other.

By the time Maston O'Neal ground-looped his Lodestar at Tampa, NAL was becoming distinctly big time. Owing to Eddie Rickenbacker's political contentiousness, the Democratic administration in Washington had punished him by awarding a lucrative New York–Miami route to NAL, the principal airline in competition with Eastern Air Lines. Baker was buying a fleet of DC-4s and DC-6s, but all attempts to open negotiations with NAL on the four-engine pay issue broke down, as they had on other airlines. The NAL pilots, accustomed to Baker's peculiarities, continued plugging along. Among them were Herschel Clark (chairman of the negotiating committee), Charley Ruby, Bobby Knox, Jack Isbill, Dave Burch, and Mac Gilmour. Mac Gilmour reflects on the hazards of negotiating with Baker:

> I started with National in 1939 after working with the Skywriting Corporation of America. I was the eleventh pilot on the line. I found out quickly that if you projected too much unionism, you didn't last long on National. Negotiating with Baker was hairy; he had let so many of the ALPA chairmen go on one pretext or another. It seemed every time somebody got elected ALPA chairman, he was gone.
>
> I wound up in the hot seat in 1940. We fought so hard, Charley Ruby and I, we fought it out with Baker and won. I'm from a union background, the coalfields of Kentucky. I figured getting fired was worth it, if that's what it took. If it hadn't been for Mr. Disher of Pan American Grace Airways [Panagra], Baker would probably never have signed. I guess there were about 40 pilots on the seniority list in 1941, and just after Pearl Harbor there was a big

expansion of military contract operations. Mr. Disher came to see me and said if we didn't get a contract with Baker, he'd hire every one of us. He was downstairs waiting for us at our last conference with Baker, and we were fixing to walk out on National as a group and go with Panagra. That was how we got a contract. If we'd walked out, we'd have at least left a framework for somebody else.

After that, it seemed like Mr. Baker never forgave us for threatening to walk out and ground his airline. He was so antipilot; something in his personality made him hire executives who were hard on pilots. You couldn't be granted any kind of favor; seniority meant nothing. We had some real rough times. Baker wanted a pilot pool, wanted to assign people to trips, and it took us an awful long time to get bidding.

The strike in 1948 was just like walking into a sand trap and not knowing it was there. We'd taken so much heckling from Baker, and ALPA wasn't strong enough then to do anything about it. We had such a few men fighting for such a great cause. We were building a house to live in. We were fighting for ALPA's future. If we'd lost in 1948, there wouldn't be an ALPA today.

At the last minute, just before the NAL pilots were scheduled to walk out on Feb. 3, 1948, Baker might have offered to rehire O'Neal. O'Neal claims that an eleventh-hour deal was worked out to rehire him, but that it fell through because nobody at the temporary strike headquarters in the Everglades Hotel would talk to either Kershaw or Baker. Despite his subsequent financial success, Maston O'Neal remains a bitter man, angrier at Charley Ruby today than at the late Ted Baker, who fired him so long ago.

"You've got to remember," he says with some heat, "that I was 31 years old, I was broke. I had nothing going for me, and I had gone through this hell for three years. All I wanted was my job back. ALPA wanted that strike, wanted to teach Baker a lesson. That's the truth."

Perhaps. But it is also true that ALPA had come to O'Neal's aid in 1945, three years earlier, when Baker had said, "I have no doubt that Maston O'Neal can go through a pilot checkout course and be approved to fly on my airline again. But I am not going to reemploy him as a pilot because he lacks judgment. I have offered him other nonflying employment with NAL."

Baker made the statement on Sept. 17, 1945, right on schedule, just as O'Neal's company-imposed two-week grounding ended. The ALPA loyalists had been through a lot with Baker; they had watched him maneuver, lie, cheat, and steal. Charley Ruby, who was at NAL's creation in 1934, probably knew Ted Baker better than anyone. He'd heard Baker make similar deathbed statements and so thought it better to walk out, get a firm commitment to rehire O'Neal, and then cancel the strike. Dave Behncke agreed that a short walkout might have a therapeutic effect on Baker, but the decision to strike was entirely a local one.

What followed was the longest and costliest pilot strike in ALPA's history up to that point. Most of the NAL pilots thought the strike would be short. The winter tourist season, traditionally NAL's most profitable time, was in full swing. The NAL pilots thought they had Baker at such a disadvantage that he would have to submit to save his airline from catastrophic loss. Charley Ruby knew better:

> You ask if I knew that Baker would try to break the strike. I will tell you flatly, yes, I knew. I knew the man, and I knew the only way he would *not* try to break us was if he couldn't get pilots. When he began to get people to fly, I knew there was going to be trouble. I didn't say anything to my own crowd for the simple reason that it would have created a panic. We might have held Baker if some of our guys hadn't jumped the fence. When the first three decided to strikebreak, Baker knew he could use them as a nucleus to train other crews. What hurt was that one of the guys who scabbed on us was Fordyce, and he had a job only because of ALPA. Fordyce repaid us by scabbing.

Baker sent telegrams to the strikers informing them that they were fired. Then he began advertising far and wide for pilots. Through the Military Pilots Association and other contacts, Baker began signing on pilots to break the strike. The first 77 strikebreakers hired averaged 34 years old, with several listing 5,000 hours of pilot time and claiming recent time in the DC-4. (The backbone of NAL's fleet was still the old Lockheed Lodestar, but Baker had four new DC-6s ready for operation.) By March 1945, he was operating a token schedule of 14 flights daily. Passenger traffic was light, and he was obviously losing money. So he appealed to the CAB for financial aid in the form of increased mail subsidies, which was his right.

The unwritten story of the NAL strike of 1948, as it would be of the Southern Airways strike of 1960, was the role friendly bureaucrats played in sustaining the two companies. The federal government, in effect, underwrote the costs of the strikes by bailing out both Baker and Frank Hulse, head of Southern Airways, after the strikes induced by their own mismanagement brought their companies to the verge of bankruptcy. These bureaucrats were beyond the immediate power of the political process and were traditionally more at home with management than labor. In the long history of federal bureaucrats moving from a supervisory role in government to a high-salaried job in the industry that they formerly regulated, none is more blatant than the case of Edward P. Warner, the noted MIT professor who served on CAB until 1945. As a CAB member, his rulings invariably went against the pilots. In October 1945, Warner quit his $10,000-per-year government job to accept a $22,000-per-year appointment with the International Civil Aviation Organization (ICAO), largely upon the recommendation of the airline industry.

Robert J. "Bobby" Knox, who retired as a 747 captain in 1975, believes CAB was instrumental in helping Baker get his airline back in the air:

As soon as Baker found out he could get a few crews qualified, he lowered the boom. The CAB started helping him every way they could. I remember we didn't get those telegrams right away, and these three people, Fordyce, Wedge, and Royall, were just scared to death. I talked with those guys, trying to impress upon them the importance of staying together, that they were going to hurt their reputations around the country by being scabs. After that, the feeling got so heated that you didn't talk. I mean, if somebody saw you talking to one of those guys, they'd think you were a traitor.

Knox was well known as a banner-towing pilot. Mac Gilmour would write in smoke "DON'T FLY NATIONAL," while Knox towed a banner reading "NAL PILOTS ON STRIKE," timing their flights to coincide with NAL's. The Century pilots back in 1932 had done something similar by painting "CENTURY IS UNFAIR TO PILOTS" on the side of an aircraft. They used this aircraft to fly formation with E. L. Cord's Stinson Trimotors. By 1948, of course, such a tactic would have invited retaliation from CAB, so the smoke writing and banner towing were more appropriate.

By March 1948, the ALPA loyalists on NAL knew they were in for a long struggle. Some pilots left the battle to go back into the military; others wouldn't help with the picketing. ALPA paid the strikers as much as $500 per month, so there was no extreme financial hardship. But there was a considerable psychic hardship, particularly as the strike dragged on without resolution.

In May 1948, ALPA secured an overwhelming majority vote from the pilots of all airlines to respect the NAL pickets wherever they appeared. This would have crippled the industry to such an extent that Baker would have been forced to settle. ATA secured a court injunction against this tactic, however, and on May 10, ALPA lost another round when CAB approved increased mail payments to NAL. The bureaucrats were obviously going to subsidize the strikebreakers.

Dave Behncke became involved in the NAL strike only after it was in progress. Behncke, as we have seen, had a multitude of troubles in 1948, and the last thing he wanted was a distraction on a carrier like NAL. But the fight with Baker was well tailored to his strengths, for it ultimately involved an appeal to politics, something Behncke was adept at. After Baker completely replaced his ALPA crews, Behncke had but one recourse left—to take his case to Washington, bring maximum political pressure to bear on Baker, and, ultimately, seek to deprive Baker of his operating certificate if he continued on his course.

The exact pattern of Behncke's influence with the Truman administration is impossible to reconstruct because it was exercised indirectly, through the American Federation of Labor's political arm. Behncke moved adroitly to ally ALPA with the labor movement that was the key to Truman's faint hope of victory in 1948, and he did this when most airline pilots probably were becoming more conservative because of their economic status. Behncke courted Truman assiduously in the pages of *The Air Line Pilot,* repeatedly running stories favorable to his administration, candidacy, policies, and even his family.

Shortly after CAB agreed to subsidize Baker's strikebreaking by increasing his mail subsidy, Truman appointed an emergency fact-finding board, as called for under the provisions of the Railway Labor Act. On July 19, 1948, the emergency board reached its verdict. "What ALPA sought was reasonable," the board declared. "It did not seek the reinstatement of O'Neal, but only an impartial determination of the propriety of his discharge. Such a determination has not been made to this day. Failure to afford it caused the strike, and the responsibility rests with the carrier." The board also criticized Ted Baker's "juvenile" attitude in the matter, but that was as far as it could go. Its function was merely to offer a proposal to end the dispute, and it had no power to force either party to accept the proposal. The emergency board's suggestion of arbitration was the only reasonable one, but Ted Baker was having none of it.

The sad fact about the 1948 strike on NAL was that it lasted much longer than necessary because it coincided with a presidential election. If Dewey were to win, Baker would win—it was that simple. Dave Behncke was a long-time Democratic loyalist, but he was open-minded enough to support Republicans who voted right on ALPA's issues. In 1948, Behncke knew that a Democratic victory was ALPA's best hope. The Republican Congress of 1946-48, Truman's hated "do-nothing Eightieth Congress," did more than nothing on the labor front. It passed the Taft-Hartley Act, with its "right-to-work" clause, severely damaging the labor movement. Consequently, labor leaders were unanimous in their endorsement of Truman. Although nobody gave Truman much of a chance, he somehow managed to pull the greatest political upset in American history. The little man from Missouri owed it all to organized labor. Now he had to pay his debts, and part of the bill coming due would be charged to Ted Baker's account. The consensus among veteran ALPA members who participated in the 1948 strike is that, had the Republicans won, the pilots would never have gotten back their jobs.

The immediate object of Baker's concern after Dewey unexpectedly lost to Truman was CAB's dismemberment hearing, which would have revoked NAL's operating certificate and awarded its routes to Pan American, Delta, and Eastern. Behncke had no interest in destroying NAL, for that would have made the ALPA loyalists' job loss permanent. But he made certain that ALPA pressed its political advantage fully so that Baker would realize that he must either abandon the luckless scabs to fate or lose his airline.

"Patriotism," Samuel Johnson once said, "is the last refuge of a scoundrel." In Baker's case, religion was. In as curious an episode as ever happened in the history of aviation labor relations, Baker suddenly announced that, owing to a deep religious conversion that had put Christian love in his heart and forgiveness in his soul, he now wished to settle. He became a devoted admirer of Dr. Frank Buchman's Moral Re-Armament, a religious movement then much in vogue among corporate executives. Immediately after the presidential election, when Baker realized that he had backed the wrong horse, he departed for Buchman's Moral Re-Armament headquarters on Mackinac Island, Mich. As Ed McDonald remembers it:

> Not more than two days after the election I remember I was walking a picket in downtown Miami at the ticket office. Somebody inside called me and said Baker was on the phone. He wanted me to come up to Mackinac Island. About 50 people flew up there— about 20 pilots, the rest stewardesses, ramp personnel, ticket agents. Seems like Baker had been up there about 10 days. We got there and had a brunch, then old Baker put in an appearance. We all stood around in a circle, holding hands, promising to let the power of God settle our differences and let bygones be bygones. We stayed up there about four days, but we didn't see Baker any more after that.

Ed McDonald sounds somewhat cynical about the genuineness of Baker's religiosity. As we shall see in the next chapter, there was good reason for his skepticism. "Baker was the kind of guy who would drive a hundred miles out of his way to get even," Maston O'Neal remembers. As the unhappy aftermath of the NAL strike would show, Baker was capable of driving farther than that.

On Nov. 24, 1948, an agreement signed in Washington between NAL and ALPA ended the strike. The principal points of settlement included binding arbitration in the case of Maston O'Neal and the rehiring of all NAL strikers ahead of the strikebreakers, who would drop to the bottom of the seniority list. Baker had promised the scabs "permanent" employment; they now faced furlough. For the majority of the 168 scabs on Baker's payroll, the furlough was the only thing about Baker's promise that was permanent. Just 17 managed to survive on the airline after being recalled.

For Maston O'Neal, the outcome proved to be but one more disappointment in a long series of disappointments. The arbitrator, or "neutral," assigned to his case found against him down the line.

Another part of the settlement required each side to drop all pending litigation. Baker had sued Behncke for slander, seeking $5 million in damages after Behncke had said that NAL's planes were unsafe. Behncke had, in turn, countersued for $1 million, alleging that NAL's "willful attempt to break a lawful union contract" caused ALPA financial loss. As much as ALPA spent on the NAL strike, Baker had spent far more, reporting an operating loss of nearly $3 million for the 9-month, 21-day strike. James M. Landis, former chairman of CAB and future dean of the Harvard Law School, acted as mediator during the negotiations. (ALPA would be seeing more of James

Landis in the future—in 1960, he would try to unseat Clarence Sayen as president of ALPA.)

Despite Ted Baker's "sweet talk," as Sid Wilson puts it, which included an offer to let every striker buy 100 shares of NAL stock at a huge discount, there remained a suspicion that his new attitude was premised more on necessity than on conviction. Behncke had forced upon Baker a settlement that Baker hated and would shortly try to subvert.

As for Dave Behncke, the year 1948 marked his last political hurrah. He had cultivated politicians and fellow labor leaders for years. The NAL strike was the ultimate test of Behncke's ability to have the larger labor union movement serve ALPA's interests. Without the American Federation of Labor and the careful efforts of Dave Behncke to exert the power of the national labor movement in Washington, the battle might well have been lost.

In January 1949, Mr. and Mrs. David L. Behncke were official guests of President Truman at his inauguration. They stayed in Washington for a week, seeing the sights, relaxing, and attending a number of official parties and galas. Larry Cates, an ex-military pilot who flew a Beechcraft Bonanza regularly and who had replaced John M. Dickerman as ALPA's Washington representative, took Dave and Gladys Behncke flying. They flew down to the Virginia coast, where Behncke had participated in bombing exercises in 1928, and over the old Langley Field area, where the Behnckes' first son had been born in 1927. They finished the flight as the sun set, sailing slowly over the western suburbs, watching the lights come on over the city's marble monuments and edifices.

It was Dave Behncke's moment.

CHAPTER 14

The Ordeal of E. P. McDonald

Three little words—"You are fired!"

They can bring on a sinking feeling, for hardly any salaried professional is in a position to say "take this job and shove it" (to quote a well-known country-and-western song). Salaried professionals, such as stockbrokers, accountants, and college professors, can always find another job doing pretty much what they were doing before. Not airline pilots. A fired airline pilot rarely gets another job. ALPA has therefore worked very hard to make those three little words as difficult as possible for management to utter. ALPA established its Grievance and Conciliation Department in 1944, and only a pilot in serious trouble can understand how reassuring its existence can be.

Not every pilot ALPA has defended over the last 50 years deserved to be reinstated, but the lodestar of its policy has always been that the pilot deserved a full, fair, and orderly hearing. Sometimes Dave Behncke was a bit reluctant to defend a pilot accused of drinking on duty, but he never failed to do it. Historically, an argument can be made that management is far more likely to overlook safety violations than is ALPA—*if* you consider safety in totality, not just in the single area of pilot performance. And ALPA has never knowingly insisted upon the reinstatement of an incompetent pilot—it has just made sure that management, or the Federal Aviation Administration (FAA), proved actual incompetence beyond a shadow of a doubt.

At times, Behncke defended cases that rankled ALPA members. One such case involved an American Airlines pilot named Sisto, who jokingly engaged the gust lock of a DC-4 flying between Dallas and Los Angeles in 1948, causing it to roll inverted. Sisto lost his job, but Behncke defended his right to a full hearing, even though many ALPA members grumbled that such blatantly unprofessional conduct hardly merited ALPA's intervention. Behncke insisted, however, that every possibility of extenuation be exhausted before a pilot's termination. Even Sisto could argue, with some justification, that testing an airplane's performance with the gust lock engaged might add to aviation's overall knowledge. A revenue flight was hardly the place to conduct such an experiment, but nevertheless, a full, fair hearing is the way to establish that.

Edward Patrick McDonald's case provides the classic example of how an ordinary pilot benefits from ALPA when somebody tries to fire him for no good reason. Of all the incidents in which ALPA has defended pilots over the years, McDonald's case must necessarily be the microcosm, the one that illustrates all the others.

Ed McDonald is 66 now, retired from National Airlines (NAL) and living in Vero Beach, Fla., with his wife Edythe. His elegant shock of snowy hair, ruddy complexion, and cultured southern accent make Ed McDonald seem like one of those small-town bankers in a Tennessee Williams play—the kind whose beautiful daughter is about to run off with a handsome ne'er-do-well.

Ed McDonald might have been forced to become a businessman, had it not been for ALPA. The story of how he survived on NAL to become a 747 captain despite Ted Baker's attempt to fire him is a fascinating one. In the aftermath of the 1948 strike, Ted Baker vowed to "get" Ed McDonald and selected other strikers, including Charley Ruby and Bob Rohan. Baker's religious "conversion" notwithstanding, he would stop at virtually nothing to dismiss the "ringleaders" of the 1948 strike.

Robert J. "Bobby" Rohan, who was actively involved in ALPA's affairs on NAL from 1945 until his retirement, puts it simply: "The aftermath of the strike was worse than the strike itself."

They called it "The War of the Blues and Grays," and survivors of the NAL strike of 1948 unanimously agree that only a miracle prevented somebody from getting killed before it was over. Behncke's promise that ALPA loyalists on NAL would "never have to fly with a scab" proved impossible to keep. The back-to-work agreement required the scabs to go to the bottom of the seniority list (which meant, of course, that most of them would be furloughed). The 168 scabs had Baker's "promise" of a permanent job, but his promises in this area were no better than similar ones he had made earlier to ALPA pilots. There was one hitch, however. In the interim, until the ALPA loyalists could be requalified, the scabs would continue flying. This gave both the scabs and Baker a clever idea. What would happen, they wondered, if Baker could afford to keep all 168 scabs on payroll long enough to petition the National Labor Relations Board (NLRB) for an election to "decertify" ALPA as the airline's bargaining agent? There were only 145 ALPA strikers to begin with, and by the time the strike was settled, that number had shrunk to 126. That meant that the scabs could outvote the regular ALPA pilots, establish a new "union," and abolish the old seniority rules. Baker agreed to do it. So began "The War of the Blues and Grays."

The nickname referred to the color of the pilot uniform. As a token of his pledge of permanency to the scabs, Baker had changed the NAL uniform from gray to blue after the strike began. He had never paid his pilots an allowance for uniforms anyway, so this meant that on top of everything else the returning pilots would be out a good chunk of money for new working clothes. They rebelled at Baker's vengeful pettiness, returned to work wearing the prestrike gray uniform, and defied Baker to fire them. He backed down—it was only a few weeks since his miraculous "religious conversion," and he wasn't yet ready to shed what he called "the armor of faithful righteousness." So for the foreseeable future, the scabs would wear blue and the ALPA loyalists gray. Occasionally, this confused the passengers when a mixed scab-ALPA crew flew together. Had the passengers known what was going on in the cockpit, they would have been within their rights in asking for a parachute.

"We didn't get along very well," says Bobby Knox with considerable understatement. "We learned to control our trips to the bathroom pretty well. We used to sit in the cockpit and never get out, because you couldn't trust those fellows. Some of them would try to make a monkey out of you."

"They were simply looking for any excuse to fire us," says Charley Ruby. "If the weather got bad and you needed help in the cockpit, you couldn't depend on them. They'd sit there with their hands folded. One guy tried a stunt with me, tried to jimmy the squeeze handle on a DC-4 landing gear so it would retract automatically. We were going into Wilmington, and I told him to put the gear down. Then I saw his hand sneaking down. I hit him so hard I thought it would break his arm, just as he touched the squeeze handle. We were about 50 feet off the ground at that time."

There had been occasional fistfights on the picket line, and there would now be blows in the cockpit. It was probably a bad idea to mix scab and ALPA crews, but NAL's management insisted on it. This difficulty was actually a minor one, however, compared with Baker's attempts to fire ALPA's leadership group on NAL outright, in clear violation of the settlement.

His first tactic was medical. As part of the settlement, each ALPA striker had to take a standard medical exam with a physician of the company's choice. Charley Ruby smelled a rat in Baker's choice of the examining physician:

> Baker went after a lot of pilots who had been particularly active, or whom he had a grudge against for some reason or other. He didn't pick on me, but it was obvious that since I was a leader, a phony physical exam would only attract attention to what he was trying to do. We got Dr. C. T. Thompson of Miami to give our pilots physicals the day before they were assigned to go to that doctor on the beach. It was funny; sometimes our guys would finish their physicals at 8 p.m. and take the physical from this quack over on the beach the next morning, so you know nothing could have changed their condition in the meantime, unless they fell over dead. He turned down every one. We ultimately had to send our people up to either the Mayo Clinic or Johns Hopkins. Every one of them who was turned down by Baker's doctor passed. We made them look awfully foolish, and the doctor should have lost his license to prac-

tice medicine, but for some reason the medical fraternity didn't choose to blackball this crook. They were just trying to make more spaces for scabs to come in. We weren't about to lose what we had won. We anticipated they'd try to use medical exams, so we really had a loaded gun at their heads.

A more troubling tactic initially used by the company was to try to certify the "National Pilots Association," rather than ALPA, as the bargaining agent. The scabs hired a lawyer, incorporated under Florida laws, and petitioned the NLRB for a representational hearing, citing terms of the settlement both sides had signed after the strike election. ALPA went to federal court, charging that the company union was a violation of a duly signed contract. The court agreed, thus excluding the scabs from further participation on the grounds that only those pilots who had been working when the strike began were eligible to vote.

"I can understand a guy saying he's antiunion on principle," Mac Gilmour declares. "That's what all the scab boys said at first. Then they turned around and tried to form a union to save their jobs. That's one thing I can't forgive. I flew with some of these scab boys, treated them just like I would anybody else. But I could never forgive their abuse of the idea of union. That's a sacred thing to me. Maybe it's in my blood, from the coalfields."

Charley Ruby remembers it this way:

> This was all happening during the checkout period. Legally, under Title II of the Railway Labor Act, there was no way they could succeed with this decertification deal. The legal end of it was handled through the Chicago office. At our end, we handled it a little differently. You see, it's the captain's decision whether or not an engine is running a little too hot, and if it is, why, he can just enrich the mixture. We passed the word to all our guys as they began coming back on the line to run 'em rich. Now, I surely don't have to tell you how much fuel a 3,350-horsepower compound engine will burn if you never lean it out. We were burning more fuel than Baker could buy. Finally, Rosenthal, Baker's industrial relations man, called me and said, "We give up—you're breaking us."

But Baker hadn't really given up—he had merely staged a tactical retreat owing to economic necessity. Originally, the ALPA strikers feared that Baker would use the checkout process to eliminate them. They anticipated that trick and avoided it by contractual guarantees in the settlement. All check rides would be given by pilots from other airlines, temporarily assigned to NAL with ALPA's concurrence. Since the backbone of NAL's fleet was still the old Lockheed Lodestar, an aircraft few airlines operated anymore, this presented something of a problem. Two pilots, Leo Cullen of Mid-Continent (later Braniff) and Buck Steers of Northeast Airlines, were eventually found to begin checking out the returning strikers.

"Within about six weeks most of us were back on the line, and the scabs were just standing around, never getting a flight, still on payroll and costing Baker a bundle," says Bob Rohan. "That didn't mean they were through trying. Lou Dymond was top of the breed, and Ed McDonald was strictly a victim of Lou Dymond trying to get him. It was a setup."

Flight 406 from Miami to New York departed at 8:20 p.m. on Dec. 21, 1949. The captain of the DC-6 was Ed McDonald, and his copilot was an excaptain, a scab named Hettenbaugh, who was also president of the scab union. McDonald had been, in his own words, a "rabble-rouser" for the strike, and he was on Ted Baker's "hit list." Jesse Mays, a nonpilot flight engineer, rounded out the crew. But riding in the jump seat was NAL's Vice-President for Operations L. W. Dymond, a "captain" who had never flown on an airline before the strike and who subsequently "checked out" as a scab. His pilot qualifications were minimal, and he had already had one accident as a copilot, hitting the approach lights during landing at New York's Idlewild several months earlier.

On Dec. 29, 1949, McDonald received a letter from Joe Bailey, NAL's chief pilot, informing him that he was fired because of a report submitted on his performance by Dymond. The report alleged that McDonald had committed six "unsafe" acts during the December 21 flight, including "poor flying technique, and extreme poor judgment" during an ILS (instrument landing system) landing at Newark. In a move reminiscent of the Maston O'Neal case, Bailey wrote: "We desire to retain your services with the company, but not in a flying position. I will be happy to discuss the nonflying position with you at your convenience." (Maston O'Neal speculated the nonflying position Baker had in mind for him was baggage handler.)

McDonald promptly appealed to his local ALPA council for help. It had taken a full-scale strike to get a neutral hearing for Maston O'Neal, but McDonald was luckier. His future as an airline pilot would ride with the judgment of Saul Wallen, a professional arbitrator assigned by the National Mediation Board (NMB).

As Sid Wilson put it: "Eddie was just damn lucky he got an honest neutral." Saul Wallen *was* an honest man, and unlike the arbitrator who had found against Maston O'Neal at Winter Haven, Fla., a few months earlier, he also knew something about aviation. (ALPA saw to that.) NAL had secured a neutral's favorable opinion in the O'Neal case largely because the neutral was ignorant of aviation. NAL counted heavily on a similar neutral in McDonald's case. Every ALPA loyalist who lost a job opened up one more position for a scab who was on the payroll but not flying, so it was to the company's advantage to bring dismissal charges. The scab union, we must remember, was still trying to unseat ALPA as the bargaining agent for NAL's pilots.

McDonald admits that he had trouble with the ILS that night, but every veteran of the 1948 strike seemed to have trouble with ILS approaches, particularly during check rides. They just couldn't keep the needles crossed and centered. Neither could the check pilots. Most of the NAL strikers believe the extreme sensitivity of the ILS needles was no accident, as Charley Ruby explains:

> Nobody could fly the ILS worth a hoot. We finally found out that somebody had hooked up both heads of what was supposed to be a dual repeater sending signals to both sides of the cockpit to just one head on the pilot side. It became so supersensitive you were either on that thing or way off. Well, we got that straightened out, and then we found that somebody was tampering with the sensitivity screw just before check rides. It got so bad nobody would go up for a check ride alone.
>
> The airline was small enough that I knew everybody, knew the guys who were super, the ones who were marginal. It was the supersharp ones who were having trouble with checks. So we pulled the panel off and found this tampering, and I marched into Rosenthal's office and threatened to bring the roof down. We put the fear in them, so the tampering stopped, at least temporarily. Nobody in management knew how to fool with the instruments anyway, so they had to use some technician. Whoever had actually done it was afraid he'd get caught after we figured that little game out. He knew nobody in management would ever own up to putting him up to it. This involved safety violations of the worst sort. That ruckus with Ed McDonald was, if anything, worse because they were laying for him, interfering with his function as pilot-in-command, and they got the guy so worked up, yelling at him, that it was a miracle he got the airplane on the ground at all.

"We were under this old-time crazy deal of 500 feet on top," McDonald says of the approach and landing which would get him fired. "I was trying to concentrate on instruments, and one of them would say 'Hey, look out for that airplane over there!' I'd go off instruments to look, and the plane would be way off, no danger, but by then my needles would be gone to hell." He made two approaches, broke out wide of the runway on the second approach, but still managed to land. A stewardess testified that McDonald landed two-thirds of the way down the runway.

From Ed McDonald's viewpoint, the whole thing was avoidable. The afternoon before the flight he asked Dymond to replace Hettenbaugh as his copilot. When Dymond refused, he went to other company executives, but all of them refused too. The documented fact that McDonald had asked for a replacement copilot weighed heavily with the neutral referee, Saul Wallen, when Wallen began digging into the details of what actually happened that night.

"Hettenbaugh and I had gotten into a fistfight in the cockpit," McDonald says quietly.

That was a day or two before. The morning of the flight, I went

right into Dymond's office and told him about it. I said I didn't want
to fly with the guy anymore. Dymond said, "Well you're going to,
and if you can't handle the job, why don't you quit?" Then I went to
the airport that night and Dymond came walking in, went over to
Hettenbaugh, and started being very lovey-dovey. I knew right
then I was out in the woods by myself.

I should have called Ruby or Rohan and said, "Hey look! I want
to go on the record right now. I'm rigged. They're going to try to
fire me, they're going to cause trouble tonight." I'd give anything if I
had.

But I went up there, with all the interruptions and lack of cooperation and antagonism in the cockpit. You know, Dymond hol-
lering, "Look out for Calco stack!" And the stack is two or three
miles away. And, "There's an airplane over there; there's one over
there!"

I had enemies riding with me and I knew it, and they had me dis-
tracted pretty damn bad.

In an extensive brief answering the six charges against McDonald, ALPA
argued that he had done nothing critically wrong during the approach and
landing and that managing to get the aircraft safely on the ground at all was
"in the best tradition of airline flying," because he was coping with an
emergency tantamount to mutiny in the cockpit. "Captain McDonald was
not given the cooperation from other crew members which a pilot is entitled to receive," the ALPA brief stated.

One of the six charges against McDonald was that he "caused the flight to
be placed in extreme hazardous proximity to surrounding obstructions
during the missed approach procedure, thereby endangering the lives of
all aboard." The company cited the nearness of Calco stack. Another
charge, leveled by Dymond, was that McDonald had allowed the course
deviation indicator to deflect full-scale and that his decision to land after
breaking out of the overcast "75 to 100 feet to the left of the runway could
have resulted in a fatal accident."

Fortunately for McDonald, not a single passenger aboard Flight 406
complained about the rough, long landing Hettenbaugh and Dymond allegedly had observed. Also, the flight engineer, Jesse Mays, contradicted
both of Dymond's assertions in sworn testimony. Neutral Wallen's conclusions relied heavily on the testimony of Mays, who must have been a courageous individual. Wallen concluded:

Jesse Mays was in a difficult position. As an individual without the
protection of a labor organization, who flew during the strike with
the "blue" pilots before the return of the "gray," and dependent
solely on the good will of management for his job, it was not surprising that he was uncomfortable. But even he testified that the
glide path indicator was *not* high to the extent of a full deflection,
as Dymond vehemently asserted, but to the extent of crossing

about at the second dot below the bull's-eye.

If the sharp corrections attributed to McDonald by Dymond had been made, it is hardly likely that the motion of the ship would not have been apparent to Mays.

The testimony of both Dymond and Mays refutes the charge that McDonald caused the flight to be placed in extreme hazardous proximity to surrounding obstructions. Dymond stated that the pull-up for the missed approach during the first attempted landing began at least a mile before the stack and that in that mile the aircraft would have climbed to 1,200 feet above the stack, while a 500-foot separation would be reasonable.

Neutral Wallen could make these factual assertions because ALPA had financed a full flight test demonstration in a DC-6, with Mr. Wallen himself sitting in the jumpseat so he could observe exactly how dangerous it was to bend the plane around to land from "75 to 100 feet left of the runway," as NAL claimed. The simulation of McDonald's flight took place on May 29, 1950. Let Ed McDonald tell about it:

> Well, you know, 100 feet is not a lot to be off to one side of the runway. They blindfolded Wallen until they told him 'Okay, there it is,' when I would have broken out at an altitude of 400 feet, and then the guy just bent it around and pulled the prow up and landed the damn airplane. They did that three times, showing him that you could be off 10 feet and get a full-scale deflection if you're close enough.
>
> And they just explained it to the neutral like that. He and I never conversed at all, although I sat right there in the audience for two weeks at the Monte Carlo Hotel in Miami. Oh, he'd speak to me: "Good morning Captain McDonald, good morning Mrs. McDonald," you know, but there was always a bunch of good ALPA people to speak for me, guys like Slim Babbitt and Jerry Wood of Eastern.

As for the company witnesses, Neutral Wallen all but called them liars, particularly with respect to their charge that McDonald landed "4,000 feet up a 6,600-foot runway." Wallen declared that these charges were "without substance," and he criticized "Miss Turner's obvious exaggeration," which had McDonald landing "three-quarters of the way up the runway."

Wallen summed up his findings as follows:

> While Captain McDonald made a somewhat more ragged approach than normal, Dymond, an observer, usurped the function of the captain and issued instructions that conditions did not warrant.
>
> The conditions precedent to the flight were in large measure responsible for McDonald's performance. A review of his record shows not one blemish, reprimand, warning, or caution. In his

eight years with National Airlines, he has never damaged an airplane, and on the trip which terminated in his discharge, there was no damage to the aircraft nor complaints from the passengers.

The System Board is convinced that the presence of Hettenbaugh and Dymond in the cockpit resulted in an atmosphere of tension that was not conducive to a perfect approach and landing. On a previous trip, Hettenbaugh had argued with McDonald during the flight and had delayed in executing his orders. This conclusion is amply supported by Flight Engineer Cunningham's testimony about the Dec. 18, 1949, trip.

The job of flying a DC-6 airplane, beyond all other employments of which the referee has knowledge, requires the closest cooperation between crew members. McDonald talked to Dymond regarding Hettenbaugh's conduct on the December 18 flight shortly before Flight 406 departed on December 21. Both Dymond and Captain Royall had foreknowledge of the difficulty between the two men. Neither took the sensible precaution of separating them, although either of them had the authority to assign another copilot. To permit men overtly hostile toward one another to undertake such a flight when the safety of the public is involved is a serious mistake. But that is exactly what Dymond and Royall did.

The evidence is ample that McDonald did not have the cooperation of his crew mates. All concerned admit that Hettenbaugh did not call out airspeeds during the approach and would not inform the tower of timely maneuvers without prompting from McDonald.

Finally, the System Board is of the opinion that Dymond's behavior in the cockpit was not helpful. His shout "Look out for the Calco stack" seems to have been needless. His cry "Reverse the props" was of questionable value. A comparison of pilots' records shows that the carrier has retained in its employ other pilots who have been involved in mishaps more serious. Among these is Dymond, the chief witness against McDonald. There was no background of antagonism between the crew of which he was member to explain an approach short of the runway at Idlewild on Apr. 30, 1949, shearing off certain runway zone lights and damaging the undercarriage. Despite this hazard to life and damage to equipment, no examination of Dymond's judgment and technique took place, and he was subsequently promoted.

In McDonald's case, a much stricter standard of judgment, under circumstances of lesser hazard and damage, seems to have been applied. Fair treatment to pilots seems to require a uniform approach to such cases.

It is our conclusion that the weight of the evidence does not demonstrate that the discharge of Capt. E. P. McDonald was for just cause.

Neutral Wallen's opinion is the most devastating indictment of management's vindictive injustice toward one of its pilots that exists anywhere in the annals of commercial aviation. He ordered McDonald reinstated with full back pay, his personnel record cleared of all references to his dismissal, and a return to active flying after a checkout by "an unbiased check pilot."

Where would E. P. McDonald have been without ALPA? Would his fellow NAL pilots have bridled at the obvious injustice done to him and gone out on strike once more, as they did in the case of Maston O'Neal? Ed McDonald is realistic about it:

> They wouldn't have done a thing, and I can't much blame them. They were so beaten down by nine months and three weeks of walking the picket lines, and then the fiasco of that doctor saying some of them had heart attacks, they were just, you know, a little shot down. And the CAA [Civil Aeronautics Administration], we tried to get somebody to show up and testify, just _sit in._ No-o-o. These CAA inspectors were scared to death of their jobs, afraid of people like Baker. No help at all. It was strictly ALPA, the national office. Without them I'd have been a goner, without old Dave Behncke, God bless him.
>
> About a year ago at a pilots' luncheon, Dymond showed up. The old-timers who retired, all of those who were on the picket line, were sitting around a big bar at The Brothers Two in south Miami, and Dymond came in. He walked right straight across the room to me and stuck out his hand. And I shook it. My feeling was, I guess, that we were in a public place, don't start any trouble, don't embarrass your friends, so I went along with it. I shook his hand.
>
> But I wish I hadn't.

And what of the principals in this little drama? Hettenbaugh lasted only a few months before drifting away into obscurity, like the great majority of the scabs. Dymond, who had been a nonpilot executive before the strike, never flew the line again after ALPA's loyalists returned to work.

"When I took the chief pilot's job in 1954," Charley Ruby says emphatically, "I sent Baker a letter stating categorically that my main condition was that I would take orders from him and nobody else. I sure wasn't going to take orders from an amateur like Dymond who was never anything but Baker's flunky anyway. He was persona non grata as far as I was concerned. Baker thought it over for awhile, then said 'O.K.'"

Maybe Ed McDonald got the last laugh after all. ✈

CHAPTER 15

The Fall of Dave Behncke

S ome kinds of history are easier to write than others. A history based on oral sources, such as this one, comprises not only memories gone astray, but also the highs and lows in the lives of its notables. Happiness, the flush of victory, and calm satisfaction are emotions that are fine to remember and wonderful for setting the fires of enthusiasm dancing in the eyes of those who have seen their full share of seasons. These emotions are also fine for a historian—good vibrations resonate easily across long gaps of time, and it's easy to feel them and to share the good old times with those who remember them so well.

But what about the bad times? They are as much a part of the story as the good ones, but they don't rekindle the friendly fires of yesteryear. Rather, they bring pain and pursed lips, sudden awkward silences, wrinkled brows, and even deliberate evasions, the kind designed to stifle memory and to bury things that, hard enough to live through, are no easier to remember.

Such a time was the ouster of Dave Behncke from the presidency of ALPA. Not once, in all the interviews that make up this history, have those who participated in the ouster expressed any sentiment other than sorrow. There was no joy in it for anybody, no flush of victory, no satisfaction. A generation later, people still remember the ordeal of Dave Behncke with only one emotion—deep, abiding pain.

The pilots who removed Behncke from office *liked* the "Old Man," deeply respected him for what he had done, and hoped against hope that he would see that his time had passed and that he must make way for a new day. They all agreed that, by trying to hang on, Dave Behncke was destroying not only ALPA but himself as well.

But Dave Behncke didn't know how to do anything but fight, he had been fighting all his life, and he couldn't stop.

By 1950, ALPA was entering a new era of high technology and rapid change. The Association claimed approximately 6,000 dues-paying members, and was at the apex of an industry that was growing faster than anybody would have believed possible just a few years earlier. So far as intercity passenger transportation was concerned, the handwriting was already on the wall—the railroads must inevitably give way to aviation. That meant

149

that ALPA affairs would no longer concern only elite travelers, but everybody.

The new world of commercial aviation was a big one, and Dave Behncke was increasingly lost in it. His worst failing in these years was an utter inability to delegate authority. The 1944 convention had authorized a full professional structure for ALPA, consisting of 11 departments. Among the 44 people employed full-time by ALPA, a fair number were professionals, like Ted Linnert of Engineering and Air Safety, who should have been allowed to manage as they saw fit. But Behncke had to have a hand in *everything* that went on in every department, usually even minute details.

Even worse was Behncke's habit of becoming fixated on particular problems. For example, the early troubles of the Martin 202 caused Behncke to devote far too much time to engineering problems. He habitually ordered other ALPA staffers to "drop everything" to help when a critical problem arose. Although that might have been justified occasionally, Behncke did it constantly.

"He would call me at all hours of the night," Ted Linnert says, "particularly after a crash. He was very much affected by the Winona, Minn., crash of an NWA [Northwest Airlines] Martin 202. A metal fatigue problem caused a wing to come off. We went to the Martin factory; they were beautiful airplanes, all upholstered and painted. He went into the cabin, and I was behind him, and I'll never forget how he turned around after a long silence and said, 'Ted, can you imagine the experience of this plane tumbling out of the sky, the way those 50 people felt, and the pilots?'"

As we have seen, a measure of dissatisfaction with Behncke's leadership was already manifest by 1947, when Willis H. Proctor of American Airlines (AAL) challenged Behncke during the convention. Proctor's bid for the presidency was the first serious challenge to Behncke since the early days, when a number of pilots favored Frank Ormsbee for the permanent presidency of ALPA. Ormsbee almost single-handedly organized Pan American World Airways (PAA) pilots in 1931 and got fired for his trouble. Behncke subsequently hired Ormsbee to be ALPA's Washington representative. He was so effective that many early pilots thought he was a better choice than Behncke for the ALPA presidency. Ormsbee was, after all, unemployed, so he wouldn't have to give up a job as Behncke would. And Ormsbee was extraordinarily sharp. He was the first to suggest, among other things, that the locus of ALPA's activities in the early 1930s should be Washington, not futile and dangerous strike confrontations spread around the country. He also argued from the very beginning that ALPA should concentrate on securing a pilots' amendment to the Railway Labor Act of 1926. Behncke subsequently adopted both of Ormsbee's ideas, although he delayed much too long in the latter. Ormsbee's powers of intellection, persuasion, and analysis were formidable. He also had something else going for him, something Behncke couldn't help but envy—Ormsbee had won the Congressional Medal of Honor in combat during World War I as a naval aviator.

In 1934, Behncke fired Ormsbee on trumped-up charges of "conduct unbecoming a member" (although Ormsbee was not technically a member of ALPA, since he no longer worked for PAA). Behncke's jealousy of Ormsbee and his fear that Ormsbee might be a competitor for the leadership of ALPA led him to the first major display of the kind of vindictiveness that would later become more evident, and it left many early airline pilots feeling uneasy about Behncke's mental balance. They knew perfectly well that Ormsbee had been guilty of nothing more than doing an excellent job and that this excellence had inspired Behncke's jealousy.

Given Behncke's nearly hysterical reaction to the Ormsbee affair, Willis Proctor's challenge in 1947 was pure déjà vu, even to Behncke's preferring charges against him for "conduct unbecoming a member" after the convention was over. An immediate and irate reaction, particularly among the large AAL membership, forced Behncke to abandon his vendetta against Proctor. Proctor was a poor candidate for the ALPA presidency in any case, for he was even older than Behncke, and a great many younger AAL pilots were clearly lukewarm about his candidacy. Were it not for the survivors who remember the Proctor challenge, historians today would have no way of knowing it ever happened. Behncke totally eradicated all mention of it from most ALPA records, including *The Air Line Pilot.*

The big question on everybody's mind by the late 1940s was Behncke himself. Things were not going well with ALPA: contract negotiations were generally deadlocked everywhere, and ALPA's administration was suffering from Behncke's increasingly eccentric paperwork. Behncke seemed unreceptive to new ideas, particularly those of the younger leaders emerging from the local councils.

Something had to be done about the Old Man, but what? In one of those compromises that foreshadowed the end while seeking to avoid it, the 1947 convention mandated changes in ALPA administrative structure, the most important being the new office of executive vice-president. The delegates to the 1947 convention envisioned this new officer as one who would handle ALPA's day-to-day affairs, relieving Behncke for more general work. In short, the membership was already trying to kick Behncke upstairs to less taxing work, to make him the de facto "president emeritus" as early as 1947.

The 1947 convention, the first one held since 1944, took place at the Edgewater Beach Hotel in Chicago in February. Aside from mandating the new office that would eventually be filled by Behncke's successor, Clarence N. Sayen, the 99 delegates to the 1947 convention also made changes in ALPA's governance that would be important in Behncke's ouster. The most important change was the creation of the Executive Board to replace the old Central Executive Council, which had begun as an ad hoc advisory group in the early 1930s and became only slightly more regular as the years passed. The new Executive Board was composed of two representatives from each airline, a captain and a copilot. This arrangement proved cumbersome owing to the large number of people involved, so the 1950 convention reduced its size by 50 percent. A single delegate would represent each airline under the 1950 revision, with a captain and a copilot alternating each year. (We will discuss the changing status of copilots— who became known as "first officers" owing to the dispute over crew complement with the flight engineers' union— when we take up Clarence Sayen, who was never more than a copilot.)

If any man could be called ALPA's "kingmaker" during the 1940s, it would be Vern Peterson. Now 73 and living in Florida retirement, Peterson brings a special perspective to Behncke's problems in the late 1940s, since he was largely responsible for the changes made at the 1947 convention:

> Dave Behncke was still in full possession of his faculties, he was the same person he had been in the early days. The problem was that everything else was changing. He always worked day and night, worked himself to death over details. Later, by the time we had to relieve him of the ALPA presidency, around 1950 or so, he was much changed, a different man really, clearly suffering from some sort of mental breakdown.
>
> The big problem, we believed, was simply one of overwork. Our decision to mandate a new officer, the executive vice-president, was prompted mostly by the fact that Behncke needed assistance, there were many things he couldn't get around to, and he would delay, delay. Things were often on dead center. Our thinking was that if he had a good assistant, he would be able to get things done.

Behncke agreed to the creation of the office of executive vice-president (he really had no choice), but he didn't like it, and he delayed filling the position for over a year. Even after he selected Sayen, a Braniff copilot, for the office, Behncke continued pretty much as he had before. So the old problems of tardy paperwork, inadequate attention to important matters, and excessive concern with minor ones continued to plague ALPA. And Behncke's health kept getting worse. In 1949 he was in and out of the hospital on several occasions.

Vern Patterson recalls, "Sometime around 1950, I saw Behncke after quite a spell. The problems with him had been sort of hard to put your finger on before, but this time his appearance had really changed. He had lost weight from well over 200 pounds to a mere wisp of 150 pounds or so. There was some question as to his physical ability to carry on."

The frustrations with Behncke's failings as a leader were fed by considerable concern among the membership over technological unemployment. The new, faster aircraft coming rapidly into service in the late 1940s had reduced the need for pilots. Junior pilots commonly faced furlough, and the problem was on everybody's mind. Behncke was the focus of much exasperation among junior ALPA members, partly because he seemed incapable of formulating a workable solution and partly because his ideas seemed totally inadequate, even archaic.

Behncke forced an industrywide deadlock in contract negotiations over what he called the "mileage limitation." It was reminiscent of the deadlock which brought on the 1946 Transcontinental and Western Air (TWA) strike, but by 1950 the membership was in no mood to endure a strike that would not result in a permanent solution to the problem. Essentially, the proposal measured work loads on all new aircraft against what a pilot could accomplish in the DC-3, which Behncke still insisted (as late as 1951) was the "standard" airliner. If a pilot could fly a DC-3 at 160 miles per hour under the guideline of 85 hours per month established by Decision 83, Behncke reasoned, he could legally fly 13,600 miles per month. Behncke therefore proposed a new negotiating standard for all future ALPA contracts that would contain this mileage limitation regardless of the type of aircraft. A pilot might fly many more passengers in a DC-6 than in a DC-3, but he would not fly them any more *miles.* This would reduce pilot work loads, reduce technological unemployment, and probably lead to the hiring of more pilots.

There wasn't a chance in the world that the airlines would ever agree to the mileage limitation. Many airline pilots thought the reasoning behind it was faulty, even though it was clear enough in its direction and would obviously accomplish some of ALPA's purposes. Remember, most airline pilots were as committed to the abstract idea of "progress" as they were to the well-being of their respective airlines. The mileage limitation idea was clearly backward looking, and it bothered many pilots. The jets were already something more than a gleam in the eye of aircraft manufacturers. What would be the effect of a 13,600-mile-per-month limitation once these aircraft became a reality? So Behncke got nowhere when he began proposing mileage limitation during contract negotiations in 1947 and 1948. By 1950, every ALPA contract in the nation had lapsed owing to Behncke's dogged determination to include the mileage limitation. Also, for the first time in the memory of ALPA old-timers, there were rumbles in the local councils that Behncke was out of his league.

Jerry Wood recalls Behncke's intransigence as a negotiator:

> Dave was inclined to run everything into a deadlock so he could get a presidential emergency board and get it arbitrated. He was also inclined to tell us what we could do and what we couldn't do. Beginning about 1950 you couldn't do things that way anymore. You had to negotiate them out. We had trouble with Dave. He was a great one, the right man at the right time, but with the coming of four-engine equipment and complicated work rules, these weren't things you could leave to arbitration, because chances are,

the arbitrator wouldn't know a damn thing about it. Dave was inclined to want to do things that way.

As ALPA's contracts with every airline in the nation began to expire, the
mileage limitation (or "mileage increase determination," as Behncke
labeled it) was the millstone dragging down everything else. The airlines
stood ready to negotiate such issues as gross weight pay, a minimum
monthly guarantee, landing pay, deadhead pay, even the long-sought new
method of computing copilot pay. TWA's Director of Flight Operations
Frank Busch told Karl Ruppenthal that if Behncke would withdraw his insistence on the mileage limitation, Ruppenthal would "guarantee a new
contract in three days."

It all came to a head on AAL. The AAL pilots, doggedly loyal to Behncke's
line at that point, voted overwhelmingly to strike. On Jan. 13, 1951, acting
under terms of the Railway Labor Act to prevent a shutdown (the Korean
War was in progress, so a strike was clearly impossible), President Truman
appointed an emergency board. David L. Cole served as chairman of the
board, and the other members were Frank P. Douglass and Aaron Horvitz,
all experienced professional arbitrators. The hearings, which lasted until
April 27, 1951, covered excessively complex issues. No agreement between ALPA and AAL emerged during the hearings. While the hearings
were in session, things began unraveling for Dave Behncke. A revolution
was in the making.

The catalyst in Behncke's downfall was the ALPA professional staff. Tired
of continuous operations at all hours of the night and day with no overtime
pay, of Behncke's bullying, and of being away from their homes for weeks
at a time with regular vacations an impossible dream, they decided to form
their own union, the ALPA Professional Employees Association. Behncke
angrily refused to recognize them, so they planned a strike. But first they
approached a group of senior captains. Ted Linnert, dubbed "Fair-and
Square Linnert" by all who knew him, insisted that senior pilots know of
the chaotic conditions Behncke was causing before the staff went on strike.

The emergency board was in the midst of its work when the employees
met with the committee of senior pilots, which in turn approached
Behncke about the professional employees' grievances. A stormy session
followed, during which Behncke insisted that only a couple of "troublemakers" were responsible for the problem. He said that he would sign a contract specifying reasonable working conditions for ALPA employees, but
he refused to do so immediately. Instead, he directed Clarence Sayen to
handle the problem.

The next day, Dave Behncke suddenly left New York, returned to Chicago, and checked into a hospital. He left orders with Sayen to discontinue
ALPA participation in the emergency board hearings, canceled all credit ar-
rangements at the hotel where ALPA's dumbfounded employees had been

staying, and ordered the staff to return to Chicago. Behncke was, in short, breaking off ALPA's participation in a major presidential emergency board while it was in full progress, at a time when it would have a major impact on the nation owing to the Korean War. An ad hoc committee of ALPA's biggest guns, including First Vice-President Jerry Wood, rushed to New York to straighten out the mess. They were determined that the board was going to proceed with or without Behncke.

Henry Weiss worked closely with Behncke during these emergency board hearings, and he was shocked at Behncke's behavior:

> A group of pilots met with Behncke in my presence and told him "Now look. You've got to stop interfering with this board. It's got to go forward at all costs, because if it breaks down, we will look like idiots in front of the industry and the world." They urged him to take a leave, because he was sick, physically sick, and he looked it, and was in fact advertising that he was sick. But they said, "This thing has got to go on, even without you! We don't want to hurt you, we want you to continue as our president, but you have to make a choice—either go on a holiday and let our general counsel (meaning me) and our executive vice-president handle this thing, or else."
>
> Well, Dave said that he understood, that he would allow Clancy Sayen to handle the board. But they didn't trust him, and they kept a member of that senior group of pilots there, almost as a guard during the whole board, seeing that Behncke did what he said he would do.
>
> What stands out in my mind very sharply is that about an hour after that meeting, Dave and I were alone in his suite and I said, "Dave, I'm sure they meant well by you." I remember his gesture. He took the forefinger of his right hand, and ran it across his throat like a knife. He said, "When this is over, I'll do it to every single one of those bastards."

Somebody had to do something about Dave Behncke now—but *who,* and how? By the time of the AAL presidential emergency board, concern among ALPA members from many different airlines was strong. Most of it came from men who held office in ALPA and who were consequently aware of the deteriorating situation. Against their will, these men were rapidly becoming revolutionaries—there is no other word for it.

At the time of Behncke's bizarre breakdown before the AAL emergency board, there were two separate governing bodies in ALPA. When one captain and one copilot from every local council (no matter how small) assembled on command of the national headquarters, they were officially the "convention." When this constituency voted by mail ballot, it became the "Board of Directors." In either guise, these individuals were the supreme authority in ALPA. By their very nature, these bodies were incapable of decisive action because there were infrequent meetings and little communication between members and because the vast majority of their members were not in sufficiently intimate contact with affairs outside their own airlines to understand the magnitude of the breakdown at the top.

Only the Executive Board was capable of decisive action, but its mandate was vague. Consisting of a single pilot representative from each airline, whether large or small, the Executive Board was essentially an interim advisory committee. Six tiny airlines with a handful of pilots could match the representatives of the six largest airlines representing over 90 percent of ALPA's membership. The Executive Board was, in short, a fragile vessel from which to launch a revolution against Behncke, but it was the only one available. Behncke had generally made little use of the Executive Board; a few members on it knew each other, and even Jerry Wood, the ALPA first vice-president (and technically second in command to Behncke), did not have a list of addresses. (In fact, Behncke once pointedly refused to give him such a list.) Should concerned ALPA members try to use the Executive Board to remove Behncke, they would face formidable legal obstacles, for the recall provision in ALPA's constitution and by-laws was cumbersome, requiring several steps and much time and expense. Indeed, the Executive Board lacked even autonomy, since it could not call itself into session. Should Behncke refuse to call a meeting, the Executive Board could not assemble, no matter how chaotic the situation became.

Then fate played into the hands of the revolutionaries. Partly because Behncke thought he had more support on the small airlines than on the large ones, he announced a meeting of the Executive Board in Chicago on June 12, 1951. (The convention voted by numbers, but the board voted by airline.) The immediate cause of Behncke's announcement was the presidential emergency board's finding against ALPA's position on the mileage limitation in its final report, which appeared on May 25, 1951. "This is an urgent meeting and vital questions will be decided," Behncke wrote, obviously referring to the possibility of a nationwide strike.

When the members of the Executive Board began assembling at the Sherry Hotel in Chicago, anxious ALPA professional employees sought them out. Most of the board members had no direct knowledge of the staff's circumstances, its attempt to form a union, or the previous attempt of a group of senior captains to mediate between the staff and Behncke. Several of the board members knew how serious the breakdown at the top was, but they played a close hand, allowing the remaining members to learn for themselves. The ALPA employees were the teachers. Among the 20 pilots who answered the roll call at the board's session, Karl Ruppenthal of TWA, Charley Barnes and H. B. Anders of United Airlines (UAL), and Paul Ambort of PAA were already convinced that Behncke must go. Gradually, they convinced Elmer Orndorff of Braniff, Jim Hale of West Coast Airlines, and Larry Shapiro of UAL (who was not a regular member, but held a proxy). They planned to focus the board's attention on ALPA itself, not on the presidential emergency board's rejection of the mileage limitation that Behncke had called them together to consider.

Almost immediately after the roll call, the board members insisted on hearing the full story of the ALPA employees' grievances. Behncke resisted, but was unable to prevent passage of a resolution calling for the creation of a committee to "survey the general management and business affairs of the Association." The resolution called for the committee to report no later than July 2, and it also permitted the board itself to remain in continuous session until then. The revolutionaries were not going to allow Behncke simply to refuse to call them back into session and thereby defuse the special investigating committee's findings. Charley Ruby, a member of the board, helped to persuade Behncke that he would have to accept this committee's existence. Behncke insisted that he be allowed to appoint the committee, but Ruby argued him out of it. The board subsequently named the following pilots to the special investigating committee: Karl Ruppenthal of TWA, Grant LeRoux of PAA, and Sterling Camden of Eastern Air Lines (EAL), a man of such stature and experience with ALPA that his mere presence on the committee would tend to give it legitimacy. As everybody knew Behncke would, he resisted this inquiry every step of the way.

The special investigating committee had the authority to look into all areas of ALPA's business, including one which was rapidly becoming infamous—the new building located at the corner of 55th and Cicero on the edge of Chicago's Midway Airport. The idea of an ALPA building had obsessed Behncke for years. The 1947 convention approved $250,000 for it, thus fulfilling Behncke's dreams. As the committee investigated further, it found that the building itself was one of Behncke's major problems. Many committee members suspected that Behncke's sidewalk supervising at the building site caused the lengthly administrative delays in ALPA's paperwork. Behncke wanted the building to be extraordinary, built to aircraft specifications. His outrageous demands, such as lining up the nuts, bolts, and screws with north and south and recutting expensive marble, exceeded the budget the convention had approved by as much as sevenfold. Behncke wanted the building to be a monument to his leadership. Ironically, it would become more a tomb.

The committee discovered that Behncke had been able to spend money never appropriated by the convention, because ALPA had no budget. There was virtually no internal control on expenditures, and Treasurer Bob Strait habitually signed blank checks because his predecessors always had. This was unorthodox, but not criminal—nobody ever accused Behncke of fraud. Rather it was a case of inefficiency, confusion, waste, and most of all an unchecked president so involved with day-to-day construction of his dream building that he had lost contact with reality.

Karl Ruppenthal, who holds a law degree and a Ph.D. and now teaches in a Canadian university, insists that Behncke lost several grievance cases because he spent so much time at the construction site that he forgot to file the cases in time. On one occasion, Ruppenthal declares, Behncke had a stenographer backdate a letter on a TWA grievance deadline that had expired and then threw away the original. He subsequently used the carbon copy to "prove" that the original had been lost in the mail.

The investigating committee explored ways of improving ALPA's administration by consulting Dr. A. A. Liveright, director of the Union Leadership Project at the University of Chicago. They considered keeping Behncke on as president while removing him as a source of delays and confusion. Liveright pointed out the difficulties of this approach. Nevertheless, the investigating committee couldn't bring itself to recommend removing Behncke. Instead, it made one last, desperate try to save the Old Man's pride—it came up with the idea of Behncke as a powerless figurehead, a "president emeritus" who would serve at full salary for life. (Subsequently, the emergency convention would vote to double his salary if he would accept the position, but Behncke refused, calling the offer a bribe.)

By the time the investigating committee finished its work, Behncke was in Washington. Grant LeRoux of PAA (who died in 1963 of a heart attack in the cockpit), was the chairman of the committee, so it was his responsibility to let Behncke know its conclusions. Behncke refused to return his calls or answer his letters. Sterling Camden, who died in 1953 of a heart attack while working at ALPA headquarters in Chicago, got the message. Behncke was going to dig in and fight.

The investigating committee was ready to recommend Behncke's ouster to the Executive Board when it reconvened on July 12. Behncke countered by mailing to the entire Board of Directors a ballot that would empower him to stop the meeting of the board, which he described as "a group using insidious tactics to march in and take over." He declared the July 12 meeting of the Executive Board to be illegal, and he threatened a court fight.

If Behncke's ballot would carry, the ouster movement would surely fail. The revolutionaries organized an intensive campaign to defeat the ballot that would in effect abolish the Executive Board and declare the work of the special investigating committee invalid. They were probably overly worried—Behncke's "ballot" was 18 pages long, rambling and incoherent, and most ALPA members had clearly had enough of communications of this sort, which they seldom read anyway.

On the morning of July 12, a quorum of 21 Executive Board members assembled. Frank Spencer of AAL, ALPA's secretary (the first national officer in history who was not a captain), convened the meeting in Behncke's absence. Spencer's first action as interim chairman of the board was to hire an attorney, because there were rumors that Behncke would begin immediate legal action against them if they convened. Sure enough, the meeting had only barely begun when Behncke's lawyer appeared and read a statement declaring them to be an illegal assembly.

Then a bombshell hit—Behncke sent a telegram from Washington firing ALPA employees Wally Anderson, Scruggs Colvin, and Executive Vice-President Clarence Sayen, accusing them of conspiracy. Nothing could have been further from the truth. Whenever Sayen had been in the company of individuals complaining about Behncke, he always changed the subject. He was completely loyal to Behncke throughout the investigating committee's life. "I never heard Sayen say one unkind word about Behncke during the entire time," Paul Ambort declares.

The Executive Board promptly rehired Sayen, Anderson, and Colvin, and summoned the Board of Directors to meet in convention on July 16, just four days later. But before the Executive Board could adjourn, new word reached them from Washington—Behncke was filing suit for $2 million in damages against Frank Spencer, Clarence Sayen, Larry Shapiro of UAL, and every member of the investigating committee except Dean Barnette. "He didn't sue me because I was just an ignorant little kid from the West Coast," Barnette laughs.

But for Frank Spencer and the others, the $2-million lawsuit was no laughing matter. It was a frightening sum, and the legal action itself would almost surely tie the principals up in court and cost enormous amounts of money. They were to appear in court the next day. Spencer and the others appeared at the designated hour of the court hearing, but typically, neither Behncke nor his lawyer was there. Just after the judge assigned to the case left, Behncke and his lawyer finally appeared.

Owing to Behncke's late arrival at the hearing, the court refused to issue an injunction to block the special meeting of the Board of Directors. So on July 16, 1951, at the Del Prado Hotel on Chicago's South Lakeshore Drive, the drama of Behncke's ouster played out. After reviewing the work of the investigating committee, the convention amended the constitution by inserting an immediate recall provision. The roll call vote was 5,562 in favor to 269, with pilots representing over 75 percent of all ALPA members in attendance. Then, acting under provisions of the recall clause they had just inserted, the delegates removed Behncke from office and elected Clarence Sayen as his successor. Capt. A. J. "Tony" O'Donnell of PAA gave a moving summary of Behncke's career and contributions to persuade the delegates to continue paying Behncke his full salary for life. They raised it to $15,000 per year, partly as a tribute to O'Donnell's oratory.

There were few dry eyes in the crowed ballroom of the Del Prado (many nondelegate pilots were also there to observe). Karl Ruppenthal remembers Ed Hackett, the labor lawyer Frank Spencer had hired to advise them, saying, "Better watch out, or he'll have them reelecting the guy."

Jerry Wood, ALPA first vice-president, presided over the convention:

I flew up on July 15, met with the guys, and got briefed. By this time, I agreed fully that there was no use trying to get the Old Man to capitulate—he wouldn't even talk a minor compromise. So there was just nothing to do but remove him from office. Whether we could do that legally or not remained to be seen.

The recall went through, and we elected Clancy Sayen and adjourned at 2:00 a.m. By 8:00 a.m. the next morning the newspapers were after us with all kinds of charges and countercharges. It really hit the fan. By the middle of the afternoon everybody had gone home. Clancy and myself and a few others sat there. That's when we found out that Behncke had filed another suit, tied up all our funds. We didn't have any money whatsoever. We chipped in $100 apiece to get a mailing out to the membership to tell them what had happened. We didn't even have any money to pay the hotel bill.

We didn't know where to go from there.

Where the revolutionaries went from there was to court. On the advice of Roy Dooley, the Chicago chairman of the AAL pilots, the revolutionaries moved quickly to transfer jurisdiction over the welter of lawsuits to federal courts. Dooley knew that Behncke had powerful political connections and that if his suits wound up in Illinois state courts, the revolutionaries would almost certainly lose. The lawsuit filed against Behncke by Captains Talton, Lafferty, Beatley, Barnes, Ambort, Orndorff, Cochran, and Karlberg was designed to transfer the matter to federal courts, based on the diversity of state citizenship of each of the complainants.

But it was the human drama, not the legal one, that mattered. Initially, Dave Behncke ignored the revolution, acting as if nothing had happened. He came to the office every day, issued orders to the ALPA staff, and sent letters far and wide insisting that he was still the legal president. When a group of pilots tried to take over the ALPA offices at 63rd Street, he called the police, who showed up in full riot gear. Behncke's son, David Jr., a tough ex-Marine, acted as his father's bodyguard, and there were several near fistfights. But Behncke was playing a losing hand, one a more rational man would have folded.

The case of _Talton et al._ v. _Behncke_ was filed on July 25, 1951. It requested an injunction to prevent Behncke from interfering with the changes made at the convention of the Board of Directors earlier that month. By implication, the suit would legalize the immediate recall provision that had removed Behncke from office. Of necessity, the court would declare the revolution against Behncke legal if it should grant an injunction, illegal if it should refuse. The case wound up being assigned to Judge Walter LaBuy—a terrible bit of luck. LaBuy was an old friend of Behncke's lawyer, Dan Carmel. Judge LaBuy assigned the case to a master in chancery named Victor LaRue. Under his control and the supervision of a court-

160

appointed "supervisor" named Manuel Cowen, ALPA would continue operating for the next year with *two* presidents. Both Behncke and Sayen would sign checks, while Cowen approved all other important transactions, including the completion of the ALPA building at 55th and Cicero. Under this cumbersome arrangement, the long court battle took place, while Clarence Sayen struggled to carry on a semblance of ALPA's normal business.

The initial round went to the pilots, when Master in Chancery LaRue found that the revolution had been legal and Behncke was no longer president. It took LaRue until April 1, 1952, to complete his investigation. He issued his report on May 20, 1952. But LaRue's opinion was merely advisory, directed to Judge LaBuy, who could accept it, reject it, or make changes. Nevertheless, the pilots felt like celebrating, for a federal judge rarely overturned a master in chancery's work totally.

But Judge LaBuy did just that. On June 25, 1952, he totally reversed LaRue, found exclusively for Behncke, and issued an injunction against the revolutionaries prohibiting them from interfering with Behncke's control of ALPA. Since the anti-Behncke forces would soon be locked out of ALPA's headquarters by court order, they quickly ran off copies of the membership list and collected $100 from each pilot they could locate for an "emergency fund." Its purpose was to wage a last-ditch battle against Judge LaBuy's ruling and, in the event of failure, to create a new pilot's association. If Dave Behncke could be stubborn, tough, and dogged, he was about to discover that his opponents could play the same game, even though their attorney was recommending surrender.

In a burst of frantic activity, the pilots set up the Air Transport Pilots Association (ATPA) and started collecting "authorization to act" cards. In short order, they had an overwhelming majority of EAL and PAA pilots, who together accounted for a substantial percentage of ALPA's total membership and, owing to their heavy financial commitment during the ouster, were supplying nearly 40 percent of all ALPA dues. W. T. "Slim" Babbitt, widely respected for his probity and long service with ALPA, agreed to head this alternative union. Although Behncke might win the court battle, he would ultimately wind up presiding over an empty house. It was a foregone conclusion that a majority of the nation's airline pilots would eventually join ATPA.

While they set up the alternative union, the revolutionaries (most of whom, we must remember, were on the Board of Directors), pursued further legal action. On the advice of Henry Weiss, who had stayed out of the scrap so far, Sayen and Ruppenthal prepared to appeal Judge LaBuy's injunction. They chose U.S. Court of Appeals Judge Walter C. Lindley, sitting in Danville, Ill. Lindley was a Republican, appointed to the court by Herbert Hoover. But Democratic Sen. Scott Lucas, whose law firm was handling the case for the anti-Behncke forces, recommended Lindley, despite their partisan differences.

Simultaneously, under emergency conditions, the revolutionaries were plotting other strategies. The easy out was simply to continue ATPA, name Sayen president, and let Behncke have the empty shell of ALPA. But Sayen refused, citing the large number of grievance cases that would be lost by pilots who still depended on him. Sayen would stay till the bitter end, he told Ruppenthal. Only after exhausting the last legal remedies, Sayen insisted, would he surrender ALPA.

Sayen and the Executive Board were pursuing other remedies. Judge LaBuy had ruled in favor of Behncke partly on the grounds that the July convention had illegally adopted the provision permitting immediate recall of ALPA's president. So, using the list of ALPA members' addresses that had been spirited away from ALPA headquarters before Behncke had the locks changed, Sayen prepared a recall ballot under the complicated old rules that required a petition signed by 30 percent of the membership to approve a subsequent mail ballot. It would take time, but eventually this approach would garner far more than the minimum necessary to circulate a full ballot. The legality of Sayen's action, owing to Judge LaBuy's injunction, was questionable, and he was risking a contempt of court citation by taking any action at all.

Everything depended on Judge Lindley of the court of appeals. Extralegal remedies like ATPA would eventually defeat Behncke, of course, but in the process the whole structure of airline pilot unionization might dissolve. Judge Lindley alone could prevent a catastrophe for the unionization of airline pilots, and he was a Herbert Hoover Republican. Small wonder that Henry Weiss warned Sayen and Ruppenthal not to let their hopes get too high. An appeals court seldom overruled a lower court on cases such as this anyway, Weiss warned.

While Judge Lindley was considering the request of Sayen and the Executive Board for a stay of Judge LaBuy's injunction, Dave Behncke took formal possession of ALPA's new headquarters building. In palmier times, Behncke had described the building as "something which will last a thousand years, which will never become obsolete."

On Thursday, July 31, 1952, Judge Walter C. Lindley ended Behncke's career. "I cannot see that either party can be injured if a restricted stay order should be entered," the judge said. This legal circumlocution meant that he was returning ALPA to the status it had enjoyed under Master in Chancery LaRue, who had found against Behncke. The judge required Sayen and his petitioners to post a $10,000 bond (supplied by Karl Ruppenthal of TWA; Breezy Wynne and Roy Dooley of AAL also chipped in money at various times—only $5,000 was in the emergency fund at the time of Judge Lindley's ruling).

The effect on Behncke was negligible. He simply ignored Judge Lindley, remained in possession of ALPA's new building, and defied anyone to remove him. The Old Man stood utterly alone at this point, with virtually no support among airline pilots and with the weight of the federal courts opposing him.

Whatever affection and respect the pilots had once felt for Behncke were rapidly dissipating amidst the tangle of lawsuits. They moved to have Behncke cited for contempt. Judge Lindley complied, and Behncke was found guilty on Aug. 15, 1952, by a three-judge court.

Sayen had meanwhile gone ahead with plans for the regularly scheduled convention in October. He was operating ALPA from the Sherry Hotel, courtesy of the owner, Mrs. Bellows. She knew the revolutionaries could not immediately pay their bills, but she figured, correctly, that they would eventually win and feel grateful, thus generating future convention business for the Sherry. Also, her husband was a successful Chicago lawyer who had no use for Behncke's legal team of Carmel, Levinson, and Despres.

With these mounting difficulties, even Dave Behncke saw the end coming. He now faced a jail term for contempt of court, and in barely a month the 1952 convention would meet. Its legality would be unassailable, and it would certainly not reelect him to another term. So Dave Behncke did what was once unthinkable, probably the hardest thing he ever did in his life. He quit. He was tired, he was sick, and he was beaten.

On Oct. 8, 1952, the Board of Directors convention met on schedule in the Sherry Hotel. Through an intermediary, Behncke sent word that if the convention would vote to pay him the pension of $7,500 annually that had already been set up some years before, he would resign. Behncke insisted that his wife Gladys also be taken care of, but he would not accept the $15,000 salary for life that the emergency Executive Board and subsequent convention had approved in July 1951. To do so would be an admission that these were legal assemblies, and Behncke would never admit that. Behncke would not accept anything from those "rump" sessions. The 1952 convention agreed to Behncke's terms. And so it was over—the Behncke era was at an end.

Behncke lived only another six months. He died of a heart attack after a sauna and massage at a Chicago YMCA in April 1953. At his own request, he was cremated, and his ashes were scattered along his old Omaha–Chicago airmail route.

To this day, most old-timers insist he really died of a broken heart. ✦

CHAPTER 16

The Sayen Style

Was Clancy Sayen ALPA's "accidental" president? He would be 62 during this half-centennial of ALPA's birth if he had not died as a passenger in a 1965 airline crash. In a sense, Sayen was a victim of the Behncke ouster. As ALPA's executive vice-president, second in the administrative hierarchy when the Old Man went down, Sayen was almost obligated to pick up the pieces—nobody else could. There is absolutely no evidence that he sought Behncke's job, that he played anything other than an inadvertent part in the movement that unhorsed Behncke, or that he was ever anything but a perfectly loyal ALPA employee. But the legacy of the Behncke ouster—bad feelings, legal expenses, and lawsuits, some of which weren't finally settled until 1958—inevitably fell to Sayen.

Such a legacy was a pity, for Sayen had a history of achievement in every field he entered, whether it was education, politics, or flying. Had he not chosen to leave Braniff temporarily for the new ALPA executive vice-presidency in 1949, he no doubt would have obtained a captaincy, risen steadily in ALPA's affairs, and eventually become a formidable contender for the presidency in his own right. These things were already apparent by 1949—that's why Behncke chose him.

Clarence Nicholas "Clancy" Sayen came out of the Michigan forests, the son of a lumberjack who had never benefited from an education, but who nevertheless permitted his son to continue in school when he might have easily insisted that Clancy go to work to help support the family. Sayen's boyhood was rigorous, but it included lots of hunting and fishing, things any healthy boy who didn't live in the North woods might have envied. The only untoward incident of this idyllic youth came when he was 10 years old: the first two-thirds of his right index finger were lopped off in an accident. It proved to be no handicap. Sayen went on to become a standout high school athlete. After graduating in 1936, his path seemed to lead directly to college. But the need for a job (and perhaps a bit of postadolescent desire for adventure) led him aboard a Great Lakes steamer instead. By the time the gales of December swept across those inland seas, Sayen had gotten his fill of that life, and he was off to college. He played football, basketball, and baseball at Northern Michigan University in Marquette. But he was no mere jock—Sayen also wrote regularly for the school newspaper, maintained a solid A average in his courses, and developed what would prove to be a lifelong taste for the academic life. Upon graduation, he married his college sweetheart, Marjorie Alvord, and set off to make what everybody assumed would be a considerable mark on the world. Dark, intense, and articulate, carrying his 180 pounds on a compact six-foot frame, Clancy Sayen looked like a winner.

Sayen's career as an airline pilot was short. He started to work for Braniff in June 1944, after learning to fly in the Civilian Pilot Training Program. Before going with Braniff, he had put in a stint as a flight instructor for a local flight school in Kalamazoo, Mich. It was a significant period in Sayen's life, for he was discovering what he liked best—teaching. His students were naval aviation cadets, mostly older men who had already attended college. Sayen liked the contact with them and liked the atmosphere of the classroom, even if it was the cockpit of a trainer.

While flying copilot for Braniff, Sayen earned a graduate degree in geography and climatology at Southern Methodist University in Dallas. To write his master's thesis, "Commercial Aviation in South America," Sayen also studied economics at the graduate level and taught himself Spanish. He was an impressive graduate student, the kind senior professors like. He seemed more a colleague than a student. Academicians prized Sayen's ability to communicate clearly in writing. His article "Commercial Aviation in Texas," published in *Texas Geographic* magazine in 1946, was a model of research and clear expository writing. So, while working full-time for Braniff, Sayen was already establishing himself as a person of rare academic promise. His department chairman at Southern Methodist, Professor E. J. Foscue, hired him as a lecturer in 1946. For the next two years, Clancy Sayen scheduled his trips around a classroom assignment teaching undergraduate meteorology courses.

By 1947, Clancy Sayen faced a major career decision. He had found a home, both emotionally and intellectually, in the university, but he obviously could not pursue a full-time career in college teaching unless he quit flying. The geography department at Southern Methodist would schedule evening classes for him because he was so promising, but they could not accommodate him forever. To rise in academic life, Sayen would have to pursue a doctoral degree, a demanding, full-time course of studies that would require as long as four years. Sayen liked flying, his fellow pilots thought highly of him, and although the money wasn't all that good for a copilot in 1947, it was already better than the salaries of some professors. Sayen was 28 years old, and he didn't know whether to follow his heart or his pocketbook. Perhaps this dilemma explains why Sayen began devoting himself to ALPA work on the local level. It was a kind of halfway house between academic work and flying. He was elected copilot representative in 1946, attended the convention in 1947, and began attracting considerable attention.

The other delegates noticed Sayen largely because he almost single-handedly picked apart one of Behncke's pet projects, a pilot's amendment to the Railway Labor Retirement Act. Behncke had been slow to move on pensions. For many years, his favorite rationale for high salaries for pilots was that flying was so dangerous, and the physical requirements were so exacting, that no airline pilot was likely to survive to anything like a normal retirement age. Behncke had often expressed the opinion that nobody could continue flying much beyond the age of 40.

By the late 1930s, this thinking was already obsolete. Many people over 40 flew, people for whom retirement was becoming something more than just an abstraction. ALPA had no retirement policy at all until the 1946 convention met belatedly in February 1947. Behncke argued strongly for inclusion in the federal rail workers' plan, which would require a fixed monthly payment and was, in effect, a tax like Social Security. A pilot would have no residual interest in the federal pension system. Dealing with a consultant named Murray Lattimer, who was apparently connected to the Railroad Brotherhood's pension system, Behncke introduced the idea to a mixed reaction. The nation was reeling under the first great postwar inflationary assault triggered by the Eightieth Congress's dismantling of the wartime system of price and wage controls, and a federally guaranteed fixed pension plan like the one Behncke favored had severe drawbacks. Young Sayen spelled out these drawbacks. He was so persuasive that the convention voted to put off further consideration of the Behncke-Lattimer plan. The convention did vote sufficient funds to hire a pension expert to study the question.

We must remember that this same convention saw Willis Proctor's challenge to Behncke and the creation of the new office of executive vice-president (much against Behncke's will). Quite naturally, a number of senior "movers and shakers" (such as Jerry Wood and Slim Babbitt of Eastern Air Lines [EAL]), were eyeing the available talent for this office. Henry Weiss, who was increasingly involved with ALPA's legal affairs, remembers clearly the impression Sayen made:

> Clancy proved extraordinarily adept at rationalizing difficult subjects such as the pension proposal Behncke was pushing. He had the knack of making these questions comprehensible to pilots. He struck me as quite brilliant, really a man of extraordinary intelligence. I have often thought that that might have worked against him somewhat in the long run. He thought so quickly, grasped an argument, and reduced it to its essentials so fast. His brain was faster than his heart. I guess what I am trying to say is that he could be quite abrupt with people who were not as smart as he was, who didn't think as clearly or see things as quickly as he did. There were some pilots who saw him as more of a professor than a pilot, and I

think that hurt him politically. In that sense, he was out of step with some pilots, but by no means all of them.

The plain fact about Clancy Sayen is that he was not the kind of man who suffered a fool gladly, and consequently he made enemies. His air of intellectual superiority didn't help matters either.

A number of people were pushing Sayen for the new executive vice-presidency after 1947. As we have seen, Behncke opposed the creation of the new office, and dragged his feet filling it. William P. Kilgore's temporary appointment, begun in March 1947, lasted over two years. Not until May 1949 did Behncke finally choose Sayen from a large field that included several people who had been nominated but had no interest whatsoever in serving. Sayen desperately wanted the job. He was bored with being a copilot, Braniff was not growing, and Sayen wanted to work temporarily at what he hoped would be a more intellectually challenging job. He expected several more years as a copilot, and he hoped to kill at least a couple of them doing something more interesting than grinding back and forth between Dallas and Chicago in the right seat of a DC-6B. In early 1948, he had even applied for a federal government position.

After a considerable hassle with Braniff (which wanted to allow him only a three-month leave of absence), Sayen got permission to work for ALPA for a year. In August 1949, Sayen arrived in Chicago to assume his duties on a probationary basis at a salary of $8,000 per year. Sayen had been earning only $4,500 per year with Braniff.

Behncke's inability to delegate authority was infamous. Still, ALPA was becoming so big that he simply couldn't do everything himself, no matter how hard he tried. So Behncke found himself leaning more and more on Sayen, particularly for the routine things he didn't like to do. Sayen rapidly developed into a capable executive assistant, working closely with Wally Anderson, who was very experienced. Together, Sayen and Anderson began a quiet revolution of efficiency in such mundane areas as bookkeeping and routine announcements and mailings to the councils. Behncke took a great personal liking to Sayen as the months passed. He often called Sayen into his office for "educational talks." Although some people might have regarded these bull sessions as a waste of time, for Behncke they were therapeutic.

By February 1951, Behncke was writing letters of high praise to Sayen, informing him of his reelection to the executive vice-presidency. Sayen had cast his lot totally with ALPA by this point, formally resigning from Braniff. His presence accounted for much of ALPA's effectiveness as Behncke declined in his final months.

Henry Weiss recalls Sayen's work during this period:

> I remember clearly that in the final months of the Behncke presidency, Clancy just about single-handedly kept the ship afloat. Dave

was closing avenues of negotiation and compromise, while Clancy kept working, very adroitly and diplomatically, to keep them open. There were certain issues where, if Dave thought something was not in the cards, he would just shut off contact with management, have absolutely no discussions with them. Clancy was developing relationships with airline management during this time. They were beginning to see that Sayen was a man they could deal with, while Behncke was not. With Sayen, they could work out difficult issues to everybody's mutual benefit. With Dave, it was confrontation—total victory or total defeat.

Now, I do not for a moment want to give you the impression that Clancy was undercutting Behncke. Clancy was a genius at explaining issues, at rationalizing them, a very adept negotiator. Frequently he would subordinate his own views to Dave's even when he was completely in disagreement with him, and argued Dave's case very creditably and effectively—much better than Dave himself could have—so what I'm trying to say is that Clancy was loyal to Dave, completely so, I believe.

The Behncke ouster was very hard on Sayen. Not only was he living on a shoestring, frequently supported by what amounted to charity from his friends because ALPA's finances were tied up in the courts, but also he had to contend with Dave Behncke's enmity. There is ample evidence that Sayen was fond of Behncke and was hurt when Behncke tried to blame Sayen's alleged personal ambition for the ouster. Sayen was hurt less because the allegations were untrue than because Behncke was obviously a man who needed help, both psychologically and physically. But there was nothing Sayen (or anybody else) could do to reach Behncke. So Sayen concentrated on righting ALPA's listing ship, negotiating contracts, and settling grievances. There is some evidence that Sayen stayed with ALPA at this point only out of a sense of obligation. He was 32 in 1951 and obviously still interested in other career choices. His file of personal correspondence bulges with letters to his former professors, both at Northern Michigan and at Southern Methodist, in a wistful tone that indicates his career uncertainty. The lure of academic life was strong for him, and he was always a ready volunteer as a guest lecturer.

The first challenge facing Sayen was the 1952 convention. Despite the widespread support among pilots for Behncke's ouster, there was no consensus that Sayen should replace him. Historically, ALPA had been a captain's organization, and copilots were distinctly second-class citizens. Sayen was never more than a copilot, and moving directly into the ALPA presidency without ever having occupied the left seat was anathema to some pilots. Until 1938, copilots had the privilege of paying ALPA dues and not much else. After that, they received half a vote, but they could not serve as chairmen of either local or master executive councils, and there could not be more than one copilot on any ALPA standing committee. The discriminatory policy went back to the dawn of commercial aviation, when captains looked upon copilots as interlopers out to steal their jobs. By the end of World War II, the copilot was obviously not merely an apprentice, but a necessary member of the crew. Indeed, on some airlines, stagnant promotion lists made the career copilot a possibility. Recognizing this, ALPA dropped all discrimination against the second man in the cockpit, but residual prejudice against Sayen because he was "only a copilot" lingered for a long time and eventually made quite a lot of trouble for him, particularly on American Airlines (AAL).

Clancy Sayen faced his first challenge at the 1952 convention where Behncke formally "resigned" in return for his pension. Although a majority of delegates believed Sayen deserved a full term in the presidency because of the superb job he had done during the Behncke ouster, a substantial minority was determined to replace him. In a portent of trouble, the opposition to Sayen centered in the AAL group. The AAL pilots were strong critics of Dave Behncke, and they alone were responsible, many old-timers think, for driving Behncke into a defensive shell. "The American pilots got after Dave so hard on this mileage limitation thing after 1950," says Jerry Wood, "that he had several sick spells." In short, the AAL pilots entered the Sayen era already believing that their share of control over ALPA was less than fair.

In 1952, these vague and inchoate resentments surfaced in the candidacy of H. Bart Cox of AAL. Cox had had a long and distinguished career in ALPA. He had worked on virtually every important technical committee, and in 1947 President Truman had selected him to serve on the presidential commission on air safety. Bart Cox was a pilot's pilot, a man who was widely respected, and if ALPA had needed a figurehead president, one who would preside symbolically while a corps of dedicated technicians ran ALPA, he would have been an ideal choice. But 1952 was such a crucial year for ALPA, coming as it did upon the heels of the Behncke ouster, that the consensus was that a figurehead president wouldn't do. Whoever headed ALPA after 1952 would have to be a full-time executive who knew as much about administration as he did about flying, the delegates concluded.

"Clancy was a little reluctant to move into the top spot because he had never flown as a captain," remembers Jerry Wood.

> He was just a little ill at ease because he knew there was a wave out there in the membership that the place should be filled by a fellow with considerable experience. Because I was first vice-president and I had been flying for 24 years, Clancy tried to talk me into taking it. He very frankly told me that he was getting an adverse reaction, particularly from the pilots on American. I told him that in the past it might have been true that you needed pilots running things, but with the coming of more complicated equipment, more com-

plicated negotiations, we had to have someone with more of a business and economics background. I argued that the pilots should be there as a backup to the president, to provide him with experience and guidance. The airlines weren't being run by pilots anymore, so why should ALPA? He wanted the job and was willing to take it, but he was a little concerned. He said to me, "You take it for a term, and I will stay on as your executive vice-president." I convinced him that wasn't the way to go, that he should become president. Actually, I wasn't the only one trying to convince him; there were lots of others. The decision to run Clancy against Bart Cox was a group decision. He was strongly supported by the TWA [Trans World Airlines], EAL, and PAA [Pan American World Airways] pilots.

I think the AAL pilots felt somewhat resentful toward us for that, but that goes back a long way, too. AAL was pretty much the mainstay of ALPA in the 1930s, and they more or less got used to the idea that they were the dominant airline. Even as early as 1944—and this is not generally known—Bart Cox had some tentative ideas about running against Dave. Two or three of us took Bart to dinner in 1944 and told him, "Maybe later, but not now." The war was going on, and frankly Dave was doing a pretty good job. Then, of course, in 1947 Willis Proctor came along and did what Bart threatened to do in 1944. I think some AAL pilots resented that we had put a stop to Cox's challenge in 1952.

Although Bart Cox's candidacy in opposition to Sayen was the centerpiece of the 1952 convention's politics, there were far more important matters afoot. Chief among them was finishing formally the reorganization of ALPA's governance begun by the special investigating committee during the Behncke ouster. The Executive Board had mandated the investigating committee to study ways of "democratizing" ALPA's structure. In the past, Behncke tended to rely on a few chosen insiders on each airline. This was hardly a conspiracy on his part, for the truth was that the average airline pilot then (and probably still) wasn't overly interested in the day-to-day running of ALPA. Behncke tended to do things undemocratically because that was the way most pilots wanted them done—so long as there was no fuss, there would be no bother about whether things were done "dictatorially." The investigating committee probed these questions before recommending a series of changes designed to allow more direct participation in ALPA's governance by rank-and-file members.

Dean Barnette of Hughes Airwest, the junior member of the investigating committee, remembers the dilemma of "democratization:"

Everybody is in favor of "democracy." When things go bad people say, "Give us back our democracy." ALPA is the same way. Unfortunately, my experience with that committee was that we found that people had not gotten involved in ALPA because they didn't want to. The deeper I probed, the less I found that Dave Behncke was a dictator, although he had certainly manipulated the bylaws to make his position more secure. Often we found that important changes in the bylaws had been made on the last day of the convention at midnight when everybody was tired and didn't fully understand what was happening. But that was really the way people wanted it; they just didn't want to be bothered.

Nevertheless, Sayen felt obligated to ruthlessly "democratize" ALPA's structure, even though it would require years of work to bring this ideal to fruition. At the 1952 convention, Sayen told the delegates that a complete revision of the ALPA constitution and bylaws would require many months of careful study. The goal of this revision, he insisted, was "positive control by the membership."

> That, however, imposes a great responsibility. Sometimes I wonder if the members are entirely ready to live with democracy. It takes more participation and alertness. Decisions by the majority have to stand despite the disgruntled member who calls the national officer in the middle of the night and says, "My council is completely wrong, they don't know what they are talking about, and you have to do something about it." We cannot have democracy and have government by influence. Some members aren't yet ready to live with democracy, but I think the vast majority are.

Young Clancy Sayen had no way of knowing that his battle to democratize and "reform" ALPA would never really end.

The most pressing task confronting Sayen was contract negotiations, and not just on current equipment. It was obvious that jet equipment was coming. Unless ALPA did a lot of advance spadework, the professional airline pilot would enter the jet age at a grave bargaining disadvantage. Sayen was instrumental in the creation of what would ultimately be ALPA's single most important tool for coping with jets—the jet pay study committee.

The necessity for pilot involvement in the development of jet design criteria and operating standards was already apparent by 1953. Sayen promoted the activities of ALPA pilot committees and staff engineers who met with government representatives to present the pilots' viewpoint before certification of the first jets for U.S. commercial operation. By 1955, the emphasis of ALPA's concern had switched from operations to the impact of the jet transition on pilot pay and working conditions. A resolution to form an official committee to study the jet pay question was recommended by the Executive Committee meeting in January 1956 and approved by the Board of Directors in February. By March the "Turbo-Prop and Jet Study Committee" (TPJSC) had been formed and had begun preparing a report that became the most important issue of the 1956 convention. Eight pilots with wide experience served on the TPJSC: Jerry Wood (EAL), Tom Latta (AAL),

Ed Tappe (United Airlines [UAL]), John Carroll (TWA), Dick O'Neill (Northwest Airlines [NWA]), Grant LeRoux (PAA), Charley Barnes (UAL), and Bobby Rohan (National Airlines).

TPJSC prepared a 124-page report that each of the 247 delegates received when they arrived in Chicago for the November 5-12 meeting. TPJSC had employed a respected consultant, the economist S. Herbert Unterberger, for advice in its report on wage theory, collective bargaining, and the relative economic status of the airline pilot of the future. Professor Unterberger attended the convention, and two full days were taken up considering the TPJSC report, with Unterberger himself answering questions at length.

Economist Unterberger provided mathematical rationales for increasing pilot compensation based on the concept of increased responsibility. As Unterberger correctly pointed out, salaries in American industry are directly related to unionization and the strength of the bargaining agent. By 1956, a considerable number of airline pilots felt they had fallen behind badly, in a relative sense. "I don't think pilots are making enough money, and I feel even more strongly about economists," Unterberger said to laughter from the delegates.

Unterberger made clear to the delegates that wage increases had to be gradual and steady—not all at once, even for jets. Following his advice, TPJSC had recommended abandoning the "ultimatum system of negotiating" and gearing the new system to existing reciprocating engine equipment. This did not mean that pilots would abandon the strike threat. The AAL pilots, who were openly hostile to the report because it did not provide a big enough initial raise or enough time off, argued that they were 85 percent in favor of "throwing down the gauntlet" to management. As John Carroll of TWA (who would later contend for the ALPA presidency in 1962 after Sayen's resignation) said, "I am a member of this committee, I participated fully in all its meetings, and I subscribe to all its findings. I tell you frankly that no one can say that I am not in favor of using a strike vote and, if necessary, a strike. Believe me, that is not implied [in the TPJSC report]."

The 1956 convention approved the complex formula for negotiating jet contracts. The delegates knew it would be difficult and time consuming to return to their local councils to attempt a full explanation. It would be far better, they thought, to have members of the committee explain the report. Jerry Wood has vivid memories of the first "road show," the cross-country trip he and other members of TPJSC took:

> One of the most difficult problems was making pilots see that the increment method, where you get paid a unit of pay for a unit of work, was the way to go. There were so many ideas about having flat salaries or having it all tied to the payload of the airplane, all kinds of crazy ideas. I say crazy because they wouldn't work. Some

very sincere and intelligent guys would advance them, but they hadn't had a chance to think them through. We had to demonstrate that the structure could accommodate any amount of money that would be negotiated, based on increased responsibility and productivity. We had some charts which projected an initial jet pay scale of $35,000 a year, based on speed and weight. This looked like a pretty impressive increase to people flying the DC-7, which paid about $16,000 a year.

Despite the careful work, not everybody was satisfied with the report. The AAL group was particularly upset and, in a first hint at the split that was to come in 1963, appointed its own jet study committee. "They came out with an awful, shallow job of investigating things," Jerry Wood says. "They just sat down and wrote out their feelings. It was about eight pages long. We had spent time, visited every factory—Lockheed, Douglas, Boeing, Consolidated. The American pilots were just pretty much against everything unless they could run it, but they eventually voted for it."

One of Sayen's hallmarks as an administrator was careful follow-up. It was one thing to negotiate a fine contract, but it was another to make sure that management adhered to it on a daily basis. Likewise, it was one thing to form a splendid negotiating tool like the TPJSC report, but it was quite another to keep it continually updated. To that end, Sayen oversaw the creation of a permanent successor to TPJSC, called the Wages and Working Conditions Policy Committee, to conduct "further and continuing evaluational study" of wages and working conditions. Its seven members, appointed by the Executive Committee, reported to both the president and the Board of Directors. In January 1957 the Executive Committee appointed Jerry Wood of EAL, Carl Cochran of Ozark, Dick O'Neill of NWA, John Carroll of TWA, Ed Tappe and Charley Barnes of UAL, and Jack Christie of the headquarters staff. All but Cochran had served on TPJSC. These ALPA heavyweights would, over the next few years, lay down a solid corpus of doctrine that has guided contract negotiations ever since.

Some of the most enduring work of TPJSC was in the area of crew complement. What were the crew complement issue's origins, and why did the men who ran ALPA in the 1950s consider it to be crucial? Clarence Sayen would back his Wages and Working Conditions Policy Committee to the hilt on crew complement, even to the extent of nearly getting ALPA thrown out of the American Federation of Labor and handing the AAL dissidents the weapon that they would ultimately use as an excuse to secede from ALPA.

Clancy Sayen beat back the challenge of yet another AAL pilot in 1956, this time Wiley Drummond, but it was almost his last victory.

"They had become paranoid about Sayen," says Roy Dooley of his fellow AAL pilots. Dooley explains:

From about 1955 on they were convinced Sayen was out to get them, and the crew complement thing was a big part of it. They were just using it to take an action that the leadership group, Shipley, Cox, Drummond, the rest of them, had already determined that they would take. Drummond always wanted to be president of ALPA. I knew him well, flew copilot with him. He had worked hard for ALPA, and he thought he deserved the presidency in 1956. The trouble was he hadn't counted his votes, hadn't done his homework, and that was typical of the American leadership. So he didn't get rid of Sayen, and right after that he jumped in bed with management as the vice-president of flight. Keep in mind that management was doing everything it could to get the AAL pilots out, because they knew Sayen was sharp and smooth at the same time, and he could really turn them inside out.

Management didn't like it, and the good old country boys running the AAL master executive council didn't like it either. They were always somewhat more militant in the 1950s about striking than any other pilot group. They liked to pass hairy-chested resolutions, and they were very exasperating to deal with. That wasn't Sayen's style. Oh yeah, he was gonna have trouble with them over crew complement, that was sure. ✦

CHAPTER 17

Safety and Crew Complement in the 1950s

Featherbedding is an ugly word. It conjures up images of cynical union bosses extorting wages from helpless employers on behalf of lazy, corrupt workers. From the very beginning, ALPA's crew complement policy has suffered from charges that it was pure featherbedding, merely an attempt to make work for pilots who would otherwise be unemployed. The third man in the cockpit, critics said, might as well be at home in a feather bed.

Only a fool would deny that ALPA was worried about technological unemployment when the crew complement issue first arose. When it became apparent that the DC-3's days as the standard airliner were numbered, junior pilots began worrying about layoffs. Although the DC-3 has probably been overly romanticized, it was nevertheless a comforting machine for a whole generation of pilots. C. V. Glines spoke for most when he wrote in *The Legendary DC-3*, "We formed an attachment for this ingenious collection of aluminum, rivets, wires, and gadgets." In an economic sense, airline pilots were attached to the "Three" because its relatively low productivity meant jobs.

The size, speed, and capacity of the first generation of four-engine aircraft represented a quantum jump from the typical airline pilot's experience with the DC-3. These large, impressive machines intimidated some pilots, particularly those who began flying in the days of open cockpits. The legendary E. Hamilton Lee reportedly took one look at the first DC-4 at United Airlines (UAL) and said, "That's too big for me, boys. When the last Three retires, so do I." But most airline pilots made the transition to larger equipment after the war without undue difficulty. There was something tentative about the first operations, though, as any veteran airline pilot will tell you.

"There is always concern on the part of a pilot making a transition to a new airplane," says UAL's George Douglass ("Mr. V" among the Key Men), who retired in 1958. "We had a tremendous amount of trouble with the first big four-engine planes right after the war, all the bugs and engine failures and fires and unknown crash causes. I personally dumped enough gas following engine failures on the Boeing Stratocruiser to have kept Varney, my old airmail outfit, operating for two years."

So, although a desire to maintain employment was a small part of the crew complement issue, the difficulty of operating these new, more complicated aircraft in increasingly crowded airspace was by far the most important reason for ALPA's crew complement policy. We must remember that ALPA was always dominated by senior captains, and as Clancy Sayen's troubles prove, it remained pretty much a captain's club even after copilots achieved theoretically full equality. Particularly just after World War II, when the insistence on a third crewman first arose, the senior captains who ran ALPA were not worried in the least about being laid off. They wanted a third crewman to help them get home safely, not to featherbed.

In fact, ALPA's crew complement policy represented something of a threat to senior captains because it exposed them to competition from young eager beavers fresh out of military service, some of whom actually had more time in military versions of four-engine aircraft than older pilots did. In 1946, *Business Week* declared that airline pilots, "many of whom are getting along in years," feared competition from "fiery newcomers who need minimum training." So, it would have seemed logical for ALPA to insist on two-pilot crews instead of three, thus limiting access to the cockpit for a competing generation of fliers.

ALPA's first position on crew complement goes back to the Behncke era. In 1932, Behncke urged airlines not using copilots to do so "in the interest of public safety." Arguing that copilots were an "essential safety backup," Behncke also appealed to the airlines' self-interest by pointing out that it was a cheap way of "preparing young men for promotion to first pilot." Behncke got nowhere with this appeal to sweet reason. Airlines that had not used copilots continued to resist them until technological changes and government mandate forced them to do so. As some airlines began advertising that their planes had "copilots fully qualified to take over in case of emergency," the pressure of competition forced laggards to respond.

The serious student of the airline profession's history should be aware that some of the resistance to ALPA's crew complement policy has come from pilots themselves. As early as December 1932, Behncke criticized pilots who resisted flying with copilots. He cited a letter to headquarters from the pilots of "a western airline" who denounced copilots as "half-baked kids." "I want it clearly understood," Behncke said, "that this does not in any way exemplify the attitude of the Association toward copilots." Obviously, ALPA had to get its own house in order on the crew complement issue before confronting management, which has always resisted increases in crew complement on purely economic grounds. For thoughtful pilots, even as far back as 1932, the crew complement issue was about safety—not economics.

Pan American World Airways (PAA) played only a small role in the early history of the crew complement issue, even though it was the first airline to fly with multiple crews. When PAA's Paul Bauhlstrom commanded the first transpacific China Clipper flight in 1936, he carried not only a radio operator and navigator, but also a "flight engineer." The first "flight engineers" on PAA were in reality mechanics who could, in an emergency, make repairs on remote Pacific islands where no regular facilities were available.

In 1937, the well-known aviation medicine specialist Dr. R. E. Whitehead began describing symptoms of "aeroneurosis" among PAA pilots owing to the "concentrated flying" of the first year of Pacific operations. PAA pilots had to fly 135 hours in a two-week period during a Pacific roundtrip, the equivalent of nearly two months of domestic flying. The first leg alone, from Alameda to Honolulu, was nearly 20 hours. Instead of resting for 24 hours, as was the common practice under domestic operations, the next morning the PAA pilots pushed on, sometimes with as little as 8 hours of rest. Not surprisingly, the PAA pilots complained of fatigue and urged installation of suitable in-flight rest facilities for the crews. This remedy required full replacement crews of flying officers. PAA resisted this "fix" to the crew complement problems, citing the expense and the tradition of single command at sea.

In 1945, when it became apparent that the four-engine aircraft developed during the war would become a significant factor in postwar international travel, the Civil Aeronautics Administration (CAA) mandated that all "over-ocean" flights would have to carry a "flight engineer." The CAA's decision extended wartime rules. Civilian crews operating four-engine aircraft under contract to the military were required to carry a "crew chief" in addition to at least two pilots. The crew chief's responsibilities were essentially the same as those of PAA's prewar flight engineer. PAA set no precedents, however, because it always operated under special international rules. The nature of PAA's operations seemed irrelevant to domestic operations, although everybody wondered how much PAA pilots should be allowed to deviate from domestic airline norms.

The modern parameters of the crew complement issue began to take shape in July 1940 with the introduction of the Boeing 307 Stratoliner, which had a distinct flight engineer station. During the brief operation of the Stratoliner on Transcontinental & Western Air (TWA) (before the aircraft were commandeered by the Army owing to the war emergency), the flight engineer was neither fish nor fowl. He obviously was not aboard to make emergency repairs at remote bases, as was the case with PAA's flight engineers, and his in-flight functions were essentially those of an airman. So was he a mechanic or a pilot? TWA had no need of mechanics in flight —they were available at every TWA Stratoliner stopping point.

Through inadvertence, TWA staffed the Stratoliner flight engineer position with a "mechanic-trained" crewman. Everybody admitted that a "pilot-trained" crewman could carry out his functions just as well, but it seemed an unimportant matter at the time. They were wrong. The nature of the training of the crewman who would fill the "third seat" was the first phase of what would prove to be one of ALPA's most vexing controversies. It was also a crucial part of what would be ALPA's greatest crisis in the modern period, the defection of the American Airlines (AAL) pilots in 1963.

Charley Ruby, elected to ALPA's presidency in 1962, inherited this buzz-saw of an issue from Sayen:

> On National, the first four-engine aircraft we had was a C-54 we got from the military for crew training. Now, there were no flight engineer positions on the DC-4. On the C-54, really the same airplane as a DC-4 except that the Four had larger engines, higher gross weight, and a very much larger fuel capacity, there was a station for what the military called a flight mechanic. He could reach the throttles, landing gear, flaps, things like that. Pan Am had previously used what they called flight engineers on some four-engine aircraft. They really were mechanics, and they used to look after the aircraft in places where flying facilities were poor and minor repairs had to be done.
>
> There was confusion about what the flight engineer's function was really supposed to be. Was he a mechanic along to make a repair, or was he a guy who was supposed to help you fly the airplane? There was never any doubt in my mind, because I was a mechanic before I was a pilot, and I can tell you that whether the airplane was big or small, that third crewman's job was *not* to be a mechanic—it was to be a third pair of eyes in the cockpit. Ted Baker was always harping on the added cost of the flight engineer, but as the airways got more complex and as you spent more time talking on the radio, it was a safety factor to have the third man. Really the third man, *if he was a pilot too,* could be depended upon to do a lot of things.
>
> It was my judgment then, and it still is, that any place you have high-density traffic you are better off with a third guy from a safety standpoint.

By the time ALPA awakened to the seriousness of the crew complement issue immediately after World War II, the controversy was about to sharpen. On the one hand, the airlines would argue that the third crewman was unnecessary; on the other hand, a new breed of "airman" would argue that the third crewman should hold a special license and have mechanical background previously required only of ground maintenance personnel. This new breed of airman, the flight engineer, could also argue logically enough that since he was not really a pilot and not really a mechanic, he ought to belong to neither ALPA nor one of the unions representing ground maintenance personnel. In 1946, before ALPA was quite aware of what was afoot, a group of enterprising flight engineers secured an American Federation of Labor (AF of L) charter under the title Flight Engineers International Association (FEIA). So the crew complement issue was destined to become a three-sided struggle among ALPA, management, and FEIA.

Almost unnoticed, a competing union had slipped into the cockpit with ALPA. Although a good case could be made that ALPA had exclusive jurisdiction over all cockpit jobs as a result of its original 1931 charter from AF of L and that FEIA's charter was thus illegally granted, Behncke wasn't sufficiently on top of things to make that argument. Sayen later would declare that FEIA was an "illegal union" under AF of L's own rules and threaten disaffiliation because of it. By then, however, the "camel had his nose inside the tent," as Jerry Wood put it.

Ironically, were it not for ALPA's concerns about safety, no airline would have been using *any* flight engineers—pilot or mechanic. A series of fatal airline crashes in 1947 forced President Truman to appoint a special presidential board of inquiry into air safety under the chairmanship of Civil Aeronautics Board (CAB) head James M. Landis. Three domestic airline crashes during a two-week period in July 1947 killed 145 people. Truman appointed Bart Cox of AAL, Bob Buck of TWA, and Jerry Wood of Eastern Air Lines (EAL) to the board, which met for seven months to investigate the general safety of U.S. commercial aviation. Ernie Cutrell of AAL also played an important technical role in these proceedings.

In October 1947, while the presidential board of inquiry was in session, one of those rare crashes occurred that focuses attention on a larger problem. A UAL DC-6 flown by Capt. E. L. McMillen and First Officer G. C. Griesbach crashed near Bryce Canyon, Utah, after an in-flight fire. It was one of a series of baggage compartment fires in the new pressurized aircraft. Fortunately for posterity, McMillen and Griesbach lived long enough to give accurate radio descriptions of their predicament and to give investigators enough clues to pinpoint the combination of design and operating deficiencies that caused the DC-6 crash. Fuel for the cabin heaters came directly from a main wing tank. A malfunction in this system caused a fire that broke out in the baggage compartment. One of the passengers who died in the Bryce Canyon crash was an ALPA employee, Fred Munch, a young attorney. In a situation reminiscent of the Cutting crash of 1935, thoughtful investigators wondered whether the crash might not have been averted if a third crewman had been aboard whose primary function was to monitor auxiliary systems such as the cabin heater.

After the Bryce Canyon crash ALPA turned its full attention to securing a third crewman for the DC-6. CAB hearings on the subject ran concurrently with the presidential special inquiry hearings. ALPA stood alone in the industry arguing that the DC-6 was too complicated to operate with only two pilots and that if such operations continued, more Bryce Canyon disasters would surely result. The aircraft manufacturers, the airlines, and initially the CAB took the opposite view. Douglas had designed both the DC-4 and DC-6 with only two crew positions. The airlines argued that a third crewman on the jump seat would have nothing to do and that modifying the DC-6 to include a flight engineer's station would cost $57 million.

Taking time out from his duties on the Truman board, Jerry Wood helped ALPA Treasurer Bob Strait of TWA, A. W. Stainback of UAL, and Bill Masland of PAA testify during the CAB hearings. They made excellent use of the Bryce Canyon crash during the three-day hearings. As if to emphasize their concern, in November 1947, an AAL DC-6 made a successful emergency landing in New Mexico after an in-flight fire similar to the fatal one at Bryce Canyon. The CAA grounded all DC-6s after an investigation proved conclusively that the cabin heater had a design error that could be compounded by pilot distraction.

This information arrived just when the industry, the CAA, and public opinion were on the verge of pinning nearly total blame for airline accidents on pilots. The Sisto incident added fuel to the antipilot fire. In October 1947, Capt. Charles R. Sisto of AAL was riding in the jump seat of a DC-4 enroute to the West Coast from Texas. As a joke, Sisto engaged the gust lock. Capt. Jack Beck was flying in the left seat when Sisto pulled his prank. Beck made minor trim corrections over the next few minutes owing to light turbulence and occasional movements of the 49 passengers. Copilot Mel Logan, who also held an airline transport rating, muttered about the peculiar handling characteristics of the airplane.

"I finally decided the joke had gone far enough," Sisto said later. But when he disengaged the gust lock, the unusual trim tab settings caused the DC-4 to nose over inverted into an outside loop. Luckily, Jack Beck's seatbelt was loose, so when the force of the DC-4's downward tuck slammed him to the cockpit roof, he accidentally feathered three of the four engines, thus averting a power-on dive. Copilot Logan's quick thinking saved them. The control pressures were too high to move the elevators, but the ailerons were working. So just as the DC-4 reached the horizontal plane of its outside loop, he rolled the plane upright, and they screamed along above redline limits 400 feet over the west Texas desert. Sisto's career as an airline pilot was over, although to the puzzlement of many pilots, Behncke defended him to the bitter end. "This incident could have been averted," Behncke argued, "had the DC-4 been equipped with a properly designed gust lock system."

So had it not been for the courage of Captain McMillen and Copilot Griesback, who managed to radio enough clues to allow investigators to pinpoint the cause of the mysterious, fatal fires aboard the DC-6, CAB probably would have once again fixed "pilot error" as the cause of a series of unexplained crashes. The Sisto case certainly pointed to that, as did the crash of a nonscheduled Burke Air Transport DC-3 in July 1947. The investigators found that the Miami-based airline's two pilots had been airborne for 23 hours during the previous 37, and that the crash almost certainly occurred because both exhausted pilots were asleep. This incident was actually more a case of CAA's lax supervision of nonscheduled airline operations than of pilot incompetence, but the public didn't see it that way.

In his testimony before yet another federal board investigating safety, Behncke told the so-called Finletter commission, a blue-ribbon panel appointed by Truman to look into aviation, "Pilots have become the scapegoats." He savagely attacked the CAB's investigation of accidents and recommended the firing of CAB Chairman James M. Landis, who was then heading the full investigation of air safety. Behncke kept pounding away, defending any and every pilot, including the unfortunate Sisto. Luckily for ALPA and the industry, the DC-6 that landed safely with a baggage compartment fire in New Mexico defused a growing sentiment to institute far more rigorous supervision of pilots and to make their dismissal easier. A study made by the CAA of the working habits of 240 airline pilots was also troubling. The CAA employed professional psychologists who tried to find out what kind of man made a "safe pilot." Behncke denounced the study, vowing never again to allow "attempts to make ALPA members guinea pigs for psychological careerists." The pattern of blaming the pilot for crashes was reasserting itself with a vengeance, and had it not been for strong ALPA political pressure, it might have worsened.

Exerting every ounce of political influence, Behncke sought the firing of CAB Chairman Landis. Landis had been noncommittal about the idea of a third crewman in four-engine aircraft, but ALPA regarded it as crucial in improving air safety. Admittedly, Landis had other enemies besides ALPA. Airline management was angry with him because he was niggardly with subsidies and because he favored an early form of "deregulation" that would permit nonscheduled airlines to compete more directly with the scheduled airlines. Against this Landis proposal, Behncke and the airlines could make common cause, for the "nonskeds" were almost totally non-ALPA.

Behncke's steady drumfire of criticism took its toll. For ALPA, the December 1947 emergency grounding of all DC-6s proved that pilots weren't the only problem, as the Landis-approved psychological study had seemed to argue. In January 1948, Truman reacted to the mounting criticism of Landis by curtly refusing to reappoint him to another term. This step was unusual, because Landis was a Truman appointee and a protégé of the powerful Joseph P. Kennedy, Sr. (father of future President John F. Kennedy). Ironically, Behncke and Landis patched up their differences, and Landis became one of the principal architects of the victory over Ted Baker during the National Airlines strike of 1948. After a long absence from aviation when he became an important financial adviser to the Kennedy family, Landis would reemerge in 1960 to challenge Clarence Sayen for ALPA's presidency.

After Landis's departure from CAB, ALPA policy solidified in favor of the three crewmen concept for all four-engine aircraft. After a series of hearings in early 1948, CAB ruled on April 4 that on "all aircraft certificated for more than 80,000 pounds maximum gross takeoff weight, and on all other four-engine aircraft certificated for more than 30,000 pounds where the Administrator has found that the design of the aircraft or the type of operation is such as to require [it] for safe operations," a flight engineer would be mandatory, whether there was a specific crew station for him or not. The Lockheed Constellation series had such a crew station, but the Douglas series did not, which had put Lockheed at a serious economic disadvantage in the competition for domestic orders. (Internationally, we must remember, it made no difference, owing to CAB's previous ruling that all "overwater international" flights must have a flight engineer.) CAB's ruling left the nature of the flight engineer's qualifications completely up to each airline, subject only to the vague licensing CAA had issued in March 1947, when it granted the first "flight engineer certificate."

ALPA regarded the April 1948 CAB ruling as a great victory for safety—not for "featherbedding," as AAL's C. R. Smith contended. AAL fought the CAB ruling to the bitter end, challenging it through a lengthy series of hearings and arguing that there was "nothing whatsoever for a third man in the cockpit of a DC-6 to do" and that he could only "get in the way."

Other airlines began complying at once, as soon as the DC-6 was returned to service after major modifications. There was, however, no agreement among them as to whether the flight engineers should be pilots or mechanics. Some, like Delta Air Lines (DAL), employed only pilots from the beginning, but others, like Chicago and Southern, employed only ex-mechanics. UAL got the worst of both worlds when "Pat" Patterson decided to employ *both* pilots and mechanics. To qualify as a "pilot" flight engineer on UAL, an applicant had to have 500 hours of pilot time, a commercial license with an instrument rating, and, of course, a flight engineer's certificate. UAL had no difficulty qualifying pilot flight engineers under the provisions of 1947 regulations. In a change of titles that ALPA would subsequently copy, UAL also decreed that henceforth copilots would be known as first officers and flight engineers would be called second officers, thus eliminating semantic distinction that might further muddy the waters.

The scene was now set for conflict with FEIA during the 1950s over the twin problems of second officer qualifications and a rival union's right to represent them. This cross would become Clarence Sayen's to bear. It undermined support for him among pilots who were particularly strong in their support of "brother airmen." This disaffection was particularly evident on AAL, as Frank Spencer remembers:

> It was during the early 1950s that the leadership of the American group became extremely dissatisfied with Sayen. One thing they were unhappy about was the third crew member concept. They somehow got the idea that Sayen was misleading management to

the effect that they might settle for something less than they wanted in exchange for a deal on crew complement. They misrepresented Sayen's position to the rank-and-file AAL pilot. Sayen was very refined, and airline presidents and big officials in government always treated him with kid gloves. You could tell that they considered him to be better than the people he worked for. That didn't sit well with a lot of AAL pilots.

Aside from Sayen's problems with some pilots, which, as Frank Spencer suggests, might well have been due more to personality than policy, the troublesome conflict with FEIA remained. A jurisdictional dispute between two unions is always messy, and historically there are seldom any clear winners. In this case, ALPA won the fight with FEIA, but it was so bloody as to be Pyrrhic, if not for ALPA itself, then at least for Clancy Sayen. Put simply, FEIA had to be controlled, and Sayen had to do it. With a competing union in the cockpit the captain's authority could always be directly challenged in theory, and it was frequently in practice. Armed with a complicated series of work rules and engineering performance charts, an element within FEIA set out to establish the "professional" flight engineer as a coequal force in the cockpit. Of course, this element did not include every nonpilot flight engineer, but it included enough of FEIA's leadership to alarm thoughtful ALPA members. Sayen's great burden was that he had to confront the FEIA leadership head-on to establish firmly ALPA's primacy in the cockpit. Many pilots who had worked side-by-side with nonpilot flight engineers never understood the true nature of the FEIA leadership's challenge, and they resented what they regarded as Sayen's "shafting" of fraternal co-workers and their union. This was particularly true on AAL and constituted a major weapon in the hands of the anti-Sayen element there. "It was bull----," says AAL's Roy Dooley, in a typically outspoken denunciation of the AAL leadership during the later 1950s. Articulate and tough, Dooley is a towering six feet five inches tall. He survived health problems in his mid-50s and returned to line flying. He never joined the splinter union that replaced ALPA on AAL, and he is still bitter about the way Sayen was treated:

Tom Latta and I were not in tune with the leadership group on AAL, but we did know ALPA policy. Clancy wanted us to represent ALPA in negotiations with management on this third crew member thing in 1956. Of course, he couldn't just send us over—the MEC [master executive council] would have to do it. Well, the MEC wanted no part of Dooley and Latta, so we were dead as far as representing our airline. Sayen typed up this list of major things about the crew complement policy and asked me to take it over and give it to Tommy Boyd, who was a vice-president, trying to explain to him just exactly what the third crew member thing was and why he thought it was important to airline management. I personally gave it to Tommy Boyd, just so AAL would never be able to say they

didn't know what ALPA meant. Sayen absolutely could not depend
on the MEC relaying straightforwardly what our policy was.

Stewart W. Hopkins of Delta Airlines (DAL) knew a crunch was coming
with FEIA almost from the beginning. Hopkins, now 72, retired from DAL
in 1969, if you call his active life since then "retirement." Hopkins probably
understood ALPA's crew complement policy as well as anybody, and he
subsequently preferred formal charges against an AAL MEC chairman for
violating that policy in negotiations with management. Hopkins recalls the
conflict:

> The really great problem came on the Lockheed Constellations be-
> cause it was absolutely imperative that a third crew member be in-
> cluded, there was a great deal of work back on that panel, and he
> had several controls to operate. On Delta, I think they made the
> right decision to use pilots, although it was mainly a matter of luck,
> not well thought out.
>
> On C&S [Chicago and Southern], we used mechanics. I was MEC
> chairman at the time, and I was approached by a number of the
> mechanics, nice guys, who said some of their boys wanted a crack
> at the third seat. We didn't object because at that time ALPA had an
> affiliate union for flight engineers. The understanding was that
> we'd support mechanic flight engineers if they'd affiliate with the
> ALPA group. But we were double-crossed. As soon as they got their
> licenses they jumped over to FEIA, and from then on it was just a
> bloody mess.
>
> There were these people in FEIA who were trying to build up a
> little empire. They tried to make it as complicated as possible, ac-
> cumulating great masses of manuals, and they'd haul this stuff
> aboard every flight, and they were trying to isolate that area from
> pilots. The first thing you knew they were in a pretty strong eco-
> nomic position, because you couldn't operate the plane without
> them.
>
> I think that to a certain extent the mechanic flight engineers did
> a pretty good job of brainwashing average pilots with the idea that
> what they were doing back there was so special that a plain old pi-
> lot couldn't begin to know how to do it. Well, that was baloney. But
> they almost got away with it by infiltrating FAA [Federal Aviation
> Administration] with their people up there in engineering posi-
> tions that were also policy-making positions.
>
> I remember Clancy called me up to the Feinsinger board on the
> flight engineer problem. We were in a war with FEIA at the time. So
> I took along Phil Morgan, who's dead now. There were people
> from ATA [Air Transport Association] there, and they sat back and
> kept their mouths shut. They weren't about to get involved in the
> conflict. FEIA had a parade of witnesses, and they were trying to
> make something bigger out of the flight engineer's job than it

ALPA's second president, Clarence
N. Sayen *(below)*, was elected in
1952 after serving as the
Association's executive vice-
president during the trauma of
Behncke's ouster. With some
reluctance, Sayen left a promising
career in academia for the right
seat in a Braniff cockpit. Behncke
chose him for the executive vice-
presidential post in 1949.

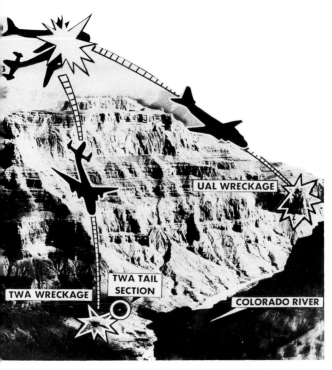

TWA WRECKAGE
TWA TAIL SECTION
UAL WRECKAGE
COLORADO RIVER

The Southern Airways strike of 1960-62 was the longest and costliest in ALPA's history—and the most important for the pilots' wage policy on regional airlines, reaffirming ALPA's principle of equal pay for equal work. Much of the expense of the strike was incurred by Superior Airlines, ALPA's effort to compete directly with Hulse and his strikebreakers. President Clancy Sayen and ALPA staffer Carl Eck *(opposite, top)* inspect one of Superior's de Havilland Doves. Picketing pilots *(opposite, bottom)* braved taunts, fistfights, and even gunfire during the 27-month strike. Among the key figures during Sayen's tenure, Capt. Stu Hopkins of Delta *(left)* was intimately involved with ALPA's crew complement policy. Capt. Jerry Wood of Eastern *(below, left)* served as the Association's first vice-president during much of Sayen's administration and formulated much of ALPA's jet pay policy. Henry Weiss *(below, right)*, ALPA's long-time general counsel, directed the legal maneuvers that eventually forced Southern's management to negotiate with the strikers.

ALPA's worst fears about "VFR on top" flying were realized on June 30, 1956, when a TWA Super Connie and a United DC-7 collided over the Grand Canyon *(top)*. The crash claimed 128 lives, then the highest toll in aviation history, and forced the federal government to supervise commercial aviation more closely, as legislated by the Federal Aviation Act of 1958.

John Carroll of TWA *(right)* lost the ALPA presidency to Charley Ruby in 1962 largely because many members considered him a link between TWA and the dissidents on American Airlines. The American dissidents eventually used the issue of crew complement as the wedge to split their pilot group from ALPA: with the issue apparently settled satisfactorily on every other airline, the American negotiating committee agreed with management that nonpilot flight engineers, represented by the Flight Engineers International Association, need not earn a commercial license and an instrument rating.

For travelers, jetliners like the DC-8 Super 63 *(above)* shrank continents and narrowed oceans. For pilots, the new equipment increased productivity, increased pressures, and—thanks to ALPA's careful preparations throughout the 1950s—increased pay scales.

In November 1956 the Board of Directors established the annual ALPA Air Safety Award for "outstanding contribution by members in the field of air safety." Thirteen years later, the winners to date gathered at a ceremony honoring the 1969 winner *(top, from left):* E. A. Cutrell, J. D. Smith, L. H. Mouden, J. L. DeCelles, B. V. Hewes, W. L. Collier, Ted Linnert, J. R. McDonald, J. W. Meek, R. C. Gerber, R. H. Beck, and 1969 winner D. A. Heine. Plaques at ALPA's Washington office *(above)* are inscribed with all the winners' names.

"Eight million people were scared airplanes were going to start falling on their heads like raindrops," said J. D. Smith, ALPA's Northeast air safety chairman. The sensational news reports during the investigation of the Brooklyn-Staten Island crash *(left)* fed the public's fears. On Dec. 16, 1960, a United DC-8 collided with a TWA Super Constellation in midair. The tragedy provoked accusations of pilot error from FAA Administrator Quesada, but the investigation uncovered faults in the air traffic control system and led to sweeping changes.

When the Board of Directors convened in 1962, Charles H. Ruby *(below)* didn't have his sights set on ALPA's highest office, but he answered the call when the delegates made him the Association's third president.

The personal animosity between American Airlines's MEC Chairman Gene Seal *(far right)* and ALPA President Clancy Sayen bore fruit in the American Airlines split of 1963. Dissident American pilots trumpeted Sayen's alleged bungling of the case of Capt. Wayne Allison *(right)* to rouse the rank and file against ALPA's officers. As the first to fly jets like the Boeing 707 *(below)* in domestic service, American pilots were the first to feel the pressures of the jet age, which may have contributed to their alienation from ALPA.

Capt. Robert W. Wilbur, Jr., *(below, left, with President Ruby)* and F/O James E. Hartley, Jr., *(below, right)* exhibited extraordinary courage when their Eastern Air Lines DC-9 was hijacked between Boston and Newark on March 17, 1970. The hijacker shot both pilots but was killed when Hartley, who had been mortally wounded, wrestled his gun from him before collapsing in the right seat. Despite gunshot wounds in both arms, Wilbur managed to land the plane safely in Boston. ALPA honored him with its Gold Medal Award for Heroism in 1970. Hartley was the first pilot to be honored with ALPA's highest award posthumously. Eastern's Miami training facility is dedicated to James Hartley.

On April 21, 1969, Charles A. Lindbergh, "whose contribution to aviation sparks the imagination of all who hear his name," was made an honorary ALPA member. Accepting the presentation from ALPA President Charley Ruby *(top, right),* Lindbergh said, "I don't know anything that would mean as much to me . . . I have always regarded my profession as that of a pilot, and . . . as a transport pilot."

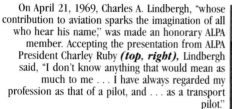

Although ALPA's move from Chicago was the subject of intense internal debate between 1962 and 1968, the check that purchased a plot of land in Washington, D.C., *(below)* proved an investment in the future of the Association. Twenty-four years after construction of the headquarters building was begun during Charley Ruby's term of office *(right),* the value of the property at 1625 Massachusetts Avenue surpassed $20 million.

really was. My god, you'd think a flight engineer had to have a Ph.D. in engineering!

FEIA embarked on a consistent policy of mystifying the flight engineer's function, and it led directly to a conflict over authority in the cockpit. What it boiled down to was we put a monkey back there on the panel, and when we turned around he was King Kong.

Since the early 1950s, the crew complement issue has confronted every ALPA president from Behncke to J. J. O'Donnell. The cornerstone of ALPA policy was laid in 1954, when the Board of Directors mandated that the third crew member, regardless of his function, ought to have a commercial pilot's license. It stood to reason, the board believed, that people working in the cockpit ought to be fully cognizant of the nature of the pilot's work. The goal, of course, was to make the flight deck fail-safe inasmuch as humanly possible. Although this policy did indeed have some adverse impact on FEIA, ALPA never adopted measures that specifically eliminated the competing union from the cockpit. But ALPA was determined in the interest of safety that, regardless of previous experience, the flight engineer must be able to take over temporarily for another crew member. As ALPA conceived the policy, it would also be a superb training device, allowing junior pilots to handle the controls regularly while serving primarily as flight engineers.

On AAL, C. R. Smith's recalcitrance, plus the resistance of the MEC, meant that to be the first airline to operate the Boeing 707 domestically, there were briefly *four* crewmen aboard instead of three: three pilots plus a nonpilot flight engineer who was a member of FEIA. (Technically, National Airlines was the first to operate the Boeing 707, owing to an interchange agreement with Pan Am.) FEIA resisted cooperating with ALPA in any way, even denying its members the right to take flight instruction paid for by the company, which was ALPA's policy.

Says EAL's Jerry Wood:

We never tried to get the old-time flight engineers out of the cockpit. We did want three pilots on the plane, and the point was to get the flight engineers qualified as pilots. FEIA tore up the industry because of that, not ALPA. We weren't trying to tear up their union either, because some of them are still around on some airlines, still represented by FEIA.

It was the right way to go, I believe, even though it was tough. The leader of FEIA was named Jack Robertson, and he was a lot like Behncke in that once he got an idea into his head, there was no way you could get it out. We employed 500 nonpilot flight engineers on EAL, and we had taken care of them. But Robertson called them out, all 500, and we had no choice but to break them. We gave them every opportunity, and eventually 104 of them came back.

The company paid every penny for their flight training, thanks to ALPA, and some of them are retiring right now as captains. The 10 or so who were unable to check out as captains did have to get their commercial and instrument rating to keep their jobs, but they maintained the same jobs they had as flight engineers with all protection.

Jerry Wood served on the 1956 Turbo-Prop and Jet Study Committee, and he personally wrote every word of the crew complement section of the report. "I had been more or less continuously involved with the issue since 1947, and strangely enough, Behncke left me 100 percent alone on that one," Wood adds with a chuckle. "As Dave put it, 'Boys, we're getting the plough under a pretty big stump.' And that was certainly the case on crew complement."

The hidden tragedy of the crew complement issue is the effect it had on Clancy Sayen. He was a dogged administrator, and he always carried out the mandates the pilots gave him to the fullest extent of his abilities. He never complained about the implementation of an ALPA policy once the board mandated it, no matter how much he might have disagreed with the policy personally.

"Clancy was very, *very* much opposed to what we were starting out to do on crew complement, incidentally," says Jerry Wood. "He told us that we were really getting ourselves into a period that was going to be rough. He was right—it turned out to be a bloody war."

Perhaps it was premonition that made Sayen oppose the mandatory crew complement policy. Eventually, it indirectly cost him his job. ALPA's crew complement policy was the rock upon which the AAL dissidents built their secession from ALPA in 1963, and they made Sayen's life so difficult that he resigned ALPA's presidency in 1962.

And what happened to the hundreds of professional flight engineers who declined flight training and persisted in the FEIA's fruitless strikes against the ALPA crew complement policy on several airlines?

"They picketed for about two years," says Jerry Wood. "Eventually they lost their cases in court, and the companies trained pilots to fill their jobs. They were just too stubborn to change. Those individuals who went along with the ALPA policy came out smelling like a rose, and those who didn't scattered to the four winds, and nobody knows what they are doing today."

In short order, a group of ALPA pilots on Southern Airways would be in a similar predicament—staking everything on the judicial process. It was a troubling episode with ramifications extending far beyond the question of whether 100-odd airline pilots would keep their jobs and be paid a decent wage. ✦

CHAPTER 18

The Southern Airways Strike of 1960

Frank W. Hulse, president and founder of Southern Airways (SOU, now merged into Republic Airlines), wanted no truck with labor unions. As a hustling "new South" entrepreneur, Hulse had to deal with labor unions because his various enterprises did a lot of work for the federal government. But whenever possible he made life miserable for union members. In 1958, Hulse broke the mechanics' union on his airline after a wildcat strike.

In early 1959, the SOU pilots figured they were in for trouble. Their ALPA contract was in negotiation, and they knew Hulse's destruction of the mechanics' union had made an easy settlement unlikely. ALPA was now the last labor union on Frank Hulse's property. Seven years of Republican administration in Washington had filled the Civil Aeronautics Board (CAB) with economic conservatives who were sympathetic to Hulse's antiunion stance. There were also some disquieting rumors reaching the SOU pilots that Hulse wanted a strike to see whether his pilots were "overpaid." Hulse had been known to mutter that they were and to speculate openly that in an open, free market he could hire cheaper qualified pilots. There seemed to be a lot of them around. Eastern Air Lines (EAL) had just furloughed 300 pilots, and practically all airlines had long furlough lists. In the recession of 1959, some pessimists thought the furloughs would be permanent. The airlines were encouraging their furloughees to return to the military for extended tours, since a steady job flying for the military beat none at all. In addition, there were still lots of World War II fliers left over, men who had never managed to get an airline job. Many of them had been living hand-to-mouth as gypsy aviators, working for rickety outfits in the Middle East and Latin America. Many of these pilots held current qualifications in the DC-3, the only planes SOU flew. All in all, it looked like big trouble for SOU's pilots.

In Chicago, Clancy Sayen was worried about the situation on SOU. By itself, SOU was just a small airline with only a few pilots. But ALPA's structure on the regional airlines (or "feeders," as they were called then) was always shaky. In a situation reminiscent of the National Airlines (NAL) strike of 1948, if one of them succeeded in breaking ALPA, Sayen expected others would surely try. In fact, he had already picked up disquieting hints that the regional carriers' association would definitely provoke a strike, on either SOU or Trans-Texas, just to test ALPA's mettle. Taking no chances, Sayen assigned Jim Pashkov, one of his best young negotiators, to the SOU case full-time in early 1959. The only other airline assigned a full-time staff negotiator was American Airlines (AAL). Obviously, more was at stake than just a small strike on a small airline employing a mere 140 pilots.

Fortunately for the pilots of every regional airline today, the SOU pilots stood firm against Frank Hulse's attempt to reduce them to second-class economic citizenship. For the airline piloting profession, it was a turning point.

The fundamental issue at stake in 1960 was equal pay for equal work. Historically, one of ALPA's most persistent quarrels was with the small airlines who argued that they couldn't afford to pay the high salaries that AAL, Trans World Airlines (TWA), and the big boys paid. Dave Behncke made resistance to this notion the cornerstone of ALPA's wage policy. ALPA has always insisted on the principle that the pilots of every airline, big or little, deserved the same pay for flying the same equipment. The smaller airlines never reconciled themselves to this idea, and from their beginning in the 1940s the new "feeders" paid substandard wages—at least until ALPA began (much to their surprise) to organize their pilots in the 1950s.

As a rule, the first ALPA contracts with the regionals were quite moderate. Clarence Sayen was a patient negotiator who was always willing to bargain. For first contracts with the regional airlines, Sayen was willing to accept inferior salary scales to win recognition of ALPA as the bargaining agent. He would be back later for better salaries. Frank Hulse knew this, but he had other ideas. Harry F. Susemihl, master executive council (MEC) chairman at the beginning of the strike, recalls:

> He *wanted* the strike—he engineered it. But let me tell you, this same man, if he were to walk into my living room this evening, would be very personable. He was a very enigmatic personality, friendly one minute and distant the next. Before the strike, he always called me by my first name, even if he met me out on the street. But after the strike, it was different. Many people who worked for him felt as if they knew him. But I don't think anybody really did, not any employee on any level. It's my understanding that when he sold Southern to North Central, even his top executives didn't find out through a personal phone call. He sent a courier over to the executive offices and played his message on a tape recorder, advising them that Southern Airways had been sold. I believe he was negatively affected by losing that strike to us in 1960. Mr. Hulse was not a good loser. In point of fact, we were pretty well beaten, economically, at that point. We had been out of work for more than two years, he was flying his routes, and he seemed to have won. We had to look for a solution in the political arena.

Nobody will ever know the full cost of the SOU strike of 1960. It was aw-fully high. ALPA spent over $2 million; SOU spent much more (and was technically bankrupt at one point during the strike). The federal govern-ment contributed nearly $10 million in direct subsidies to SOU during the strike. As we shall see, a substantial percentage of this huge outlay of tax-payers' dollars went directly to support strikebreaking.

But how do we measure the cost of the SOU strike in human terms? How can you put an honest price tag on the anguish of seeing a less qualified pi-lot take your job, of two years of hassles and fistfights and quarrels with local airport authorities over picketing rights, of having to make speeches to hostile audiences in the deep South? The South in 1960 was not the kind of place where people were sympathetic to strikers. Imagine what it must have been like trying to explain the strike to the Chamber of Commerce in Greenville, Miss. In the South, whipped up by propaganda, many people came to believe that labor unions were Communism's secret weapon to subvert America—even though there were no labor unions in the Soviet Union, and the American labor movement had long since gotten rid of its own Communist elements. Frank Hulse was more than willing to capital-ize on this kind of antipathy toward labor unions. The unionization of his pilots in 1951, only two years after he founded SOU, shocked him.

"He never forgave us for that," says John Boyd, who retired from SOU in 1976 and who is called "Senator John" because he spent so much time lob-bying in Washington during the strike. A mixture of admiration and resent-ment plays across his face as he discusses the early days with Frank Hulse. Boyd, who learned to fly in the Army during World War II, is well qualified to speak about those years, because he was working as a pilot for Hulse be-fore SOU existed:

> Mr. Hulse got a certificate late in World War II, but he did nothing with it until 1949. We got paid practically nothing at first, but in all fairness to Mr. Hulse, he really didn't have it. A couple of our early pilots had worked for other airlines. They were the prime movers on getting us thinking about ALPA. People like Sam Buchanan, W. S. McGill, and Jack Kendall, who had worked for better wages on AAL, began talking up union, and we got an election and went ALPA. Sam Buchanan was later discharged for another reason, but I'm quite sure he was discharged for forming the union, if you un-derstand what I mean. He later got killed flying corporate. Mr. Hulse didn't want Buchanan on his property because he thought Sam had double-crossed him.
>
> Most of the first batch of pilots, only about 50 of us, had known Mr. Hulse for years. We knew all the executives, people like George Estey, who was treasurer and who was my close personal friend. George is dead now, so I'm not going to hurt him by saying this, but he called me one night and said, "Listen, Mr. Hulse wants you to oppose forming the union." I said, "George, I can't do that; I

have to go with the pilots." George went back and told Mr. Hulse. After that, I found out I was no longer his friend; I was betraying him by going over to the union. That was the kind of atmosphere we were working under, and Mr. Hulse would have fired us all, I'm sure, except that under federal law he couldn't. He also needed us because our routes were basically Memphis to Atlanta with stops at Birmingham, Ala., Tuscaloosa, Ala., Tupelo, Miss., and Columbus, Miss., smaller towns that didn't even have paved runways, just grass cow pastures, mostly VFR [visual flight rules] flying. You couldn't just bring anybody in to fly those routes; you had to know them real well.

During the mid-1950s, relations between the pilot group and SOU's management were decidedly cool, and salary scales lagged considerably behind the national average. ALPA's policy of raising wage rates on one airline at a time, the familiar routine of "jacking up the house one corner at a time," worked less well on the regionals than on the majors because, although the majors received some CAB subsidies during the 1950s, the regionals were almost totally dependent on federal dollars. In that era of tight economic regulation, an airline's overall operating costs were closely scrutinized by the CAB. Airline management, particularly on the regionals, had to go hat-in-hand to Washington for annual bailouts. This provided them with an argument for low wages, which most pilots bought. In the event of extraordinary costs, they might have to submit to what the CAB called "crisis supervision," which could mean pilot layoffs.

CAB's goal was to make the regionals independent of the federal dole, but that came very slowly. Optimistic assessments of the eventual profitability of regional airline services had pretty well stopped by the mid-1950s. Adding to their poor economic performance was the aging of the DC-3, still the standard aircraft on most regional airlines. The regionals had equipped themselves with cheap cast-off Threes from the majors in the late 1940s and early 1950s. By the mid-1950s, they were wearing out, and obviously the regionals would soon have to start replacing them with modern equipment like the Martin and Convair twin-engine aircraft. That was going to require heavy financial outlays. The bankers exerted strong pressure on the regionals to cut costs and get their balance sheets in better order against the day when the banks would underwrite large loans for new equipment. ALPA's wage policy on the majors, who already operated the new equipment the regionals must soon acquire, would make pilot compensation an even larger expense if ALPA could force the regionals to pay comparable scales.

That, in a nutshell, was why the regionals began resisting ALPA's wage demands so strenuously in the late 1950s and why a nasty strike on one of them was inevitable. From ALPA's point of view, pilot productivity was going to increase markedly once the DC-3 was phased out, but the time to start breaking the regionals to the harness of contemporary wage policy was before the new equipment arrived. The strategy of the famous wage policy guidelines adopted by the 1956 convention was to proceed gradually and peacefully.

Conversely, from the regional airlines' point of view, the time to break ALPA was now, in the late 1950s, while the DC-3 was still in service and there was an abundance of pilots holding air transport ratings for it. To wait another year or two, until after the new equipment began arriving, would put ALPA in a commanding position and make strikebreaking impossible, since ALPA would command the loyalty of the only pilots capable of flying on short notice. Although a conspiracy is difficult to prove, every SOU pilot believes that the regional airlines did conspire to force a strike somewhere, simply because it was "now or never." In addition, the regionals reasoned that ALPA was so embroiled in the nasty dispute with the Flight Engineers International Association (FEIA) that it wouldn't be able to support a local strike on a small carrier effectively.

Clancy Sayen tried to avoid trouble by insisting that regional pilot groups seek only modest wage increases. Far better, Sayen believed, to concentrate on work rules rather than wages. Higher dollar amounts could come later, he reasoned, once new equipment was in operation. For the present, the smart thing to do was to win agreement on the principle of "trip rigs," which were already in use by most of the major airlines. SOU, like all the regionals, still used old-fashioned block-to-block pay computation. Against this attempt to modernize the method of pilot compensation, the regional airlines closed ranks, as former MEC Chairman Harry Susemihl recalls:

> We had complete confidence in Clancy Sayen. He wanted to pursue this as a classic labor dispute. But the company presented us with a "take-it-or-leave-it" package, and they had brought in an attorney to handle negotiations whose specialty was breaking labor unions. They were not negotiating in good faith. The opinion of Clancy Sayen, and of the Executive Committee too, was that ALPA was being given an ultimatum by the regional carriers' association. We felt pretty sure that a strike on one of the regional carriers was unavoidable. The judgment was that ALPA would be better off if the strike came on SOU because our pilot group was very nearly unanimous. I think we only had two nonmembers at the time the strike started. The other carriers had a much higher percentage of nonmembers. That is why the SOU pilot group won the dubious honor of going to the trenches on this one.

For nearly a year, from July 30, 1959, when SOU's agreement came up for renewal, until June 5, 1960, when the strike began, SOU's pilots were in almost constant negotiation and mediation, always hitting a brick wall. Hulse apparently believed that when push came to shove, his pilots would not walk out. He was also exploring the possibility of hiring scab replacements. When the SOU pilots finally notified the company that they had taken enough abuse and were therefore left with no alternative but to "withdraw from service" (in the quaint phraseology of the Railway Labor Act), SOU's management moved immediately to hire replacement pilots. As Bill Himmelreich (or "H," as his fellow SOU pilots called him) recalls, management fully expected the "new hires" to scab:

> I was 30 years old, getting right on the border line as far as whether I would be employable. I was furloughed by EAL in March 1960. Those of us who were laid off first were lucky, because we got what few flying jobs were available. An EAL crew scheduler called me and said that he had heard through the grapevine that SOU was going to hire new pilots very shortly. He warned me that SOU was a Mickey Mouse little outfit, but he pointed out that EAL wasn't always what it is today. Director of Personnel Everett Martin had told me during ground school that there would probably be a strike. He said to me, "In your case, with your background, we can make you a captain overnight." It didn't surprise me that right after the strike started, I got a message to call Everett Martin. I didn't, although I'm usually very conscientious about returning phone calls. The union had asked the probationary copilots to come out with them, and we did.

Taylor Abernathy, currently base chief pilot for Republic Airlines at Memphis, was a new hire, like Bill Himmelreich. Neither of them was yet on the payroll when the strike ballots were circulated, so they were walking into what would prove to be a very trying rite of initiation. Abernathy came from a union background, so he was neither shocked nor surprised at having to go out, but he admits to being uneasy:

> We had a vice-chairman named Al Hill, who was a very nice, low-key person, and he talked with the people who had been here just a few months. It was more or less expected of us to go out on strike. It was a big question mark, I think, from the company's point of view, as to what we'd do. They really thought that we would stay. We reluctantly went out because Al Hill talked with us, but there was no pressure.

The new hires thought the strike would be short. In fact, the first pickets turned out in a festive mood, and the temporary strike headquarters in Memphis's Holiday Inn looked like a cocktail party. The typical pilot on SOU had not been involved in the day-to-day negotiations over the last year and had no idea of how intractable management had become. The pilot leadership group was under no illusions, however.

Furthermore, the ALPA negotiating team was in temporary disarray owing to the death of Jim Pashkov, the staff negotiator Sayen had assigned full-time to the SOU case. Pashkov, in addition to being an attorney, was also a naval aviator. He was killed while flying a Reserve training mission when negotiations were at a critical point.

The SOU strikers began to realize that they were in for a long struggle when V. A. Knudegard and Wallace Wigley, chief pilots at the Atlanta and Memphis bases, respectively, resigned from SOU, refusing to be party to SOU's unfair bargaining tactics. Wigley had been frantically trying to avert the strike, and he believed he had settled all the outstanding issues. But much to Wigley's surprise, Hulse injected a new note into the negotiations. Like Ted Baker in 1948, Hulse demanded an end to seniority and the right to "discipline" leaders of the strike. That was too much for Wigley, who not only resigned, but angrily removed a sport coat given to him by Hulse and left it behind. ALPA added Wigley to its strike benefit fund, even though technically he was not eligible for it since he was not an ALPA member.

Wigley couldn't know, nor could any of the other strikers, that the pilots of Southeast Airlines, a small intrastate carrier in Tennessee, were about to be unemployed. Southeast was folding because CAB had refused to "certificate" its runs and awarded them instead to SOU. Its 24 pilots, all qualified to fly DC-3s, were available. Hulse believed they would go to work for him immediately, as did Everett Martin, SOU's personnel director, who warned the SOU pilots that he could replace them in a month. With these unemployed pilots as his ace in the hole, Hulse was extraordinarily truculent.

"Morale was good at first," says Phil Moss, who was on the negotiating committee. "I can still remember meeting Wallace Wigley at the airport after he had gone down to Birmingham to talk to Mr. Hulse. He got off the airplane and he had tears in his eyes. At that point the carnival atmosphere went out of it. I knew it was going to be a long, cold winter."

"I told the guys at that time," agrees John Boyd, "that the woods were full of the bodies of men who had underestimated Mr. Frank Hulse."

Round one went to the strikers. The chairman of the Memphis council, Jim Harper, had taken care to contact the Southeast pilots Hulse was counting on. Although they needed jobs badly, most of them refused to scab. Only a few of them crossed ALPA's picket lines to apply for jobs. Hulse began running advertisements in trade journals offering employment to qualified DC-3 pilots age 28 to 50. A fair number of men who had been fired for cause from other airlines began showing up in SOU cockpits. Hulse was offering the equivalent of sweatshop wages, but pilot employment opportunities were so limited that he could get away with it. The Federal Aviation Agency (FAA) bent every rule in the book to help him. FAA Administrator Quesada and his successor Najeeb Halaby, both of whom were notoriously antipilot and promanagement, aided Hulse's attempt to break ALPA.

The most celebrated FAA dereliction involved a scab named Hulihan, who had somehow wangled a job with only a private license and no instrument rating. As the strike deepened, the SOU pilots began setting up their own files on the scabs, doing the job FAA refused to do, carefully checking the scabs' backgrounds with an eye to discrediting their competence. A contact in the FAA records section checked on Hulihan and found that he held only a private license. By the time United Press International's Robert Serling broke the story, Hulihan was a captain. It created a dandy stink. Hulihan was promptly fired, but his flying for several months as a captain was an indictment of both SOU and FAA.

The SOU strike was simply too complex at all levels—at Memphis, Atlanta, Washington, and Chicago; in the legal system; in the stock market; and of course, ultimately, in politics—for any historian to do it justice. In some ways it was a repeat of the NAL strike of 1948, with the same techniques of banner-towing aircraft ("Don't Fly Southern"), fights between scabs and strikers at the airports, minor vandalism to SOU's property, and ALPA and SOU suing each other. But in some respects, the SOU strike was much harder because it went on so much longer. For example, although there were a few brief fisticuffs during the NAL strike, there was actually gunfire during the SOU strike. While assisting striking SOU pilots, Delta's George F. Metts was wounded by a shotgun-toting scab.

The SOU strike broke out at a bad time for ALPA. The FEIA dispute was in full flower, the major airlines were gearing up to resist ALPA under their Mutual Aid Pact (in which they would support each other financially during a strike), and the subsurface antagonism toward Sayen by a substantial minority of the ALPA membership was about to emerge. The financial burden of supporting the SOU strikers was heavy enough to exacerbate other problems.

"There was no way of turning the SOU spigot off," says Charley Ruby, who became president during the final stages of the strike. "We had to try to control the problem with a minimum of expense and still do a respectable effort. Our financial situation was so precarious that I didn't waste any time, once I got to Chicago, in chomping down on a lot of things."

One of the reasons the SOU strike cost so much was an ill-starred attempt to compete directly with SOU by running a rival airline. Superior Airlines, as the ALPA-sponsored outfit called itself, was an absolutely unique experiment in the annals of modern labor disputes. Superior operated eight-passenger de Havilland Doves in direct competition with SOU's most profitable routes and departure times. It capitalized on public apprehension about Hulse's strikebreakers, something that was much in the news by March 1961, owing to the Houlihan case and a couple of nonfatal accidents involving scabs. (FAA Administrator Halaby, stung by the bad publicity, publicly warned SOU to clean up its hiring, but he still maintained that the scabs were "qualified.") Offering free champagne and intensely personal service, Superior Airlines tried to keep ALPA's case before the public.

"Our purpose is to give good service and make money," Jim McCormick told the press. McCormick was Superior's treasurer as well as a striking new-hire SOU pilot (who was also on furlough from EAL). Nearly all of Superior's employees, whether they were driving baggage trucks or taking tickets, were SOU strikers. "Their purpose is purely harassment," Hulse fumed in return. Wallace Wigley, formerly Hulse's chief pilot, now filled the same role for Superior. Technically, the airline's president was an Indiana fixed-base operator named Willard Rusk, but it was an open secret that ALPA financed the venture. After losing nearly $1 million, ALPA folded Superior's wings in March 1962, although it hung onto the de Havilland Doves until United's Scotty Devine sold them after he became ALPA treasurer in June 1962.

"In retrospect, Superior Airlines was a gross error," Devine says. "Sayen was forced into it. He was a pretty good businessman, and I doubt that he ever thought it could be successful. A lot of our total expenditure for that strike came from trying to run that airline, and it didn't have much effect on the settlement of the strike either. But we had to fight like that because Hulse was trying to do what Wien tried in Alaska, and he had to be beaten one way or another. The SOU strike was a national issue, not a local one."

Sayen was forced to try direct competition with Hulse because of a series of adverse court and CAB rulings. Initially, Sayen hoped that the threat of a boycott of all airports serving SOU would end the strike. There was substantial sentiment among the pilots of several airlines to simply refuse to fly into any picketed airport. The courts squelched this approach. The other avenue lay in ALPA's charge that SOU had bargained unfairly by injecting into the negotiations a demand that "ringleaders" in the strike be "disciplined." This was clearly illegal under the terms of the Railway Labor Act.

But in September 1961 CAB Examiner William Cusick ruled in Frank Hulse's favor, dismissing ALPA's claims of unfair bargaining. As far as Cusick was concerned, the SOU strike was now over, and the strikers were permanently out. ALPA promptly appealed Cusick's ruling to the full CAB. Eventually, nearly two years later, this appeal would bear the fruit that would defeat Frank Hulse. But this story contains another one that involved politics at the highest level.

The SOU strikers had jumped into national politics by publicly endorsing John F. Kennedy during the 1960 presidential election. JFK was inclined to support them, but he had a few other things to contend with—like the possibility of World War III. Until vacancies occurred on CAB, it would continue to have a 3-2 Republican majority that had already shown itself to be hostile to ALPA in the SOU strike. Everything depended on JFK's appointments to CAB.

Harry Susemihl puts it very succinctly: "If Richard Nixon had won in 1960, neither I nor any other SOU pilot would ever have worked again." JFK owed his election to organized labor, and ALPA would now benefit from the AFL-CIO connection, as it had so many times in the past.

The unsung hero of the successful campaign to put a prolabor member on CAB, which would shift the five-member board's majority in favor of the SOU strikers, was a nonpilot named Charlie Overholt. Early in the strike, Sayen approved a request by the Memphis SOU pilots to put Overholt on their payroll as a publicist. He had worked for *The Memphis Union News,* a local AFL-CIO newspaper, so he knew labor's ropes well. Overholt's job was to run what the SOU strikers labeled the "Labor Contact Program" to line up labor support. It was entirely the idea of Jim Harper, the quiet, calm chairman of the Memphis council, and it paid handsome dividends in terms of national support. Before Overholt was through, practically every labor organization in America except the Teamsters had applied pressure in support of the SOU strikers. (The Teamsters finally admitted, in August 1962, what everybody in ALPA already knew—that they were bankrolling FEIA. Thanks to Attorney General Robert F. Kennedy, the Justice Department was now in full pursuit of Jimmy Hoffa, keeping Hoffa so busy in court that the Teamsters had no time to fish in aviation's troubled waters.)

No one will ever be able to measure the impact of organized labor's combined pressure on Congress and the President. If the pressure had not been constant and heavy, perhaps JFK might have tried to mollify the business community with his CAB appointment. Sacrificing a union local with a mere 140 members would be a small price to pay for better relations with businessmen. AFL-CIO pressure prevented it.

The problem on CAB was that one of the Democrats, Alan S. Boyd, had previously proven hostile to the interests of organized labor. In February 1961, when JFK made his first CAB appointment, he named Robert T. Murphy, a Rhode Island attorney, thus creating a 3-2 Democratic majority. JFK had known Murphy when Murphy was a Senate staff member. Insiders said he was a good choice for ALPA, since Murphy was well-regarded by the Rhode Island AFL-CIO. So JFK had made a good appointment, but a great deal still depended upon the pressure he placed on Alan Boyd. That's why the Labor Contact Program was so important: JFK had to feel pressure from organized labor so he would, in turn, pressure Boyd, whom he had recently appointed CAB chairman. The appeal of the anti-ALPA ruling was in progress then.

"The Kennedy Administration proved very helpful to us in the Southern case," says ALPA attorney Henry Weiss.

> One person who made a lot of difference was Professor Nathan Feinsinger, whom Kennedy appointed to a special fact-finding board on the strike. The Feinsinger hearings were very important in bringing out some of the illegal bargaining tactics used by SOU and also in dramatizing the extent to which the federal government was underwriting the strike through its subsidies. This accumulation of evidence was very important in swinging a majority on

CAB in our favor. I think it's fair to say the SOU strike was resolved through a combination of pressures — political, legal, and financial.

The Feinsinger commission, named for Professor Nathan Feinsinger of the University of Chicago, was created by President Kennedy to investigate the crew complement dispute among ALPA, FEIA, and the airlines. Secretary of Labor Arthur Goldberg had been responsible for JFK's selection of Feinsinger to head the President's commission on the airlines controversy. Because of intense political pressure from A. S. "Mike" Monroney, the Democratic senator from Oklahoma, JFK agreed to place the SOU strike within the jurisdiction of the Feinsinger commission.

Finally, the Feinsinger commission got around to hearing the SOU case in March 1962. SOU's principal witness was Earle Phillips, the attorney whose intransigence as a negotiator had created the strike in the first place. Phillips was obviously at pains to dodge key questions about SOU's subsidy payments from CAB. Eventually, under the patient questioning of Feinsinger, Phillips was forced to admit that since the strike began CAB had paid SOU over $9 million!

This sum staggered Feinsinger, who wanted to know what effect these taxpayers' dollars had on SOU's ability to withstand the strike. Plenty, as it turned out. CAB's chief counsel admitted under Henry Weiss's cross-examination that it simply did not know how much went for strike-breaking.

"There is no breakdown of so much for strike expenses or so much for maintenance," the CAB lawyer answered. How Frank Hulse spent the taxpayers' money was none of CAB's business, the lawyer insisted, so long as he rendered "honest and efficient service."

Phil Moss, who was in Washington during the Feinsinger hearings, remembers it as a turning point in the strike:

> The question arose as to how they accounted for the way those monies were spent. There was a CAB representative on the stand, and he said he could care less how they were spent. Once the money left CAB, it went to the carrier, and if Mr. Hulse wanted to light his cigar with a $100 bill, then it was perfectly all right with them. And Feinsinger said, "Would you repeat that please?" And the guy immediately knew he had said the wrong thing.

The Feinsinger commission provided all the factual information that would be necessary to overturn the finding made by CAB Examiner Cusick in 1960. CAB finally considered ALPA's appeal of Cusick's decision in May 1962, 23 months into the strike. The outcome was by no means a foregone conclusion, however, for although JFK had appointed people to CAB who were known to be prolabor, once they were seated he had no further control over them. Moreover, for CAB to overturn Cusick's findings would be a precedent—never before had CAB invoked its legal powers to determine whether an airline had "bargained in good faith."

The history of CAB's legal powers began with the Railway Labor Act of 1926, under which interstate carriers had to "exert every reasonable effort" to settle labor disputes. But the 1926 law gave the government no power (other than going to court) to force the carrier back into negotiations. Under the terms of the Civil Aeronautics Act of 1938 (as amended in the Federal Aviation Act of 1958), the airlines were required to comply with the provisions of the 1926 rail law. This gave CAB a power, called "cross-referencing," to enforce provisions of law spelled out in other acts, even though they were not originally written to cover aviation. CAB did not have specific statutory power to intervene in labor disputes. But CAB did have the power to shoot SOU out of the skies by canceling its "certificate of convenience and necessity." Without this certificate, SOU was not eligible for the CAB subsidy, and without the subsidy, it could not operate. Thus, through an indirect strategy mapped out by Henry Weiss, CAB could force SOU to negotiate with its strikers (not settle, merely negotiate).

In its final decision, CAB noted that SOU's prompt hiring of strikebreakers was evidence enough of "bad faith" on SOU's part. When SOU pilots, through the efforts of Wallace Wigley and others, had settled all outstanding disputes and were ready to return to work, they were prevented from doing so by Frank Hulse's insistence on the right to "discipline" strike leaders and to deprive them of seniority. "The demands of Southern relating to seniority are illegal," CAB stated flatly, for they "contributed to the prolongation of the dispute," in direct defiance of the 1926 Railway Labor Act. The crucial CAB ruling was made along straight party lines, with Democrats Boyd, Murphy, and Minetti voting in favor, and Republicans Gurney and Gillilland voting no.

Despite this favorable ruling, the issue was not yet firmly decided. ALPA promptly appealed the CAB decision to the courts. The reason for this apparent anomaly was that Henry Weiss feared SOU's lawyers would appeal it, and he wanted to place it under the jurisdiction of a judge more sympathetic to organized labor than the southern judge that Hulse's attorneys would likely choose. The court that receives an appeal first has jurisdiction. "We made sure the petition was dated and timed," says Weiss. "Nobody who knew Frank Hulse believed he would quit."

ALPA had one ace left in the hole, one that would eventually induce Hulse to surrender. Midway in the course of the strike, somebody mentioned to Clancy Sayen that ALPA had spent nearly enough on the strike to buy SOU. In fact, the dollar value of SOU's outstanding stock wasn't much more than the $2 million ALPA had already spent. So why not buy SOU? SOU's stock on the open market was quite low in 1961, owing to Hulse's purchase of a fleet of secondhand Martin 404s on credit. SOU was also just that much more vulnerable to CAB's threat to cut off its subsidy, and this weakness gave ALPA's national leaders the idea of buying up SOU stock to pressure Hulse further for a speedy settlement.

The stock purchase program was the brainchild of Memphis council Chairman Jim Harper. Originally, its purpose was to get striking pilots, who were also holders of token amounts of SOU stock, into the stockholders' meeting to raise a little hell. Under Clancy Sayen, this token purchasing program became quite another matter. Using various fronts to disguise the stock acquisition program, ALPA eventually accumulated about 22 percent of all SOU common stock—enough to threaten Hulse's control of his own airline!

Hulse awakened to this threat simultaneously with the CAB ruling against him, when a Baltimore investment group holding nearly 30 percent of SOU's common stock approached ALPA's new president, Charles Ruby, and Treasurer Scotty Devine about a deal. Hulse was beaten now, and he knew it, so he gave up. There would be no more trouble, he let it be known, if ALPA would agree to sell him its SOU stock at market value. There would be no repeat of the poststrike hassles that the NAL pilots experienced in 1948. He would throw the scabs to the wolves, excepting only that they would come to work for him at the bottom of the seniority list when openings became available. Hulse was, in short, following the historical pattern of businessmen who make promises to scab pilots—the promises were good only so long as they were convenient. The scabs were now on their own, and nothing they could do would save their jobs. They tried forming their own union and filing suit against CAB, just like the NAL scabs had done in 1948. It didn't work for them either.

And so the longest strike in ALPA's history was over. The majority of the luckless scabs would never work for SOU again, despite Hulse's earlier promises. Those few who managed to remain on SOU's payroll must surely take small comfort that the high salaries they enjoy today were bought with the sweat and anguish of others.

"About 30 of them altogether managed to hang on," says John Boyd, with more than a hint of disdain. "They were the kind of people who could convince themselves that there wasn't anything wrong with what they did. The ones who couldn't convince themselves were the ones who couldn't take the pressure and quit."

"A few of them were young when they scabbed," says Bill Himmelreich, who was just as young himself. "I know that some of them would join if ALPA had a program like the typographers, where a man could get into the union after scabbing if he paid dues for the entire time that he scabbed and all the assessments. Several of them have told me that they'll regret what they did for the rest of their lives, and if ALPA would let them in they'd be down to see their bankers the next morning, ready to pay whatever it took."

ALPA fought the SOU strike like there was no tomorrow. Something much more important was at stake than just a small strike on a small airline. In a sense, the 1960-62 strike was the Magna Carta of ALPA's wage policy, and the struggle the SOU strikers waged in those years has paid dividends ever since for pilots of regional airlines.

Perhaps the final word on the SOU strike of 1960-62 is best spoken by Jim Harper, who was so deeply revered by his fellow SOU pilots. In an interview before his death, Harper put it all in perspective:

> The pilots built SOU with their dedication. Management tried to destroy it with greed. It was a real shoestring operation in those days. We'd take company scrip in lieu of money, and on our off days we'd all load into an airplane and blitz a town. By that I mean we'd move into a community and try to sell SOU. We did it for free, on our own time. We built that airline. We put our guts into it. But we'd have gotten nothing out of it if it hadn't been for ALPA. That's why we pilots should be committed to the labor movement, perhaps more definitely than a plumber or a carpenter. ALPA is known, of course, as an "Association," but we are part of the labor movement. We have to have _union_.

CHAPTER 19

Internal Politicking, 1960–1962

C lancy Sayen was 41 years old in 1960, a year of decision for him. He had drifted into the ALPA presidency almost inadvertently in 1951, and like many men who have careers thrust upon them, Sayen was dissatisfied. It seemed almost as if he had never made a choice of his own, as if his life were drifting away from him, under the control of others. If he were ever to seek a career of his own choosing, it would have to be soon.

"Clancy had become increasingly unhappy with the job over a number of things," says Jerry Wood of Eastern Air Lines (EAL). "The constant attacks by dissident members hurt him. The age 60 thing hurt, too, because he was caught in the middle. The junior guys wanted to get the old guys out, but this was done tacitly in the inner workings of ALPA without the press and public ever knowing how deeply split we were."

Sayen was ALPA's focal point for every variety of discontent, both internal and external. He felt stifled and impotent, battered from every side by people with special grievances, all of whom seemed to blame him for their problems. Put simply, by the end of Sayen's third term, he was burned out on ALPA. He had lately received offers to enter private business with friends, and he was eager to accept. With his restless energy, quick mind, and facile executive style, Sayen would be a natural in the business world, as more than one airline executive with whom he had dealt realized. Sayen felt a strong urge for personal growth and development, as his academic career while he was a Braniff copilot had proved. But the lure of academic life had weakened for Sayen. At his age, he was too old to seek further graduate education, and in any case, the fast track in the business world attracted him more. Had it not been for two factors, Sayen would almost certainly not have sought reelection to a fourth term as ALPA's president in 1960.

The first factor was the Southern Airways (SOU) strike. By mid-1959, the situation on SOU had deteriorated so badly that a strike seemed unavoidable. Sayen felt obligated to the SOU pilots to see them through the crisis, and the timing of developments there forced him to delay making a firm decision to resign. Then, by early 1960, the second factor caught up with Sayen, one that would rouse his competitive instincts and force him into a hotly contested race for the presidency. For the first time in ALPA's history, a prominent nonpilot, an outsider, was seeking the ALPA presidency. Former Civil Aeronautics Board (CAB) Chairman James Landis, a man with powerful connections and a formidable background in the legal profession, was the candidate of a strong anti-Sayen group that emerged in certain EAL locals.

James M. Landis was pure, up-from-the-depths Boston Irish, a comer who fought his way to the top through the thickets of politics and law. Enroute, he became a close political ally of Joseph P. Kennedy, Sr., the former ambassador to Great Britain, Democratic party power, and father of John F. Kennedy. Landis was entirely capable on his own, but the patronage of the elder Kennedy led to Truman appointing Landis to CAB in 1946. When Truman and old Joe Kennedy had a falling out in 1948, Landis lost his CAB chairmanship. Dave Behncke had warred continuously with Landis during his tenure at CAB, but once Landis left office they became fast friends. Behncke had an eye for legal talent, and in his prime Landis was among the best lawyers in the country.

During the late 1940s, Landis served ALPA well on several occasions, the most famous being the National Airlines (NAL) strike of 1948. After that, Landis represented individual pilots in numerous grievance cases. All the while, he was working as a principal financial and legal adviser to the Kennedy family. When John F. Kennedy won the Presidency over Richard Nixon in 1960, Landis headed a blue-ribbon commission on government reorganization during the transition. After the inauguration, Landis filled a permanent slot on a similar presidential commission, one function of which was to look into the regulatory agencies, particularly CAB. In his capacity as a Kennedy campaign adviser, Landis began to make contacts with dissident ALPA members in early 1960. In short order, a diverse coalition of anti-Sayen elements hatched a plan to run Landis against Sayen at the upcoming Miami convention in November 1960. From the dissidents' point of view, Landis had everything. He was well-connected politically, he had a highly recognized name among pilots, and he was a legal expert at dealing with regulatory agencies like CAB. Their major hurdle was that Landis was not a pilot and never had been.

"It was an odd episode in the odd life of Jim Landis," says Henry Weiss, who knew the former Harvard Law School dean well.

> When Kennedy was elected President, Landis was selected as an in-house adviser, although I'm quite convinced he was there only as a sop to old Joe Kennedy. He never had that much influence on Jack Kennedy, perhaps none at all. His attempt to unseat Sayen was actually something of an embarrassment to the administration—here Landis was, out running for the presidency of a union at the same time he was advising the future President! There were several efforts made to get him to withdraw, and just before the convention in Miami, I was contacted by someone in the administra-

tion and asked to persuade him to withdraw. Of course I kept Clancy fully informed of the administration's lack of interest in seeing Landis replace him.

Perhaps Landis was unaware that JFK himself was trying to keep him from challenging Sayen, and certainly the dissidents supporting him were unaware of it. Their promotion of the Landis candidacy was motivated more by dislike of Sayen (and their repeated failures in 1952 and 1956 to replace him with another pilot) than by any particular attachment to Landis. Possibly Landis, feeling very much an outsider and an anachronism among the youthful JFK entourage, sought to escape from an intolerable situation, and he saw the ALPA job as an easy one from which he could draw a nice salary by trading on the influence and reputation he still had.

In September 1960, while the JFK-Nixon campaign was in full swing, Landis declared his candidacy for the ALPA presidency, announcing what amounted to a "platform" calling for various improvements in the way ALPA was run. Landis made it clear, however, that he was challenging Sayen for the ALPA job because Sayen had failed as a leader. Landis insisted that he had the support of the "majority of the nation's working pilots." He said ALPA had fallen badly behind under Sayen, that it lacked "leadership, organization, and a program for the future." He called for "decentralization and the recruiting of experts" to run ALPA, and he chided Sayen for failing to provide the "public relations" the pilots needed. This latter comment was, of course, a thinly veiled hint that ALPA would have a friend in the White House should JFK win. Pilots from 16 airlines were named as the "campaign committee" for Landis. Without exception, they were part of the anti-Sayen faction that had never been able to command a majority in any convention before. With Landis, they hoped to change that.

When reporters asked Landis to cite specific examples of Clancy Sayen's failings, he mentioned the SOU strike, then three months old. A smile must have crossed Sayen's face in Chicago when he read that remark. In fact, the SOU pilots idolized Sayen. Furthermore, Landis cited the 1960 wildcat strike by EAL pilots over Federal Aviation Agency (FAA) Administrator Quesada's demand for unannounced check rides by inspectors in the new jets. Slim Babbitt and Jerry Wood must have smiled at that one. They were still among the biggest of EAL's big guns, and they were committed to Sayen. But to anyone who understood how democratic ALPA's internal politics were, the Landis candidacy was no joke. Landis was campaigning vigorously, visiting local councils all over the country.

Vern Peterson still bridles at the mention of Jim Landis. The men who had built ALPA were going to take no chances on losing control of it to an outsider:

Landis had the age 60 thing to work with, and he gave the impression that he could do something about that in Washington. It created quite a bit of hard feelings. [His supporters] said, "If you're not for Landis, you're against the age 60 retirement rule." Sayen, of course, opposed the rule. I got quite embroiled on that thing on our own airline, because the thinking was pretty balled up. The vote was actually very, very close, and we suffered quite a few pains and uncertainties.

Jerry Wood first heard of rumblings of the Landis candidacy in the summer of 1960, before the anti-Sayen dissidents announced it openly. Wood began quietly politicking on Sayen's behalf. He also kept his ear close to the ground, trying to ascertain just how much support the anti-Sayen movement enjoyed among the rank and file. Wood admits opposing Landis's candidacy with some regret:

> Jim Landis was a good friend and a nice guy. Under other circumstances I could have supported him, but I thought we needed someone with Clancy's qualifications more than we needed a brilliant lawyer. The main attack on Clancy was coming from people who disagreed with our wages and working rules policies. I was chairman of the committee that originated those policies, so I was in a position to judge which man was better suited to carry them out.
>
> Jim Landis's candidacy was spearheaded on EAL by Chuck Basham, Bob Silver, and Bill Frye. Also, Joe Stewart of NAL was very active in getting Landis to take a shot at the presidency. However, after the campaign got going, the American [AAL] crowd got behind Landis.

When the convention met in Miami on Nov. 14, 1960, the key vote on the Landis candidacy was a purely procedural one. A provision of the ALPA by-laws required a two-thirds majority of the Board of Directors to make a nonmember eligible for president. If Landis lost on the procedural question, no vote on his actual candidacy could be taken. Before the key procedural vote came up, Landis's backers tried to win a suspension of the rules, allowing Landis to address the convention directly. They argued that in the name of democracy all sides of every question ought to be heard. The opposition, led by Jerry Wood, countered with a display of hard-nosed politics. They knew that Landis was a formidable rhetorician who might well sway the convention with his eloquence. So they staked everything on a vote denying him the right to address the convention until after the vote on the constitutional amendment. They knew they had the votes to win, which would make Landis's candidacy moot. After that, Landis's eloquence wouldn't matter.

Capt. Jack Young of EAL clearly stated the case for allowing Landis to address the convention:

> There is no question that Mr. Landis is well-qualified for this job. The fact that he has had the confidence of three former Presidents

of the United States, and President-elect Kennedy as well, is an indication that he is qualified. If I want someone to fly an airplane, I go to a pilot. If I want someone to handle my affairs, I'm going to find someone who is an administrator. This is why I turned to Mr. Landis. I think if we do not even consider Mr. Landis, we will do ourselves great harm.

Sayen's supporters pulled out all the stops to beat back the Landis candidacy. They argued that the special character of ALPA required a pilot as president and that its unique position within the labor movement would be lost if a nonpilot should become president. One by one, men who had been involved in ALPA from the beginning came to the front of the hall to express their views with extraordinary clarity and historical purpose. Most people are not well versed in history, even their own. But the delegates to the 1960 convention who opposed the Landis candidacy knew the history of ALPA and how to use it.

Chuck Woods of United Airlines (UAL) argued cleverly that the only reason an outsider was interested in the ALPA presidency was because the pilots themselves had already made a success of it. "I take tremendous pride in ALPA," Woods declared. "I have seen it develop people within its own ranks who have become experts in every field. Mr. Landis's qualifications impress me, and I wish I had some of them. I do not, however. I am an airline pilot. I would like to keep this organization for the pilots. I think we can develop among our membership whatever leadership we need."

Paul Reeder of UAL had been an ALPA member from the beginning. "The history of pilots' organizations goes way back to the 1920s," Reeder reminisced.

I was in on the birth of ALPA. Dave Behncke ran for office in the NAPA [National Air Pilots Association] and was defeated by Dean Smith, who was with Byrd at the South Pole. Dave then spread off and organized a group especially for airline pilots, and that was the birth of ALPA. From that day to this, we have managed to run our own affairs. I believe we should keep it that way.

The transcript records that each of these speeches was followed by applause, neatly noted in brackets by the stenographer. Obviously the dissidents supporting Landis did not have the votes to present him to the convention. But at the same time, there was no point in totally alienating them. Before the actual vote was taken, Capt. Ray Hutchison of Pan American magnanimously suggested that EAI's Chuck Basham, Landis's most prominent supporter, be allowed to speak his piece fully.

"Mr. Chairman," Hutchison said, "we have with us here tonight a member in good standing who has been the campaign manager of what I believe will be the cleanest campaign that you in your lifetime will ever see for the presidency of ALPA. Therefore, I request that Chuck Basham be allowed to speak to this body."

Basham proved adept at enunciating his position, probably performing as well as Landis himself could have done:

> Gentlemen, I think there is an issue here stronger than Mr. Landis. There is a lot of emotion on the floor, and I think we ought to bury it. It is going to be very difficult to explain that we were scared to make Mr. Landis eligible for a 51 percent majority. That is all that is being asked, a democratic approach. You have a leverage of a two-thirds majority, which should protect us from every Tom, Dick, and Harry from outside. But we selected Mr. Landis because he is a man of great stature and dignity, the top administrator in the United States. You are insulting him if you do not get rid of this two-thirds lever and make him eligible. I believe you have every legitimate right to want a pilot as president, but this is a time of specialists. Mr. Landis is a specialist, and that is why he was asked by President-elect Kennedy to handle jobs far in excess of the complications of ALPA. Needless to say, I do not have to make a pitch for his background.

But Basham's argument swayed nobody. Landis lost on a voice vote, one Basham and his supporters were willing to accept. But from the AAL councils, the demand emerged for a roll call vote. The leader of this movement was Nick O'Connell, the man who would lead the AAL pilots out of ALPA in 1963 when he became master executive council (MEC) chairman. O'Connell's parliamentary tactics were futile, and they occasioned a lively dispute with Henry Weiss, the convention's parliamentarian. Whatever good will was engendered by the graciousness of Landis's supporters in defeat was quickly dissipated in O'Connell's parliamentary nitpicking.

"I feel like I have completed my obligation," O'Connell said afterward. "It is an honor to be on the losing side."

After the roll call a massive desire for internal harmony made Sayen's election nearly unanimous. The victors were magnanimous toward Landis's supporters. After the vote, the convention gave a standing vote of appreciation to Judge Landis.

The members rose and applauded Basham as he left the convention floor. The Landis episode was over, and but for the lingering animosity of the AAL group, which had become chronic in ALPA affairs since the late 1950s, a spirit of harmony prevailed. Of the convention's business, only renominating and electing Sayen to another four-year term remained. He had no announced opposition at this point. Stewart Hopkins of Delta made the principal nominating speech, masterfully summing up Sayen's strengths and weaknesses:

> Gentlemen, what you said was that you wanted an airline pilot. But I think you should realize that in Clancy Sayen, you also have an

outstanding administrator. Some of you can remember 1953, when this Association was a bankrupt shambles, torn by factions, about to go under. The last 10 years of progress did not come out of thin air.

In addition to being an administrator, Clancy Sayen is a teacher. I do not know how many of you are aware of it, but your whole complex of loss of license, mutual aid, insurance, and retirement is practically a product of his mind. He not only conceived the program, but he taught the staff and negotiation committees that implemented it.

Clancy has very little patience. He refuses to create a father image. He refuses to hold anyone by the hand. He treats you like adults. I know how hard he works, how basically honest he is, and how brilliant he is.

Sayen was elected by a voice vote. The AAL pilots constituted the core of nays. A subsequent voice vote to make the election unanimous saw the AAL councils remain silent. It was an ominous sign.

Thus, Clancy Sayen was elected to a fourth full term in an office he never really wanted in the first place. What he thought we can only imagine, but the ambiguity in his acceptance speech gives more than a hint of dissatisfaction, both professional and personal. While the climactic debate over the Landis vote was in progress, Sayen had absented himself from the convention. He was, quite frankly, smashed when the delegates called him back to the floor:

Gentlemen, I have been in the bar. If I seem a little incoherent, there are several reasons. One reason, I have been in the bar. . . . The other reason is that we have had some rough years, and I do not think they are going to get easier. If I said so, I would just be trying to kid you and me. One reason is that we fight so hard among ourselves, and our fights with other people are getting harder, the pressures are getting greater, the mistakes getting bigger.

I hope that out of all this we can learn something. The essence of democracy is controversy. If there's not any controversy we're not doing very much. As long as the controversy takes place within acceptable bounds and when it is over people will with dignity accept the result and work together, then we have the very essence of democracy.

You have heard me make speeches enough. I do not want to make any more.

As even the casual reader can tell from the tone of this impromptu acceptance speech, the heart had gone out of Clancy Sayen. He had had it with ALPA, both professionally and personally. Only his competitive instincts led him to accept a fourth term, and though his supporters couldn't know it, he had no intention of serving out his full term.

Perhaps only Henry Weiss was fully aware of Sayen's state of mind at that time:

> Clancy was a man who really had no great taste for politics within his organization, even though he was literally idolized by a great many people in ALPA. He was competent and devoted to his duty, but he didn't have a sense for going out and dealing with the rank and file; in fact, he disliked it. In the first four or five years of his presidency, Clancy would not venture out of his office, and he avoided spontaneous, face-to-face meetings with officers of the government, airlines, and sometimes his own people. In other words, he essentially started out dealing with his own people in a very insecure way. That insecurity never did leave him, but you had to know him quite thoroughly to know that.
>
> In early 1960, Clancy told me he was going to retire as president of ALPA. I had two serious approaches by the U.S. government, asking me to sound out whether Clancy would be interested in taking a position with the Kennedy administration. I did sound him out and came back with the answer that he wasn't ready to make up his mind. He was very close to Lane Kirkland, who is now president of the AFL-CIO and who was very close to the Kennedy camp. I feel sure that Clancy was under consideration for an undersecretary of labor and could have had it for the asking.
>
> But he had other notions that he confided to me. He was such a top-notch, extraordinary individual, and he had worked his rear off for 11 years, and he was not prepared to commit himself at that point to the future. He and Lane Kirkland had some thought of a common enterprise, possibly sometime in the future, but first he wanted a break. He wanted to buy a boat, go sailing in the Caribbean, do many things. He was bored, and he told me, "I'm getting tired of getting a thousand dollars more a year for pilots who already have enough money. What am I doing with my life?"
>
> But nonetheless, he continued in office in 1960 and 1961, and the culmination of his boredom and the fact that some pretty bad boys were nipping at his heels caused him to resign. They never had a majority, but they made life very unpleasant for Clancy, and after 1960 there were repeated confrontations on the Executive Committee that were really ugly. He was, in effect, almost driven from office.
>
> Finally, Clancy asked me to draft a letter of resignation. I sat on the damn thing, stalling him. He finally sent me a note saying, "Hey, if you don't write it, I'll write it myself."

Sayen announced on Oct. 31, 1961, that he intended to resign from the ALPA presidency effective with the next Board of Directors' convention, which was soon after rescheduled for Miami in late May. This set off a furious round of internal politicking, most of it purely personal. Technically, Sayen's resignation in midterm (between conventions) would have meant that First Vice-President John Carroll of Trans World Airways (TWA) would become president. Sayen's decision to delay his resignation until the next board meeting meant that Carroll would have to campaign for the office like any other candidate. The anti-Sayen forces, which we must remember never commanded a majority at any convention, launched a vigorous assault on Sayen, claiming that he should step down immediately.

"We had confrontations where the Executive Committee refused to adjourn unless Clancy resigned then and there," recalls Henry Weiss.

But Sayen wouldn't resign in favor of John Carroll. He regarded Carroll as a link between the AAL dissidents and the TWA councils, and he feared that if Carroll became president, TWA would slip into the AAL orbit. Sayen was not alone. Although Carroll was widely liked on a personal basis, he still excited a vague distrust among many people. This distrust had more to do with doubts about Carroll's judgment than anything else. As later events proved, they were probably justified.

During the fight over crew complement in the early 1960s, the Flight Engineers International Association (FEIA) argued that nonpilot engineers were necessary aboard airliners to keep pilots from misbehaving. To support their argument, FEIA officials produced in-flight photos that showed stewardesses at the controls, in the laps of pilots, and generally horsing around. Under Quesada and Halaby, FAA cracked down on this sort of thing. ALPA strongly endorsed the crackdown, agreeing that such behavior was unprofessional and contrary to ALPA's own code of ethics. A number of pilots against whom this kind of misconduct could be substantiated had their licenses suspended and were fined. Thanks to ALPA, none lost his license permanently. These celebrated incidents brought up by FEIA never endangered an aircraft, but they embarrassed the profession nonetheless.

John Carroll would eventually lose his job with TWA because he allowed an "unauthorized person" (his son) in the cockpit during takeoff. This was long after he failed to supplant Sayen, but it gives some inkling why people felt misgivings about Carroll, even though they couldn't be specific.

Slim Babbitt, long one of Sayen's protectors, was resigned to Sayen's leaving ALPA, although he didn't like it. He believed John Carroll would never do:

> I had great respect for Sayen, even though I had some differences with him. But they weren't big differences, and the things he did wrong didn't compare to all the good things he had done. He left on his own; we would never have let them drive him out. He left because he had several things brewing in his mind. He didn't leave in any kind of disgrace. He was a genius, I'll always say that about Sayen, with figures and pensions and insurance, things like that.
>
> John Carroll was a wonderful guy, but I had done too much ALPA work with him, and I just couldn't see him being ALPA president. A likable guy, but he didn't have all his facts. In Executive Commit-

tees he'd bring up stuff and, my God, I used to want to go up there and spend no more than a day, and because of John I'd be stuck for three or four. He was the kind of guy you ask what time it is, and he tells you how to build a watch.

The general opinion of TWA pilots about John Carroll is mixed. Out of loyalty, many of them agreed to support him for the ALPA presidency, but the tone of their conversation indicates that, to a man, they weren't sorry he lost. Dave Richwine speaks for most TWA pilots when he says:

John Carroll represented himself as the unofficial spokesman for all TWA pilots. John was a big, tall guy, like Carter Burgess [TWA president], and they hit it off very well on a personal basis. Once Burgess invited John to a meeting with all TWA vice-presidents, introduced him, and asked him to make some comments on the state of the company. John got up and looked around and said, "I can see what's wrong with TWA. There's not enough brains in this room to run a peanut stand."

Now, I got this story from a man who was there. Also, John Carroll was the only pilot I know who had to wait a year after he was eligible for ALPA membership before he was accepted. John had been so free with his opinions that people weren't sure they wanted him. You still find people on TWA who are strong fans of his, because he had a fine mind and was very articulate. But he was hard to keep in the right channel and that frightened people. He was also extremely autocratic and pretty well disliked by the co-pilots, flight engineers, and stewardesses. As a matter of fact, the hostesses turned him in on the thing that got him fired. Now, I've represented guys in trouble, some of whom had serious drinking offenses, but I was not involved in John's case, and I am very, very glad I wasn't. Imagine putting an unauthorized person in the right seat for takeoff! Many people felt very strongly that John got what he had coming to him. The guy was so intelligent, but when it got down to the tough ones, his ego overcame his judgment. I was not the only TWA pilot who was not too happy about John Carroll being president. I was certainly not enthusiastic about him, even though we were obligated to support him in 1962. He had some strong points, but his shortcomings were such that I didn't think he would have worked out.

When I saw Jerry Wood walk into that hotel with Charley Ruby at his side, I knew what was happening. They would buy anybody that Jerry brought in there who was a viable opponent to John.

When the 1962 Board of Directors' meeting convened, the delegates confronted probably the most intense presidential politicking in ALPA's history. Although a narrow consensus had emerged in opposition to Carroll, there was no obvious alternative candidate. Many delegates favored Kay McMurray, a former UAL captain who had resigned to go into the insurance business and later signed on full-time with ALPA. He had served Clancy Sayen in the same capacity in which Sayen had served Behncke, executive vice-president. McMurray had done an excellent job, was widely respected, and knew ALPA intimately. But he had two things working against him. First, McMurray, unlike Sayen, didn't have the crisis of Behncke's ouster to explain his decision to leave the cockpit permanently. Second, McMurray bore many of the same handicaps as Jim Landis, and an attempt to make him president would alienate the sizable group that had supported Landis, since it would smack of discrimination. (Technically, because McMurray was an "inactive" ALPA member, he would need the same constitutional two-thirds majority that Landis would have required to be eligible to serve.)

Another major candidate for the presidency in 1962 was UAL's Chuck Beatley. Although a reluctant candidate, Beatley was willing to stand in until ALPA's power brokers could find someone else. Operating under the old axiom that you can't beat somebody with nobody, the opposition to John Carroll needed Beatley to serve as a foil until they united on a choice.

Ironically, Charles Ruby of NAL thought he too was supposed to be merely a stalking horse for somebody else:

> They said I was supposed to split the vote. John Carroll had been politicking for a year. I had known John Carroll only through meeting him at various conventions. A bunch of people had approached me about stopping Carroll, but I didn't think too much about it. When they asked me to allow my name to be placed in nomination, my next question was, "Can I draw few enough votes to be safe?" Actually, I found out before I finally committed that the people on Eastern, Pan Am, and National who were pushing me didn't have a preferred candidate other than me. But I still thought I wouldn't be elected. I didn't figure that Sayen would come down to the convention and talk to them. Sayen said, "It can go wild if John Carroll gets in." I wasn't even a delegate, and my name didn't even surface until about two days before the vote. LeRoux of PAA [Pan American World Airways], Babbitt and Wood of EAL, and Bobby Rohan of my own airline did the politicking. Sayen didn't specifically advocate my candidacy, he just let people know what he thought about Carroll.
>
> I still figured that there were so few of these guys who had ever heard me or seen me, and fewer still who knew me, that I wouldn't get it. I went around to all the MEC caucuses, and people started greeting me and I started to get more concerned—about winning. I was as close to being retired as a man could get, flying the DC-8 just four and one-half trips a month. So winning the ALPA presidency was a sad day from my standpoint. Frankly, I wanted Chuck Beatley. He was a good guy, he had a lot of experience, and he made sense.

The vote was close, but Charley Ruby, then 53 years old and a pilot for NAL since the day it was created in 1934, was ALPA's new president. His victory was the product of a combination of forces that will be dealt with in a later chapter. But for now suffice it to say that Charley Ruby was like a comfortable old shoe. In troubled times, people need reassurance and a steady hand. Ruby laid no claim to brilliance, nor did he outline dramatic changes or new departures for ALPA. He was a status quo candidate, and his victory was, in effect, a vindication of Clarence Sayen. All Ruby promised was that he would do the best he could. Everybody who knew Ruby respected his granite-like integrity. For the moment, that would be good enough for ALPA.

What of Clarence Nicholas Sayen, released at last from the yoke that bound him to a job he never wanted? At 43, Sayen was ready for a new career. He would take a long vacation first and then go into the trucking business on the West Coast with his old friend H. B. Anders of UAL. In a few months, he would tire of the business and begin flirting with politics. In 1964, Sayen headed "Pilots for Johnson" against Barry Goldwater, but once again he turned down offers from the Democratic administration to come to the political arena of Washington to employ the skills he had exhibited as ALPA's president.

In early 1965, Sayen did what many smart insiders figured he would do all along—he joined airline management. EAL employed Sayen as vice-president in charge of West Coast operations to open that territory under new CAB route awards. But Sayen never worked a day for EAL. After accepting the job from EAL President Floyd Hall (the former TWA pilot and ALPA member) in New York, Sayen was enroute to Chicago when the Boeing 727 on which he was a passenger crashed into Lake Michigan. It was a clear night, there was no distress call, and the accident has never been explained. Everybody aboard died.

The brilliant career of Clancy Sayen, just 46 years old and with a seemingly limitless future, was over. ✦

CHAPTER 20

Charley Ruby's Hour

One theory of leadership holds that events make history and that specific people, no matter how famous, are merely bit players in a larger drama. The converse of this theory, sometimes labeled the "great man" thesis, holds that at a certain point in history, an individual emerges whose personality is so vibrant that he dominates the times and molds events. Napoleon, according to the first point of view, would have remained an obscure Corsican soldier had it not been for the French Revolution. The French Revolution, according to the second point of view, might have remained an obscure footnote to history had it not been for Napoleon.

Of course, these theories seek to explain the complexity of history by simplifying it, but the truth lies somewhere in between. In 1962, ALPA was entering what can be called its "mid-life crisis," and Charles Ruby seemed to most members to be the best choice for those particular times. In a sense Clancy Sayen had been a Napoleonic personality, and 53-year-old Charley Ruby was attractive at least partly because he seemed unlike Sayen. To use another analogy, Ruby would play Lyndon B. Johnson to Sayen's John F. Kennedy—a calmer man of an older generation succeeding a more exciting man of a younger generation.

If conciliation, tact, and the ability to reconcile conflicting opinions and factions are prerequisites of leadership, then Charley Ruby was foredoomed to failure. Blunt as a bullet, plainspoken to the point of embarrassment, and unwavering in his course of action once convinced of its correctness, Ruby was no diplomat. Perhaps these personality traits sprang naturally from his Quaker background, along with his abstinence from strong drink, strong language, and tobacco. But as even his detractors admit, Charley Ruby possessed a granitelike integrity and a bulldog tenacity. He wasn't showy or apt to overwhelm people with his verbal brilliance, but Ruby had native shrewdness and toughness. Of course, anybody who had grown up in the airline business dealing with Ted Baker on National Airlines (NAL) was likely to be tough, but Charley Ruby was exceptionally so.

Why did ALPA turn to this man in 1962? Scruggs Colvin, a career ALPA employee who worked for every president from Dave Behncke to J. J.

O'Donnell, has some ideas about that:

> Charley Ruby was a man for the times; he was a calming influence,
> wasn't pushing for any big programs. Sayen was like General Pat-
> ton, always pushing, making tremendous strides in work rules and
> retirement. Those were times when you could reach way out and
> accomplish things. Ruby was completely different. He was a care-
> taker, cleaning up all the details that Sayen didn't have time for.
> Sayen wasn't much of a detail man, you know. Ruby was really man-
> dated to come in and straighten things out. Sayen had rushed out
> and planted the flag. Charley Ruby was the logistics man, the one
> who had to bring up the blankets and toilet paper and get every-
> thing in the right spot.

Colvin pauses in his analysis, a smile flickering across his face because of
the unintended humor of his metaphor. "All ALPA presidents have been different, but I can certainly say that Behncke was the most different. And he
was right, the appropriate man for the time. I honestly think that's been
true with each president."

Was Charley Ruby supposed to be a mere caretaker, marking time until
ALPA sorted itself out? His initial mandate was to strengthen the precarious
financial situation. Beyond that, Ruby was pretty much on his own, free to
either push forward or hold the line. ALPA was still in the midst of a period
of severe internal discord, despite Sayen's departure. The anti-Sayen faction that had backed John Carroll of Trans World Airlines (TWA) against
Ruby was still poised to make trouble, so Ruby necessarily went slowly in
certain areas. The Southern Airways (SOU) strike was still dragging on,
draining ALPA's leaders emotionally and demanding nearly all their time.
The crew complement issue was hanging fire as usual, this time with respect to the Douglas DC-9 and the BAC-111. ALPA's treasury was hemorrha-
ging so severely that any president who saw himself as merely a caretaker
would soon have nothing to take care of.

Charley Ruby was not constitutionally suited to preside over a period of
drift. Although he didn't know his own mind as to the shape and direction
of ALPA's long-haul policy, neither did the average ALPA member. The
short-haul problems were enough to occupy Ruby completely at first. One
thing he had to do without delay was to restore to ALPA's internal affairs
something like harmony, or at least civility. Both qualities had been lacking
during the latter part of Sayen's tenure. The minutes of the Executive Committee during those days make harsh reading. The smoldering resentments of the American Airlines (AAL) group toward Sayen often flared into
the open. Sayen, stung and angry, often replied in kind, giving as good as
he got.

In such a time of crisis, the transparent good will and easy manner of a
man like Ruby promised to defuse mounting tensions. As it turned out, he
proved unequal to the task of keeping the AAL group within ALPA (as we

shall see in the next two chapters), but it was not for lack of trying.

If Sayen's personality was at least partly to blame for the AAL pilots' dissatisfaction, it made sense that his successor be as unlike Sayen as possible. But those who thought deeply about such things knew that the new ALPA president must also be a battler, someone who could hold the center when the flanks were giving way. No one doubted that Charley Ruby was a fighter, certainly not NAL boss Ted Baker, who had spent so many years with Ruby gnawing at his ankles. The questions about Ruby's capacity to lead ALPA arose not because he lacked the will to battle, but rather because the area in which the fight was likely to occur, the purely political sphere, was not his strong suit.

"Ruby was a man who essentially disdained the whole arena of politics," says ALPA attorney Henry Weiss. "He had no taste for politics and basically was indifferent to it—to the point where he almost got recalled."

That recall effort against Ruby at the 1968 Board of Directors meeting was something several old-timers on NAL half expected when Ruby emerged as the consensus candidate in opposition to TWA's John Carroll in 1962. One NAL pilot (who prefers to remain anonymous) put it this way: "Most of us admired and respected Charley because he had done a lot more than his share for ALPA. When the going got tough, there was nobody better than Charley at digging in. You just couldn't move him, like an old hickory stump. But some of us worried about his rough edges."

When Charley Ruby flew his last DC-8 trip for NAL on July 4, 1962, he ended an airline piloting career that spanned nearly the whole history of commercial aviation in America. The third ALPA president had been with NAL since its birth in 1934, and in a sense he was a throwback to the Behncke era. Now 71 and retired in Jacksonville, Fla., Charley Ruby still retains the erect posture, penetrating gaze, and earnest, unhurried way of talking that characterized him during his presidency. His opinions, always strong, are no weaker now with the passage of time.

These days, Charley Ruby spends a lot of time with the prized pair of white Studebaker Avantis he and his wife drive. They are exquisite, mechanically perfect cars, the kind that stop auto afficionados in their tracks. When one Avanti is completely overhauled, Ruby begins work on the other. He has prudently stocked spare parts in his garage, from axle springs to engine components. This behavior comes naturally, because he was a mechanic before he was a pilot. In the early 1930s, Charley owned one of Florida's best automobile garages. His work was so good that customers brought more business than he could handle, particularly in his specialty—luxury sedans. "I had to get into aviation to get some rest," Charley says, only half joking. "I could have worked 24 hours a day and never caught up."

But auto mechanics wasn't Ruby's destiny. Fresh out of high school in 1928, he went to the school run by the Robertson Aircraft Corporation in

St. Louis to learn flying. In those days, the course included mechanical training, and since there were more jobs for mechanics than for pilots, Charley, always practical, opted for mechanical work. Returning to Florida with an A&P license and a smidgen of flying time, he tried to wangle a pilot's job on Pan American (PAA). He got nowhere. Under Juan Trippe in its early days, PAA self-consciously projected an "aristocratic" image modeled on the military's, and its pilot corps was practically a naval aviation auxiliary. The idea of a kid with a high school education flying one of his Clippers didn't appeal to Trippe, but he needed mechanics. Let Charley Ruby tell you how frustrating it was to be a mechanic when he really wanted to fly:

> In 1929, I went down to Miami with my mechanic's license and took a job with PAA. I told them I was looking for a pilot's job. I knew I didn't have enough pilot qualifications to suit them, but I wanted to upgrade. Well, they made promises since they were quite short of mechanics, because it was tough to get people to go down to Haiti and places like that. The job paid $100 a month. I figured out pretty quickly that they were never going to let me upgrade—in fact, what they had in mind was retrograde. They needed mechanics more than pilots. I worked for PAA about a year, and they kept putting pressure on me to go down to Central America, and I told them, "Listen, I have no intention of moving to any of those places. Sure, I'm single, but I'm not going to go down there and hibernate in some jungle. This is not such a fine job that I've got to keep it. You're getting two weeks' notice." So the crocodile tears were all over the place; they were promising me I could fly, but by then I really didn't believe them.

That's when Charley Ruby went into the auto repair business. As a sideline, he also ran a little aviation repair shop and bought and sold a bit on the used airplane market. In the process, Ruby learned about the flying game the hard way and met the man who would later become his boss, George T. "Ted" Baker, the founder of NAL. Baker was dabbling in aviation in the late 1920s before moving from Chicago to Florida. His primary interests had been the automobile business, but he also owned a nonscheduled outfit he grandiosely labeled the National Airlines Taxi System. After moving to Florida, Baker resurrected it, but with no more success than he had had in Chicago. However, he had nerve and a high roller's sense of the possible, something Charley Ruby lacked. But for that, Charley Ruby might have been the founder of NAL. There are those who hint that his long animosity toward Baker, and vice versa, stemmed from this.

When the Post Office Department opened up the airmail routes for bidding after the cancellation crisis of 1934, Ted Baker jumped in. Charley Ruby's great mistake was that he was too practical.

A wealthy friend offered to stake Ruby's bid on the route that Baker later developed into NAL. John Thompson was a midwestern businessman who wintered in Florida. He owned one of Walter Beech's Travelairs, but since he wasn't much of a pilot, Thompson went in search of one. He found Ruby, and over the next few years they became friends. From 1931 to 1934, Ruby flew John Thompson and his wife all over the country in all kinds of weather. In the process, Charley became a proficient, self-taught instrument pilot. He also understood the economics of the aviation business too well to undertake the risks Ted Baker unblinkingly accepted. The initial Post Office contracts were let to bidders whose low initial proposals were simple gambles. Like the Braniff brothers and the other small bidders for mail contracts in 1934, Baker was prepared to eat his losses initially, hoping against hope that the government would rescue him later by raising the mail subsidy. Charley Ruby refused to take the gamble, so he turned down John Thomspon's offer of financial support. NAL would become Ted Baker's airline, not Charley Ruby's.

Ruby went to work for Ted Baker at the beginning, leaving the employ of John Thompson (although he continued to maintain Thompson's airplane). While flying for Thompson, Ruby had met Dave Behncke, but the idea of joining ALPA held no attraction for Ruby at first. As essentially a corporate pilot, Ruby had nothing to gain from ALPA. Nor was ALPA particularly active among NAL's first group of pilots—there were only four of them. But the early NAL pilots knew about ALPA, and as their employment conditions failed to improve along with NAL's fortunes, they became eager converts.

"Ted Baker probably did more to ensure the solidarity of the airline pilots behind ALPA than anybody else after 1934," says Jerry Wood of Eastern Air Lines (EAL), who had known Baker in Chicago. "We would be split all over the place, and then Ted Baker would do something rotten, he was that kind of guy, and pilots all over the country would rise up and stand together."

Charley Ruby's long involvement with ALPA reached a climax during the 1948 NAL strike. As master executive council (MEC) chairman, Ruby was in almost daily contact with Behncke. The heavy press coverage of that bitter dispute made his name well known throughout ALPA. In fact, Behncke offered the newly created post of executive vice-president (which Sayen eventually accepted) to Ruby.

"In his later days," says Ruby, "Behncke was a little off mentally. He wouldn't trust people because he didn't think there were many to tell him the truth. He hung onto me pretty tight after 1948, and the difference between me and Sayen was that he [Sayen] wanted the job pretty badly and I didn't."

When the dust finally settled after the protracted 1948 NAL strike, Ruby became Baker's chief pilot. From October 1954 until July 1961, Ruby was in management. That he could hold such a position and not fatally damage his standing with NAL pilots is a tribute to Charley Ruby's essential fairness. That he could also work with Ted Baker indicated hidden wellsprings of tact and diplomacy beneath Ruby's blunt exterior. That Ruby and Baker were both frugal probably had something to do with their seven years of harmony.

In 1962, when the delegates to the ALPA convention of Miami Beach began searching for a "stop John Carroll" candidate, Charley Ruby emerged as the logical choice. He was an authentic expert with management experience, he had a high name recognition factor among pilots and a demonstrated ability to manage money, and he had brought the feuding on NAL to an end. He seemed to have all the qualifications for the ALPA presidency.

As we have seen, Ruby's election was accepted by the Carroll forces because they thought it was temporary. There was a wide assumption that Ruby was merely an interim candidate who would be content to serve a single term, leaving office in 1966. But another factor in Ruby's election to the ALPA presidency requires elaboration. Today, everybody knows that the airline a pilot works for is largely a matter of accident. But in the old days, there were real differences among the pilots of each airline. W. A. "Pat" Patterson of United Airlines (UAL) and Juan Trippe of PAA both ran relatively "aristocratic" operations. That is, they liked their pilots to be ex-military, preferably with college degrees. EAL's Eddie Rickenbacker, considering his own limited formal education, never made much of an issue over his pilots' nonflying background, and the AAL and TWA managements were even less interested in their pilots' extraneous qualifications. Down the scale from there, the backgrounds of each airlines' pilots became more mixed. For example, Capital Airlines, before its merger with UAL, had the reputation for hiring pilots from hardscrabble backgrounds, the kind who had learned the trade by hanging around airports as kids, trading odd jobs for occasional hops. The same could be said of NAL, Braniff, and other airlines that had sneaked into business after the airmail crisis of 1934.

Petty jealousies, often based on intangible factors, were a source of disunity in ALPA's early history, moving Dave Behncke to preach his "band of brothers" sermon frequently. After World War II, these differences between pilot groups began to evaporate, since airlines like Trans Texas and SOU were as likely to have a 40-mission bomber pilot with a Harvard degree as were Continental and Delta. But ALPA's political structure meant that internal division between pilot groups would be a long-term problem. Put simply, a pilot representing a large airline carried more weight and authority at an ALPA convention than did the pilot of a small airline.

So the divisons between the various pilot groups lingered, as antique prejudices tend to do, exacerbated by the lower pay and lower prestige that the pilots of smaller airlines suffered because of the equipment they flew.

But, in a curious way, the sheer voting strength of the large airlines worked against them in 1962 and helps to explain Charley Ruby's election. The pilot groups of major airlines have tended toward a certain parochial distrust of the pilots of other majors, fearing them as competition. This distrust opened the way for the pilots of small airlines to play balance-of-power politics. In 1962, this factor worked to Charley Ruby's advantage. The AAL pilots, long accustomed to being either the largest or next to largest group in ALPA, sank a rung after the merger of UAL and Capital in 1961. The merged UAL pilot group now far outstripped the AAL pilots, and the mutual antagonisms of these groups made it unlikely that the leader of any other major group, such as TWA's John Carroll, would be able to command the votes of either one. Suppose the TWA and AAL group united to freeze out the UAL group, denying them a fair share of power in ALPA? It was a worrisome prospect.

So, the pilots of the regional airlines would be able to broker the convention, provided they could unite at least one major airline behind a candidate from one of the smaller "trunks." When the EAL group moved to Ruby under the prodding of Jerry Wood and Slim Babbitt, the PAA pilots fell into line also, partly because of the strong support of the influential Grant LeRoux and partly because of the PAA group's distrust of both UAL and AAL (their distrust of TWA went without saying). The votes of EAL and PAA, both large airlines, along with those of the small airlines, were nearly enough to put Charley Ruby over the top. NAL threatened nobody because, although technically a major, it wasn't much larger than some of the regional airlines. A smattering of support for Ruby on TWA and UAL was all it took to seal his victory.

Many challenges confronted Ruby when he took office in 1962. He handled some better than others. The bitter SOU strike was in the course of being settled owing to Sayen's spadework, but Ruby closed it adeptly, as we have seen in a previous chapter. In the matter of ALPA's finances, Ruby was well suited to clean things up. Put simply, he was a notorious penny pincher, so frugal that he irritated some pilots. "Charley never spent a nickel that didn't have to be accounted for," says EAL's Jerry Wood.

Charley Ruby's first duty upon taking office was to order a thorough audit. What he heard was good news—ALPA's financial situation was tight, but not desperate. There was a cash flow problem owing to the heavy expenses of the SOU strike and the flight pay loss associated with the protracted UAL-Capital merger. But both these episodes were winding down, and as Ruby discovered to his delight, the value of ALPA's real estate holdings in Chicago, principally the building at 55th and Cicero, put the ledgers well into the black. As for administering ALPA's internal affairs, Ruby was better than Sayen. Careful, calm, and deliberate, a "detail" man in the best sense of the word, Ruby brought to the Chicago headquarters a clarity of purpose that was in the best tradition of the "nuts-and-bolts" types who had made ALPA's technical committees models of productivity for so long.

Why then did he only narrowly survive recall in 1968 and lead a badly divided ALPA through the end of his presidency in 1970? Nobody blamed Charley Ruby for the defection of the AAL pilots in 1963, so that played little part in the growing dissatisfaction with his leadership. The major source of contention by 1965 was that Charley Ruby seemed incapable of dealing effectively with the ever more restrictive environment in which modern airline pilots worked. The modern airline pilot's fate depended on a complex web of relationships between the public at large, his employers, and government. Let us consider the noise abatement problem.

For the public at large, the overriding concern about the new jets was that they were noisy and that a modern jetport was a bad neighbor. The solution to this problem was complex, but at least one component of it was good public relations, something Ruby's critics said he was incapable of providing. A crisis occurred when the village of Hempstead, N.Y., sued in federal court to impose its own noise abatement standards upon the airline industry and the Federal Aviation Administration (FAA). Had the suit succeeded, it would have effectively closed Kennedy Airport and crippled FAA's ability to be master in its own house.

Working with government and management, Ruby led the fight that beat back Hempstead's suit. "This was one of the few times that the airlines, ALPA, and the whole bunch were all in bed together," says Jerry Wood, who was the major expert witness called by the government against the suit. "It was an interesting variation to what we'd been used to."

Defeating Hempstead's lawsuit was one of Ruby's first highly visible actions as ALPA president, and it was about the last that won universal approval from the membership. By 1965, the rumblings of discontent with the nature and style of his leadership began to reach levels like those under Sayen.

What were the major issues, who were the leaders of the anti-Ruby faction, and why did they come within a single vote of forcing Ruby's resignation in 1968?

A number of external issues arose in the mid-1960s to trouble Charley Ruby. Among them were relations with FAA, problems with air traffic control (ATC), and the perennial problem of aircraft and airport certification. But topping the list of external problems was skyjacking (which we'll explore more fully in a subsequent chapter). As an old-fashioned, law-and-order conservative, Charley Ruby was outraged to the point of incoherence by the epidemic of skyjacking, and although most airline pilots fully shared his outrage, they worried because it made his public statements seem irresponsible. Like Dave Behncke's, Charley Ruby's English was nonstandard, couched in southern cadences. Although Ruby could use language subtly and with extraordinary metaphorical power, to the kind of pilot who was college educated and accustomed to Sayen's flawless academic delivery, Ruby's appearances before congressional committees left a sour aftertaste.

Even Ruby's defenders admitted that in the heat of debate he often sounded like a bumpkin, and they understood that the impression he made, particularly when dealing with management, was not nearly so favorable as Sayen's. "The first reaction to Charley was always 'Where did you come up with this hayseed?'" recalls Jerry Wood. "But after a while, you'd find these same people, in management and government, coming back to him for advice and usually acting on it."

Nevertheless, by January 1966, discontent with Ruby's leadership had reached such proportions that his supporters moved to defuse it. It was an election year, and skirmishing over the presidency had already begun. Many ALPA members thought Ruby would voluntarily vacate the office to return to flying. His supporters, aware of the widespread feeling that his caretaker presidency was ending, decided to move boldly to keep him in office by putting the critics on the defensive and answering previous charges against Ruby's stewardship. The device they chose was a special committee of 15 pilots, all of whom had long experience in ALPA affairs, who would investigate Ruby's performance and evaluate his fitness for a second term. They forced a resolution through the Executive Committee creating the "Committee of Fifteen" (as it was informally called), allowing Ruby to choose the pilots who would serve. This controversial move was bound to draw fire, partly because it was premised on the notion that no matter who is president, "unanimity of purpose is difficult to achieve." The idea that *any* ALPA president would likely have trouble wasn't what the anti-Ruby forces wanted to hear, but for the moment the Committee of Fifteen outflanked them. Also, the anti-Ruby forces were about to discover one of the oldest truths about politics—you can't beat somebody with nobody. Nobody emerged as a strong challenger to Ruby in 1966, the Committee of Fifteen gave Ruby a clean bill of health, aside from criticizing his laxness in educating the membership about ALPA's "history and need," and the "bad lack of communications between the President's Department and the staff."

In one sense, the Committee of Fifteen was a great success because it drew opposition fire from Ruby to itself. Since Bobby Rohan of NAL, Ruby's old airline, chaired the committee, and since several of the members (like J. P. Talton of EAL) were nearing retirement and hadn't been active in ALPA affairs recently, the critics leveled charges that it was composed of "has-beens." Several MECs passed resolutions denouncing the Committee of Fifteen as "illegal" and "a self-serving political body." The committee replied in its final report: "We accept none of these allegations, and we also respectfully urge those who have submitted resolutions aimed at destroying this study group to review their bylaws and try to at least learn the basic structure of the Association."

Although Ruby's critics eventually forced a resolution through the Board of Directors dissolving the Committee of Fifteen by a vote of 84 to 63, there were 87 abstentions. As the large number of abstentions emphasized, Ruby's opponents built their case not on another individual but rather only on opposition to Ruby. That approach wouldn't work, and since no viable alternative candidate emerged at the November convention, he was re-elected to a second four-year term without opposition. The anti-Ruby forces, led by Gus Muirheid of EAL and Rich Flournoy of TWA, were flab-bergasted at the ease with which the Ruby forces defeated them in 1966. "Our strategy was to get Ruby out, and then pick somebody else," says Flournoy. "That was the wrong approach."

One section of the Committee of Fifteen's report dealt with an obvious failure on Ruby's part, one that the anti-Ruby faction felt strongly about and would subsequently use against him. "The Association is not taking advan-tage of the benefits to be derived through our affiliation with the AFL-CIO," the report stated. That sore spot offered another opening to the anti-Ruby group. Although ALPA owed everything to its connection with organized labor, the increasing affluence of its members as jet pay came in had made them receptive to the ideas of the Republican party and other antilabor elements. Charley Ruby admits to distancing himself from the AFL-CIO on the grounds that "they never had anything to offer us and didn't know any-thing about our business." Ruby's thinly veiled antiunionism rankled many ALPA members, although probably not a majority.

"It was obvious a political crunch was coming somewhere down the road," Rich Flournoy recalls, "and our view was that Charley was just not of-fering any leadership at all in this area. Ruby was offended by the whole idea of political action, but later on he did accept the fact that we were a labor union, and had to function like one, and that meant getting our nose bloody, if it came to that."

Other areas of controversy between Ruby and Flournoy simmered. The age 60 retirement rule was badly handled, according to Flournoy, al-though Ruby admitted opposing it with only "limited pressure," owing to the stagnant promotion lists that made many younger pilots support it. "Most of us felt that Ruby was completely under the thumb of Henry Weiss on this issue, and that blanket opposition to the age 60 rule was all wrong. What we wanted was a system of waivers to the rule, so that a pilot who was over 60 and able to pass rigorous relicensing tests could get a waiver and keep flying." But Ruby and Henry Weiss, perhaps more aware of the diffi-culties of a selective approach to opposing the age 60 rule than was Flour-noy, decided to fight it out "all or nothing."

The move to Washington, D.C., also caused friction between Ruby and the group led by Flournoy and Muirheid. In 1962, the Board of Directors mandated a move of ALPA's headquarters from Chicago to Washington "as soon as practical." There were good reasons for the move to Washington, among them the steady growth of the Washington office owing to the heavy volume of work assigned to it. But on the other hand, there were good reasons against the move. Although there was never any real reason for ALPA's headquarters to have been in Chicago (other than it being Dave Behncke's home), ALPA had built up a large and loyal staff who would not leave their home city. The expense of the move was also a troubling question.

Opposition to the Washington move was led by Homer Mouden of Braniff. As one of ALPA's most respected nonpolitical "nuts-and-bolts" types, Mouden's views commanded wide respect, but probably not a majority opinion—at least in 1962, when the board mandated the move. The 1964 board rescinded the move to Washington, only to have the 1966 board reinstate the move whether or not the majority of ALPA's members still favored it. By then, what had been a vacillating policy was "set in stone." The best efforts of Mouden, Dave Richwine of TWA, and many others to force a reconsideration of the move failed. Charley Ruby, caught in the middle of the flap over moving to Washington, admits to having mixed emotions about it. "When you boiled it all down," Ruby recalls, "there were advantages to it, but being there only made it easier than if we had to pay hotel bills and travel. It didn't really change things all that much."

The board's 1962 mandate of the move and Ruby's resistance for one reason or another until 1968 provided one more round in the intensifying debate over Charley Ruby's fitness to lead ALPA. Eventually, Ruby's alleged recalcitrance over the Washington move provided a major charge against him in a formal vote of confidence.

The August 1968 meeting of the Executive Committee saw the introduction of a formal resolution calling for Ruby to resign. Rich Flournoy of TWA led the move, alleging that Ruby had failed to carry out the 1962 Board of Directors' requirement that ALPA move to Washington. In a bitter and heated session lasting an entire day and into the next, the Executive Committee debated the formal censure of Charley Ruby "for his continuing refusal to respond to proper Executive Committee expression of its powers and duties." The remedy for Ruby's alleged misdeeds was "that in the best interest of the Association, the president announce his resignation."

The crucial individual in the debate was Stewart Hopkins of Delta Airlines (DAL). "Stu Hopkins opposed us very reluctantly," Flournoy says. "His feeling was that Charley was no prize, but that he'd be gone in two more years anyway."

"Ruby was kind of a country boy," says Hopkins, "and I don't think he came off too well in some areas, but he worked hard and he was trying, and the guys who were trying to get him out didn't have anything very specific to go on."

Hopkins' decision not to join Flournoy, Muirheid, John Nevins (master chairman of TWA, serving as a proxy for ALPA Secretary J. G. Fickling of

Piedmont), Seth Oberg of Western Air Lines (WAL), and Gerry Goss of
Frontier Airlines (FAL) meant that Ruby himself could cast the vote that
would tie the censure motion. Voting against Ruby's removal were
Hopkins, Bill Davis of UAL, Marge Cooper (vice-president of the Steward &
Stewardess Division), and Don Nichols of UAL.

In the final analysis, the Ruby forces were able to beat back the 1968 recall attempt because the insurgents, led by Flournoy of TWA and Muirheid
of EAL, lacked broad support from the rank and file. Stewart Hopkins
sided with Ruby because he was bothered by the insurgents' methods. In
Hopkins opinion, an ALPA president owed his office to the conventions of
the Board of Directors, which met specifically to elect him. The Executive
Committee, in Hopkins's opinion, had no business reversing the 1966
board that had elected Ruby. As if to confirm Hopkins's view, the 1968
board meeting in convention would subsequently refuse to recall Ruby
during a "formal" proceeding.

And so Charley Ruby and his supporters overcame the rising centrifugal
forces that threatened not only his presidency, but ALPA's cohesiveness as
well. Ever since the AAL defection in 1963, ALPA had lived under the haunting fear of another major separatist break. In the considered opinion of
ALPA insiders, another such defection would doom the organization. Furthermore, thoughtful observers of ALPA affairs believed that the Executive
Committee itself, owing to its status, was largely responsible for the
teetering instability that marked the period. As Wally Anderson, who has
been at the right hand of every ALPA president since Dave Behncke, puts it:

> My own recollection of those days, and I sat through every Execu-
> tive Committee meeting, was that personal and political activities
> surrounding the committee caused the internal schisms. There
> was a growing feeling that the structure of the Executive Commit-
> tee and its stated responsibilities were at fault. The regional vice-
> president concept, which provided five members for the Execu-
> tive Committee, was at the core of most problems. For years the
> Executive Committee was a thorn in Sayen's side. It continued
> through the presidency of Ruby, generating significant political
> problems and harassment. There was little improvement after
> O'Donnell became president, with the regional vice-presidents
> frequently attacking and destroying the effectiveness of the man-
> agement structure. This Executive Committee structure was the
> core of most of the presidential problems between 1958 and 1968.

As we shall see, the Board of Directors meeting in convention would
subsequently pull the Executive Committee's teeth, but not until 1974.
Until then, Ruby and his successor, J. J. O'Donnell, would be dogged by an
Executive Committee whose constitutional responsibilities were murky
enough to allow it to interfere in daily administration. Both the Committee
of Fifteen and outside management experts hired to study ALPA's adminis-

tration (notably Professors George Shultz and Arnold Webber of the University of Chicago) had cited the inherent dangers of allowing a committee whose real purpose was to "advise and consent" to involve itself in direct administrative matters. If a camel is a horse designed by a committee, then the constitutionally induced weakness of the ALPA presidency was the result of government by committee, rather than government by a central officer charged with responsibility and authority. Put simply, the Executive Committee had some constitutional authority, but no direct responsibility to run ALPA.

After Ruby's trouble with the Executive Committee, the Board of Directors began to recognize the basic problem. In 1968, the board amended the bylaws to spell out the president's responsibilities and authority. As a counter to the Executive Committee, the board provided for regular meetings of the 30-odd master chairmen (the Executive Board) and gave them new policy-making power. But the Executive Committee, made up of the five regional vice-presidents and the national officers, was only curbed, not destroyed. Finally, in 1974 the continuing troubles generated by the committee led the Board of Directors to replace the regional vice-presidents with five executive vice-presidents elected from among the members of the Board of Directors while in biennial session. The division of authority and responsibility between regionally elected vice-presidents and master chairmen thus came to an end, but not before it had caused nearly two decades of turmoil.

If only the 1974 reforms had come earlier, ALPA's history in the 1960s might have been vastly different. Although nothing is more uncertain than the "might-have-beens" of history, timely structural reforms in ALPA's governance might even have prevented the defection of the AAL pilots in 1963. Holding ALPA together after that earthquake might well have been Charley Ruby's finest hour. A lesser man might have lost ALPA altogether. ✦

CHAPTER 21

Origins of the American Airlines Split

In the Japanese film *Rashomon,* the survivors of a violent adventure emerge with totally different accounts of what happened, remembering words nobody spoke and events that never occurred. Or were the words spoken, and did the events occur? Strong emotions trigger distortion, and *Rashomon* illustrates the ambiguity that often characterizes eyewitness accounts influenced by fear and anger. Whom does one believe, for example, when two old enemies, with the fires of indignation still burning in their eyes, recount differing versions of history?

The defection of the American Airlines (AAL) pilots from ALPA in 1963 has a *Rashomon*-like quality because there were no dispassionate observers on either side. According to the ALPA loyalists on AAL, men like A. M. "Breezy" Wynne, Frank A. "Doc" Spencer, Carl Rubio, and Roy Dooley (to name but a few), the dissidents who took control of their pilot group in the late 1950s were simply wreckers, no better than the ignorant barbarians who sacked Rome and amused themselves by destroying priceless works of art.

On the other hand, the AAL leaders of that era, some of whom are still active in the cloned version of ALPA called the Allied Pilots Association (APA), tell a totally different tale. They insist that the proper history of their separation from ALPA should begin by recounting Clancy Sayen's tyranny and the treacheries of other pilot groups out to "get" AAL. The separatists often cite the strike benefits denied them after the December 1958 walkout. ALPA loyalists insist that the AAL separatists knew in advance that they wouldn't be eligible for strike benefits.

Where does the truth lie? How can we purify the facts to reveal what went wrong in 1963? For make no mistake about it, the separation of the AAL pilot group from ALPA was a crisis on a grand scale. All the prerequisites for ALPA's total dissolution were present in 1963.

Historians can often tell what happened, but not why. The trouble that led to AAL's separation from ALPA in 1963 began with a bitter personality conflict between C. E. "Gene" Seal, the AAL master chairman elected in 1956, and Clancy Sayen. Why the two men hated each other is lost to history and perhaps unrecoverable, since both men are dead.

Tom Latta of AAL attributes the split to Sayen's refusal to "mollycoddle an idiot." But then, Latta was no admirer of Gene Seal, and as one of the die-hard ALPA loyalists, we must expect him to have a low opinion of the secessionists. Fairness requires us to remember that Sayen could be professorially impatient with slow learners, and there is some indication that Gene Seal fit that description. Clancy Sayen did not suffer fools gladly, and whether or not Gene Seal was a fool, Sayen certainly thought him one. Almost certainly, the initial trouble between Sayen and Seal arose because of some quirk in the mental makeup of each man, some "chemistry" that makes one man instinctively dislike another. For whatever reason, within a year of Seal's accession to the AAL master chairmanship, his relationship with Sayen can only be described as poisonous. Nearly 20 years later, the fruit of their split lives on in a dangerous and quite unnecessary division in the ranks of professional airline pilots.

ALPA's history up to 1963 had been a remarkable story of unification across company lines. The cooperative spirit of the first generation of professional airline pilots was their greatest single resource, and without it Dave Behncke's scheme to unionize pilots would have died aborning. But after World War II, and certainly by the 1950s, the old spirit of shoulder-to-shoulder solidarity among pilots was beginning to erode. Of course, ALPA had seen its share of fractious skirmishing even in the best of times. But the old guys knew how to put their intramural quarrels aside. By their nature, the first generation professional airline pilots were independent free-thinkers who always applied the arts of conciliation and compromise imperfectly. When the chips were down, however, they knew that an imperfect compromise to preserve unity beat none at all. Bitter experience had taught them that without the strength they derived from each other, they would stand alone before the impersonal power of giant corporations whose personnel policies could be quite predatory. Aside from the Transcontinental & Western Airways (TWA) pilots' foray into company unionism in 1933 (and even that, we must remember, was owing to severe management pressure), there had never been a serious threat of disunity before it erupted on AAL in 1963.

But by 1963, everything was changing. Inevitably, a new generation arrived made up of pilots less steeped in past struggles and more complacent about the professional status ALPA had created for them. The new generation was also increasingly indifferent to ALPA and its administration. Pioneer pilots, by and large, paid close attention to ALPA affairs, and they couldn't understand the lackadaisical attitude of younger pilots, particularly when it came to governance at the local level. By the late 1950s many pilots simply took for granted that somebody else would do the hard work needed to sustain ALPA. While complacent pilots golfed or pursued second careers, a minority ran ALPA's local affairs on each airline. Although most of these individuals were dedicated to making ALPA work, on some airlines a few pilots used ALPA as a gimmick for personal aggrandizement. The indifference of the rank and file and the poor attendance at local council meetings meant that a minority on any airline could, with proper planning, seize control and eventually dominate the master executive council (MEC) itself. The danger was that a well-organized clique could speak for an indifferent majority of pilots.

The old-timers worried about ALPA's future, but by 1963 they were either retired or verging on it and could only watch in disbelief as the tragedy of 1963 unfolded. "The young turks brought it off," says Albert E. "Prince" Hamer of AAL, who joined ALPA in 1931. "I had been inactive in ALPA for a number of years because I was in the chief pilot's office, but in 1963, a year before my retirement, I went back on the line. I went to a couple of these 'get out of ALPA' meetings and talked against it. I said I thought that was playing the company's game. I was just blown off the floor. They said I was an old man who didn't know what he was talking about."

John J. O'Connell, the last loyal MEC chairman on AAL (who is definitely not to be confused with Nick O'Connell, the MEC chairman who led the 1963 defection, or John J. O'Donnell, who was elected ALPA president in 1970), is a soft-spoken man who chooses his words carefully. Operating under the old idea that if you can't say something good about somebody, you shouldn't say anything at all, O'Connell has refused public comment on his old opponents in AAL ever since his retirement in 1968. But in an interview at his Sun City, Ariz., home, O'Connell pulls a sheet of paper from his pocket and begins reading capsule descriptions of the leading actors in the AAL defection. Words like "opportunistic, treacherous, hypocritical, dishonorable, chauvinistic, and cynical" dominate his summary. If these words accurately describe the men who displaced ALPA loyalists like O'Connell from positions of leadership in AAL during the late 1950s, what events brought them to power?

Pilots on AAL had felt a pervasive sense of injury for a long time. As the backbone of ALPA in the early days, the first to organize 100 percent, the first to negotiate a contract, and the only pilot group to stand absolutely rock firm during the threatened nationwide strike of 1933, the AAL pilots felt superior to other pilot groups. Their devotion to ALPA was so strong in the early days that from the election of Clyde Holbrook as ALPA's first first vice-president through Tom Hardin's selection as member of the first Air Safety Board, they dominated ALPA affairs in all areas except the presidency itself. The AAL pilots' dominance, in turn, produced something of a backlash that manifested itself by the late 1940s in an almost automatic anti-AAL voting block in most conventions. Willis Proctor of AAL failed in his challenge to Behncke in 1947, although in truth even many of Proctor's fellow AAL pilots were lukewarm about his candidacy. During the Sayen era, both H. Bart Cox in 1952 and Wiley Drummond in 1956 mounted formidable but unsuccessful challenges for the presidency. Both of these AAL pilots were men of wide reputation and long service to ALPA, and their rejection left many AAL pilots feeling aggrieved.

"In retrospect," says Jerry Wood of Eastern Air Lines (EAL), "there was no conspiracy [to deprive AAL pilots of the presidency]; it just happened, and guys like Wiley Drummond, who was a real gentleman, understood and didn't let it bother them. American was pretty much the mainstay of ALPA for so long that they got used to the idea of being dominant, and this led to some disgruntlement when they couldn't be any longer. Up until 1956, the dissidents were in the minority, and I can still remember Wiley Drummond leading them back into the convention that year to make it unanimous for Clancy."

Shortly after 1956, Wiley Drummond, H. Bart Cox, and other old-time ALPA loyalists on AAL began either to retire or to graduate to management ranks. Drummond, for example, became director of flight agreements (he died in an automobile accident in the early 1970s). "I talked to Drummond at the time of the split," says ALPA loyalist Tom Latta of AAL, "and he was appalled, but like a lot of the older guys he had no way to express himself."

"The 1956 convention was sort of a landmark in the trouble between American and the rest of ALPA," says Stewart W. Hopkins of Delta Airlines (DAL). "Every convention they would lose the presidency or the vice-presidency or whatever, and their people reacted badly. I think some opportunists started using this to take things over and just guided the rank and file along. I remember writing Clancy a letter after the 1956 convention saying, 'These guys are beaten and bloody and you had better hold out the hand of friendship.'"

As men like John O'Connell began losing the reins of power on AAL, a series of MEC chairmen (Gene Seal, Paul Atkins, Nick O'Connell), each a bit more inclined toward the dissidents' point of view than the last, took control. John O'Connell had made himself persona non grata by criticizing the performance of the AAL negotiating committee, on which the dissidents were entrenched.

"I had a lot of contact with the dissidents because they took control of the negotiating committee late in my term as MEC chairman," O'Connell remembers. "It took them 14 months to negotiate one contract, and whenever I sat with them in New York, they did nothing, absolutely nothing! They were just leaning back, taking it easy in suites up in the Russell Hotel at ALPA's expense, keeping Jack Christie [ALPA's director of negotiations] tied up."

The passing of the older generation of leaders like Wiley Drummond made things easier for the generation of dissidents on AAL. After 1957, they made opposition to Sayen the key to their internal politics, largely because their anti-Sayenism struck fertile ground among rank-and-file pilots. No AAL leader ever seemed to lose support through an open display of hostility toward Sayen, whose habit of socializing with prominent United Airlines (UAL) pilots like H. B. Anders and Chuck Woods led AAL pilots to believe that he was plotting against their interest somehow.

"Sayen did spend a great deal of time over at United when they ran into trouble," says Frank A. "Doc" Spencer of AAL, "but that was only because they were handy. The American pilots, when they wanted something done, perceived Sayen as too busy to attend to their difficulties. At the time, we were either the biggest or the second biggest airline, paying a quarter of the dues of the whole Association. They figured they only got about one-twentieth of Sayen's attention."

AAL's management, whose grudges against ALPA dated back to the Behncke era, clearly encouraged their pilots to believe that Sayen was singling out AAL for harsher treatment than other airlines, particularly UAL. AAL and UAL were competing fiercely during the 1950s for dominance, both technologically and economically. This competition cost both airlines money unnecessarily, particularly in inaugurating jet service. Although Pan American World Airways (PAA) was the first to fly large numbers of jets, AAL was nominally the first to use them in domestic service. (Actually, National Airlines [NAL] pilots were the first to fly Boeing 707s commercially in U.S. airspace, owing to an interchange agreement with PAA.) To beat UAL into service with jets, AAL had to avoid a strike by bowing to ALPA's crew complement policy. But yielding to ALPA exposed AAL to a strike threat from the Flight Engineers International Association (FEIA), so for many months AAL had to operate the new jets with four crew members, three pilots and an engineer.

There is very persuasive evidence that AAL's management so resented ALPA's crew complement policy that they began actively encouraging the separatist movement among their pilots as early as 1955. This is not to say, however, that the coming schism in ALPA was a management plot. Rather, one can conclude from certain company actions that management aided and abetted the separatist movement by making things easy for pilots who were hostile to ALPA, thus assisting their rise to power within the AAL pilot group. Nick O'Connell, the MEC chairman who led the defection, was allowed a work schedule that was extraordinarily favorable, according to ALPA loyalist Roy Dooley, who in 1964 made a carefully documented post-mortem study of the secession at the request of Charley Ruby. Dooley puts the circumstantial case for AAL management's complicity this way:

> I don't think American's management at the local level could control anybody's flying assignments. I think C. R. Smith and Bill Whitacre [vice-president for operations] did it from the top. Whitacre was a pilot in bombers who became a general in World War II, but he did not fly the line, and he was recognized by the old-timers as a pilot hater. By the time this came up, he was in a position to do what he could to influence people, and I think he was told by American's top management, C. R. Smith, to do what he could to

help these guys to get out of ALPA, to embarrass ALPA, screw it up, and maybe destroy it. I think there was a definite effort by management to get the American pilot group established with their own union. Not long ago I was told this personally by a man who was high in management. He said, "Well, you know, Roy, I was there when this was going on and I was always against it and I always told those people they shouldn't do it." Sayen told me in 1961 that he knew damn well they [the dissidents] had a deal with American, but he couldn't prove it.

Dooley's suspicion of C. R. Smith rests on abundant historical precedent. As a protégé of E. L. Cord, Smith took a crude view of labor relations. Although Cord gained effective control of AAL in 1932, he had made so many enemies in Washington after the Century Airlines strike of that year, that heading AAL himself might jeopardize its mail contract. So Cord delegated C. R. Smith to front for him. The old-timers on AAL, some of whom had worked for Cord before, knew they were in for trouble. No matter who was nominally in charge, a Cord operation was a Cord operation, whether it was Century Airlines, Auburn Auto, or Checker Cab, and that meant labor baiting and low wages.

True to form, Smith announced a pay cut coupled with more restrictive work rules almost immediately after taking over. The Great Depression made a handy excuse, but in good times or bad, Cord's enterprises adhered to the "iron law of wages." Put simply, that "law" of classical economic theory holds that the proper wage for any worker is an amount so low that only the most desperate unemployed person will work for it. Ipso facto, since plenty of unemployed pilots asked AAL for work in 1932, C. R. Smith figured he was paying pilots too much.

In fairness to Smith, we must acknowledge that he was not alone in wanting to "reform" the pilot pay system in 1932. The operating companies, faced with declining revenues as the Great Depression deepened, sought to end the system inherited from the Post Office in 1926 that paid pilots base pay plus mileage. Some airlines, like Northwest Airlines (NWA) and PAA, already paid pilots monthly salaries. Although this "reform" did not cut salaries drastically at the time, every pilot knew it would work out to a substantial reduction as newer, faster aircraft came on line.

Dave Behncke staked ALPA's whole future on the fight against flat monthly salaries. If he could not deliver on this vital issue, the typical pilot of that era would see no reason to join ALPA. In a supreme test of nerve and will, Behncke threatened a nationwide strike early in 1933. He knew ALPA could not win. "I figure we would have lasted about five days," Behncke later admitted to the 1934 convention.

By persuading the National Labor Board (NLB), predecessor of the National Labor Relations Board (NLRB), to intervene in the case, Behncke averted the strike. NLB's function was essentially to keep labor peace, and only by convincing its investigative staff that there really would be a nation-wide strike was Behncke able to present the ALPA case. If the NLB investigators had concluded that Behncke's strike threat was merely a bluff, they would have stood aside, the strike would have gone forward, and ALPA would have been broken. Students of aviation history today would know about pilot unionization only as an odd episode that ended in an abortive strike in 1933. Labor history is littered with similar examples of unions that destroyed themselves with premature strikes.

But largely thanks to the AAL pilots, that didn't happen. The first AAL pilots were tough, with the nerve to stand up and spit in C. R. Smith's eye. More than the pilots of any other airline, the AAL pilots of 1933 stood firm behind the strike threat. "I believe they would have walked out to the last man," Behncke said later. Even on UAL, Behncke's own airline, a dozen pilots stood ready to scab, and on other airlines there were even more. Fortunately for ALPA, the NLB investigators interpreted the steady resolve of the AAL pilots to shut down C. R. Smith's airline as typical of the whole industry. The AAL pilots were truly the rock upon which ALPA was founded.

Was C. R. Smith, many years later, creating the conditions upon which ALPA would founder?

After the 1956 convention in which Clancy Sayen defeated AAL's Wiley Drummond for the presidency, several ALPA loyalists openly complained about AAL management's involvement in the campaign on Drummond's behalf. Apparently fearful that these manipulations would lead to more difficult labor relations once Sayen was reelected, AAL's management tried to mollify Sayen. "It was not our desire to inject ourselves in any way into the internal affairs of ALPA prior to the convention," wrote Paul Kayser, vice-president of personnel on AAL. Many ALPA loyalists were skeptical of Kayser's sincerity.

Clancy Sayen could not help but resent the increasingly hostile attitude of the AAL group after 1956. There is good evidence that Sayen tried to undermine the AAL leaders with their rank and file. Writing to Walt Cary in 1956, Sayen bemoaned "the willingness of the average intelligent pilot to permit the lunatic fringe to run his affairs. I noticed, for example, in the minutes of the last AAL Council 22 meeting that of some 350 pilots in this council, there were 17 present. Most of them were of the unstable, noisy minority which promotes irresponsible action."

As one might expect, Sayen's meddling in AAL's internal affairs played into the hands of the dissidents, who quickly exploited the notion that ALPA's national officers were persecuting them. Rank-and-file AAL members naturally felt closer to their own elected leader (even though he was elected at poorly attended council meetings) than to ALPA's national officers. Moreover, the local leaderships' nearly absolute monopoly on the sources of information gave the typical AAL pilot a distorted view of

Sayen's protracted quarrel with Gene Seal and his successors, Paul Atkins and Nick O'Connell.

Much later, as an illustration of this point, Bob Harrington of AAL wrote to Charles Ruby, "The only people I know with the Association are the ones I elect and send up there. I, like many others on American, do not like the present schism, but whom do I believe?"

ALPA loyalists in the late 1950s had a hard time combatting what Tom Latta called "the spoon-fed hate" that the AAL leadership directed against Sayen. "There was a series of events dating back a long way for which Sayen was not responsible," agrees Frank A. "Doc" Spencer of AAL. "But the American pilots felt he was and they would not listen to the other side of the story."

ALPA loyalist Tom Latta, an engineering graduate of Virginia Polytechnic Institute with a distinguished record of service on AAL's "nuts-and-bolts" committees, places primary blame on the AAL leadership:

> It all started because the leadership group on AAL after J. J. O'Connell's term was so poor that Eastern and Delta tended to dominate ALPA. They put up good people like Jerry Wood and Stu Hopkins. The AAL group spent all their time making asses of themselves with this "dump Sayen" movement. It began with the eight-hour controversy, which was a very emotional thing with us. A lot of the guys wanted to cut C. R. Smith's throat, drag him down to Times Square, and string up the body like Mussolini's. Clancy _did_ pretty well hold the fort on the eight-hour issue, but everywhere I went after that episode there were loud screams about Sayen. The American leadership fomented every conceivable distortion against him, trying to cover up their own stupid, boneheaded errors. It was awful, the way they said things about Sayen which they knew weren't true.
>
> The average pilot, by the early 1960s, by the time this prolonged propaganda campaign began to work, was ready to believe anything. Seal and his crowd on the MEC monopolized the sources of information flowing to the AAL group, and they stopped at nothing to make Sayen look bad, to distort the record however they could. That propaganda campaign got the whole AAL pilot group to where they just couldn't think straight.

By 1961, it was obvious that some concession would have to be made to the AAL group to preserve ALPA's unity. Since the dissidents had made Sayen the principal focus of their complaints, it seemed logical that a change of leadership might palliate them. As we have seen, Sayen was also tired of ALPA and actively seeking another career. Although Sayen's friends, still in the majority in ALPA, would never have let the AAL dissidents drive him from office, his decision to resign in mid-term seemed to be in the best tradition of internal compromise to preserve unity.

Although fair-minded pilots were appalled at the virulence of the AAL leaders' assault on Sayen, they accepted his resignation as an unpleasant fact of life. The reaction of William M. Masland, one of PAA's most respected pilots, indicates the esteem that most ALPA members felt for Sayen. Masland spoke for a majority of airline pilots when he congratulated Sayen for what he had done for the profession. Masland pleaded with Sayen to reconsider his decision to resign, perhaps to take a sabbatical and then resume the presidency:

> You have weathered the Quesada attack on the profession and established it as a force in the industry. The next years will determine which way it goes from here. Are there alternatives you would consider? If there are any such ideas that you yourself hesitate to propose, there are many of us who would be willing to do so if we only knew what they were. We in ALPA all seem to start from scratch each election. The result is that most of the term is spent in learning the job, and in the process the incumbent repeats all the errors of his predecessor. You have carried yourself very well indeed, and most of us back you. You have created a new form of labor union, a showpiece and example.

The positive reaction to Sayen was international. Capt. A. D. Mills of the Canadian Air Line Pilots Association (CALPA) wrote to Sayen offering to step down if Sayen would agree to accept the presidency of CALPA. Mills declared that CALPA wanted Sayen, "money no object," after a "sabbatical among various misty and sun-drenched isles." (Sayen resisted this tempting offer, however; as noted in Chapter 19, he operated a trucking business, dabbled in politics, and became an Eastern vice-president before his tragic death in 1965.)

Sayen's mid-term departure from the ALPA presidency in 1962 meant that ALPA was, in effect, meeting the AAL dissidents and their supporters halfway. The next step was up to the AAL leadership.

CHAPTER 22

American Airlines Goes It Alone

Clancy Sayen's departure from the presidency should have created a moment for reaching out, for compromise and conciliation. If ever there was a time for new beginnings, it was when the 1962 convention elected Charley Ruby, an obvious compromise candidate.

It was not to be. The American Airlines (AAL) delegates sat stonily through the session that defeated their chosen candidate, John Carroll of Trans World Airlines (TWA), and then silently refused the traditional gesture of unity—a procedural voice vote making Charley Ruby's election "unanimous." This ominous sign indicated that the AAL group's habit of opposition would not be broken easily. As later events would show, the AAL leadership had already decided on either total autonomy within ALPA or a formal break. Charley Ruby was going to have no honeymoon.

How do we explain the AAL leadership's persistent hostility toward ALPA? A case can be made that the anger they had directed at Sayen for so long (and would now transfer to Ruby) was a by-product of emotional tensions brought on by the jet age. AAL was the first airline to put the new jets into widespread domestic service, and the pressures on AAL pilots by 1956 were tremendous. Of course, other airline pilots would soon be moving into the jet age, but the AAL pilots were first, they were worried, and they might well have sought some psychological relief from their predicament by scapegoating.

Traditionally, scapegoating begins with a cause célèbre, something which seems particularly outrageous to the affected group. Modern political revolutionaries have used the cause célèbre to stir up their followers against established authority. The AAL dissidents found their cause célèbre in the firing of Capt. Wayne Allison.

Walter M. Cary, one of the few Sayen supporters on AAL, wrote to Sayen in 1956 warning that the Allison case was becoming political and cogently analyzing the situation on his airline:

> Hostility toward ALPA is based on fear of the future. With the jets coming fast, we will be hit "firstest with the mostest," and the boys are afraid. Your calm attitude is extremely important, but a lot of our guys don't have the patience. We need your experience, because the next few years are going to be rough. There are a few

dead cats in the closet which a few radicals would like to drag out and fling around. The most notable one is the Allison case.

The Allison affair had its roots in AAL's "screening" program for senior pilots at the Ardmore, Okla., training base. From the beginning of the Ardmore school in July 1947, AAL pilots suspected that its real purpose was to get rid of troublesome senior pilots. With Dave Behncke's strong support, Wayne Allison, the local council chairman at Tulsa, led the fight against the Ardmore school, and AAL backed down. But from then on, Wayne Allison was a marked man.

Tom Latta probably knows more about the Allison case than anybody, for he sat through every grievance hearing as the ALPA representative. "What Allison did wasn't smart," Latta explains, "but there's no doubt that if he'd been anybody else, the company wouldn't have fired him. We proved they'd been keeping a file on him with the avowed purpose of building a case so they could fire him. Then he pulled this stunt that gave them a perfect excuse."

Allison's "stunt" was something that might have earned a "good company man" a pat on the back. While enroute to California in a DC-6, Allison lost an engine over Arizona. The weather was perfect, so Allison, *after consulting with the dispatcher,* proceeded to California on three engines. The company much preferred having the aircraft in California to having it in Arizona, so Allison humored them. Admittedly, the AAL dispatcher's advice to continue was ambiguous, and Allison's cocky urge to display his own airmanship warped his judgment.

"Allison's great violation had been in failing to land at Winslow," says retird AAL Capt. John O'Connell, "but before he got to Burbank he had violated about every rule in the book."

Federal authorities heard that an AAL plane had continued a trip in violation of federal regulations and suspended Allison, pending a hearing. AAL then promptly fired Allison.

"Wayne Allison was kind of a 'cowboy type,'" says AAL's Roy Dooley. "But he was a strong ALPA man and a good pilot, not one of the typical old bull-headed pilots nobody could teach anything, who regarded company regulations as something to be ignored."

"Allison was a very difficult person," adds John O'Connell, "but he had a lot of friends, and he had a good showing at the first hearing held in New York, maybe 150 pilots."

Clancy Sayen actively involved himself in the Allison affair from the start, partly to prove to the AAL pilot group that ALPA would stick up for one of the AAL pilots' heroes. But Allison proved a disappointment. Rather than pursuing his case through the normal channels, Allison chose to file suit against AAL on his own, seeking a large sum of money. As is normally the case when an individual and his lawyer go up against a battery of high-priced corporate legal talent, Allison lost. Sayen had meanwhile arranged a deal by which AAL would take Allison back, but the terms were so humiliating that Allison would not accept that solution. So Sayen, perhaps frustrated by his dealings with Allison, washed his hands of the case.

"Sayen did a heck of a job for Allison," insists Tom Latta. "In effect, he got [Allison's] job back. All Wayne had to do was say, 'I'm sorry, I'll be a good boy in the future.' But that wasn't good enough. Allison didn't want to just come back to work, he wanted retribution, wanted the people who had fired him fired."

So Allison was out, but his case and the resentments it aroused among poorly informed rank-and-file AAL members continued to dog ALPA's leaders well into the Ruby era. In 1956, the dissidents began using the Allison case to discredit ALPA's national officers. ALPA loyalist Breezy Wynne tried in vain to talk sense to the AAL pilots. As chairman of Council 39 at Chicago, Wynne sent a newsletter in September 1956 to all council members, stating:

> I get tired of hearing people bellyaching that "ALPA let us down" and dragging up long-dead issues, trying to make a stink. The effort taken to work up the stink is effort taken from trying to get radar in the [Convair] 240s and [DC]-6s. But who cares? The stink is the thing, not the radar; politics, not dull, dreary representation. Remember how Allison refused the aid he had coming in order to try for a $494,450 settlement in court? He lost his court case, as many forecasted, and now he wants his job back. Whether Allison gets his job back or not, I am concerned overall about the time and energy being spent [by the MEC, master executive council] on his case when it could be spent on the proposed training program for jets. I just wish the MEC would show as much compassion for those of us who still have jobs as they do for Allison.

Despite the best efforts of ALPA loyalists like Wynne, the rank-and-file AAL pilot had no real chance to be educated about the Allison case. The AAL MEC, which was exploiting the case for all the anti-Sayen sentiment it was worth, monopolized the channels of communication to AAL pilots with distorted accounts.

Against this background, the celebrated 22-day strike of Dec. 18, 1958, to Jan. 10, 1959, took place on AAL. The 1956 convention had narrowed the grounds under which strike benefits could be paid. The 1958 Eastern Air Lines (EAL) strike over ALPA's crew complement policy had caused such heavy expense that the Executive Committee recommended, and the Board of Directors approved, that in the future, an airline on strike for purely economic reasons would have to be out at least half of the month to be authorized benefits. This policy was no secret, and the AAL negotiating committee and MEC were well aware of it. Although the AAL pilots deserved strike benefits under the "properly authorized strike" clause, they did not meet the half-month standard in either December or January and hence could not collect strike benefits. Naturally the AAL pilots, who had been hearing the assessments of the Capital and EAL strikes, felt cheated. Their outrage should properly have been directed at their own leadership rather than ALPA's, for Clancy Sayen had specifically warned them about the strike benefits problem before they went out, as Doc Spencer recalls:

> It is positively *not true* that Sayen manipulated the American pilots out of strike benefits. There were changes in policy having to do with strike benefits to protect the Association's exchequer and to make sure that pilots wouldn't leave the Association in droves if they were going to be hit with very high strike assessments. The current leadership on American wanted to strike, but Sayen believed we just couldn't have three airlines striking at once, so he refused to allow the strike all fall, and the guys got extremely dissatisfied with the delay. Around Christmas there was a confrontation between Gene Seal and Sayen during which Seal said, "We don't think you'll let us strike." And Sayen said, "Pick a date." So they did pick a date, and it was just before Christmas. The guys on American were so excited that they gave no thought to how this would affect their strike benefits. I can remember clearly sitting in the downtown hotel in the coffee shop when strike benefits were being discussed. Sayen said, "Do you guys know what you're doing, because if you strike now you're going to cut yourselves short on strike benefits?" Well, they said, "We don't care about any of that stuff, we want a strike." The only people present were those guys on the negotiating committee, and their minds were completely off everything but that Sayen had agreed to a strike. After Sayen left, I brought up the subject again of the inappropriateness of going on strike at that time because of the change in the policy, but they would have none of that.

The final brick in the wall that AAL pilots built between themselves and the rest of the profession was crew complement. As we have seen, AAL management fought the original Civil Aeronautics Board (CAB) order to carry a third crewman on DC-6s to the bitter end, and they never forgave ALPA for winning that fight in 1948. ALPA's second victory on the crew complement issue came in early 1961, when the Feinsinger commission appointed by President Kennedy essentially agreed with the idea that the third crewman on turbine equipment should be "pilot qualified." ALPA's policy (discussed fully in Chapter 17) required the companies to bear the expense of qualifying flight engineers as pilots. Naturally, the companies resented this training expense, preferring to "grandfather in" existing flight engineers, many of whom were ex-mechanics, and to hire only pilots as flight engineers in the future. By opposing ALPA's policy (which protected individual flight engineers while allowing them to upgrade), airline management made common cause with the Flight Engineers International

Association (FEIA), which feared destruction of a functioning union. ALPA endured several strikes over crew complement, notably on EAL, and won its point by dint of main economic force.

By the early 1960s the battle was all but won, and the FEIA was a fading force in the industry. Crew complement was Sayen's baby, and in carrying the field with it he had possibly become, as *Aviation Daily* rather breathlessly described him, "the most powerful man in U.S. civil aviation today."

Ironically, the AAL split of 1963 came just when the crew complement policy was all but settled industrywide. Put simply, the AAL negotiating committee lost its nerve and succumbed to management blandishments. A further irony is that the committee did so in the name of "saving our old friends, the professional flight engineers, and a fraternal union, the FEIA." But once the AAL group had bolted, they essentially turned their backs on FEIA, and AAL's management hired only pilots as flight engineers. In return, management offered the AAL negotiating committee a "sweetheart" contract as a reward.

How was the AAL negotiating committee able to "run away" on crew complement and sign a contract that was in total violation of a policy that ALPA had risked bankruptcy to uphold? The first reason was timing; the second reason was conspiracy.

Almost at the same time that Clancy Sayen announced his intention to resign in 1961, the AAL negotiating committee secretly decided to disregard ALPA crew complement policy. In a transitional time, with the prolonged Southern Airways (SOU) strike still unsettled and the relations between Sayen and the AAL group strained generally, it is not surprising that nobody would be watching the shop carefully. But, in addition, a staff member allegedly assisted the AAL negotiators' deception of ALPA's national officers. Sometime during his detached service, this staff member ceased informing ALPA headquarters of the course that AAL negotiators were taking on crew complement. In November 1962, as the dimensions of the AAL group's breach with ALPA policy became clear, the Executive Committee directed Ruby to fire the staff member forthwith. (He later went on the Allied Pilots Association [APA] payroll.)

As we have seen, Charley Ruby came to office in July 1962 with no real understanding of the advanced state of the betrayal being perpetrated by the AAL negotiators. "I had only a very skimpy knowledge of the thing," says Ruby, "but the American MEC spelled it out to me pretty quickly. My only rejoinder was that if every airline member of the Association had the same philosophy, we would be split up into separate airline representations, none of which would have muscle. I told them they'd either have to learn to live with a unified effort or suffer the consequences and that my job was to enforce ALPA policy."

Almost immediately, the AAL pilots became aware that dealing with Charley Ruby was a new ball game. As Arlin V. "Al" Read, another ALPA die-hard on AAL, put it, "They [the AAL dissidents] knew Sayen well enough to know they could bluff him, and they did bluff him time after time. But Charley Ruby couldn't be bluffed."

The AAL dissidents and Charley Ruby were thus on a collision course, one that the new ALPA president could not shift. Either he would force AAL to toe the mark established by other pilot groups in costly strike actions, or he would meekly surrender to the AAL group's extortionate demand for special status within ALPA. Ruby knew that submission to the AAL group would destroy ALPA's internal discipline and open the way for rapid disintegration. Faced with that prospect, there was no alternative to a fight with the current AAL leadership.

By 1962, the new AAL MEC chairman was Nick O'Connell, a long-time anti-Sayen. In June 1962, even before Sayen's successor was known, the AAL MEC apparently made a firm decision to leave ALPA if the new president did not grant them total autonomy in contract negotiations. Nobody at ALPA headquarters knew about the course negotiations were taking until August 1962, when a member of the negotiating committee, Capt. Harold R. Miller, broke ranks with the dissidents.

Acting on Miller's information, in August 1962 Ruby called AAL Master Chairman Nick O'Connell to account for the actions of the negotiating committee. O'Connell arranged a joint meeting between Ruby and the AAL negotiating committee, during which Ruby informed them that their approach on crew complement was jeopardizing recent hard-won gains. The AAL negotiators, with the full support of Master Chairman O'Connell, then were on the verge of signing a contract that would effectively junk ALPA's mandatory crew complement policy. Instead of requiring three crewmen, each with a minimum commercial and instrument rating, the AAL contract would call for "some additional training" for the nonpilot flight engineer as a fail-safe measure, with such training being left up to the company. By not having to provide nonpilot flight engineers with a commercial and instrument rating, AAL's management would save an estimated $10 million. The AAL negotiating committee, headed by Dick Lyons, assured Ruby that the FEIA supported the negotiating committee's settlement.

Lyons's assertion later turned out to be incorrect. The previous May, the so-called Taylor board had affirmed the broad outlines of both ALPA policy and the Feinsinger commission by requiring the company to provide nonpilot engineers with a commercial license and an instrument rating on company time and expense. The decision of this arbitration board, composed of George Taylor, Edgar Kaiser, and AFL-CIO chief George Meany, apparently settled the crew complement issue once and for all, to everyone's satisfaction. Ruby thought it surprising that the AAL negotiators stated flatly that the nonpilot flight engineers on AAL were opposed to the Taylor board's decision.

It was a classic case of *Rashomon*-style ambiguity again. ALPA was about to find itself in the awkward position of upholding the rights of AAL's flight engineers, whose union, FEIA, had until lately been engaged in a bloody war with ALPA. Even more incredibly, ALPA would be fighting its own pilots on AAL, *who also claimed to be fighting for the "rights" of professional non-pilot engineers to be let alone!*

After checking with Joe Manning, leader of the AAL flight engineers, Ruby learned that Manning was enraged with O'Connell. Manning called O'Connell "Big Daddy" and insisted that the AAL flight engineers preferred dealing with ALPA.

Although Charley Ruby had no intention of allowing the AAL negotiations to proceed, he had operated previously on the assumption that Nick O'Connell was an honorable man who was sincere when he spoke of the AAL pilots' desire to "protect" the flight engineers on AAL from having to undergo mandatory pilot training they did not want. Manning flatly told Ruby that O'Connell was a liar. Ruby was in a quandary. If the AAL leadership was trying to deceive him with so obvious a lie, what did it portend for the future?

Charley Ruby saw no alternative but to begin formal expulsion proceedings against the AAL leadership. In October 1962, ALPA's Executive Committee passed a resolution affirming the crew complement policy once more and ordered the AAL dissidents to "reshape" negotiations to comply. Nick O'Connell attended the meeting. Faced with a warning that AAL's course could lead to serious trouble, O'Connell agreed to acquaint the AAL negotiating committee with the Executive Committee's views. He flatly refused, however, to obey the Executive Committee's order to recess the negotiations.

Two tense months passed, during which the AAL negotiators defied the ALPA Executive Committee and continued meeting with the company. In a final attempt to restore internal harmony, Charley Ruby asked for a meeting with the full AAL negotiating committee in New York early in December 1962. The meeting was inconclusive. A few days later, on December 11-13, Ruby met with the AAL MEC in Chicago. Ruby warned the AAL pilots that adherence to ALPA's crew complement policy was vital. "As a means of making clear to you the great stake we have in this area, not only for the American pilots but for the pilots of other trunk carriers," Ruby told them, "we called together the master chairmen of every airline for a thorough discussion of the crew complement issue." Ruby told the AAL pilots that they were jeopardizing the Association's whole future for short-term gains. Then, turning tough, Ruby declared:

> In a further attempt to resolve this most troublesome question, I have convened the Executive Committee to meet with you. It must be clear that this cannot be for the purpose of further debate. The pilots of other airlines affected by the crew complement policy have in no instance made an agreement for less than a commercial

license and an instrument rating for the third crew member on jet equipment.

As your president, I have attempted to mediate and conciliate for many months to persuade people of good will to resolve these problems. I assure you that personal experience has taught me that the fruits of serious dissension among us are plucked by management and do not yield gains to any of us. But there should be no misunderstanding—I am bound to implement policy and this I intend to do. The Board of Directors, the Executive Committee, and the master chairmen have affirmed a course from which I cannot and will not deviate.

The AAL negotiating committee, having previously informed the Executive Committee that it had "no intention of prejudicing a contract beneficial to American pilots," denounced ALPA's national leaders for "interference" with their efforts to achieve a "complete solution of the crew complement issue." To no avail, Ruby again pleaded with the AAL pilots to get back on the crew complement reservation. "I think it behooves all of us," Ruby wrote to O'Connell, "to do our utmost to solidify ALPA's position and solidarity if we are to become an effective force over the years."

Ruby's appeal to 1930s-style unity fell on deaf ears. A few days later Ruby called Bill Whitacre, the AAL executive who was negotiating with the runaway committee. Noting that the AAL negotiating committee was proceeding in violation of ALPA's constitution and bylaws, Ruby warned Whitacre that signing a contract would lead to legal action under the Railway Labor Act.

Ruby's threat gave Whitacre pause—no corporate executive wants to be responsible for costly legal action. In a conference between the AAL leadership and Whitacre on Jan. 3, 1963, the company apparently promised to sign a favorable contract with the pilots if the pilots would in turn agree to leave ALPA and form a company union.

During its January 8-11 meeting, the AAL MEC faced the moment of truth. For years they had been threatening to go the route of company unionism. Now, at long last, they had to decide. The company was dangling an enticing package of wages and working conditions, premised on their pilots' willingness to deny the AAL flight engineers the benefits of the Taylor board settlement. The AAL dissidents took the bait.

"Therefore be it resolved," the AAL MEC declared, "that the entire AAL pilot group goes on record as authorizing the AAL negotiating committee to conclude a contract and to further advise AAL management that the AAL pilots are agreeable to implementation of said contract *with or without formal approval from ALPA.*"

The die was cast. On January 11, the Executive Committee authorized Charley Ruby to file suit against AAL for violation of the Railway Labor Act. Also on January 11, Ruby wrote to AAL President C. R. Smith, ALPA's old nemesis, that "any negotiations or agreements on behalf of the pilots in your employ must be conducted and made only with the consent of this Association, which is the authorized bargaining agent."

On January 18, Whitacre answered Ruby's letter. "The company has no alternative but to conclude an agreement," Whitacre said, "since the persons in question occupy official status as members of the Association's negotiating committee and appear to represent a majority of the company's pilots."

Ruby promptly appealed to rank-and-file AAL pilots over the heads of their own elected leadership. Beginning in late January 1963, he sent a series of bulletins to the AAL pilots in an attempt to "halt the steady diet of half-truths and misstatements about the Association, its officers, and policies." But only the AAL pilots could save themselves from the uncharted seas of company unionism. The ALPA loyalists on AAL began to rally for a desperate last-ditch attempt to stop their own runaway leadership, which was already circulating "authorization to act" cards among the rank and file. The ensuing contest between the AAL pilots left deep scars that persist to this day. Suffice it to say that the struggles of the minority of ALPA loyalists on AAL were foredoomed to failure, for the dissidents had been too long in control, and their propaganda campaign against ALPA had become too ingrained in the mental patterns of rank-and-file AAL pilots, whose indifference to ALPA affairs had left them poorly equipped to make judgments.

The initial ad hoc loyalist committee, made up of Harold Miller, H. E. "Doc" Merrill, Jim Jewell, Lloyd Wade, and Frank A. "Doc" Spencer, found itself totally on the defensive, trying to answer rumors. The AAL leadership had recently circulated the story that Clancy Sayen was still on ALPA's payroll. _"Fact!"_ wrote the loyalists in their newsletter. "Mr. Sayen was terminated from the ALPA payroll immediately upon completing the transition period stipulated. Since that time, he has had no direct ALPA assignment. He did represent the Braniff stewardesses for two days at a grievance hearing, for which he was paid by the stewardesses $252.39."

As any political pro knows, if you can keep your opponent answering unsubstantiated charges, the mere refutation of them gives a sense of their validity to unthinking people. "Have you stopped beating your wife yet?" is an unanswerable charge.

But more important than the political tactics used by the separatists was the company's offer of an enticing package of wages and working conditions in return for the AAL pilots' desertion of ALPA.

"You can always get a sweetheart contract if you agree to break a union," says Carl Rubio of AAL, who retired in 1980 after paying full dues to ALPA his entire career. "This profession didn't get to where it is by forming company unions. By remaining loyal to a real labor union, I found it easier to live with myself. And, anyway, the contract we got from the company in

1963 hasn't held up all that well. Under the APA contract, American's pilots can still go to work at 6 p.m. and wind up flying a tight approach at 7 a.m. the next morning."

However, the majority of AAL pilots didn't see things Rubio's way. The AAL leadership argued that they were the wave of the future, that other airlines would quickly follow them out of ALPA. The AAL group made formal overtures to Pan Am, but the Pan Am group turned them down cold. The AAL leaders then approached TWA, where John Carroll, the former master chairman and defeated presidential candidate, fronted for them. Carroll argued strongly in favor of the AAL approach to crew complement policy in a letter to TWA Master Chairman Russ Derickson, denouncing the Taylor board settlement on TWA.

In response to Carroll's propagandizing in favor of the AAL separatists, ALPA loyalist Tom Latta declared, "Crew complement is *not* the issue," in a letter to Derickson:

> The Turbo-Prop and Jet Study Committee *never* contemplated lesser qualifications than a commercial and instrument for the third crewman. When the recommendations were made to the 1956 convention, the AAL master chairman, C. E. Seal, stood up on the floor after the voting and asked that the record show that AAL had voted "unanimously" in support of the crew complement portion of the recommendations. Mr. Paul Atkins and Mr. Nicholas O'Connell were in attendance. Mr. O'Connell had a vote. I presume he knew that his vote was "for." The average member of AAL has become completely frustrated concerning what he can expect from ALPA because of "maverick" leadership. He hears only the anti-ALPA representative calling cadence and never knows he is out of step. Recent events show clearly that the AAL leaders are willing to sell every other pilot in ALPA "down the river." The AAL pilot does not know how rocky the road his representatives have chosen for him is.
>
> I simply wonder how much political hay John Carroll is trying to cut. The recent actions on AAL confound reason and press upon the AAL pilot an unwarranted reputation of not caring what happens to his fellow pilots on Eastern, United, TWA, or Ozark. John's advice should be "get back in ALPA."

One further motive in the AAL leadership group's desire to leave ALPA must be mentioned. ALPA loyalists on AAL insist that the leaders had engaged in a consistent pattern of financial misconduct that Sayen had accepted but hard-nosed Charley Ruby would not. At Ruby's request, Roy Dooley of AAL made a carefully documented study of the flight pay loss requests of the AAL negotiating committee and MEC. What Dooley found later led him to urge AFL-CIO President George Meany to seek prosecution of the AAL leaders under the financial misconduct sections of the Landrum-Griffin law. Charley Ruby remembers:

I noticed a tendency for the American MEC to hold a lot of meetings, and when you get into a big airline that's awfully expensive. As I looked over the flight pay loss, some airlines, like Northwest and Continental, were stingy with the Association's funds. Well, on American those boys didn't care, moneywise. I started putting the squeeze on them and it ruffled their feathers, because they were spending money in ways I just wouldn't stand for. I went to the American MEC early and told them they had a responsibility to control their own expenditures. I said I was going to be breathing down their necks on flight pay loss and that some of the ridiculous things they had been pulling better not happen again.

What "ridiculous things"? Early in the Ruby administration, the new treasurer, Scotty Devine of United Airlines, approached former Master Chairman John O'Connell for some answers on the flight pay loss requests coming from AAL. O'Connell remembers:

Well, I kept quiet until I could get back to the Los Angeles base to check it out. I found a man who could only hold a copilot bid who was applying for captain's pay loss *at 100 percent night, at 84 hours and some minutes!* The person who actually flew those trips was in the top 10 on the seniority list, and this guy was hundreds of numbers down the line. It was just plain theft, and it was very common among that crowd, although I didn't know it at the time. I would have taken it to the membership if I had had more evidence than this one case. It actually took Roy Dooley months to assemble all the evidence.

The basement of Roy Dooley's home in suburban Chicago is spread with dossiers on members of the various AAL committees. It takes an expert understanding of the AAL system to interpret the flight pay loss requests.

"In each case you'll notice that the authorizing signature is [the same]," Dooley points out.

You couldn't just hand in a bill and say, "My [local council] chairman asked me to go out and count the runway lights at O'Hare." But if you put down that Ted Linnert authorized it, if accounting had any question they would go to Linnert, who was head of ALPA engineering. [The staff member later fired] was the American guy, the staff negotiator whose duty it was to ride herd on the contract. The fact that he went with them when they split is very interesting. He was a Trojan horse. They were always close to 85 hours, which was the most ALPA would pay and a lot closer than most line pilots are able to get. They would bid trips that had such rotten working conditions it would be impossible to fly, but nobody would ever know about it. It came down to a moral judgment in that case, but suppose you give ALPA a bill for a trip that isn't even on your bid sheet, or one that didn't even exist? They used ALPA to increase their salaries without having to go sliding down any wet runways at night. All these folders show a pattern of deliberate excessive compensation at ALPA's expense. They didn't have the right to that money, and they weren't using it for anything that was of any benefit to the American pilots. It was fraud, not just an interpretation of the rules. I'll put it plain—they were a bunch of thieves.

Human motivation is complex. We will never know to what extent the AAL leaders' decision to secede from ALPA was motivated by fear that Charley Ruby, whose reputation for granite-like financial integrity had preceded him, would expose their flight pay loss habits to the rank-and-file AAL pilot. By the time Roy Dooley, Breezy Wynne, and others had mounted a campaign to acquaint the rank-and-file AAL pilots with their leaders' peculiar flight pay loss habits, the situation was so ripe with charges, counter-charges, and lawsuits that nobody believed them.

On Feb. 5-7, 1963, the Executive Board met in emergency session in Chicago to endorse Ruby's position, to denounce the AAL leadership group, and to advise AAL management formally that they "are not the bargaining representative of the American pilots." Nick O'Connell and other members of the AAL group were present at the meeting. It was the last time AAL leaders and ALPA leaders met formally. Kay McMurray, Ruby's executive assistant, came to the February 21 negotiation between the AAL dissidents and management in New York. McMurray informed the gathering that they were in violation of the law and then left the room.

On March 1, 1963, ALPA filed suit against AAL, the AAL negotiating committee, and Nick O'Connell personally, alleging that there had been "influence and coercion by the company in the choice by pilots of their representatives" in violation of law. On April 26, 1963, O'Connell and all other members of the AAL negotiating committee were expelled from ALPA (with the exception of Harold Miller, who had resigned from the committee in February).

In response, the AAL dissidents announced formation of APA and petitioned the National Mediation Board (NMB) for a representative election. For the next two months, the dissidents waged a fierce campaign against ALPA among the rank and file, alleging misdeeds that the committee headed by Harold Miller found impossible to counter effectively. The results were predictable: in June 1963, NMB reported that 84 percent of AAL's 1,571 pilots had authorized APA as their bargaining agent.

The overwhelming majority the dissidents secured from AAL pilots was probably decisive in the legal proceedings. The U.S. district court of Judge Inzer B. Wyatt found against ALPA in August 1963. There was nothing for ALPA to do but appoint "trustee councils" on AAL to look after the interests of the 236 anti-APA pilots on AAL. Subsequently, the ALPA diehards were permitted "apprentice" status and retained on the roster. Many of them eventually drifted into APA, until finally only a dozen or so remained.

Among the loyalists who played prominent roles in trying to stop the split were Carl Rubio, A. M. "Breezy" Wynne, Roy Dooley, Tom Latta, Ted Sorenson, E. S. "Pye" Swanson, Jim Jewell, George Eckhardt, Arlin V. "Al" Read, John J. O'Connell, Stan Neilsen, Evan W. Chatfield, Sheldon E. "Ed" Pangburn, Frank A. "Doc" Spencer, Roy Patterson, Charles Doudt, Fred Johnson, Bob McDaniels, Lloyd J. Wade, H. E. "Doc" Merrill, and S. V. Ballard. In addition, a number of old-timers like Albert E. "Prince" Hamer, Hamilton C. Smith, Walt Braznell, J. F. Bledsoe, Wiley Drummond, and H. G. Robinson, who had been in management most of their careers, were known to oppose the split. Eventually, many of the loyalists found it necessary, both for protection and to establish a sense of community, to join APA. But for the most part, these marriages were not of the heart.

"Today's AAL pilot typically wasn't even hired yet when the split happened," says Carl Rubio. "They take as a kind of 'received wisdom' that ALPA never did anything for the American pilots. From time to time I would be ostracized, accused of allowing APA to carry me. I'd just get out my ALPA card and say, 'ALPA is carrying APA.' APA really has had no impact at all nationally. During Operation Accordion, when they tried to shrink the size of oceanic airlines to Europe, ALPA stepped in and stopped what was going to be a serious safety violation. I'd point this out to the APA types, and they'd say, 'What good is that to us? We don't fly to Europe.' I'd say, 'Yeah, but how about your wives and kids? Do they ever fly to Europe?'"

By late 1963, many ALPA members were heartily sick of the AAL group. Capt. E. R. Epperson of Delta expressed this feeling when he wrote to Charley Ruby: "Let them go. Hell, we don't need that bunch of patsies. Concentrate on ALPA. They will learn."

But Charley Ruby, like most ALPA members, felt the average AAL pilot should not be punished for the sins of his leaders. "There is a sizable element of American pilots who do not wish to leave ALPA," Ruby replied to Epperson. "We cannot in conscience abandon them."

In the aftermath of the split, the President's Department of ALPA functioned as the MEC for the dues-paying ALPA members still on AAL, and permitted a special delegation of loyalists (headed by former Master Chairman John O'Connell) to attend the 1964 convention. A number of lingering problems, such as the disposition of the substantial property—typewriters, office equipment, and the like—remained to be settled. ALPA's Executive Committee, on Aug. 24, 1963, established ALPA's policy toward AAL that persists to this day. ALPA resolved to stick by its loyal AAL members, "to hire outside legal counsel to protect their representational rights as long as there are members requesting such services on American."

This conciliatory policy toward the defecting AAL pilots reflected the views of most ALPA members. The old-timers had not forgotten the contributions of the AAL group. As Master Chairman L. B. Gordon of Trans Texas (later Texas International) wrote to Ruby: "At a time when it appeared we had no one else to turn to and were about to be scabbed, the American pilots made it known in no uncertain terms that they intended to back us all the way." Gordon urged Ruby to "keep the doors open" for the AAL group.

"I still entertain hopes that eventually the American pilot group will become aware of the overall problems pilots face," replied Ruby to Gordon. "Pilot objectives are the same, regardless of the airline, and I am optimistic that the American pilots will one day see fit to return to full ALPA membership."

For labor historians, ALPA is a stunt done with mirrors. In the face of an almost constant oversupply of pilots, ALPA has somehow managed to protect the minority of pilots with airline jobs from the "iron law of wages." The old guys, the first generation of professional airline pilots, made ALPA's living denial of the iron law by careful application of the difficult arts of conciliation and compromise. Their fundamental goal was always unity across company lines. Dave Behncke never tired of preaching this gospel. The second generation of professional airline pilots, those who came to maturity around 1963, somehow forgot this fundamental lesson, perhaps because they have never been exposed to the predatory personnel policies that made life so difficult for their predecessors. The old guys knew that without the strength professional airline pilots derived from each other, they would all stand naked before their enemies.

In the brave new world of deregulation, that's a lesson worth pondering.

"APA has never been tested," says Tom Latta. "If the company ever decides to bite them, they'll go down. All that's kept the American pilots afloat so far is that there's an ALPA to go back to. ALPA's still there, still setting the pace for the industry."

If the past is truly prologue, then perhaps it is time for the AAL pilot group to come home. ✦

ntering the
dministration of J. J.
'Donnell *(right)*, the
ssociation faced issues
at transcended the
oncerns of pilot groups
n individual airlines and
lled for unified,
dustrywide action.

A member of the AFL-CIO's select Executive Council, President J. J. O'Donnell *(below, with AFL-CIO President George Meany in 1977)* strengthened ALPA's ties with organized labor. "I sit here with 30,000 votes, while organized labor has 15 million . . .," O'Donnell has said, ". . . and that is a powerful force that has been helpful with many of ALPA's problems." In Atlanta in January 1981, ALPA First Vice-President Gerald Pryde spoke at a meeting to promote Operation USA *(bottom)*. Flanking Captain Pryde at the rostrum were *(left to right)* F/O Jerry Lawlor (TWA), Treasurer John J. Magee, Secretary Thomas M. Ashwood, and F/O Rick Dubinsky (UAL).

On Oct. 21, 1980, uniformed ALPA pilots from 23 airlines marched on the White House to protest potential safety hazards in the policies of Langhorne Bond, then FAA administrator. The demonstration awoke the press and the public to these and other threats to aviation safety, without disturbing this Braniff pilot's child *(left)*. ALPA Secretary Tom Ashwood *(below, in sunglasses)* led one column of marchers. Ten months later, ALPA again spoke out on a national issue when President O'Donnell *(bottom)* called a press conference in Washington, D.C., to reassure the American public that "the system is safe" in the aftermath of the Professional Air Traffic Controllers Organization walkout.

In the 1960s, terrorists saw the jetliner both as a symbol of wealth and power and as a vulnerable target for violence. The forward section of TWA Flight 57 *(right)* was decimated in March 1972 when a time bomb exploded inside the evacuated aircraft at McCarren Field in Las Vegas. Two years earlier, the Black September movement was born in explosions in the Jordanian desert as Arab terrorists blew up empty hijacked planes, including a BOAC VC-10 *(below)*. As President O'Donnell's executive administrator, Jack Bavis *(bottom, at a 1972 SOS news conference,)* integrated Eastern's flight security program into a national one.

The 1972 Board of Directors meeting in Las Vegas brought together hijacking victims *(opposite, top, standing from left)* S/O Jim Hankins, F/O Don Salmonson, F/O Greg Colliton, and Capt. Lee Hines and *(seated, from left)* Capt. Dale Hupe, Capt. Bill Haas, and Capt. Oscar Cleal, who was blinded in a 1961 hijacking. Hupe, Salmonson, Hankins, and Colliton received the Gold Medal Award for Heroism, ALPA's highest honor *(opposite, center)*. F/O Freddie Jones *(opposite, bottom)* was honored with a gold medal after he was killed by a crazed gunman in a 1974 hijacking. The courage of these and other pilots—some of whom sacrificed their lives—was the price of the Antihijacking Act of 1974 *(opposite, far right)*.

Today, as in the beginning of the Association, ALPA pilots continue to be vital and visible advocates of air safety. The influence of today's ALPA pilots on such projects as the National Airspace System Plan *(right)* and a collision avoidance system such as the Boeing-designed concept *(below left)*, will affect the profession through the next generation. The input of Captains Richard B. Stone (DAL), Joseph Oliver (DAL), George Terhune (PAA), and Mel Hoagland (UAL) *(bottom, seated, left to right)* helps designers like George Sexton of Lockheed-Georgia *(standing)* plan the flight decks of the future. At hearings on the 1982 Air Florida crash *(opposite, top)*, Capt. Don McClure (EAL), F/O Augie Stasio (UAL), F/O Tom Kreamer (USAir), Harold Marthinsen (director of ALPA accident investigation), and F/O Jim McWilliams *(clockwise around table, from left)* carried ALPA's concerns to NTSB. Testifying on Capitol Hill, President O'Donnell *(opposite, center)* and ALPA representatives *(opposite, bottom, left to right at table)* Capt. Bill Melvin (DAL), John O'Brien (director of ALPA's Engineering and Air Safety Department), F/O Jack Howell (EAL), and Capt. Pat Clyne (NWA) have proven influential proponents of the interests of pilots.

CAPT ODONNELL

ASTP

ALPA's Washington office *(top)* allows pilot spokespersons convenient access to Congress, government regulatory agencies, and other interest groups in the aviation community. The first floor of the eight-story building houses a sophisticated computer system *(above)* that, through its terminals at the Washington office and in field offices across the country, provides members with up-to-date information on pay scales, retirement benefits, and other vital issues. Although ALPA's founders probably never anticipated using such technology in their union, they articulated, in the preamble to the Association's constitution, the ends it serves: to unite airline pilots for "the protection of their interests and the promotion of their general welfare" and "to cultivate a spirit of harmony and understanding between air carriers and airline pilots. . . ."

CHAPTER 23

Jets and Thin Ice

Rites of passage are never easy. Ask the old helmet-and-goggle airmail types what it was like to go from open cockpits to Ford Trimotors and instrument flight. Then ask their successors, the second generation of professional airline pilots, what it was like to go from the DC-3 to the Super Constellation. By the late 1950s, airline pilots were about to undergo another baptism of fire under new technology—the jets were coming.

For 20 years the jets gestated in the world's military services. Their coming to commercial aviation was inevitable, part of a long trend stretching back to the Wright brothers and their bitter competition with Glenn Curtiss. Always pushing each other, the pioneers extended the frontiers of aviation until development became an all-consuming passion, a kind of religion that saw men sacrifice their lives and fortunes to fly faster and higher. No man could restrain this rush to progress.

After World War II, sleek military jets were at the cutting edge of aviation development, but commercial exploitation of the jet's potential would have to wait until the needs of national defense abated. This was a far cry from the 1930s, when the "Douglas Commercial" series, the planes that made the first real profits, were at the peak of existing technology and were totally a product of the private sector. The military aspect of jet aviation was troubling to many airline pilots, largely because of an "image" problem. The popular media depicted jet pilots as hard-living, bushy-haired, physically flawless specimens of young manhood (rather like airline pilots had been depicted in the 1930s). Magazines, movies, and television saturated the 1950s with sensational accounts of the physical ordeal that high-altitude jet flight put these young military pilots through, endlessly making the point that flying these hot new aircraft was a "young man's game."

No small wonder, then, that staid, middle-aged airline pilots should feel apprehensive about their futures once the new jets came on the line.

In fact, the transition to jets was something most pilots would take in stride. A big airplane was, after all, just a big airplane, and the pilot who had mastered Douglas DC-7s or Boeing Stratocruisers was usually sure enough of his own abilities to handle new power plants and increased speed. But there were exceptions, and everybody who lived through the jet transition knew of a pilot whose career had been short-circuited, usually by that deadly handmaiden of insecurity, alcoholism. There were even a few cases where a suicide might have been the result of the feelings of inadequacy that the giant new jets could instill in an older pilot.

Consider the massive changes that the new jets brought to air transportation. Big and swept-winged, operating smack up against the sound barrier and on the threshold of the stratosphere, the new jets were able to shrink continents and oceans like no passenger plane had ever done before. By the mid-1950s, the old prop planes had already extended their technological parameters as far as possible, and the traveling public was growing weary of their time envelopes. Coast-to-coast, the props still ate up 10 hours between boarding and deplaning for the ordinary passenger. But the jets could cut that time down to less than a working day, about five hours of air time, and maybe an hour on each end to get to and from the airport (provided that the antiquated ground transport systems weren't too crowded). For international travelers, the differences were even more astounding. London was only 7 hours away from New York for a jet setter, but for a prop passenger it was 12 hours distant.

For the engineers, the new jets were technological marvels, collections of scientific advances in dozens of fields from avionics to metallurgy to aerodynamics. For airline management, the new jets were at once a risk and an opportunity. History had shown that the airline boss who jumped in too fast, who committed to a new airplane before all the glitches were out, was taking a chance. If the jets proved unreliable, his competitors would sell more of that most perishable of commodities, passenger seats, by plugging along in their safe and sure old props. On the other hand, if the jets proved successful, and if an airline manager waited too long to place his name on the order list at the factory, he stood to lose out to the canny guy with jets who would lay first claim to passenger loyalties.

But the risks for pilots were greatest of all. Working pilots, ordinary guys who had somehow made airline piloting their calling, would ultimately have to break these new turbojet monsters to the commercial harness and would have to learn their jets' eccentricities daily out on the line, in fair weather and foul. Long after the engineers had put away their sensitive instrumentation and the test pilots had gone on to the next frontier of aviation, ordinary line pilots would still be exercising their stewardship over the new jets, learning about them much as the pilots who had come before them had unraveled the mysteries of the Ford Trimotor after the engineers thought there were none. And, as inevitably happened, some pilots would pay with their lives to advance the curve of learning. ALPA had no official role in aircraft certification.

The enormous changes wrought by the coming of jets meant new problems for ALPA, but also new opportunities. Because the new jets represented a quantum jump in pilot productivity, most ALPA members insisted that they should be paid more—a lot more. For the average pilot, the greatest impact of jets was that pay scales took off. This dramatic jump in salaries didn't happen by accident or at the largess of the companies. ALPA's hard spadework prepared the ground for higher pay scales, and most pilots fully appreciated the work done by the committee on jet pay, which provided the rationale and justification for new contracts on each airline.

But another aspect of ALPA's role in the coming of jets was never far from the mind of the typical pilot. "What will ALPA do for me if I can't cut it?" was the haunting question many pilots secretly harbored. The local council chairman at each airline domicile usually bore the brunt of this apprehension, for he was the first to know when things went sour for a pilot moving to jets.

The experience of each pilot group under jet transition was different, yet somehow the same. For example, let us consider the situation on United Airlines (UAL). William J. Moore, who had gone to work for UAL in 1946 after learning his trade in combat during World War II, served as chairman of Chicago's UAL Council 12 during 1963-64 and 1973-74. Moore's first term as local council chairman placed him squarely in the middle of the transition to jets. Now retired, Moore sums up the problem generally:

> From my experience, the jet transition was the most troubling period in the professional lives of the people I dealt with. For many pilots, the training school at Denver was stressful, although to a certain extent the stress was self-inflicted. For years I worked with people who had these problems, you know, the *fear.* There were several people who just dropped out, who couldn't take the stress, who would go up to a certain point in training, nothing wrong with their flying, and then just couldn't push beyond. There was an agreement between the companies and ALPA on the disposition of these cases, and generally if a man couldn't pass muster at the Denver school, he could bid down to the equipment he had been flying previously. It was common rumor that if a man went through the Denver training center and he didn't make it, practically any other line would take him. It was a tough school, certainly in the beginning.

The transition to jets was particularly troublesome on UAL owing to the merger with Capital in 1961. Capital (né Pennsylvania-Central) was the odd man out among large trunk carriers. Unlike its "Big Four" competitors, UAL, Trans World Airlines (TWA), American Airlines (AAL), and Eastern Air Lines (EAL), Capital was burdened with mostly short-haul routes, which meant that although it ranked fifth in almost every category, its profitability was vastly inferior. Given the tightly regulated structure of the airline industry in the 1950s, Capital's only chance of improving its profitability over what was essentially a local service route structure lay in acquiring new aircraft that were so efficient and so superior that new passengers would come in droves. Traditionally, the Big Four had led the industry in technological innovation, largely because they had financial resources that airlines like Capital lacked.

In one of the great gambles in the history of commercial aviation, Capital's president, J. H. Carmichael, ordered a fleet of British-built Vickers Viscount turboprops in 1956. Carmichael was aware that the pure jets were coming, and that neither his route structure nor his financial situation warranted their acquisition. The great advantage of jets was speed, but owing to the time eaten up by approach, landing, and ground turnaround, this advantage melted away on short-haul routes. The marriage of turbine power and propellers, however, meant that some of the pleasing characteristics of jets (quiet ride, lowered fares, better schedules) could be adapted to routes that were the natural habitat of aircraft with slower but more economical reciprocating engines. Carmichael and Capital would ultimately lose their gamble. The economic climate of 1956 dealt Capital the most telling blow. With a business recession in progress, it was a poor time to introduce the expanded service that Viscounts made possible. Also there were crashes that dampened passenger enthusiasm for the Viscount. Eventually the Viscounts performed well enough, but Capital's route structure itself was impossible. Finally, the only way out for Capital was a merger. UAL picked up the pieces in 1961.

Under auspices of the Civil Aeronautics Board (CAB), the merger of Capital and UAL brought salvation to the pilots of Capital, but they donned UAL uniforms as distinctly second-class citizens. The Capital pilots had always lived under a rather informal system that lacked the rigor UAL pilots had known. Consequently, the UAL training school, the "Denver aggravation," hit the Capital pilots hard. Ironically, the Capital pilots, who had been flying turbine equipment before the UAL group, now faced pressure to relinquish their bidding rights to the jets UAL had placed in service in 1960.

One cause of ALPA's financial malaise of the early 1960s was the bitter seniority fight arising from the UAL-Capital merger. Eventually things worked out, and the two pilot groups blended harmoniously, thanks to the careful procedures that ALPA had so painstakingly developed for settling disputes. But what was a rough period for most airline pilots was doubly so for the Capital pilots, who came to regard the Denver training school with a phobia bordering on paranoia. In short, the Capital pilots, who called their training jaunts "You Bet Your License" (after the popular TV quiz show), worried that UAL might be using the rigorous training system to get rid of them.

Dick Becker, a Capital pilot who served out his career with UAL before retiring, describes the informal Capital training system as "two hours of flying, takeoffs, and landings; they showed us where the radios were, and you learned the rest on the line." A vastly different system awaited the Capital pilots merging on UAL. "For one short period, they failed one out of three," says Jess Bradford, another ex-Capital pilot. "It was quite an expense for the company, and eventually we got one instructor fired because he was creating a stress situation."

"It got so bad some guys took up religion," adds Carl Peterson, another ex-Capital pilot who endured the rigors of the Denver school. "They had this oral examination with 120 questions, and sometimes they would flunk you in the 727 course for missing _one_ question."

"You had to get up at 4:30 in the morning," recalls Jess Bradford, "and they rarely had an airplane ready to go before 9:00, see? And some of these standards guys thought they taught the Wright brothers how to fly, and by the time you get through it's 2:00 p.m. and you do a bad job, you know, because you're tired. I was in the air 4 hours and 50 minutes during one check, and I never got out of the seat."

The rigor of the UAL training system foreshadowed a general toughening of school requirements throughout the industry. Partly the new stress on comprehensive ground training came from the campaign of Federal Aviation Administration (FAA) head Elwood "Pete" Quesada, the ex-Air Force general who seemed to bear a grudge against airline pilots—or so many ALPA members thought. Operating under the rubric that low pilot proficiency caused most of the safety problems accompanying the introduction of jets, Quesada insisted that FAA inspectors join regular crew members at random in the cockpit to conduct the aeronautical equivalent of pop quizzes.

Quesada's approach to improving pilot proficiency caused the only wildcat strike in ALPA's history. It began with Quesada's insistence that his inspectors be allowed to ride in the third pilot's seat during regular flights. When this controversy developed in June 1960, most airlines operating jet equipment carried a crew of four, three pilots and a flight engineer. The third pilot occupied a seat immediately behind and to the right of the captain. Quesada insisted that the inspector occupy the jump seat opposite the flight engineer's station. It was a clear case of conflict over command authority, since the pilots insisted that the third pilot had duties to perform, whereas Quesada argued that his inspector's function took precedence over the crew function and that in any case the FAA personnel were fully qualified to perform the third pilot's duties.

Over this conflict, the pilots of EAL, Pan American, TWA, and AAL began guerrilla actions against FAA. During June 1960, several pilots on these airlines refused to fly—when the FAA man entered the cockpit and insisted upon taking the third pilot's seat, they simply canceled the flight. Quesada again threatened dire consequences for pilots refusing to fly with his inspectors. With the problem of Electra structural failures still bubbling and the safety record deteriorating despite his crackdown on pilots, Quesada found the pilots' guerrilla rebellion against his inspectors a convenient diversion. In a spate of news releases and interviews, notably with *U.S. News and World Report,* Quesada flatly declared that "pilot error" was still the largest single cause of fatal accidents, and he threatened to lift the license of the next pilot who refused to fly with an inspector in the third seat.

Quesada's hard-nosed attitude provoked the wildcat strike on EAL. The EAL pilots who operated DC-8B equipment approached ALPA about authorizing a strike, but Clancy Sayen, after soliciting legal opinions from outside experts, concluded that there was no contractually acceptable way to strike under ALPA auspices.

The EAL pilots began walking out on June 12, 1960. EAL was forced to cancel 104 flights the first day of the wildcat strike; by the second day, over 50 percent of EAL flights were scrubbed. Despite an emergency court injunction against the walkout on June 14, EAL's scheduled flights dropped to only 30 percent of the prestrike total, as court officers had trouble finding pilots to subpoena.

ALPA had to walk a fine line during this affair, owing to the legal complexities of the contract. Clancy Sayen had to make perfectly clear that this action was the product of extracontractual problems with the federal government, for which ALPA was in no way responsible. Many EAL pilots, and others on AAL and TWA, as well, faulted Sayen for not supporting the wildcat strike more forthrightly. Years later, during Operation USA (Unity for Safe Air Travel), ALPA President J. J. O'Donnell, an EAL pilot during the wildcat strike, would apply some of the lessons learned in 1960. By defining Operation USA as an "exercise in free speech" to protest government policies, the nationwide shutdown ALPA threatened in 1981 would ultimately rest on the notion of "petitioning the government for redress of grievances" and would not technically be a strike against the airlines in question. This reasoning never occurred to Sayen in 1960. The trouble developed so quickly on EAL that ALPA was really more of an observer than an active participant.

Despite the injunction against the pilots' wildcat strike, the trouble spread to Pan Am on June 20, as 102 pilots in sympathy with the EAL pilots refused to fly. James Landis, who was at the time challenging Sayen for the ALPA presidency (as we saw in Chapter 19), injected the wildcat strike into ALPA politics by promising fully to support the wildcat strike if he succeeded in ousting Sayen.

By June 25, under threat of contempt of court citations and with Clancy Sayen reluctantly calling for the pilots to return to work, operations on EAL were back to normal. Nevertheless, EAL filed suit against ALPA, its officers, and the striking EAL pilots individually for $11,400,000 in damages. This harassing legal action eventually came to nothing, and it probably reflected the new EAL management's (Rickenbacker had just retired) frustration over losing money for the first time since 1934. As part of the welter of lawsuits emerging from the 1960 wildcat strike on EAL, ALPA filed suit against FAA, seeking to void the Quesada approach to in-flight checks. This suit, too, came to naught, and eventually ALPA would have to bargain directly with FAA over cockpit check procedures.

During the early jet era, ALPA fought FAA Administrator Quesada over many things, particularly his methods, but never his emphasis on safety. Everybody wanted safety, but Quesada's approach, in the opinion of airline pilots who lived through that era, was entirely punitive, focusing too much on the alleged inadequacies of individual pilots and not nearly enough on the shortcomings of "the system." For the pilots who ran ALPA during this period, two problems with "the system" were significant—inadequacy of training and inherent flaws in air traffic control (ATC), which the new jets aggravated.

To take the first of the systemic problems, one should be aware that airline training had historically been weak. In the early days, if a man had by hook or crook gotten a license, airline managers generally agreed that he was "trained." Even airlines like TWA, which had more rigorous recurrent training programs than others, lagged behind the military in introducing modern training programs and devices. So once again, as had happened so often in the history of commercial aviation, ALPA took the lead that management should have taken and insisted that if pilots were to be vulnerable during recurrent FAA line checks, then they should at least have adequate training to prepare them.

Capt. Ed Watson of EAL headed the first ALPA Training Plans Committee. With the assistance of committee members Steve Gondek of Mohawk (MOH) and Don Leonard of Northwest Airlines, Watson patiently put together the technical assistance to enable the individual training committees of each airline to build adequate training programs for their own pilots.

ALPA's position throughout the jet transition was that proper training alone would not solve the safety problem and that pilots themselves were less responsible for jet crashes than were defects in the ATC system. Quesada dismissed ALPA's complaints. Quesada's whole program rested on the assumption that pilots were at fault, not the system itself. Quesada, like most Eisenhower appointees, enjoyed a very favorable press with the influential Luce publications *Time, Life,* and *Fortune. Time,* for example, praised Quesada because he "cracked down mercilessly on slipshod flying procedures that have bedeviled the airlines for years." Quesada trained a corps of FAA inspectors, mostly military retirees, and then sent them out to prove, in his words, that "they can fly better than the man they're checking out." One out of four airline pilots failed the checks administered by Quesada's inspectors, who insisted, among other things, that airline pilots begin demonstrating their basic airmanship by doing approaches to stalls in routine checks. It all looked pretty good to the man in the street and the administration was willing to give Quesada's methods a chance. There was only one problem—despite Quesada's crackdown on pilots, the safety record deteriorated in the late 1950s.

Naturally, professional airline pilots resented Quesada's attack, but until he lost support by refusing to ground the Lockheed Electra during the airliner's time of trouble, it was dangerous for ALPA to attack him. Quesada had public opinion on his side, and owing to the troubles over crew complement, the public was beginning to regard professional airline pilots as an exotic species of union featherbedder. Quesada insisted that his vaunted revamping of the airways system under the 1958 law, coupled with his campaign to bring commercial aviation "up to military standards," as *Time* described it approvingly, would eventually solve all problems.

A number of ALPA activists publicly opposed Quesada. Bobby Rohan of National Airlines (NAL) attacked the requirement that FAA checks include approaches to stalls. After the crash of an NAL DC-7 over the Gulf of Mexico in November 1959, Rohan publicly warned that the probable cause of the crash was structural failure induced by Quesada's required stall maneuvers. Rohan denounced approaches to stalls as "not necessary and deleterious to the airframe" and warned that NAL pilots would no longer perform them.

Quesada threatened to end the flying career of any NAL pilot who refused to go through the full check, and he had the power to make it stick. NAL Vice-President L. W. Dymond (whom we met in the chapter on Ed McDonald's ordeal) sided with Quesada. Dymond's credentials as an airline pilot were, of course, laughable, but the public had no way of knowing that.

Then, one of those spectacular crashes that illuminates a safety problem happened. Aviation historians know it as the Brooklyn-Staten Island crash, because one plane plummeted into Brooklyn, the other into Staten Island. For the first time, two aircraft under positive radar control in full instrument conditions collided in midair. The tragedy proved that "the system" could as easily cause death as a "slipshod" pilot.

The Brooklyn-Staten Island crash was reminiscent, in some ways, of the celebrated Grand Canyon crash on June 30, 1956. The cause of the Grand Canyon crash was the old "VFR [visual flight rules] on top" flying that ALPA had been complaining about for years. The TWA Super Constellation and UAL DC-7 collision, then the worst airline tragedy in U.S. history, cost 128 lives. Like the crash that killed Sen. Bronson Cutting in 1935, the Grand Canyon crash also led to sweeping changes in the federal government's supervision of commercial aviation. The Cutting crash had led to the passage of the Civil Aeronautics Act of 1938, and the Grand Canyon crash led directly to the Federal Aviation Act of 1958.

Ironically, the Brooklyn-Staten Island crash of Dec. 16, 1960, again involved TWA and UAL. This time, a UAL DC-8 collided with another TWA Super Connie. Both planes were under full radar control from the ground.

The dead totaled 139: everybody aboard both planes, including a small boy who survived the crash only to die later in the hospital. The UAL DC-8 had entered holding at normal cruising speed, overshot the prescribed racetrack pattern, and collided with the TWA aircraft. Federal regulations did not require a reduction in speed before entering holding, even though it was aerodynamically impossible for a DC-8 to stay within the limits of the holding pattern without so doing. The UAL captain was following "the book," but obviously there was a flaw in its pages. By now, it was Quesada's "system."

Quesada had championed radar ground control as a cure-all for the system. ALPA had always distrusted absolute ground control because it robbed the pilot of authority. The Brooklyn-Staten Island crash offered ALPA an opportunity to attack Quesada's policies without seeming self-interested and vindictive.

The man who knows more about the Brooklyn-Staten Island crash than anybody else alive is J. D. Smith of UAL. Now an executive with the line, in 1961 Smith was ALPA's safety chairman for the northeast region, which included the site of the crash. During the 1950s, Smith participated in more accident investigations than any other pilot, since the most heavily traveled sector of the country lay in his region. As the spokesman for safety in the urban areas of the northeast, Smith found himself under considerable pressure:

> We had airplanes landing in the streets at Newark, and 8 million people were scared airplanes were going to start falling on their heads like raindrops. I was at home when I saw on television that some kind of plane was down in Staten Island. I got in my car and went to the site, and I spent that whole day and most of the next there. I had to do a lot of coordinating so that there would be no fingerpointing by one pilot group at the other.

Any spectacular accident will cause a gusher of sensational news stories. Often, as in the case of the crash of the AAL DC-10 in Chicago in 1979, most of the early releases will be misleading, and federal officials, hectored by reporters and feeling public pressure, will sometimes make statements that add to the confusion. FAA Administrator Quesada made just such a statement to the press. Within a few days, Quesada announced on television that the UAL plane was at fault for overshooting its holding pattern. Immediately, "Pat" Patterson of UAL blasted Quesada for being "premature."

Sensing a major controversy, the news media homed in on J. D. Smith, who was ALPA's designated spokesman, for comment on the dispute between Quesada and Patterson. "I let Quesada and Patterson fight in public with no help from me," says Smith. "The aviation reporters, the good ones, realized that speculation was premature at that point. They were a knowledgeable bunch."

While Quesada and Pat Patterson engaged in verbal battle via the headlines, the FAA investigating team, along with J. D. Smith's ALPA accident study group, patiently sought the "probable cause" of the Brooklyn-Staten Island crash. Quesada undoubtedly was seeking to regain some of the prestige he had lost recently by allowing the Lockheed Electra to keep flying despite fatal crashes involving structural failure. Quesada's position was that the Electra was safe at reduced speeds, since the harmonic vibrations from the engines that had caused metal fatigue in the aircraft's wings did not begin until maximum cruising speeds were approached. The public, needless to say, was so leery of the Electra that the plane's full commercial potential was never realized, and Quesada suffered because the public saw him as sacrificing safety to the economic interests of the airlines and aircraft manufacturers.

Attempting to recoup his lost public standing, Quesada used the Brooklyn-Staten Island crash as a further argument in favor of stricter age limitations on airline pilots, particularly those operating jets. After all, military pilots seldom flew actively once they were in their 50s, so why should airline pilots? Since the allegedly slow reaction time of the UAL captain caused him to overshoot the holding pattern, Quesada suggested once more that jet captains retire at age 55. Quesada also made much of some recent crashes where pilot incapacitation played a role, particularly an October 1959 crash involving a pilot who was taking tranquilizers and undergoing mental treatment. Since the pilot had concealed his psychiatric problems from FAA, Quesada suggested that mental incapacitation might have played a role in the accident. ALPA objected strenuously to Quesada's airing of this opinion, largely because there was no direct evidence suggesting that the pilot's mental state caused the crash. Similarly, in another crash of a nonscheduled airline's military charter, the pilot in question had concealed a heart condition from FAA medical examiners. When he died suddenly in the cockpit, his copilot proved incapable of landing the airplane safely. ALPA pointed out that any regulatory setup that would permit an airline to employ an incompetent copilot, particularly a company holding a Pentagon contract, showed, again, that there was more wrong with "the system" than with the pilots.

Against this contentious background, the final act of the Brooklyn-Staten Island affair was played out. Initially, Quesada's position, as usual, was that pilot error had caused the crash, whereas ALPA argued that the system was at fault. Quesada seized upon the lack of redundancy in radio equipment in the UAL plane (one VOR receiver was down), citing continued flight into the New York terminal area without fully functioning avionics as a prime factor in the accident. The UAL DC-8 crew, according to Quesada's reconstruction, was unable to locate the radial designating the limits of the holding pattern quickly enough because they had to reset the single functioning VOR receiver.

The investigation later proved conclusively that any time lost tuning radios by the crew of the ill-fated DC-8 was inconsequential. The UAL aircraft was slowing from cruise after entering the terminal area; although its speed had dropped only some 50 knots, it was still screaming along at over 300 knots when the collision occurred. Quesada obviously knew this speed was too fast to allow the DC-8 to remain within the racetrack pattern, so simultaneously with his denunciation of UAL, FAA promulgated new maximum airspeeds in terminal areas. The new limit was 250 knots. Had the UAL aircraft been flying at that speed or below, the crew probably would not have overshot the racetrack holding pattern.

As the man who nursed the investigation along to its conclusion for ALPA, J. D. Smith sees the Brooklyn-Staten Island crash as a turning point:

> The basic cause of the crash was that there were no specific requirements as to speed limits in the holding pattern, other than those required by the aircraft itself. The accident investigation generated greatly reduced speeds in holding and upon entering terminal areas. In a legal sense, there was no requirement for these maximum endurance-type speeds before Brooklyn-Staten Island. There were a lot of lessons learned out of that accident. It highlighted the need to develop wholly new ATC procedures.

One such procedure called for reporting the loss of avionics to ATC. The DC-8 was lacking one VOR receiver, and had there been a requirement for this to be reported to ATC, possibly the radar controller would have been paying closer attention to the plane. As it was, the radar controller simply sat and watched the DC-8 barrel past the limits of its holding pattern until it disappeared into the blip of the TWA aircraft. Naturally, this made Quesada's reliance on ground radar control suspect. While conducting his publicity campaign, Quesada quietly ordered mandatory reports from all aircraft losing radio navigation equipment, thus indicating that he knew the DC-8 crew was not wholly at fault. But publicly, Quesada continued forever after to bemoan "dangerous flight practices" on the part of civilian airline crews and to imply that they were misbehaving in the cockpit.

Bit by bit, the jet transition progressed, with episodes like the Brooklyn-Staten Island lesson adding to overall knowledge. There would be others in the future, often illustrating, as did the TWA 727 crash into Mount Weather on the approach to Dulles Airport in December 1974, that even ATC procedures that seem time tested and foolproof can have fatal consequences. But the Mount Weather crash was far in the future, and ALPA greeted the election of John Kennedy with a sigh of relief and the hope of a better working climate. The change of administrations in Washington promised an early departure for Quesada. Few in ALPA would miss him—

the "war with the general" had been one of the most trying aspects of the transition to jets.

Now a new trial awaited professional airline pilots in their taming of the big jets. These magnificent flying machines attracted a new mass clientele to the airlines. Any cross-section of Americans will always contain a few who are insane, deluded, or sociopathic, many of them subject to strange fantasies of power and omnipotence that the continent-shrinking jets seemed to encourage. How easy it would be, some of these aberrant individuals must have thought, simply to produce a pistol, take command, and rule the lives of crew and passengers, godlike, in the heavens.

The era of skyjacking was upon ALPA. It would test mightily two ALPA presidents, Charley Ruby and his successor, J. J. O'Donnell. Before the epidemic of skyjacking was over, professional airline pilots would pay with their lives.

CHAPTER 24

Skyjacking

Civilization is a delicate web held together by mutual consent. The jet airliner is modern civilization's most prominent symbol of that mutual consent, the embodiment of man's conquest of the skies, and the promise that someday technology will serve only mankind's peaceful instincts. Graceful and powerful, the jet airliner is also delicate and vulnerable.

To a certain extent, civilization has always been vulnerable to criminals, psychotics, fanatics, and misfits. Armed with bomb and gun, the few who would make war on the many have always been able to hold society hostage temporarily. By striking at the vulnerable interstices where mutual consent and common respect govern decent intercourse, Jesse James distorted the society of frontier Missouri by robbing its unguarded banks and trains. So also would the skyjackers be able to distort commercial aviation, ironically linking Jesse James's heroic status with the admiration many people felt for skyjackers.

Just after Fidel Castro seized power in Cuba, most skyjackers were people fleeing communist tyranny and hence "freedom fighters" to many Americans. For Capt. J. J. O'Donnell, who stepped from the command of an Eastern Air Lines (EAL) DC-9 to the helm of ALPA in the midst of a sickening international wave of aerial piracy in 1971, the crusade against skyjacking would be an all-consuming passion. Nearly everything ALPA did between 1970 and 1974 would necessarily take a backseat to the elimination of skyjacking. Like his predecessor, Charley Ruby, J. J. O'Donnell would face his share of intractable issues and impossible situations, but none would rival skyjacking in intensity. He would find that hard problems make for difficult solutions.

The early history of skyjacking bears some comparison to that of the safety issue. Put simply, safety is so expensive that both management and government have skimped on it because of their principal concern for profits. Historically, some of ALPA's toughest fights were with the companies and the government over the proper balance between safety and economy. In a sense, this scenario would repeat itself in skyjacking, with ALPA urging a no-holds-barred, full-forward approach and the government and the airlines always seeking the least costly solution.

By 1970, professional airline pilots the world over were infuriated at the penny-wise niggling that had characterized the response of governments and airlines to skyjacking. With an epidemic of political and economic terrorism abroad in the world, capped by the simultaneous skyjacking of four airliners on a single day by Arab terrorists in September 1970, the professional airline pilots of the world, speaking through the International Federation of Air Line Pilots Associations (IFALPA), would demand strong action to curb aerial piracy. Pilots couldn't understand why governments and airlines were so reluctant to move against skyjacking.

The lead editorial in the *New York Times* on Sept. 14, 1970, explained this reluctance by pointing out that "concern for profit" was preventing the airlines from taking the kinds of measures that would prevent skyjacking. Although Charles Tillinghast of Trans World Airlines (TWA) disputed the *Times* editorial, most informed observers knew better. Jack Bavis, who flew for EAL before coming aboard ALPA as J. J. O'Donnell's executive administrator in 1971, bore personal responsibility for overseeing ALPA's antiskyjacking program in the early 1970s. As an ex-Massachusetts state policeman, Bavis brought special expertise to the EAL flight security program. O'Donnell tapped him to integrate the EAL program into a national one. Immediately, Bavis discovered that "economic reality" stood athwart ALPA's effort to eliminate skyjacking:

> Reason and logic weren't going to work, simply because of the cost of an effective security system. President O'Donnell took over at a time when emotions had reached a high point among the pilot groups, and a lot of people who wanted action were blaming Charley Ruby for not getting it. After I got here I discovered the handicaps he was working under. What Charley had was himself, virtually no help from anybody else, because he was so busy fending off internal attacks. J. J. was free, temporarily at least, from that kind of attack, so he could spend his time on the basic problem, which was money. We not only had to apply unremitting pressure, but we also had to come up with a source of funds to pay for the ground security system. Eventually we persuaded the government to tap ADAP [Airport Development Aid Program] funds.

Expensive ground security (long backed by ALPA) to prevent skyjackers from boarding was the only answer that ever made any sense. Effective ground security systems were practical and available as early as 1963, but not until tragedy and the unrelenting pressure from ALPA forced the hand of the Federal Aviation Administration (FAA) and management did these systems begin to come into widespread use after 1973. It is one of history's supreme ironies that public apathy underlay this government and management reluctance to stand tough against skyjacking. The combined efforts of ALPA and IFALPA to create effective ground security systems would suffer, partly because the public didn't want to be inconvenienced.

Although aviation has seen random skyjacking before, the modern history of the subject begins in 1959, the year Fidel Castro seized power in Cuba. When anti-Castro Cubans began commandeering airliners to flee their homeland, most Americans heartily approved! After all, Castro was a Communist, and people fleeing his tyranny seemed to deserve sympathy. Although most professional airline pilots, regardless of their nationality, saw the dangers of skyjacking immediately, the public was having too much fun sharing a horselaugh at Castro's expense to worry about the long-range implications of skyjacking—or about the possibility of this virus spreading.

It never seemed to occur to the average American that applauding an escape to freedom accomplished with a pistol at the head of an airline pilot, albeit a Cuban Communist one, was not the wisest precedent for the nation with the world's most extensive air transportation system. All through the 1960s, as Castro consolidated his power, Cuban opponents of his regime continued to flee in everything from leaky sailboats to oversize inner tubes. Their flight became more desperate as Castro's firing squads began eliminating officials of the Batista regime. Needless to say, a man who expects to be lined up against a wall and shot will not trouble himself over the legal niceties of his departure—if a pistol must be his passport, then so be it. And anyway, for most Americans, skyjacking was something that happened only in Communist countries.

Then in May 1961, the tables were turned. A man describing himself as pro-Castro skyjacked a National Airlines (NAL) Convair 440. The skyjacker was armed with a knife and a pistol, so Capt. Francis Riley was in no mood to argue with him. Enroute to Havana, the skyjacker ranted about warning Fidel of an assassination plot. Riley later described the skyjacker as a "psychopath." After landing safely at Havana, the crew and 17 passengers were allowed to depart. The skyjacker was never seen again.

It was the first skyjacking to Cuba—it would not be the last.

On July 24, 1961, barely three months later, an EAL Electra with 38 passengers aboard was diverted to Havana. Castro promptly released the crew and passengers, but he kept the plane as a pawn in his game to have the United States return the motley collection of fishing boats, airplanes, and even naval vessels that had been hijacked to the mainland. Castro declared that he would release the Electra as soon as the United States agreed to open formal discussions about putting a halt to skyjacking. He also wanted an agreement to return hijackers to the flight's country of origin to face prosecution. The U.S. government balked. No politician in his right mind, given the public's antipathy toward Castro, dared return an anticommunist "freedom fighter" to Cuba. Nor were we about to return any of the hijacked vehicles to Castro, largely owing to legal claims filed against them by individuals seeking redress for property lost in Cuba because of the revolution. (We did, however, return Castro's naval vessel.)

After two weeks, Castro relented and the EAL Electra was released. Historical irony again—Castro made the first overture to end skyjacking, but we rebuffed him. And there the matter rested, with the news media tending to portray those who escaped from Cuba as heroes. This glorification was bound to have an influence, and the idea of skyjacking, once implanted in an unstable mind, was bound to have consequences. It would cost Capt. Oscar Cleal his eyes, his career, and very nearly his life.

On July 31, 1961, Oscar Cleal was doing what he liked best, flying his Pacific Air Lines (later Hughes Airwest) DC-3 over the company's intrastate route in California. At Chico, Calif., that day, Oscar Cleal made what would prove to be his last landing as an airline captain with a certain nostalgia. He was scheduled to return to the Martin 404 soon, so he expected to be flying again, but not in the trusty old DC-3. Cleal and First Officer Al Wheeler chugged up to the ramp and shut down, anticipating a delay owing to a late arriving passenger. (Things were pretty casual on an intrastate carrier operating out of quiet, small-town airports in those days.) Cleal and Wheeler relaxed in the cockpit, idly discussing the weather at their next stop.

As they waited, Cleal and Wheeler heard a commotion, first in the baggage compartment and then in the cabin. "I thought it was a drunk," Cleal remembers, "but [the noise] could have been a shot." Cleal looked out the window and saw station agent Bill Hicks dragging himself away from the airplane, holding his side. Then there was a pounding on the cockpit door. Cleal and Wheeler added up the odd circumstances and surmised that a skyjacking was under way.

Seizing a wrench for added fist weight, Cleal rose from the left seat to do battle. Then he heard a pistol shot and a voice saying, "Get this plane going or I'll shoot everybody."

The flimsy cockpit door was bulging as the gunman frantically tried to burst in. Cleal positioned himself behind the left seat in an alcove used to hang coats. The instant the gunman crashed in, Cleal intended to brain him with the wrench. But mindful of the hazard facing the passengers, Cleal ordered Wheeler to start the right engine and taxi away from the terminal, thus humoring the skyjacker temporarily. Wheeler complied, but the DC-3 wouldn't budge—the parking brakes were set and could only be released from the left seat. Cleal left his ambush and jumped into the left seat to release the brakes. At just that instant the door latch gave way and Cleal found himself staring straight into the barrel of a pistol.

The skyjacker was an unemployed, homesick hillbilly who wanted to go back to Smackover, Ark. The only problem was, he was broke. But he did own a pistol, and the Cuban skyjackers had given him an idea. Why not flee California, the hated land of city dudes and strange ways, by pointing the gun at an airline pilot? Once home, the skyjacker would simply disappear into the hills, perhaps to be regarded as a hero by the homefolk. Such were the thought processes of this deluded individual.

"I never had any intention of leaving the ground," Cleal says. "The only thing in my mind was to somehow to get the drop on the guy and disarm him." Using the ruse that he needed a chart from his nav kit, Cleal contrived to maneuver into a position where he could grab the gun. But when Cleal made his move, the pistol went off, and "a sea of black ink" closed over his eyes. First Officer Al Wheeler, a husky ex-policeman, jumped the skyjacker grappling with him over the gun as the taxiing DC-3 careened about the airport apron. "The last thing I recall was pushing on the brakes and pulling back the throttles," Cleal says. "Then I lost consciousness."

The skyjacker fired five shots in all before Wheeler knocked the gun from his hands. He then produced a knife, obliging Wheeler to fight on with him as Wheeler tried to control the taxiing aircraft. Finally, three passengers rushed forward to help Wheeler subdue the skyjacker. The skyjacking was over, but for Oscar Cleal the struggle was just beginning:

> When I came to in the ambulance Bill Hicks said, "Well, we made it so far." It took me an awful long time to realize that I'd never be back flying again, the thing I loved more than anything. I've thought over the things that contributed to the skyjacking. I think one of them was that the station agent had very little assistance. It was too much for one man to handle, and due to the economy of the feeder-line business at that time, well, they took advantage of these young guys to do all these jobs. When Bill Hicks was loading cargo, the skyjacker came on the airplane. When Hicks asked him to get out, he pulled the gun and shot him. There was a city-employed armed guard, carrying a 45 on his hip, and Hicks dragged himself into the airport, right by this guard *who did absolutely nothing!* The thing I would like to stress was that my first consideration was for the safety of the passengers, so I turned to this guy who had the .38 at my head, and I said, "Where do you want to go?" And he said, "Arkansas." I said, "We're not going anywhere unless I have a chart." I pointed to my nav kit, ostensibly with the thought that if I could reach down under that gun to my chart and come up fast, I would be able to grab that gun. But when I started to come up, he shot me. I just wasn't fast enough.
>
> There are an awful lot of attitudes as to how one should deal with this. Some captains don't want to mess around with a gun at all. Some people say we ought to be able to collar the guys ourselves. Others say, "I don't care where they want to go; we'll take them there." But I have to hand it to El Al; they really have the answer as far as I'm concerned. I think the captain should have at least a .38 in his possession, though I'm not saying he should wear it on his hip. I feel the flight crews should be trained in karate or judo to disarm any drunk, psycho, or skyjacker. I got a few of the pilots there at Pacific Air Lines to go through this training. If I had had this training, maybe I wouldn't have fumbled when I tried to disarm the skyjacker.

If the story of the tragedy that befell Oscar Cleal has anything like a happy ending, it is that he battled back against the darkness to become a successful stockbroker. He had been working on the Pacific Air Lines retirement committee, so as soon as his health permitted, Cleal began studying. With the help of his nurses and wife, who read aloud to him, and Recordings for the Blind, which transcribed textbooks he needed, Cleal passed the necessary examinations. Later, Cleal got hired by Shearson, working there for 13 years specializing in retirement and pension plans. Currently, he is with Kidder, Peabody & Company. "I didn't want to live off my friendships," Oscar Cleal says simply. "After 19 years of working in this business, I guess I made the right decision. But the brokerage business will never take the place of airline flying. It was a great fraternity."

ALPA President Clancy Sayen, spurred by the tragedy that befell Oscar Cleal, issued steady warnings about the vulnerability of the air transportation system. Using his influence with the Democratic administration, Sayen was instrumental in persuading John F. Kennedy to ask Congress for special antiskyjacking legislation. In 1961, a potpourri of federal and state laws impinged in some way on the problem, and this diversity of statutes was itself a source of encouragement to potential skyjackers. For example, although the skyjacker who ended Oscar Cleal's career got the stiffest sentence possible under existing law, he was a free man after a mere 15 years. "The SOB who stole 19 good years of flying from me is now out walking around," Oscar Cleal says simply, with understandable rancor.

From 1961 on, ALPA's primary goal was to make sure not only that skyjackers would pay heavily for their crime, but also that air piracy itself would be as difficult as possible. And here chance intervened, for in 1961 the skyjacking binge suddenly abated and the public lost interest. Congress was reluctant to take expensive corrective action, so it failed to mandate the necessary security measures. Thus, the skyjacking issue merged neatly with the safety issue, which always had a dollar sign attached to it.

Getting a law passed providing stiff penalties for convicted skyjackers was relatively easy. Under ALPA's prodding, Congress passed and President Kennedy signed, in record time, a new "air piracy" act. Although stiff penalties and a tough law on the books looked good, neither took any courage to pass because there was no price tag attached. FAA Administrator Najeeb Halaby imposed some middling precautionary measures in August 1961 (mainly requiring locked and bolted cockpit doors), but the Air Transport Association (ATA) opposed more stringent measures. Halaby, always sensitive to the economic health of the carriers, demurred from stiffer prevention.

With ALPA's help, Congressman Frank Leslie Chelf introduced an amendment to the Federal Aviation Act of 1958 which would have tightened screening procedures to prevent people carrying concealed weapons from boarding as passengers. Again, ATA opposed any kind of passenger screening or search. "I, for one, was tremendously disturbed by the ATA opposition to the Chelf bill," says Oscar Cleal.

By 1962, when Charley Ruby took over as ALPA president, it was obvious that the FAA was going to bow to ATA's opposition to tougher screening of boarding passengers. "We beat our brains out for years on this cockpit security thing," says Charley Ruby, "but we were getting nowhere; we were still vulnerable because it seemed as if everybody was pretending that what happened once couldn't happen again."

But it did, and ironically on Oscar Cleal's own airline—Pacific. On May 7, 1964, in a chilling preview of the violence to come, another deranged individual shot his way into the cockpit, killing Capt. Ernie A. Clark and First Officer Ray E. Andress. The skyjacker's object apparently was suicide. All 44 persons aboard the aircraft died in the crash. The FBI later traced a revolver found in the wreckage to a man who had just bought a $60,000 policy at an airport insurance kiosk. For years ALPA had been agitating against these "instant insurance" policies, but since somebody stood to make money from them they stayed in airport lobbies, a permanent temptation to the deranged.

At this point, professional airline pilots began to arm themselves. In August 1961, just after Oscar Cleal's wounding, ALPA officially came out against armed guards aboard aircraft to prevent skyjacking. If firearms were going to be aboard, most pilots preferred to use them themselves, but ALPA continued to support rigid preboarding passenger searches as the best alternative.

Charley Ruby has vivid memories of the problems ALPA encountered as a lone voice seeking effective remedies to the skyjacking problem:

> I spent an awful lot of time trying to talk people into doing the things that were *possible* to do, and I must say that when it came to doing something *effective*, ALPA was not only the prime mover, we were almost the *only* mover. The first solution to the problem just added to it potentially; that was the sky marshal idea. It was perfectly clear to everybody that the minute you have somebody with a gun who is not under the captain's direct control you've got a high element of risk. Even with the use of low-velocity bullets there's always a chance of somebody shooting out a windshield, pieces flying back in both pilots' faces. We had to fight like hell for the most basic changes in ground screening, X-ray surveillance of luggage, magnetometers. It was obvious that the companies and the FAA were going to do as little as possible, and we finally had to threaten to take action on our own, and if it meant defying the government ban on flight crews carrying handguns, well, we just had no choice, because we just couldn't tolerate it any longer. I had to fight four-fifths of the airlines on the use of low-pulse X-rays, which were just beginning to show up to screen luggage. FAA was dubious about it, and of course Ralph Nader and his ilk screamed.

The companies and FAA finally gave in after an awful lot of pressure on my part, and they only did it because I threatened to go public with it and say that ALPA has a method of dealing with this problem, which was the only one that ever made any sense, and that was to stop the skyjacker from ever getting on board the plane.

By 1965, the jet airliner had become a widely accepted symbol of the power of modern civilization. A new glamour attached itself to these sleek, continent-shrinking machines, and a new word, the "jet set," was coined to describe the elite groups of every society who flew in them. But although jet travel was still associated in the public mind with extravagance and luxury, by the mid-1960s it had become, in fact, the dominant mode of inter-city travel for everybody, from common people to nabobs. In short, jet aviation had an aura of power and romance, but everybody had access to it. It was a matter of time before psychological and political misfits, criminals, and others with a grudge against society would focus upon the jets as a means of obtaining attention and settling grievances. The airline pilot became, for many of these troubled people, a kind of heavenly father figure to whom they could appeal for redress, succor, or just attention. All a skyjacker needed either to get away or to get attention from a society that ignored him was an airline ticket, a weapon, and the will to use it. Then somebody would have to listen to him.

This threat hung over every airline pilot. Several hundred flight crews had to face the challenge of a skyjacking, ranging from the 28-hour odyssey of Capt. William R. Haas of Southern (later Republic) to the wounding of Capt. Dale Hupe of TWA, each of whom had to make life-or-death decisions to save his aircraft. But no case is more significant than that of Capt. Bob Wilbur and First Officer James Hartley, Jr., of EAL.

On March 18, 1970, in a case similar to the one which sent Capt. Ernie Clark's Pacific Air Lines F-27 plunging to earth in 1964, Bob Wilbur and Jim Hartley narrowly saved their passengers from a psychopath intent upon suicide. The deranged passenger who forced his way at gunpoint into the cockpit of the DC-9 piloted by Wilbur and Hartley on a Newark-Boston flight ordered them to fly eastward over the Atlantic. Wilbur's pleas that the plane was nearly out of fuel left the skyjacker unmoved. It became apparent to Wilbur and Hartley that their unwelcome cockpit guest intended to kill everybody aboard. The two pilots had no alternative but to grapple with the man who stood menacingly over them with a pistol.

In as desperate a combat as two men have ever waged airborne, Wilbur and Hartley subdued the skyjacker as shots ricocheted through the cockpit. Their victory was costly. Hartley, mortally wounded, still managed to wrest the gun from the skyjacker and shoot him with it. Wilbur, bleeding from his gunshot wounds and on the verge of losing consciousness, somehow managed to land the DC-9 at Boston. Jim Hartley died during the final approach.

For ALPA, the martyrdom of Jim Hartley meant that mere gestures (like the naming of EAL's new flight crew training facility at Miami after Hartley) would no longer be enough. With pilots threatening to retaliate against both the government and their employers by a "suspension of service" (SOS), or simply withholding their labor for a period of time, the tide at last turned in favor of the active prevention Oscar Cleal had first suggested back in 1961. Practical electronic screening devices had been available since at least 1963, but FAA had delayed making these passenger-screening tools mandatory because of ATA pressure against them. Although FAA had shown considerable interest in electronic "frisking" of passengers, it moved so slowly in instituting a full-scale test of the devices at Dulles Airport in Washington that most airline pilots were disgusted. ATA gave its blessing to the Dulles tests, but insisted that it not "create an inconvenience" for passengers and that the airline companies should not have to bear any of the expense of the system.

In 1969, the year before the tragic EAL skyjacking, FAA finally appointed a special task force to study electronic screening of passengers on the ground, but had it not been for Jim Hartley's death, the report of this task force would probably have been buried like others before it. The group, formally called Task Force on Deterrents to Air Piracy, was chaired by Dr. H. L. Reighard. Ultimately, the task force opted for the ALPA program of intensive ground screening, but not without unremitting pressure by ALPA. Jack Bavis recalls that initially the Reighard task force relied almost entirely on nonelectronic means, leaning heavily toward the "behavioral profile" as the primary means of spotting skyjackers:

> When I took over, the special task force had been meeting for several months, and we knew there were major weaknesses in its approach. We learned quickly that in order to get action, you had to continually chastise the government through whatever channels were available, the media, congressional hearings, otherwise they would not take the necessary steps because of the expense. The behavioral profile was fine as far as it went. Security people could be trained to spot people who would ordinarily fly tourist, but were flying out of class, Cubans with no luggage, and other likely skyjacker types. But what worked well for a while might not work later. They'd modify, change as they figured out who was being stopped from boarding, and some skyjackers just never fit it at all, so ALPA had to pressure the government hard to get them to go along with more rigorous preboarding screening. And on this we had major problems with FAA, and it finally took President Nixon overriding them, thanks to a lot of help from John Volpe (Nixon's secretary of transportation), a personal friend of J. J. O'Donnell's, the newly elected president of ALPA.

After implementation of ALPA's program, the skyjacking problem started to abate, at least on U.S. domestic flights. Combining rigorous electronic screening with behavioral profiles of boarding passengers compiled by a team of psychologists, ground security officers began to make a real dent in the rate of skyjacking. But it took a massive effort, one that caught as many innocent pranksters as serious hijackers, before the ground screening program would work. Movie star Marlon Brando, for example, wound up in trouble after joking to a cabin attendant about the "arrival time in Havana."

ALPA began to find wide public support for all its antiskyjacking ideas after the death of Jim Hartley, but amazingly, ATA and the government continued to insist, long after public opinion was clearly on the side of rigorous preboarding security, that such measures would cause a decline in passenger boardings. Perhaps the government and ATA were overly influenced by a few politicians who cited civil liberties violations as one possible aspect of preboarding screening. Sen. Vance Hartke of Indiana, a powerful force in Congress during the 1960s, repeatedly attacked preboarding screening in a strange, quixotic crusade that once landed him in trouble for failing to open his briefcase for a ticket agent's inspection. It was a bizarre episode, and similar instances probably account for the timidity of the authorities.

Although a solution was at hand to the domestic skyjacking problem after 1971, for U.S. pilots involved in international operations it was another story. Many pilots were never aware of IFALPA until they began to need its services desperately in the fight against international terrorism.

The events that finally gave IFALPA the leverage to act against skyjacking internationally came as the result of trouble in the Middle East. The curtain raiser took place in August 1968 with the skyjacking of an El Al airliner to Algeria. Once on the ground, the skyjackers held the Israeli nationals (and the two Israeli pilots) hostage for the release of terrorists held in Israel. There was an immediate outcry from the world's various airline pilots' organizations. At the suggestion of the French ALPA, IFALPA sent a delegation to Algeria to negotiate the release of the hostages. Using the stick of an international boycott of all air traffic to Algeria, IFALPA got the hostages released.

Since holding hostages hadn't worked, the radical Palestinians tried direct violence next. In December 1968, two Arab gunmen opened fire on a parked El Al airliner at Athens, Greece. One passenger was killed and a cabin attendant seriously wounded. Boasting of connections with the Popular Front for the Liberation of Palestine (PFLP), the two gunmen declared they were "under orders" to kill Jews and destroy planes. Although they were tried, convicted, and sentenced to long prison terms, the two gunmen would soon be released owing to further threats of the PFLP against Greece's air commerce, thus raising the troubling question of how any country could punish terrorists when its own planes were vulnerable.

A long series of terrorist incidents directed at air commerce then ensued. The fragile edifice of international aviation could do nothing to protect itself, since both management and various governments shrank from the kind of expensive ground security systems that were beginning to be installed in the United States. Excepting only the Israelis, whose El Al planes regularly flew with their own security (even in Europe), the airline target was still wide open to terrorism as late as 1972. At this point, the world's eyes began to turn to the United States. Only in America (and, of course, in the Communist bloc countries), was a solution to the skyjacking problem at hand. The world was ready at last to pay serious heed to the program ALPA had been advocating in the United States for nearly a decade —ground prevention. But it would come too late, and the trigger would be something the Israelis did.

Vulnerable as the Israelis were to aerial blackmail, one would think they would avoid provocation. But Israel's hardnosed security forces, finding out that two Algerian "security officers" were aboard a British airliner transiting Israel on a regular flight, insisted on taking them off the plane. Speculation was that the Israelis wanted to hold the two Algerians hostage for the release of their own operatives being held in Algerian jails, but no one knows for sure. In any case, the Israelis put themselves in the position of inviting retaliation, as IFALPA pointed out in a telegram to Golda Meir, the Israeli prime minister. The U.S. State Department agreed with IFALPA, and ultimately the Israelis would release the two Algerians, but not before Black September was born.

The Israelis had foolishly grabbed the two Algerians in August 1970. On Sept. 6, 1970, ostensibly in retaliation for the Israelis' detention of the two Algerians, Arab terrorists skyjacked four international flights simultaneously. Only the El Al jet among the four (the others were TWA, Pan Am, and Swissair) thwarted the skyjackers, when an onboard Israeli security agent shot it out with the skyjackers, killing one. The other, the notorious woman skyjacker, Lela Khaled, was wounded. The El Al plane survived only because the two grenades she had smuggled aboard in her brassiere had defective fuses. The other terrorists flew a Pan Am Boeing 747 to Cairo, where they landed, evacuated all the passengers via emergency chutes, and then blew up the plane. The destruction was supposed to be a "lesson" to the Egyptians for their cooperative attitude toward a peace settlement with Israel. The other two aircraft were flown to an abandoned World War II airstrip in Jordan, where the occupants were held inside the airplanes without air conditioning or proper sanitation for nearly two weeks while the skyjackers tried to negotiate the release of Palestinians held in Israeli jails. When the British government refused to turn over the wounded Lela Khaled to the skyjackers, another team of skyjackers seized a British airliner and added it to the collection of planes squatting in the desert. Meanwhile, the world waited tensely for the ordeal to end.

Through massive diplomatic pressure, the terrorists were finally forced to release their captives. The radical Palestinians blew up all the aircraft as a parting gesture, however, and in a sense they badly overplayed their hand. Although they succeeded in blackmailing the British into releasing Lela Khaled (who was later fictionalized as the murderous female guerrilla in the movie and novel *Black Sunday*), the Palestinians had worn out their welcome with Jordan's King Hussein. The Jordanian army subsequently crushed the Palestinian forces operating out of Jordan before the month ended—"Black September," as radical Arabs would call it ever after.

The events leading up to Black September would ultimately convince the nations of the world that skyjacking could be eradicated only by the strongest and most concerted of international efforts. In a sense, ALPA and IFALPA had won their battle to force authorities at the highest levels to make the safety and security of commercial aviation a matter of international policy. In the United States, the fruits of ALPA's labor were most apparent in the Antihijacking Act of 1974, one of the last pieces of legislation Richard Nixon signed before his resignation. The law was the result of a program of continuous pressure, ranging from the worldwide SOS in 1972, which saw many airline pilots throughout the world in symbolic and practical protest refuse to fly, to such "nuts-and-bolts" work as that done by ALPA's Flight Security Committee and ALPA's Air Safety Forum. Internationally, IFALPA would press for ratification of the Tokyo and Montreal conventions against aerial piracy, a principal provision of which was levying sanctions against any nation granting sanctuary to skyjackers.

But the Antihijacking Act of 1974, the first measure to curb aerial piracy that could be called "bulletproof," wasn't born without a great deal of pain and effort, some of which put ominous strains on ALPA's internal unity. Despite the 160 skyjackings of U.S. airliners from 1968 to 1972, which included the murder of one airline pilot and the wounding of eight others, many airline pilots were unwilling to give more than verbal support to the antiskyjacking crusade. Some pilots supported airline management when it resisted antihijacking measures as too costly. For ALPA's Flight Security Committee, headed by Tom Ashwood of TWA, this lack of internal unity, beyond mere lip service, was a major headache. By 1972, Ashwood's committee had devised a training syllabus to teach pilots how to handle skyjackers, but the various airlines resisted implementing a "standardized" program. "There are indications that airline managements are objecting to any plan of training outside their individual control," Ashwood declared in frustration.

Clearly, one of J. J. O'Donnell's biggest challenges as ALPA's president was to find out just how firmly modern airline pilots would stand together in a true crisis. It all boiled down to the question of whether or not the blood of the pioneers who had formed ALPA still coursed through the veins of their modern successors. The vehicle to reveal the intestinal fortitude of modern pilots, or the lack thereof, was the SOS crisis of 1972. The portents of this June 1972 episode were ominous, suggesting that the interline unity of professional airline pilots could not stand the kind of stress that their professional forebears had endured to form ALPA.

The idea of a temporary nationwide work stoppage surfaced spontaneously at the local level on several airlines (particularly EAL) after IFALPA's endorsement of the tactic in 1971. The SOS called for shutting down flights throughout the country for either 24 or 48 hours as a theoretical exercise in "freedom of speech or expression." For J. J. O'Donnell, who was still feeling his way into the presidency, the SOS would allow him to see if ALPA members would really stick together and follow the dictates of their Board of Directors. No airline would dare to fire pilots for a work stoppage in violation of a contract, if everybody hung together. But if some airlines refused to honor the SOS, it would weaken the whole project, drive a wedge between pilot groups, and suggest that modern pilots were incapable of unified action even in matters of life and death, theirs and those of the passengers whose lives had been entrusted to them.

For this reason, J. J. O'Donnell and the Executive Board raised the SOS idea carefully, until finally a consensus emerged that such drastic action was necessary. O'Donnell himself had become convinced by early 1971 that an SOS was worth trying, but he necessarily had to develop support among the Executive Board members before he moved. Finally, in June 1972, after a great deal of careful spadework by Captain O'Donnell, Capt. Tom Ashwood, and Jack Bavis, the Executive Board acted, authorizing ALPA's participation in a 24-hour, worldwide SOS. O'Donnell was given authority to determine how and when the stoppage would occur. IFALPA set the SOS for June 19, 1972. It was, as we have seen, a dangerous and risky step, but also one that O'Donnell felt honor-bound to carry out. O'Donnell remembers:

> The ALPA Board of Directors had passed in 1968, 1969, and in the early 1970s a series of strong policy statements on skyjacking. Because of the inability of the United Nations to act strongly the international federation, not ALPA, called for a worldwide strike on June 19, 1972. We were trapped by this date. We had an emergency Executive Board, and we all agreed. Everybody was patting everybody on the back, the suspension was going to occur. But as we got closer to the date, the master chairmen were all talking to each other, some started to weaken.

On the very day that rumors of rebellion in the ranks began to circulate, J. J. O'Donnell was scheduled to appear on *Face the Nation*. Confronted with hostile questions from the panelists, who cited comments of some other ALPA officials that they would not support the SOS, O'Donnell was in an uncomfortable position. He was also facing a court action that ATA had

immediately filed to stop the SOS. O'Donnell put on a resolute performance, partly to intimidate his opponents, and partly to buck up his own
wavering troops. He promised to go ahead. "I am not a lawyer; the injunction is for the lawyers to argue," O'Donnell said on national television. "But
I do want to say one thing. There is no way I will order my people to go to
work." The ghosts of John L. Lewis and Dave Behncke must have been applauding—but the response of some ALPA members was considerably less
enthusiastic.

When the crunch came, some airlines shut down, notably EAL, Southern
(SOU), and Northwest, but others, notably TWA and Delta, did not, although there were exceptions on every airline. Master Chairman Bill Arsenault of United Airlines (UAL) was furious at the timidity of his own master
executive council (MEC), as were others such as Bill Davis, a UAL 747 captain who walked off his plane in Detroit because he knew the company
could not get a replacement 747 pilot there. Many other UAL crews simply
walked off their planes in defiance of both the company and their own
MEC.

On some airlines the SOS broke down completely, thus threatening
ALPA's internal unity. Eastern's pilots were openly furious at Delta's, whom
they accused of cowardice. Not a few EAL pilots were heard to say openly
that if Jim Hartley had been a Delta pilot, the attitude of Delta's pilots toward the SOS would have been different.

Shortly after the SOS episode, a skyjacking occurred on SOU that drove
home just how vulnerable professional airline pilots were, perhaps giving
pause to those who refused to support the SOS and causing renewed concern about the bumbling machismo some ground security personnel had
displayed in trying to halt skyjackings.

Capt. William R. "Billy Bob" Haas and First Officer Harold Johnson had
been skyjacked by three petty criminals with a grudge against the city of
Detroit, after taking off from Birmingham, Ala., in November 1972. If this
sounds just a bit strange, wait—the story gets stranger. The three skyjackers ordered Haas to fly northward to Detroit, where they demanded
$10 million from city officials. While they waited for somebody on the
ground at Detroit to round up the money (eventually SOU's management
got a suitcase full to give them, although it was nowhere near $10 million),
the three skyjackers got roaring drunk, forced all the male passengers to
disrobe, and generally terrorized everybody aboard. After securing the
money hastily rounded up by SOU's ground personnel in Detroit, the skyjackers forced Haas to take off, thus commencing a wandering aerial odyssey that spanned the continent from Canada to Cuba. The skyjackers threatened to crash the plane into the nuclear facility at Oak Ridge, Tenn., and at
one point demanded to speak to the President of the United States. Landing in Cuba, the skyjackers thought that the Cubans would welcome them
as heroes with their suitcase of extorted money. But the tough-looking Cu-

ban soliders surrounding the airplane had unnerved the skyjackers, and a Cuban spokesman was noncommittal about their future in Cuba, so they forced Haas to take off once more. By the time FBI agents decided to keep the SOU DC-9 on the ground at Orlando at all costs by shooting out the tires they were probably justified in doing so, although this action led the skyjackers to shoot First Officer Johnson and force Haas to attempt a take-off on flat tires. Somehow Haas did it.

> They grabbed Harold out of the cockpit right after the plane started settling on the gear rims and they were cussing and shooting their pistols out each window, and one of them said, "O.K., Harold, this is it, you're gonna die," and one of them shot him. I heard the shots back in the cabin and they told me to take off or they were going to kill me, too. I said that I couldn't take off without a copilot. I thought they'd killed him, but one of them said, "Naw, he's not dead," and they then slammed him back into the seat with a bullet in his arm. I added power and somehow we started rolling. Harold was in bad shape, blood all over, and I said, "Harold, don't pass out on me." The airspeed kept rising and I figured I'd run off the end of the runway; there was a highway I could sort of set down on there, I hoped. I never figured it would fly, but somehow the airspeed kept climbing. All sorts of things were going through my head. I felt sure the oil caps were off and that the engines were going to seize up any minute. And all of a sudden the airpseed jumped and I rotated and we were airborne. I told Harold he *had* to help me, and somehow he started flipping switches, and we made it.

The crippled DC-9, smoke trailing from its burning landing gear, headed for Havana for the second time that day.

"When I got off the airplane and I was helping to put out the fire," Haas remembers, "Castro was standing right there under the wing, looking at the gear. He came up to me and said, 'I want to shake the hand of the man who kept that plane in the air.' I had been doing a lot of work on my house, and my hands were rough and calloused. He looked at them and said, through an interpreter, 'These are the hands of a man who works.' And then he gave me a big hug. He was very flattering and quite personable."

Nearly every pilot who was skyjacked to Cuba came away feeling that the Cubans were going to be very hard on their unwelcome guests. Billy Bob Haas cooperated in the ALPA program to widely publicize the comments of Cuban officials indicating that skyjackers had an unpleasant life awaiting them in Cuba. The object of this program was to dissuade potential skyjackers from trying it, and perhaps it worked.

Haas credits his survival and that of his crew and passengers partly to training he received in handling skyjackers psychologically. "It was mostly common sense," Haas recalls. "We just tried to keep them talking, humoring them, establishing personal contact, that sort of thing." ALPA was responsible for the various companies' training programs. Among the first program initiated by J. J. O'Donnell was one on "hijacking management." In 1971, the Executive Board authorized distributing educational material on aberrant behavior and cooperating with the airlines and FAA in a program for educating flight crews in handling such behavior. Haas remembers the brief formal psychological training program even though he admits to not paying really close attention, "Like everybody else, I never thought it would happen to me."

The FBI's intervention in the SOU skyjacking posed a mortal danger to Haas and his crew, despite an ALPA Executive Board resolution adopted in December 1971 requiring that "the pilot in command of any aircraft whose safety is being threatened shall have complete and final authority on all questions relating to the handling of the hijacker's demands, whether the aircraft is at the ramp, taxing, and/or enroute." This policy flowed directly from the FBI's earlier intervention during a skyjacking of a charter flight at Jacksonville, Fla., which resulted in the death of the pilot. By 1974, after ALPA's heavy lobbying had secured passage of the new antihijacking law, the FBI and other law enforcement agencies were clearly subordinated to FAA in handling skyjackings. ALPA President J. J. O'Donnell insisted that a provision of the 1974 law stated clearly that aviation authorities would have "exclusive responsibility for the direction of any law enforcement activity affecting the safety of flight."

In retrospect, perhaps the most amazing thing about the passage of the 1974 antihijacking statute was that ALPA managed to secure it despite the obvious division within the ranks of professional airline pilots. Like an athlete who manages to win even on days when he is not performing at peak ability, ALPA somehow managed to accomplish its goals. Only in the area of "automatic sanctions" against nations harboring skyjackers did the 1974 law fall short of ALPA expectations.

ALPA President O'Donnell stressed that the excellence of the 1974 law should not allow the air transportation industry "to be lulled into a false sense of complacency." Since he had been fighting the skyjacking menace steadily for nearly four years and had endured many of the same frustrations as his predecessor, Charley Ruby, J. J. O'Donnell took understandable pride in the passage of the 1974 law.

"The new law is the result of sacrifice, bloodshed, anxiety, pain, and abuse suffered by flight deck and cabin crews," O'Donnell declared in 1974. "It is the result of long, frustrating, laborious effort on the part of ALPA members, committees, officers, and staff, who made sure that the legislation did not become lost in the congressional jungle."

The response of professional airline pilots to the skyjacking menace was at once heartening and disquieting. Many pilots displayed quiet courage and a willingness to stand tough in support of effective remedies backed by ALPA. But at the same time, many other pilots proved, by their tepid responses to the 1972 SOS, that the mere theoretical threat of disciplinary action by their airlines was sufficient to deter them from strong action, even in matters of life and death.

For J. J. O'Donnell, the response of rank-and-file members to ALPA initiatives in the skyjacking crisis could not have been encouraging. But if the SOS was not a success, it was at least a learning experience, one from which O'Donnell would have to profit if he were to remain in a viable position vis-a-vis his membership. O'Donnell's strengths, it was widely agreed, were as a conciliator and negotiator, so he began patiently patching ALPA back together after the 1972 SOS episode, concentrating on a series of specific proposals to be included in what would ultimately be the antiskyjacking legislation passed by Congress in 1974.

"I've had to eat a hell of a lot of crow to keep ALPA together," O'Donnell recalls. "Mike Lyon, the vice-chairman of the PAA [Pan American] MEC, told me I wouldn't get many guys to pat me on the back as president. I am human, and I get ticked off, and I wonder sometimes why I should be doing this for these people. But pilots on every airline would see what was happening, they'd be embarrassed at the weakness of some of their own people, they would see the need for a strong Association, and they would express their appreciation. Maybe that's what's kept me going."

Nobody ever promised J. J. O'Donnell a rose garden as the president of ALPA. It was a good thing he knew it before accepting the office. ✦

CHAPTER 25

The Rise of J. J. O'Donnell

From the Association's beginning in 1931 through its first half century, just over 55,000 airline pilots have carried an ALPA membership card. Only four have risen to become president of ALPA and to speak for their fellow professional airmen. By way of comparison, the people of the United States have had 10 Presidents during that time. Given the record of intramural disputes that this history has traced, how are we to account for the relative stability and continuity at ALPA's top? A casual observer might think, from reading these pages, that ALPA's leadership would rotate with the passing seasons, as indeed some factions within ALPA have often advocated.

When Charley Ruby replaced Sayen at ALPA's helm in 1962, it was obvious that the people who made up the core of ALPA's power structure, the movers and shakers like Jerry Wood and Bobby Rohan and Grant LeRoux, wanted somebody who was as unlike Sayen as possible, yet who still would maintain the vital inner continuity. Charley Ruby fit the bill. He was a rock-solid technocrat of the old school, enormously competent as an aviator, and deeply schooled in ALPA's inner workings, but never one to stir up trouble for his own advantage. Nevertheless, Charley Ruby, like Clancy Sayen, faced tough internal opposition. Ruby went through a recall effort in 1968, which failed.

What did the first three ALPA presidents have in common? For one thing, each one of them had to fight to keep the ship afloat and to hold on to the presidency. Each president faced detractors who persistently lashed out, often seemingly heedless of the potential for destruction in the action.

Welcome to the club, J. J. O'Donnell.

Through the first four years of his presidency, J. J. O'Donnell performed well enough so that opposition to him was relatively muted, but still sufficient to raise a sharp challenge to his reelection in 1974. The majority of professional airline pilots took the random criticism of O'Donnell in stride and concluded that he had acquitted himself well in the struggle against skyjacking. O'Donnell's handling of ALPA's financial and administrative problems also was well received by most pilots, so they reelected him to a second term. It was a traditional judgment.

At the 1978 Board of Directors meeting, the only opponent to J. J. O'Don-

278

nell for the presidency was Bob Shipner of Eastern Air Lines (EAL), who withdrew after finding little support outside several EAL councils. O'Donnell was then reelected by acclamation.

Given all the bickering in ALPA's past, the majority of working airline pilots have a remarkable way of sticking calmly with leaders who have demonstrated ability, *after,* of course, allowing the opposition to have its full say. But these decisions were never easy or smooth.

In 1980, after 10 years in office, J. J. O'Donnell (who had come to the ALPA presidency via an EAL captaincy) like Behncke, Sayen, and Ruby before him, would have to face the challenge of a recall movement. Like his predecessors, O'Donnell considered the recall movement a mischievous attempt to harass him, a "scare tactic" to put pressure on him because of their disagreement with him on several issues. One of the keys to understanding the dissidents' complaints lies in the dislocations that began to afflict the profession after passage of the Airline Deregulation Act of 1978. Although O'Donnell had foreseen the problems deregulation would bring and had warned strenuously of the adverse effect deregulation would have on the established airlines once new competitors appeared, most ALPA members either weren't listening or were so committed philosophically to the conservative economic and political notions that underlay deregulation that they rejected his warnings. When, two years after deregulation became an accomplished fact, the very problems O'Donnell had earlier warned against burst upon the airline piloting profession like a thunderclap, some ALPA members began searching for a scapegoat. J. J. O'Donnell was conveniently it.

"ALPA has a tradition of eating its own young," says Stewart W. Hopkins of Delta Air Lines (DAL), the former first vice-president who struggled so mightily to save Clancy Sayen from his detractors.

Before analyzing the rise of J. J. O'Donnell, a historical caveat is in order. The historian has to separate what contemporaries must know about the past from what is merely nice to know. To do the job effectively, the historian needs distance. Good history needs aging, and the enemy of historical perspective and detachment is current events. For some ALPA old-timers (as readers of this history have surely noted), the events of a generation ago are still "current" in that they are still keenly felt and unresolved. The passage of time allows the historian perspective. At some point in the life of any living organization like ALPA, history plays out. When Charley Ruby relinquished the helm to J. J. O'Donnell, ALPA's era of current events began, and it is still in process, with J. J. O'Donnell and the people of ALPA "making history" as each day passes.

Nevertheless, the time that J. J. O'Donnell has served is long enough to allow the historian to form at least some partial judgments and make a few tentative comparisons. First, the most obvious link between J. J. O'Donnell and his predecessors is the fact that some pilots don't like him.

"If Jesus Christ were ALPA president," says former EAL Master Chairman W. T. "Slim" Babbitt, "there would still be some guys asking Him, 'What have You done for me lately?'"

Time in office has never been kind to ALPA presidents, largely because of the character traits of those who are drawn to airline flying. Put simply, the kind of man (and, lately, woman) who is likely to become an airline pilot is a self-assured individual who is comfortable with having to make important decisions in the cockpit. After becoming a successful airline pilot, the individual ALPA member is likely to assert this cocky self-confidence in other areas of life. This syndrome, often referred to jokingly as the "God complex," afflicts many airline pilots, particularly when it comes to ALPA affairs.

"Most of the people I dealt with during my tenure as a national officer," says Stu Hopkins, "came to me unhappy about something." The internal sniping at the president, any president, comes from ALPA being so democratic. A guy can get up on the floor of a convention and shoot his mouth off, and usually the only thing that cuts off debate is exhaustion."

"Attending a convention," says EAL's W. T. "Slim" Babbitt, "was usually quite an education for a pilot who was mad at ALPA. He'd come in an expert on everything, but by the time it was over he usually had a better understanding of ALPA's complexities."

In the final analysis, why would anybody want to be president of ALPA? In 1970, when J. J. O'Donnell decided to seek the office, he was fully aware of the hazards involved because he had been loyal to both Clancy Sayen and Charley Ruby during the internal bickering that marked their presidencies. "Charley's attitude was that most of the guys biting at his heels, some of whom were from my own airline, were incompetent destructionists," muses O'Donnell.

> I've had my hardest times with people from the same mold. I was just appalled that he had to waste so much valuable time massaging individual egos, time which could have been more wisely spent on resolving the problems that faced all of us. But, I guess that's the price for full democracy.
>
> A lot of the members feel the need to have a one-on-one relationship with their president, even though they have elected someone to act as their representative through the council structure. Of course, it's just impossible for me to respond to 30,000 members on an individual basis.

There is no way the president can take every telephone call from every dissatisfied pilot; if he did, he could never do the job. In every organization of ALPA's size and complexity, the chief executive has an assistant, an alter ego, who is more accessible to the rank and file. Jack Bavis, an EAL first officer who holds the position of ALPA executive administrator, has filled this role for O'Donnell.

280

Like every ALPA president confronted with the recurrent headaches of leadership, J. J. O'Donnell often wonders why he ever agreed to give up what he considers to be the best job in America—regular airline flying—in the first place. O'Donnell was born in 1925, in Dracut, Mass. During World War II, he spent over two years in the Pacific theater, leaving the Navy in 1946. Like Dave Behncke, O'Donnell still hankered for a military career and entered Air Force pilot training three years later. In 1952 he was assigned to Lincoln Laboratory, the Air Force Cambridge research center at Massachusetts Institute of Technology. In 1956, at the urging of Lincoln Lab's Colonel Carey, who recognized that O'Donnell really wanted a piloting career, O'Donnell returned to the cockpit full-time with EAL.

O'Donnell recalls that the most difficult tasks since becoming president in 1971 have been shaping the kind of efficient administrative machine that all pilots demand, and that the Board of Directors had mandated as its number one priority, and maintaining the reputation for integrity that ALPA had painstakingly established over the years. "ALPA is a representational organization with a high degree of visibility nationwide. How we are viewed by the Congress, the administration, and the public is vital to every goal we seek." Success on the Washington scene demands a delicate balance, O'Donnell believes, "which can be upset by a single misstep; the respect we have earned could be wiped out by what appears to be an insignificant comment. Respect is not a transferable commodity; it must be earned."

Almost from the beginning of his career as an airline pilot, O'Donnell was involved in ALPA work. During his probationary period, O'Donnell interested himself in EAL insurance and pension programs, found several things not to his liking, and wrote a letter to Clancy Sayen saying so. Sayen, who also rose to prominence in ALPA via an expertise in these areas, liked the tone and thrust of O'Donnell's letter and invited him to participate in subsequent negotiations with EAL. In 1958, O'Donnell's fellow EAL pilots, impressed with the quality of his work, elected him to local office. The next year, he was elected copilot representative, serving two consecutive terms as a member of the Board of Directors. From then until his accession to ALPA's presidency in 1971, J. J. O'Donnell served continuously in ALPA office as a member of the Eastern Air Lines Pilots Negotiating Committee and the ALPA Retirement and Insurance Committee, establishing a reputation for hard work, accuracy, and an ability to get along with pilots of differing views and airlines. During the Sayen-Ruby eras, which saw almost continuous intramural bickering, his almost uncanny diplomatic ability to meld the differing viewpoints of disparate airlines into a consensus attracted attention. By 1970, ALPA needed a harmonizer to lead it. J. J. O'Donnell seemed to fit that role.

By the late 1960s, O'Donnell had demonstrated the kind of skills usually associated with aggressive and high-priced legislative insiders. His appearances on Capitol Hill increased ALPA's credibility. "If you don't have an overwhelming appetite for the day-to-day pressures of the Hill, you just won't make it," O'Donnell says of his efforts to push legislation through Congress. But like every ALPA president who has entered the maelstrom of Washington politics, O'Donnell has found that not everything he has done meets with the approval of all pilots, and those who disagree with him, like ALPA members since the beginning, let him know about it—in spades.

> Criticism is not only expected but essential to an effective operating entity such as ours. But mischievous and destructive criticism can ruin any team effort. Those who continually harass their elected leaders and hinder their ability to accomplish anything are a small minority, but in the long run every pilot suffers. If the younger members, those 40 and under, could only realize some of the extreme hardships those pilots back in the 1930s and 1940s had to endure, and if the more senior pilots could only understand the fears and frustrations the junior pilots experience when faced with furlough possibilities and other uncertainties of the industry, this whole system would work better.
>
> Early in 1970, several pilots came to me asking me to run for president. I had no ambition to be president because I had been at the board when we went through Clancy's resignation and Charley Ruby's recall efforts. I knew how easy it was to sit outside and tear an organization apart, rather than to become a constructive participant and try to make it work. During the 1966-70 period, when Ruby was running into problems, I tried to help him by responding to the questions directed at him in the pension and loss of license fields. Some of the members questioned why I was assisting President Ruby. My view was that once you elect a guy, you forget politics and stick your oar in the water and try to help him do the job.

The pilots of several airlines found much in J. J. O'Donnell to admire. As it became apparent that Charley Ruby, having reached age 62, would step down, support for O'Donnell as his successor began to develop. The pilots of United Airlines (UAL), who have historically been among the most steadfast supporters of incumbent ALPA presidents from Behncke to Sayen to Ruby, were surprisingly strong for O'Donnell, largely because some of them appreciated the team spirit he had displayed in troubling times. "I think that was why some of the pilots approached me to run," O'Donnell believes. "I was working to help President Ruby, rather than being counterproductive or destructive."

Capt. Max Davis was O'Donnell's leading supporter on EAL. In early 1969, Captain Davis began trying to persuade him to formally announce for Charley Ruby's job. "I told him no," O'Donnell says flatly. "I had served continually for 14 years and that was enough. I had told my wife that I would get out of ALPA work for awhile. I had done my share. I think every member has an obligation to serve his fellow pilots in some way, to put something back into our Association for all it has done for our profession. I was ready to turn my area over to someone else."

But Max Davis refused to accept O'Donnell's "no" and began setting up meetings with the pilots of other airlines, creating, in effect, a J. J. O'Donnell campaign committee, although nobody called it that yet. If the pilots who answered the summons to the banner of J. J. O'Donnell had anything in common, it was that they were familiar with his work and respected it. One fear haunting every loyal ALPA member was that an inexperienced outsider using scare tactics and "hairy-chested campaign slogans" might capture enough temporary rank-and-file support to win the election. In short, the O'Donnell supporters (who included some of the profession's most respected and senior pilots) wanted somebody who was known as a team player, who had eschewed the wild political maneuvering that had characterized the Sayen and Ruby eras, and who was knowledgeable enough about ALPA to get the job done once he was elected.

Finally, Max Davis and others supporting O'Donnell's candidacy persuaded him to run, but only after overcoming the last-ditch opposition of Fran O'Donnell, J. J.'s wife. "Max and a couple of others talked to Fran, and she OK'd it on one condition—that if I didn't win, I would take a break from ALPA work. She believed she would have me back home for a while," O'Donnell quips.

As the campaign of 1970 developed, one of the surprising things was the extent of Charley Ruby's neutrality. Unlike Clancy Sayen in 1962, who had pulled every string available to defeat his nemesis, John Carroll of Trans World Airlines (TWA), Ruby wanted no lingering animosity from the presidential contest sandbagging the eventual winner. Ruby believed that the feeling of some pilots that he had been the choice of the Sayen "clique" in 1962 had caused him problems later, and he wanted no disability hanging over the head of his successor.

"Charley knew I was running and campaigning," says O'Donnell, "but he never pushed my candidacy, and I respected his decision. In retrospect, his judgment was correct."

In June 1970, J. J. O'Donnell made his first formal campaign swing around the circle to address various local councils.

> I visited United Council 12 in Chicago, which was the largest council. I think they had already made up their minds to support me, even though I didn't know Doug Wilsman, who was the council chairman at the time. He invited me and all of the other candidates to their local meeting. It was a very large turnout, and the members asked all the candidates questions on the issues. A great majority of the questions were directed at me, and you could sense what was happening. After the meeting I flew back to Boston, and by the time I got home there was a phone call from a friend who read me the resolution endorsing me from Council 12.

The endorsement by the largest council of the largest airline in ALPA gave a tremendous boost to O'Donnell's candidacy. Shortly thereafter, the EAL master executive council (MEC) also endorsed O'Donnell, but unlike the UAL endorsement (which had ignored UAL pilots who were also announced candidates), the EAL endorsement was qualified—Captains Bob Tully and Dick Jones of EAL later received endorsement also.

"The Eastern MEC said anybody who wants to run for ALPA president had better appear before the MEC in Boston on Cape Cod in August 1970," O'Donnell remembers. "I was the only one to appear."

The subsequent endorsement by the EAL MEC, coupled with the endorsement by UAL Council 12 in Chicago, triggered a rush of other endorsements. By the time the convention met in November 1970, O'Donnell had visited many other local councils, and a curious thing began to happen. Whenever O'Donnell appeared with an opponent, to debate and answer questions, even those pilots who supported other candidates began to admit that if *their* choice wasn't successful, J. J. O'Donnell would do. To be acceptable as second choice was an important political consideration in 1970, because there were 10 serious candidates in the running. Some of them would obviously be knocked off in the early balloting, so the candidate with the strongest secondary support had an important edge. Among the contenders, Bill Arsenault of UAL, Al Bonner of DAL, Rich Flournoy of TWA, and Dick Jones of EAL survived the first round of balloting against O'Donnell. John Campbell of Continental, Clyde Haggard of Braniff, Bob Rubens of North Central (now Republic), Joe Sheehan of Northeast (now DAL), and Bob Tully of EAL fell away as the balloting progressed.

J. J. O'Donnell became president after the longest balloting process in ALPA's history. From Wednesday afternoon until Saturday morning, the supporters of the five surviving candidates haggled, horse-traded, and plotted strategy. The Steward and Stewardess (S&S) Division, sensing the potential disruption in the lengthy balloting, began to abstain after the eighth ballot and were not a factor in O'Donnell's election. A recurrent nightmare of ALPA insiders was that the S&S Division, owing to the coming of jumbo jets that would increase the number of cabin attendants in relation to the number of pilots, would someday come to dominate ALPA. Various rule changes were tried through the years, but obviously if ALPA were to remain a pilot's organization, the S&S Division would have to go. This was, for many people in 1970, "the problem," and whoever got elected would have to deal with it. Ultimately, of course, J. J. O'Donnell would guide the S&S Division on its own way to become the independent Association of Flight Attendants (AFA), but this was not apparent yet, and the effect of the S&S vote on the outcome of the 1970 contest bothered many people. It was a mark of the S&S leaders' integrity that they voluntarily abstained from the process, lest they fatally compromise any winner who might depend upon their support.

The first vote taken after the S&S withdrawal saw no change: O'Donnell led the field with 9,000 votes, Flournoy and Bonner each had 5,000, Arsenault had 4,000, and Jones 3,000. Braniff played a curious game, shifting to O'Donnell on the sixth ballot, and then back to their favorite son, Clyde Haggard on the seventh and eighth, only to return once more to O'Donnell on the ninth.

Al Bonner suggested a deal after the ninth ballot. In return for O'Donnell's votes, Bonner offered to name O'Donnell either first vice-president or executive administrator. It was a curious proposition, for O'Donnell's total nearly doubled Bonner's at the time.

"I told Al I didn't have the votes to give," O'Donnell recalls. "It was very clear from my steering committee that if there were any deals with anybody, I would lose their support. I thought that was a fair and proper condition."

On the tenth ballot, Rich Flournoy of TWA, seeing no chance of his winning, switched his support to Dick Jones of EAL. Flournoy and his supporters expected this act to precipitate a surge away from O'Donnell to Jones, and for a while this tactic appeared to work. Through the next two ballots, there was a steady accretion of support for Jones, but not from J.J., until on the eleventh ballot Jones pulled even with O'Donnell at 9,600 votes. But O'Donnell's strength held firm at that point and Jones's stalled, still well short of a majority. Then finally the logjam began to break. Braniff, which had swung away from Haggard to O'Donnell before, tilted to O'Donnell once more on the thirteenth ballot. Braniff, which had a substantial pro-O'Donnell faction from the beginning, now precipitated the swing that everybody had been waiting for.

On the fourteenth ballot, Continental and Flying Tiger went to O'Donnell, leaving him only 2,700 votes short of a majority. Sensing that he would go over the top on the fifteenth ballot, several airlines rushed to win the honor of casting the decisive vote. Among them were Pan Am, two large TWA councils, Piedmont, and DAL. When it was over, J. J. O'Donnell had 59 percent of the vote—a convincing victory, but certainly not a unanimous one. He would thus begin his presidency without even a semblance of the unanimity that had characterized the elections of his predecessors, and for that reason he had to tread warily.

"If anybody was in position to make mischief," says J. J. O'Donnell of the period after the election, "it was Bill Arsenault of UAL. But he didn't. He was a very capable person and absolutely dedicated to a strong, unified Association. He never hesitated to express the differences we had over the long period we worked together, but his criticisms were constructive."

The newly elected ALPA president would need the help of men like Bill Arsenault, for an uncertain era was about to dawn. If ALPA were to remain a viable organization (something no pilot should ever take for granted), with working pilots calling the shots and running things in fact as well as in theory, then someone was going to have to do the thankless tasks, attend the endless committee meetings, and staff the tedious study groups. It would fall upon J. J. O'Donnell to tap those wellsprings of service among his fellow pilots, to somehow cajole them into serving ALPA's needs in a hundred ways with the time they might have as easily spent playing golf or running a business on the side.

By the beginning of J. J. O'Donnell's tenure, even the most casual observer could see that the airline industry was reaching full maturity. This coming of age meant that airline managers would begin to reevaluate the old formulas and patterns by which the industry had lived. Simultaneously, a new era of diminished expectations beset the airline business as it suffered from a series of unexpected economic shocks. The Arab oil embargo of 1973 seemed to trigger the faltering economic climate of the rest of the 1970s, and the deregulation of the industry at the end of the decade placed stresses on the airline business that adversely affected pilots. O'Donnell was quick to recognize these threats, and he came to office already pursuing courses of action that he hoped would preserve jobs and minimize the impact of economic stress upon the industry and the profession.

More than any other factor, ALPA's success has depended historically upon the notion that the airline business, was, at heart, a regulated public utility. An inherent part of this idea is that regulated businesses by their very nature ought to be immune to certain market forces. In return for good service at a fair price, government regulators would offer guaranteed profits. This idea is not new—it goes back to the era of Teddy Roosevelt.

The airline business, after the early disastrous years of free market competition in the 1920s, eagerly embraced the idea of government regulation. If the government expected airline managers to invest large sums to provide decent passenger service, managers reasoned, than the government at least ought to offer some protection against fly-by-night upstart operators who would undercut them. Dave Behncke agreed wholeheartedly with this approach, largely because he saw the opportunity to force all airlines to pay their pilots the same wages.

By the late 1920s, during the Hoover administration, government and management had agreed that the airline business would be part of the "free market" only in a limited sense. FDR's New Deal ratified this decision. The vital safety issue just would not compute in a pure free market system. Competent pilots, for example, were not supposed to be subject to the vagaries of the free market, nor were safe airplanes and trained mechanics. The essential guarantee against the "free market" was the "certificate of public convenience and necessity" issued by the federal government after 1938. Without such a certificate, no airline could operate on a given route, and the government was very stingy about giving them out until the end of the era. The Airline Deregulation Act of 1978 marked the end of the old system, which had seen professional airline pilots prosper mightily.

Historically, ALPA has always thrived when the industry was booming and faced problems when it was either stalled or shrinking. A time of prolonged stagnation in the industry would change relations between management and labor, not necessarily to ALPA's advantage. Nothing indicates these reduced circumstances better than the diminishing opportunities for pilot employment and the frozen promotion lists that characterized most of the 1970s. Although the scarcity of jobs and a massive pool of pilots aching to have them were hardly new problems, the dimensions were quite unlike anything any ALPA president had ever faced before. Historically management has used every instance of stress, no matter how fleeting, as an excuse to cut the size of its pilot work force while demanding increased productivity from those still working.

So airline pilots in the O'Donnell era would live in an age of diminishing prospects, made all the more distressing by an explosion of technology that promised, but never quite seemed to deliver, a better future. A professional airline pilot's working environment, in the purely physical sense, would change only marginally during O'Donnell's decade, unlike the abrupt dislocations that Behncke had to cope with caused by the coming of instrument flying, the problems of crew complement that Clancy Sayen faced, or the painful jet transition that was Charley Ruby's cross. But O'Donnell would encounter problems that were at once more subtle and more menacing than his predecessors had faced. Although it would be grossly unfair to say that "just anybody" can fly a modern jetliner, the truth is that the jets (once the transition period was over) were easier to fly than the airliners of the late piston era. But if the equipment pilots flew during the 1970s improved technologically, the same cannot be said for the environment in which they operated. The availability of radar and increasingly automated cockpit systems promised to make life easier for pilots, but actually they added new and formidable complications that were difficult to explain to the public. In the past, ALPA presidents had always been able to rely to some extent on a sympathetic public. Not so with J. J. O'Donnell. The ultimate loss of the third cockpit crewman, once the issue finally came before a study commission appointed by President Reagan, illustrated this point. The safety advantages of the third crewman, long the cornerstone of ALPA thinking, were lost largely because the public did not care any longer and was not receptive to ALPA's arguments. Could anyone have salvaged more than J. J. O'Donnell? Only after a long, cool view from a distant historical peak can we answer that question, and probably even then with no real certainty.

In the 1970s, troublesome, repeated strikes on Northwest Airlines (NWA), Continental (CAL), and Wien Air Alaska (WAA) would demonstrate that the limits of the old system had been reached. ALPA, under J. J. O'Donnell, would have to cling to the status quo, tenaciously resisting a variety of corporate efforts to redress the balance in management's favor. In this environment, O'Donnell pressed to preserve jobs even in face of objections from a few very senior members. The philosophy of "sharing the injury during downturns" was born.

In a sense, things had come full circle by 1981, with J. J. O'Donnell once more moving ALPA back into the mainstream of organized labor, where Dave Behncke first placed it in 1931. For J. J. O'Donnell and the future of ALPA, a close association with organized labor had become, by the late 1970s, a matter of life and death, although few professional airmen seemed to realize it. Few modern airline pilots seem to understand that ALPA had tailgated the labor movement or that today's high salaries and favorable working conditions would not exist without the concept of the airline business as a regulated public utility. Put simply, the status of the airlines as a government-supervised public utility, with guaranteed levels of profit, meant that management could pass along pilot salaries, no matter how high, to the traveling public. More than any other professional-occupational group this historian knows of, modern airline pilots owe their current status to the traditional alliance between labor and government regulators. The average airline pilot has, until recently, seemed unaware of how fragile this alliance is, but certainly J. J. O'Donnell was aware of it from the beginning:

> There is a core in ALPA that says, "What the hell are we in the AFL-CIO for anyway?" At the last Board of Directors meeting [1980], 70 percent had never been to a meeting before, and somebody always brings it up, so you have to educate a new group. I sit here with 30,000 votes, while organized labor has 15 million votes. George Meany and Lane Kirkland on numerous occasions let me go out around the country and to Congress to testify on behalf of the airline pilots with 15 million votes as my base, and that is a powerful force that has been very helpful with many of ALPA's problems. The average pilot is a very intelligent individual, and it only takes a few moments to get him to understand the need for unity during times of decline and trouble.
>
> The question of ALPA's continued affiliation with the AFL-CIO has been brought before the Board of Directors on numerous occasions during the past several decades. Each time, after lengthy and in-depth debate, the board has voted overwhelmingly that our members' long-term interests are best served by continuing our relationship with the AFL-CIO.
>
> More than anything else, the deregulation of the airline industry, coinciding with the economic decline of the past year, will bring reality home to the professional airline pilots. Unionized employees are the target of the deregulators. Those of us who understand this tried to get our membership involved and committed to de-

feating that legislation. But too many believed in the great benefits that were promised from it. All the benefits that are going to flow from deregulation are going to be at the expense of unionized workers—ALPA members—and others.

In a sense, many airline pilots were asking for trouble long before it happened, largely because they had committed the cardinal sin of forgetting their roots in the labor movement. Perhaps it is a measure of ALPA's success as a trade union that it has allowed its members an income in the same bracket as the country club set. It was natural that the values of the people with whom pilots associated (which can be summed up as conservative Republican) would rub off, even to the extent that many pilots seemed embarrassed to admit their trade union affiliation! The hard-line old-timers, who made the life-style of today's airline pilots possible, knew their dependence on the labor movement was complete. But by the Ruby era at least, modern airline pilots had begun to believe that they were professionals in the traditional sense of the word and that they did not need a labor union. If history teaches any lesson at all, it is that people who start believing their own propaganda are heading for a big fall.

The fall for professional airline piloting as a privileged occupation may have been the Airline Deregulation Act of 1978. From the beginning, the threat to airlines with established labor contracts was apparent, and J. J. O'Donnell was in the forefront of those who warned that deregulation of the airline industry would not work.

"In the long term, deregulation of the airlines is going to be a total disaster," says J. J. O'Donnell earnestly. "They will have to re-regulate five or ten years down the road, and the shape of the industry then is not going to be in the best interests of pilots. Free market forces do not bear well unless you have a whole bunch of airports that everybody can get access to."

In a nutshell, the limited nature of the environment in which commercial air transportation functions means that the free market is limited. There are only so many gates, at a fixed number of airports, connected by a finite airspace. Somebody is going to have to say who flies where and when, if not necessarily how, and with what kind of pilot. In short, the very nature of the airline industry demands regulation by somebody other than a vague and impersonal force called the free market.

And here the modern profession of airline piloting has come smack up against a crushing historical irony. By the 1970s, the typical airline pilot had become a knee-jerk conservative whose political vocabulary consisted mainly of Chamber of Commerce clichés. The absurdity of a group of trade unionists talking like independent entrepreneurs was not lost on J. J. O'Donnell, who took a considerable amount of flak from some of the ALPA membership for his opposition to freedom from government regulation.

"You have to remember where deregulation came from," says O'Donnell.

It came under Carter, but it was a carry-over from the administration of President Ford. You can't blame Ford—he truly didn't know what was going on—but it was his advisors, some young guys who wrote books on free market forces, and they wrote on local service carriers, showing how free market forces would provide better service and increased frequency at a lower cost. These free market book writers are a major part of our problem in the air transport industry today. They enlarged their ideas on local service carriers to cover the whole system. Right now, fares are up over 75 percent in the last year, service is down, and the small markets are getting shafted. It's a disaster; there is not a free market environment out there. People say, "But look at all the new airlines!" They're hiring guys at New York Air for $3,000 a month to fly a plane that a Texas International [TXI] pilot flies for $6,500 a month, and copilots are paid $16,000 a year in flat monthly salaries, but they had taken the calendar year and divided it up into 28-day months so they have 13 months. New York Air is a runaway shop, a spinoff of TXI in an attempt to start a nonunion airline.

In the wake of deregulation and the economic decline, J. J. O'Donnell faced many problems. On one hand, he had to function as a politician, and the first prerequisite of any politician is that he satisfy his constituents. On the other hand, O'Donnell also had to function as a leader. A leader must educate his followers so that they will not insist on his taking them over a cliff. O'Donnell knew instinctively that the typical airline pilot of his era was riding for a fall, and he also knew that no amount of adroit maneuvering on Capitol Hill (and O'Donnell, after a decade on the job in Washington, was an acknowledged master of the corridors of power) could disguise ALPA's reputation as a "gold-plated union" whose members were little concerned with issues of vital interest to ordinary trade unionists. The typical liberal Democrat also knew full well that the average ALPA member was not only unlikely to vote for him, but was usually an ardent supporter of the kind of conservative politician who was overtly hostile to the interests of organized labor.

Although it is impossible to prove that these feelings and attitudes governed the work of Sen. Edward M. Kennedy, the liberal Democrat whose senatorial committee gave birth to the Airline Deregulation Act of 1978, the likelihood is strong. Put simply, the liberal Democrats allowed the free market program for air transportation (long supported by their conservative opposition) to become law. Those who would ultimately be most affected and most damaged by that free market solution, namely the nation's professional airline pilots, were ideological conservatives in their voting habits, thus making it easy for traditional liberals to abandon them.

In short, the nature of the ALPA membership by its mid-century point had made J. J. O'Donnell's leadership task almost impossible. O'Donnell had, in a technical sense, wrung just about everything out of the industry that a traditional approach could muster. He realized early that the changing nature of the air transport industry made it absolutely essential for ALPA to reestablish its reputation as a good neighbor in the community of organized labor and that politically ALPA was going to have to adopt a flexible, pragmatic approach. But a leader can only lead his troops so far, and occasionally he must look back over his shoulder to see if anyone is following.

The twenty-sixth meeting of the Board of Directors in November 1980 was faced with several issues that posed serious threats to the piloting profession. As its initial course of action to combat these problems, the board directed that a nationwide shutdown be called, through a "suspension of service" (SOS), to assure that regulatory agencies would listen and respond to the concerns of airline pilots. Dubbed "Operation USA," the real purpose of the SOS program was to assess just how firm the commitment of modern airline pilots was and whether they were sufficiently resolved to stand firm in areas vital to their professional well-being. In short, ALPA's leaders had to know for sure if the membership would support the directives laid down by their representatives—the Board of Directors. Did the blood of the early pioneers who founded ALPA still course through the veins of their modern counterparts? The 1972 skyjacking SOS had left that question unanswered.

Under the terms of Operation USA, ALPA would shut down the nation's airlines for a short period if it did not get a satisfactory resolution to the major issues confronting airline pilots, which included primarily a plea for reform of the aircraft certification process and a fair resolution to the crew complement issue. The program, carefully structured to give O'Donnell the opportunity to work out a compromise with the incoming Reagan administration, suffered at first from a lack of grass roots support. O'Donnell was fully aware that this course of action justifiably scared many ALPA members, but from the volume and type of complaints received in Washington it was apparent that many MECs did little to inform their members about the action initiated at the November board meeting.

The SOS was essentially a strike, although of a very special kind, that would require an expertise in the ancient art of "withdrawing from service." ALPA had lately little experience in the grubby business of striking. During the O'Donnell era, strikes had not figured prominently as an ALPA weapon. Only on NWA, which endured nasty strikes three times during the decade, was there anything like a pool of pilots who had sufficient knowledge to carry off the organizational and administrative tasks an SOS would require. For that reason, O'Donnell, in consultation with First Vice-President Gerry Pryde of UAL, liberally sprinkled NWA pilots about the Operation USA structures, where their recent experience with shutting down an airline could be put to practical use. Bob Kehs of NWA wound up running the show, assisted by Dave Koch of UAL. The success of the shutdown effort, however, would depend on work done in the trenches by pilots like Dick Turner, Charley Young, and Gene Kragness, all of NWA, who took on the grass roots communication task in sessions at various pilot domiciles around the country, explaining the intricacies of setting up a "war board" to track every crew and every flight on every airline. As Turner and Young made clear to the Boston area pilots in February 1981, all it takes to shut down a flight is one member of the crew who walks off.

If the SOS scheduled for early 1981 had actually come off, the nation's airlines would have been crippled. For a day or so, nobody in this country would have been sure of getting anywhere. Out of this new awareness of their potential power, a rising sense of self-confidence began to spread among those who were committed to Operation USA.

As the March 1 SOS commencement date approached, O'Donnell met continuously with representatives of the new Reagan administration. But with no response from the Reagan team to ALPA's request for a special committee to review the crew complement question on the next generation of commercial airliners, O'Donnell had to continue the SOS threat. The clock was running. The supporters and believers of Operation USA continued their vigil. Two weeks before the deadline, Department of Transportation Secretary Lewis appeared before a special session of ALPA's Executive Board and announced that the administration would establish a presidential task force, as sought by ALPA's Board of Directors. ALPA agreed to abide by the task force's findings and to stand down on the SOS.

The ALPA members who had worked so doggedly on Operation USA were, needless to say, disappointed. For the first time in the professional careers of most of them, the old ALPA idea of unity across company lines had become something more than an abstraction, and they were anxious to test their mettle, to see if they actually could carry off an action that rivaled in gutsiness those of ALPA's founders.

As Jerry Lawler of TWA, who headed the SOS effort in Chicago, put it: "I love flying an airliner, and I think being a 727 captain is just about the slickest thing in the world. But there comes a time when you have to stand up and be counted, no matter what the risks."

From J. J. O'Donnell's point of view, the SOS was a mixed bag. The latent spirit of unity which Operation USA brought to the fore convinced him that when professional airline pilots could be brought to see their own interests clearly, they were still capable of taking great risks to defend them. John Ferg, the UAL MEC chairman, spoke to this idea at the Atlanta organizational meeting of Operation USA, when he said in a fiery speech, "This really ought to be called Operation Unity to Save Our Asses."

To O'Donnell, Operation USA was the card he could play if all else failed. The Reagan administration would eventually appoint a commission to study ALPA's crew complement grievance and subsequently act on the other issues raised by the pilots. Most ALPA members were heartily sick of what they regarded as harassment of airline pilots by the Federal Aviation Administration (FAA) and they also wanted to expose failures in FAA's aircraft certification process. ALPA, first and foremost, wanted an objective evaluation of the crew complement question. But what was not to be expected, and what J. J. O'Donnell as a prudent leader would not assent to, was the playing of a hole card like Operation USA as anything other than a last resort. The fissures such an action might open could very well lead to ALPA's destruction. O'Donnell had succeeded where every previous ALPA president had failed, in one sense, against the combined opposition of both FAA and the industry. ALPA won an official role for line pilot participation in the certification of a new aircraft and the monitoring of the process during its useful life.

"We started out with the assumption," O'Donnell continues, "that we would never get all the things we wanted, but my feeling was we could shut it down, unless we got a legitimate response on the important issues."

And so the circle has turned. Fifty years after its foundation in struggle, sacrifice, and tragedy, the airline pilots of America, although not quite back to square one, are still facing the fundamental questions their forebears faced in 1931. Can they stand up and fight the good fight, always keeping in mind that justice and virtue do not always prevail, and that "God," as Napoleon put it, "is on the side of the big battalions"? Are modern airline pilots made of the same stuff as the men who created ALPA during the era of wooden wings?

History is waiting for its answer. ✦

INDEX

Note: ff indicates scattered references on succeeding pages; book and periodical titles are set in italics; journal articles are set in quotes.

Air traffic control (ATC) system, 255
  failure of, in Brooklyn-Staten Island midair,
    256-58
Air Traffic Control and Airway Aids Advisory
  Committee, 110
Air Transport Association (ATA), 94, 106, 107, 131,
  184
  attempt to raise DC-3 gross weight, 115
  attempt at uniform contract, 113-15
  and NAL strike, 135
  opposition to ground security systems, 266-67,
    269, 270
Air Transport Code, 63
  hearings, 36-37
Air Transport Command (ATC), 112, 114, 122
Air Transport Pilots Association (ATPA), 161-62
Air transportation industry. *See* Airline industry;
  Commercial aviation
Allied Pilots Association (APA), 226, 239, 244, 247,
  248
  formation of, 246
Allison, Wayne (AAL), 235-37
Ambort, Paul (PAA), 156, 159
American Airlines (AAL), 42, 44, 72, 76, 77, 93,
    106, 107, 113, 124, 139, 150, 160, 162, 179,
    180, 188, 189, 251
  acquisition of Thompson Aeronautical
    Corporation, 4
  and ALPA's first employment contract, 95, 105
  DC-10 crash (1979), 257
  and jet service, 230, 235
  "screening" program, 236
American Airlines (AAL) management
  and AAL pilot defection, 174, 230-31, 232, 242
  policy toward ALPA, 4, 10, 230
  See also Cord, E. L.; Smith, C. R.
American Airlines (AAL) pilot group, 169, 173,
    218, 219
  and Allison firing, 235-37
  ALPA loyalists among, 226, 229, 233, 236, 237,
    244, 247
  and crew complement issue, 182-83, 230,
    238-45
  defection from ALPA (1963), 2, 80, 178, 220,
    224, 226-34, 235-48
  dominance in ALPA, 228-29
  early disgruntlement with ALPA, 169
  flight pay loss scheme, 244-46
  guerrilla actions against FAA, 253
  hostility toward Sayen, 169-70, 173-74, 182-83,
    204, 206, 214-15, 226-27, 229, 233-34
  and jet pay committee report, 172, 173
  and nationwide strike threat (1933), 232
  and presidential emergency board, 154-55

and strike benefit complaint, 237-38
  strike vote (1951), 154
American Airways (AAL) (later American Airlines),
    37, 43, 63, 64, 70, 107
American Federation of Labor (AF of L, later AFL-
    CIO), ALPA's affiliation with, 11, 37, 45,
    48-49, 52, 57, 62, 64, 173, 222, 288
  and Century Airlines strike (1932), 45, 48-49,
    50, 52
  and FEIA, 178
  and NAL strike (1948), 135, 138
  and SOU strike (1960), 196
American Flying Club, 27
Anders, H. B. (UAL), 156, 212, 230
Anderson, Wally, 159, 167, 224
Andress, Ray E. (Pacific), 267
Antihijacking Act (1974), 272, 276
Antiskyjacking legislation, 266-67, 272, 276
APA. *See* Allied Pilots Association
Arab oil embargo, 286
Arab terrorists. *See* Skyjackings.
Ardmore, Okla., training base, 236
Army Air Corps, 110
Arsenault, Bill (UAL), 274, 284, 285
Artificial horizon, as early instrument, 33
ASB. *See* Air Safety Board
Ashwood, Tom (TWA), 272, 273
Association of Flight Attendants (AFA), 284, 285
ATA. *See* Air Transport Association
ATC. *See* Air Traffic Control System; Air Transport
  Command
Atkins, Paul (AAL), 229, 233, 244
Atlanta Constitution, 82
Ator, M.D. ("Doc") (AAL), 66
ATPA. *See* Air Transport Pilots Association
Auburn Automobile Company, 44, 231
AVCO. *See* Aviation Corporation of America
Aviation (later *Aviation Week*) magazine, 98
Aviation Branch. *See* U.S. Department of
  Commerce
Aviation Corporation of America (AVCO), 51, 107
Aviation Daily newsletter, 239
Aviation industry. *See* Airline industry; Commercial
  aviation
Aviation mystique, 22-23

Babbitt, W. T. ("Slim") (EAL), 102-03, 146, 161,
    166, 203, 209, 211, 219, 280
BAC-111, 214
Bach Trimotor, 47
Bailey, Joe (NAL), 143
Baker, George T. ("Ted") (NAL), 8, 114, 127-28,
    178, 193, 213, 215
  attempt to decertify ALPA, 140, 142

296

contract chiseling, 131-33
as fair-weather amateur pilot, 15
and NAL employment contract with ALPA, 131
and NAL strike (1948), 6-7, 129-30, 133-38,
140-43, 148
and origins of NAL, 216-17
religious conversion, 137
See also National Airlines
Ball, Bert, 14
Ballard, S. V. (AAL), 247
Barnes, Charley (UAL), 156, 172, 173
Barnette, Dean (AWI), 159
on ALPA's democratization, 170-71
Basham, Chuck (EAL), 204, 205-06
Bauhlstrom, Paul (PAA), 176-77
Bavis, Jack (EAL), 280
and ALPA's antiskyjacking program, 262, 269
SOS, 273
Boyle, Lt. George, 25
Beatley, Chuck (UAL), 211
Beck, Jack (AAL), 180
Becker, Dick (Capital), 252
Beech, Walter, 217
Behncke, Dave, 3, 5, 93-100, 116 ff, 185, 211, 213,
214, 218, 220, 227, 228, 230, 248, 274, 279,
281, 282, 286, 287
as airmail pilot for NWA, 32, 97-98, 99
and air safety, 19-22, 35-42, 98
and Air Safety Board, 79, 83, 88, 91, 106-09
and Air Transport Code, 36-37
and ALPA's Washington presence, 54-57
and American Federation of Labor, 62, 64, 288
and ATA's attempt at uniform contracts, 113-15
and cancellation of airmail contracts, 21, 55 ff
and Century Airlines strike, 45-53
and Civil Aeronautics Act (1938), 94
and Civil Aeronautics Board, 202
and Civilian Pilot Training Program, 102
collective bargaining agreements, 81, 94-95,
115, 116, 119, 120-21
and company unions, 2
on competitive flying, 20-21, 68
before congressional committee hearings, 55
contempt of court ruling, 163
and copilots, 176
on crew complement, 186
criticism of DOC accident investigators, 38-39
death, 53, 164
and Decision 83, 54-55, 59, 81, 82, 95
and defense of fired pilots, 139-40
early contract negotiations, 105
early flying career, 97
election as ALPA's first president, 66-67
erosion of Washington political base, 105-06

and FDR, 57-58, 66
fight against Ardmore School, 236
before Finletter commission, 181
fired for absenteeism from UAL, 57
first employment contracts, 95, 104-05
formation of ALPA technical committees, 110
and four-engine pay dispute, 116, 117-21
before Howell commission, 83
inability to delegate authority, 124, 150, 167
and Key Men, 5, 10-12
and Livermore affair, 35-42
and Long & Harmon fight, 73-77, 81
and "mileage limitation," 153-54, 156-57
and NAL strike (1948), 127-29, 131, 135-38
as NAPA governor, 20, 205
and nationwide strike threat (1933), 59, 62-66,
79, 231-32
opposition to hourly wage, 66
organizing efforts at EAL, 103, 111-12
organizing efforts at UAL, 60-62
ouster from ALPA, 149-63, 164, 168
pension proposal, 166
personality, 53, 93, 117
as pilot on Boeing Air Transport, 94, 99
as pilot on UAL, 74, 93
political decline, 124-25
political savvy, 6, 57, 95
and Railway Labor Act, 94
and reserve military status of airline pilots, 105
and Rickenbacker, 6
and small operators, 70
stature as union leader, 95
and *Talton et al. v Behncke*, 160-61
and Truman administration, 135-36
and TWA pilots association, 81, 83
and TWA strike (1946), 117-18
and uniform national pay scale, 63
in U.S. Army, 96, 97, 98-99, 109-10, 112
vision of ALPA, 61
wage policies, 188, 231
winner of 1921 Chicago Air Derby, 97
Behncke, David, Jr., 160
Behncke, Gladys Mae Hensen (Mrs. Dave), 12, 45,
97, 98, 138, 163
Belding, Jim (UAL), 14, 20-21, 63-64
Black, Sen. Hugo A., 56, 75
Bledsoe, J. F. (AAL), 247
Board of Directors, 155-56, 163, 204, 224, 237,
242, 278, 281, 288
and ALPA's move to Washington, D.C., 222-23
and Behncke ouster, 158, 159
and flight engineer ruling, 185
and restructuring of Executive Committee, 225
and Ruby election, 210-12

Derickson, Russ (TWA), 244
Devine, Scotty (UAL), 195, 199, 245
Dewey, Thomas, 7, 136
Dickenson Air Lines (later Northwest Airways), 98
Dickenson, Charles, 97-98
Dickerman, John M., 55, 138
DOC. *See* U.S. Department of Commerce
Dolson, Charles (DAL), 110-11
Dooley, Roy (AAL), 160, 162, 226, 230-31, 236, 247
  on AAL pilots and ALPA, 183-84
  on AAL pilots and Sayen, 173-74
  and AAL pilot flight pay loss scheme, 244-45, 246
Doudt, Charles (AAL), 247
Douglas Aircraft, 173
Douglas C-54, 178
Douglas DC-3, 175, 187, 264-65
  ATA attempt to raise gross weight of, 115
  on regional airlines, 190-91
  as "standard" airliner, 153
Douglas DC-4, 118, 178, 179
  accidents, 119
  pilot transition to, 175-76
Douglas DC-6
  accidents, 119
  Bryce Canyon crash (1947), 179-80
  and crew complement issue, 179-80, 182
  grounding of, 179, 180
Douglas DC-7, 249
Douglas DC-8, 254
  and Brooklyn-Staten Island midair (1960), 256-57
Douglas DC-9, and crew complement issue, 214
Douglass, Judge Frank P., 123, 154
Douglass, George ("Mr. V") (Varney), 11-12, 61, 104, 175
  on Behncke's leadership, 100
Drayton, Charles (PAA), 37
Drew, Pat, 86
Driggs, J. L. (Larry), 27-28
Drummond, Wiley (AAL), 173, 174, 228, 229, 232, 247
Dymond, L. W. (Lou), 143-47, 148, 256

EAL Pilots Negotiating Committee, 281
Earhart, Amelia, 83
Eastern Air Lines (EAL), 4, 14, 31, 47, 102, 132, 136, 146, 157, 166, 170, 171, 173, 179, 180, 185, 201, 202, 211, 217, 218, 219, 221, 224, 228, 233, 251, 255, 268, 280, 282, 284
  hiring of Sayen, 212
  skyjacking (1961) 263-64
  skyjacking (1970), 268-69
    See also Rickenbacker, Eddie
Eastern Air Lines (EAL) pilots
  and Air Transport Pilots Association, 161
  endorsement of O'Donnell, 284
  first ALPA contract, 111
  furlough, 187, 192
  SOS (1972), 273, 274
  strike (1958), 237
  wildcat strike (1960), 203, 253-54
Eastern Air Transport, 46
Eckhardt, George (AAL), 247
Edgerton, Lt. James C., 25
Egge, Carl F., 16
Eight-hour issue, 233
Eighty-five-hour rule, protection of, during WWII, 113
Eisenhower, Dwight D., 255
El Al
  skyjacking (1968), 270
  skyjacking (1970), 271
Electronic airways, and early IFR flying, 33
Employment contracts, early, 104-05, 110-11, 131
Engineering and Air Safety Department, formation of, 150
Engineering and Airworthiness Advisory Committee, formation of, 110
Epperson, E. R. (DAL), 247
Estey, George, 189-90
Executive Board, 151, 170, 292
  creation of, 151-52
  denouncement of AAL leadership group, 246
  and FBI skyjacking intervention, 276
  hijacking management program, 276
  "revolution," 156, 161, 162, 163
  and SOS (1972), 273
Executive Committee, 171, 173, 191, 214, 224, 237, 239, 241, 242, 247
  call for Ruby's resignation, 223-24
  and Committee of Fifteen, 221
  confrontation with Sayen, 208-09
  formation of jet pay study committee, 171, 173
  formation of Wages and Working Conditions Policy Committee, 173
  restructuring of, 225
  as source of ALPA dissension, 224-25

FAA. *See* Federal Aviation Administration
Face the Nation (television show), 273
Farley, Postmaster General Jim, 56, 58, 75
FBI. *See* Federal Bureau of Investigation
FCC. *See* Federal Communications Commission
Federal Aviation Act (1958), 198, 256
  and antiskyjacking amendment, 266-67
Federal Aviation Administration (FAA), 4, 8, 10,

303

305

307

and pilot pushing, 39
Point Reyes crash (1939), 103
"Purge of '39," 103-04
SOS (1972), 274
transition to jets, 251-53
See also Patterson, W. A.
United Airlines pilots
and Behncke's organizing activities, 60-61, 62
and nationwide strike threat, 64
support of O'Donnell, 282-83
Universal Airlines, 81
Unterberger, S. Herbert, 172
U.S. Army pilots
and Century Airlines strike, 49
flying the mail, 56, 57, 58
U.S. Department of Commerce (DOC), 44, 49, 56
Aviation Branch, 41
Bureau of Air Commerce, 38
and Copeland committee, 90-91
early accident investigations, 38-39, 41
investigation of Cutting crash, 88-90
investigation of Long & Harmon, 75-76
and Livermore affair, 32
maximum hours per month, 36-37
reduced beacon wattage of NDBs, 86
suspension of NWA's operating certificate, 41
U.S. House of Representatives Post Office
Committee, 29, 52, 75
U.S. Navy pilots, and Century Airlines strike, 49
U.S. Post Office Department, airmail service,
15-16, 22, 26
cancellation of contracts, 21-22, 35, 55-59, 82
FDR's desire to reestablish, 56, 58, 69
inauguration of, 25
investigation of Long & Harmon, 74-75, 76, 77
pay scales, 44, 59
pilot strike (1919), 23, 24-30
See also Airmail contracts (subsidies); Airmail
pilots
U.S. Senate, airmail contracts investigation, 21
U.S. State Department, 271

Varney Air Transport (later United Airlines or
UAL), 11, 61, 100, 175
Vickers Viscount turboprops, 252
Vidal, Eugene, 88, 90
Villa, Pancho, 96, 107
Volpe, John, 269

Wade, Lloyd (AAL), 243, 247
Wages. *See* Pay scales, pilot; Pay scales, copilot
Wages and Working Conditions Policy Committee,
173
Wagner, Reuben ("Mr. P," "Rube"), 10, 11, 12, 14,

16, 19, 104
on de Havilland DH-4, 27
Wagner, Sen. Robert, 36, 65
Wagner Labor Relations Act of 1935, 36
Wallen, Saul, 143, 144, 145, 146
Wanamaker, John S., 25
Warner, Byron S. ("Mr. A.," "Pop") (NAT), 5
and birth of ALPA, 10
Warner, Edward, P., 83, 134
Warner, Roy P. (NWA), 39
"War of the Blues and Grays, The," on NAL, 140 ff
Watson, Ed (EAL), 255
Webber, Prof. Arnold, 225
Weiss, Henry, 161, 162, 197, 198, 206, 209, 222
on Behncke, 116-17, 120, 121, 155
on JFK and SOU strike, 196-97
on Landis, 202-03
on Ruby, 215
on Sayen, 166-68, 208
West Coast Airlines, 156
Western Air Express (WAE, later Western Air
Lines), 14, 31, 32, 44, 55, 57, 111
Western Air Lines (WAL), 224
Wheeler, Al (Pacific), 264-65
Whitacre, Bill, 230, 242-43
Whitehead, Dr. R. E., 177
Whittemore, Fred, 40, 41
Wien Air Alaska (WAA) strike, 195, 287
Wigley, Wallace (SOU), 193, 195, 198
Wilbur, Bob (EAL), 268
Williams, "Red" (Century), 51
Wilsman, Doug (UAL), 283
Wilson, Bruce (NAL), 127, 128
Wilson, Sid (NAL), 127, 138, 143
Wilson, Woodrow, 25, 26
Wilson, Mrs. Woodrow, 25
Wood, Jerry (EAL), 4, 6, 146, 155, 156, 159-60,
166, 169, 179, 180, 185-86, 201, 203, 204,
210, 211, 217, 219, 220, 221, 229, 233, 278
on Behncke as negotiator, 153-54
on jet pay study committee, 171, 172-73
on Sayen, 169-70
on Wages and Working Conditions Policy
Committee, 173
Wood, Rep. William, 50
Woods, Chuck (UAL), 205, 230
Woolman, C. E., 14, 70, 110-11
Working conditions, airline pilot
and Decision 83, 65 ff
guaranteed minimum, 54, 59
and Railway Labor Act, 94
World War I, 96, 101
World War II, 93, 101-15
and growth of aviation, 101-03

protection of labor gains during, 113-15
Wyatt, Judge Inzer B., 246
Wynne, A. M. ("Breezy") (AAL), 162, 226, 237, 246, 247
on Cord, 44-45

Yackey, Tony, 97
Young, Charley (NWA), 292
Young, Jack (EAL), on Landis, 204-05

PHOTO CREDITS

All illustrations *Air Line Pilot* photos except the following. Section 1, "Beginnings": Hopson (Smithsonian Institution); A-2 Swallow (United Airlines); Knight, boarding passengers, airmail office, Jenny in fog, wrecked DH-4, and Lindbergh's wreck (Smithsonian Institution); Army Private Behncke, Behncke in flight training, Aerial Revue poster, Checkerboard Field, news clippings, Holman, and Behncke's return to the Army (Behncke family photos). Section 2, "The Behncke Era": Treat (Treat family photo); 1947 Board of Directors meeting (Wayne State University Archives of Labor and Urban Affairs); Cutting crash (Acme); Frye, Douglass, and Behncke (Associated Press). Section 3, "The Sayen and Ruby Eras": Sayen (Louis W. Braun); Grand Canyon crash (United Press International); DC-8 Super 63 (Douglas Aircraft Co.); Staten Island crash (United Press International); B-707 (American Airlines). Section 4, "ALPA's Fifth Decade": O'Donnell with airliner models (Yoichi R. Okamoto); TWA Flight 57 and BOAC VC-10 (United Press International).